TRAVELERS' TALES BOOKS

T R A V E L E R S ' T A L E S

BRAZIL

TRUE STORIES

T R A V E L E R S ' T A L E S

BRAZIL

TRUE STORIES

Edited by

ANNETTE HADDAD AND SCOTT DOGGETT

Series Editors
JAMES O'REILLY AND LARRY HABEGGER

TRAVELERS' TALES

SAN FRANCISCO

Art Direction: Michele Wetherbee and Stefan Gutermuth
Interior design: Kathryn Heflin and Susan Bailey
Cover photograph: © *Nicholas DeVore/Getty Images. Rio de Janeiro, Brazil.*
Illustrations: David White
Maps: Keith Granger
Page Layout: Cynthia Lamb, using the font Bembo and Boulevard

Distributed by Publishers Group West, 1700 Fourth Street, Berkeley, California 94710.

Library of Congress Cataloguing-in-Publication Data
Travelers' tales Brazil: true stories/edited by Annette Haddad and Scott Doggett.—
    1st ed., [Rev. ed.].
      p. cm.
    Includes bibliographical references and index.
     ISBN 1-932361-05-7 (pbk.)
    1. Brazil—Description and travel. I. Title: Brazil. II. Haddad, Annette. III. Doggett, Scott.
     F2517.T68 2004
     918.104'65—dc22

                                                        2004005991

First Edition
Printed in the United States
10 9 8 7 6 5 4

Quem quer viver faz màgica.

He who wants to live works magic.

—GUIMARÃES ROSA

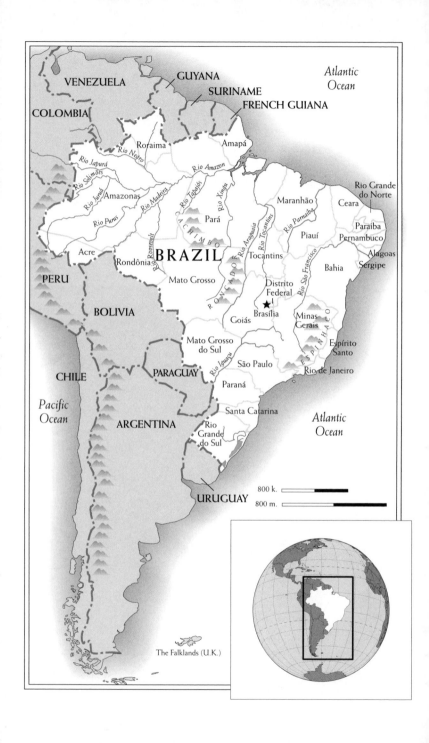

Table of Contents

Part Two
SOME THINGS TO DO

Part Four
IN THE SHADOWS

Part Five
THE LAST WORD

Brazil: An Introduction

BY ALEX SHOUMATOFF

Brazil has the seething, epic quality of other developing mega-states like India, Mexico, and Russia, but there is something uniquely intoxicating about it. As you'll discover in the travelers' tales that follow, no popular music is at once so joyous and melancholy, infectious and cathartic, as the Brazilian samba; no language is more sensuous than Portuguese on the lips of a Carioca, a native of Rio de Janeiro; no people are sweeter or more generous than the *gente humilde,* the Brazilian poor; no wilderness is as unfathomably immense or as riotously diverse as the Amazon rainforest; no culture has such a mischievous sense of fun or such a highly evolved sense of the absurd. It is no accident that magic realism was invented by two Brazilian writers, Murilo Rubião and José J.Vega; they were just responding to the surreal edge to Brazilian life. Brazil is the tropical "sex-positive" (in the anthropologist Thomas Gregor's term) society par excellence, a mecca for repressed souls from the temperate zones. And of course the soccer and the beer are without peer.

Few expressions are more overworked by travel writers than "a land of contrasts," but in the case of Brazil the disparities—between the South and the North, the crowded coast and the empty interior, the rich and the poor—are so pronounced that it is transcendently apt. The cultural menu ranges from neolithic hunter-gatherers whose villages have been spotted from the air but never entered by any so-called *civilizado,* to fully up-to-the-minute Internet surfers. In between are all kinds of gradations, like the hospitable, self-sufficient *caboclos* author Joe Kane meets in "*Bodó* Sing-Along," who live in the time of Daniel Boone along the Amazon's thousands of tributaries and sub-tributaries, trading what they grow, hunt, and fish for a few useful modern goods such as foot-powered sewing machines, shotgun shells, and transistor radios.

Brazil's tri-cultural makeup—its fusion of Indian, European, and African elements—gives it a special dynamism. It explains the genius of Antonio Carlos Jobim, for instance, and why Brazilians are more spontaneous, warm, and fun-loving than Mexicans, who lack the African dimension and are haunted by the grandeur of their past. Brazilians have zero interest in the past. They have a horror of growing old. The quintessential Brazilian putdowns are to be labeled *já era,* as having "already been," i.e., as history, and *sistemático*—anal-retentive, Germanic. What matters is the present—how vibrant and insouciantly alive you are—and the future, as Alma Guillermoprieto beautifully conveys in "Opium of the People."

So many things about Brazil are as good as it gets that Brazilians tend to have trouble adapting to foreign cultures, and when stationed abroad are soon overwhelmed by *saudade,* another key word: they pine for their food and their samba, their Antarctica lager and their *futebol.* But every culture has its shadow side, and Brazil is no exception. Underneath the sweetness lurks a very nasty streak of violence, the politicians and the police can be as venal and corrupt, the rich as cynical and selfish, as any on the planet. If you commit a crime and know the right people, you walk; if you don't you rot in jail. The racial fluidity, one eventually realizes, is only apparent; the top stratum is almost pure white-European.

So egregious are the social inequities that it is no coincidence, either, that Leonardo and Claudio Boff, two of the leading exponents of liberation theology, which prioritizes basic human rights in the here and now, should be Brazilian. As a 16th-century Portuguese navigator sailing up the Brazilian coast remarked famously, "There is no sin south of the Equator." This attitude, which Cal Fussman describes in "Rio Risqué," accounts for both Brazil's seductive charm and its chronic problems.

But it would be a gross injustice to end on a sour note of negative stereotyping. *Impunidade* is another important word for understanding Brazil, but the most important word of all is *alegria,* the loving light-heartedness that is at the soul of these beautiful people. Come discover their world in *Travelers' Tales Brazil.*

Alex Shoumatoff is the author of many books, four of which are about Brazil: The Rivers Amazon, The Capital of Hope, In Southern Light, *and* The World Is Burning. *From 1978 to 1990, he was a staff writer at* The New Yorker *and is now a contributing editor at* Vanity Fair. *He has two sons by a Brazilian woman, and lives on a mountaintop in the Adirondacks of upstate New York.*

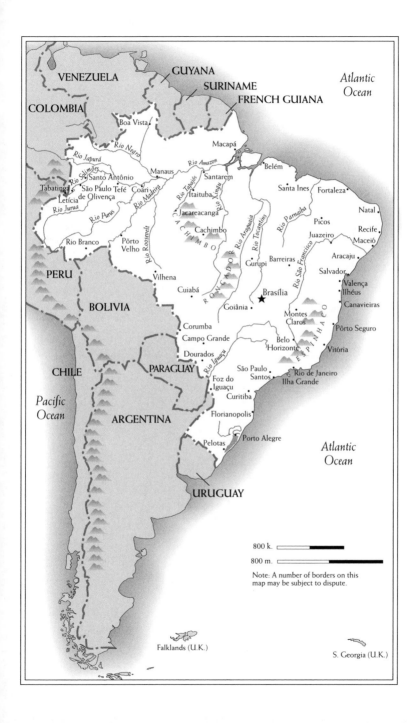

PART ONE

ESSENCE OF BRAZIL

JOE KANE

Bodó Sing-Along

*A member of the first expedition to
navigate the entire length of the Amazon River finds
the real Brazil on the banks of the Solimões.*

AT THE BORDER BRAZIL SHARES WITH COLOMBIA AND PERU, the Marañón River becomes the Solimões, and from there zigzags east some twelve hundred miles through the state of Amazonas. Brazilians consider Amazonas their Wild West. About the size of Alaska, with fewer people than Philadelphia, it contains twenty percent of Brazil's landmass but less than one percent of its population; aside from the cities of Manaus and Tefé, and a few small towns like Tabatinga, São Paulo de Olivença, and Coari, it is nearly uninhabited. Given that, and the proximity of the duty-free port of Iquitos, Peru, the lawless influence of nearby Leticia, Colombia, and the hefty taxes Brazil levies on foreign goods, a comfortable living can be made running contraband boat engines, transistor radios, hand tools, stereos, televisions, clothes, motorcycles, and crates of produce along the Solimões. A smugglers' code governs life on the river.

Early one morning, seeking directions as we kayaked along the border between Colombia and Brazil, my expedition partner, Piotr Chmielinski, attempted to overtake a dugout canoe. Its sole occupant raced for the bank and a man jumped out and shouldered a

3

rifle. He relaxed when Chmielinski explained himself, but as we left, he yelled out, "Be careful! The river is full of bandits!"

After that, when we met traffic I hung back in my kayak, secured my paddle, and put my hands under my deck. If Chmielinski felt at all threatened, he mentioned that I was armed and nodded in my direction—a signal for me to squint into the bush as if sighting a target. Though nervous during these charades, at times I had to fight to keep from laughing out loud. I had not touched a gun since I was a kid.

The forest along the Solimões may be the lushest on the Amazon. The trees tend to be tall, well over 50 feet, and the bush thicker than any I had seen in Peru. Our second day below São Paulo de Olivença we paddled dawn to dusk without spotting a single hut. The river itself was perplexing. In the parlance of the Amazon, the Solimões is a "white" river, thick with Andean silt, which gives it a coffee-and-cream color. The silty deposits have made the *várzea,* as the Amazon floodplain is known, a zigzag puzzle of natural levees and ditches (variously called *furos, paranás,* and *canals*). Navigation can be confusing, and there are few beaches on which to camp.

According to the Guinness Book of Records, the two longest rivers in the world are the Nile and the Amazon. Which is longer is more a matter of definition than of simple measurement.

The Amazon begins with snowbound brooks in southern Peru, which converge to form the Apurimac. This joins other streams to become the Ene, the Tambo, the Ucayali, the Marañón, the Solimões, and finally the Amazon. The Amazon has several mouths that widen toward the sea. If the Pará estuary (the most distant mouth and the route taken by Joe Kane) is counted, its length is 4,195 miles. The length of the Nile watercourse, as surveyed before the loss of a few miles due to the formation of Lake Nasser behind the Aswan High Dam, is 4,145 miles.

—AH and SD

That night, New Year's Eve, we traveled until dark before picking up the lights of a cattle ranch, but the frightened owner would not let us stay. We pitched camp on the bank below the ranch, in a fetid puddle of mud and clay. The air reeked of manure and mud stuck like paint to anything it touched. Black flies competed fiercely with mosquitoes for their pound of flesh.

We took what comfort we could from the routine of making camp. We erected tents, stretched a line between them, hung up life jackets and rainsuits to dry, drew water, brewed tea, sponged out our boats. Chmielinski cooked chili, and the two of us sat on a muddy log and ate it.

"In Poland this is the biggest day of the year," he said. "In Krakow everyone is dancing. The relatives are together eating a big dinner. But never are they eating chili."

"Do you miss them?"

"Yes. And they are missing me. Every year for six years they are leaving one plate empty on the table."

"For you."

"Yes."

"Someday maybe it will not be empty."

"That is something I cannot think about. It will make me crazy."

"Have they ever been able to visit you?"

"No, but they are remembering me."

"I'm sure they are."

"Happy New Year, Joe."

"Happy New Year, Piotr."

After dinner we heard distant gunshots, and that night we slept with machetes at our sides, though I did not know what I would do if I had to use mine. Frogs croaked, nightbirds yawped, bats whirred, and though I dove into my tent as fast as I could, had the netting unzipped for perhaps fifteen seconds, an insect zoo managed to establish itself on the underside of my tent ceiling. By candlelight I saw two enormous red ants, a winged ant that looked like a termite, a squadron of gnats, two black moths, and three fat mosquitoes that became two Rorschach blots on page 52 of my third notebook. The disturbed survivors flitted and buzzed until I settled down to sleep.

Late in the night a boat engine idled offshore, and a bright light ran over our camp. Voices argued loudly, but the boat sped away when Chmielinski ran down the bank.

Later still, peering through the mosquito netting, Chmielinski spotted two shadows slouching through the mud right next to our camp. He grabbed his machete, sneaked silently from his tent, and pounced, simultaneously raising his machete and switching on his flashlight to blind our attackers, who proved to be…"the life jackets, Joe! They are blowing on the drying line: I am thinking they are trying to get us!"

By eight the next morning a fierce headwind had whipped the river into chop and waves that reduced our speed by a third. Buried in the troughs, I lost sight of Chmielinski, though he paddled only a few feet in front of me. I could not time my stroke. At the moment I pushed hardest, expecting my paddle to bite water, it bit nothing but air. Then, accelerating, it struck the water awkwardly. Executing several thousand such strokes wore me out. When my paddle hit water the shock ran through wrist, up forearm, along shoulder, into neck, and erupted through lips in a frustrated oath.

Meanwhile, five days and 250 miles into Amazonas, the clay banks occasionally gave way to low sandstone bluffs, and here and there a sturdy plank-and-frame house sat defiantly on stilts, right over the water. At the mouth of the Içá River we passed a mile-long village, Santo Antônio. The main street ran between houses of brick and wood and ended at either edge of town. As we paddled by, I watched a Volkswagen bug drive slowly along the street, turn around, drive back, and so on, like a plastic duck at a shooting gallery.

Perhaps a dozen settlements dot the 600 miles of river between São Paulo de Olivença and Coari, most of them hidden up swamps and small tributaries, and all of them poor. Alan Holman, an Australian who made a solo kayak descent of the flatwater Amazon in 1982, measured these villages according to how many eggs he could purchase. A six-egg village was an oasis.

At the store in no-egg Porto Alfonso three men were leaning against empty shelves, drinking bottles of raw cane spirit called *cachaça*. One asked Chmielinski where we were going.

"Belém," Chmielinski said.

"Where do you sleep?" another asked.

"In houses, or on a beach."

The third man did not look up from his bottle. "Where are you sleeping tonight?" he asked.

"Maybe Fonte Boa."

"You will not get there today."

"A beach, then."

"That could be dangerous."

"We have big guns," Chmielinski said, "and we are twelve."

"Where are the rest?"

"With the soldiers."

"Soldiers?"

"In the airplane. The one that follows us."

The first man asked, "How do they know where you are?"

"Radio."

We had no such teammates, of course, and no radio; whether the men already knew this I could not tell.

As we left the shack we met a distinguished-looking man (he wore shoes), a Colombian engineer surveying a nearby tributary for a dam. "Three weeks, no eggs!" he said in English. "No food, nothing." He was living on instant rice.

The lepers who inhabited *Ilha do Jardim*—Garden Island—said that a drought had left them short of food, but they gave us six papayas and three bunches of bananas. The bananas were delicious (in the heat of the day they were often the only food I could keep down), but later, when I tried to eat one of the soft ripe papayas, I thought of those people, the skin dripping off their faces, and though I felt guilty for it I threw the fruit in the river.

We paddled eight hours that fourth day below São Paulo de Olivença, and our chart said we had covered 70 miles. We paddled twelve hours the next day—40 miles. On the sixth day we pulled hard, the banks slid by, the chart said we had gone nowhere. My shoulders developed a sharp, white-hot pain and made popping noises. Our chocolate melted, our bread turned moldy, and we discovered that our *comida plástica,* which I had selected from the crate support crew Zbigniew Bzdak and Kate Durrant had hauled to São Paulo de Olivença, consisted entirely of chili. After eating it twice a day for six days neither of us could stomach another spoonful.

We paddled long hours in silence, past islands of floating grass and the occasional snake chugging along with its head raised out of the water like a periscope. The wildlife was oblique—a shaking in the bush at night, a tree limb bent by a hornet nest, squawking in a treetop, a dolphin breaching, the zigzagging triangle of a shark's fin. (Several shark species breed in the Atlantic but forage as far upriver as Iquitos.)

Either it rained hard or the sun burned so intensely that in the middle of the day we dove into the river, hung on to the noses of our boats, and drifted downstream with the one-knot current. This was safer than one might think. According to a doctor Durrant had consulted in Iquitos, most Amazonian water snakes swim beneath the surface but are not poisonous, while land snakes, which sometimes are, travel on the surface and are easily spotted. Piranha are overrated—we met no one on the river who had witnessed an attack, much less death—and the despicable orifice-entering *candiru* was thwarted simply by wearing a pair of shorts while swimming.

Several fishermen insisted the *pirarucú* could eat a man. According to all available scientific evidence the species is incapable of such a feat, but having seen several of the monsters, I cannot blame the fishermen. The *pirarucú* (or *paiche,* as it is known in Peru) is one of the world's largest freshwater fish—it can grow to ten feet and 250 pounds—and in addition to gills has a single lung that it must service every few minutes, breaking the water with a loud rolling display not unlike a great scaly red-and-green log. After witnessing that act at close range several times, and being startled half to death,

In the jungle, and especially in long grass, we used to collect large numbers of ticks called carapatos. *We had heard a great deal about these creatures, none of it in their favor; and at first the revulsion they aroused in their victims was tempered with a certain pride, a feeling that their attentions, though unwelcome, constituted a part of the Real Thing.*

—Peter Fleming,
Brazilian Adventure (1933)

I was willing to believe that such a fish would eat not only a man but a horse.

On the seventh day into Amazonas, we stopped at the grassy head of hilly Acarara Island. A big-boned man named Luis paddled a canoe over from the mainland, and we asked permission to camp.

"But of course," he said. "The land is yours."

Like most of the peasants along the Solimões, Luis was a *caboclo*—a person of European and Indian blood who leads a catch-as-catch-can existence dependent mainly on a sunny disposition and traditional forms of fishing, trading, and slash-and-burn agriculture. Minutes later another *caboclo,* Mauricio, arrived on foot, at the head of a parade of goats, and also granted us permission to camp (though with somewhat more authority than Luis, as the land was actually his).

The *caboclos* spoke Portuguese (sufficiently similar to Spanish that we could converse), and while I cooked and we watched a storm approach they taught me the words for knife, fire, rain, and thunder. The English equivalents pulverized them with laughter. *Rain* was hilarious, *fire* induced near-hysteria, and *thunder*—Luis could pronounce it only as "sunder," and collapsed in a fit of snorts and giggles. Later, as he paddled away, his voice carried across the water and up to our bluff. "Sunder!" I heard, followed by his mulish laugh, and I in turn experimented with my new words—*faca, fogo, chuva, trovão*—rolling them around like exotic fruit.

Late that night the storm hit with a fury. It would have blown me right off the island and into the river if Chmielinski had not planted my kayak next to my tent as a protective wall. Hearing the commotion, I stuck my head out, shone my flashlight, and spotted Chmielinksi running around in the rain stark naked. When I called to him, he yelled back, "I like this being wet!"

Our hosts the next evening, the *caboclo* Francisco Gomez and his family, lived in a thatch-and-palmwood house set well back from the river. Several pocked tin pots hung beside the fire pit in back, next to five huts containing mosquito nets and nothing else. The house itself was a single room with a table along one wall and, against another, a wooden mantel that held two laminated pictures of a blue-eyed Virgin, a hammer, a wind-up cuckoo clock that did not work, and two bottles of antivenin. Below it were five machetes and three beaten cardboard suitcases. That appeared to be the sum of the family's possessions.

We put up our tents in the house, studying the chickens that ran beneath the floor, and Francisco introduced his tough old wife, Fatima, then a young woman with a baby, then another young woman, very pretty, who wore a short skirt, eye shadow, and a jaguar-tooth necklace. Fatima chased her from the room. Three boys came in, and two young men.

"Francisco," I asked, "how many people live here?"

Two more boys entered, a girl, a young mother with a baby.

Francisco thought for a moment. "Thirteen."

In walked an older man, António, who like Francisco appeared middle-aged. He had a small boy with him.

"I count seventeen," I said to Francisco.

He thought for a moment. "Yes," he said. "Seventeen."

"All live here, in this house?"

"All live here."

"All one family?"

He smiled. "Two families."

"Three," António said. "But I am not always here. I have children in other places."

"How many children?" Chmielinski asked.

"Forty-four," António said.

"*Forty-four?*"

"Yes. I have forty-four children. With ten women." He nodded seriously.

"Where are your children?" Chmielinski asked.

"Everywhere!" António said. "That is why I come to Francisco's home. Only two of them live here."

An hour later all seventeen inhabitants had crowded into the room. The women and children sat along the walls and the men huddled around Chmielinski, who spread open our chart on the table. The men exclaimed when Chmielinski showed them their house, marked by a square. The chart also indicated a canal near Francisco's home, but it was not clear whether the canal cut all the way across a bend in the river. If it did, we would save a day by following it. If the canal petered out too early, however, we would lose two days backtracking.

Did any of the men know about the canal?

"Yes," Francisco said. He pointed knowingly to the chart. "There it is."

Chmielinski sighed. "But does it exist?" he asked. "Is it on the river?"

Francisco shrugged. António, however, said it was, and the other men nodded vigorously.

"Six hours from here," António said.

"Four hours," one of the younger men said.

"One day," Francisco said.

Chmielinski knew that routine. He gave up and cooked our chili, cooked all we had left, and Fatima brought bowls and *farinha,* the lumpy powder made from toasted manioc that can be, as this was, nutty and delicious. She passed the bowls around and we distributed our chili and everyone sat on the floor and ate. She gave me a Portuguese lesson: knife, spoon, stove, rain, yesterday, today, tomorrow.

I read my Portuguese *Berlitz:* "Waiter, my fish is cold."

"Your fish is cold," Francisco said. "But you have no fish."

I read on. "Are you alone tonight?"

"Stupid question," António said.

After dinner Chmielinski continued to work with the map, but I was tired and said goodnight. I crawled into my tent and wrote in my notebook. I woke up with my nose on the page. When I rolled over on my back four tiny faces were staring down at me through the netting. I closed my eyes and sometime later woke to António and Francisco arguing about, I think, a calf. Then the young men got into it, and the women, and the place was in an uproar. Finally, Chmielinski called out from his tent, in slow, precise Spanish, "Excuse me. I know this is your house, but you have invited us to stay, and we have much work tomorrow. So please."

The Gomez family retired. I fell asleep. When I woke again, an hour before dawn, they were sitting along the walls.

Chmielinski and I spent all the next day searching for the canal, and all the next two days backtracking. Perhaps we had misunderstood the Gomezes, lost something in the cracks between Portuguese and Spanish. Perhaps the canal had simply dried up. Or perhaps in their generosity the Gomezes had given us completely false information, because it was what they thought we wanted to hear.

The next night, our tenth on the Solimões, we stayed with a 32-year-old *caboclo* named Eduardo. He had silver-blue eyes and strong square features, and he lived in a stilt house right on the river, at the mouth of a lake the color of his eyes. Six other houses along the water made up *Cabo Azul,* or Blue Cape. Eduardo's wife had gone away somewhere, and in both celebration and sorrow he was drinking rum.

A monkey troop of young boys stuffed our boats into Eduardo's house and fetched water from the river while Eduardo cooked *bodó,* a fish with a lobsterlike exoskeleton. The meat flopped out in a steaming hunk, redolent of peppers. When we finished, the boys washed the plates in the river. Then, as one, they demanded, "A song!"

Eduardo pulled a guitar from beneath a pile of rags and badly but loudly played four-chord ballads of romance, drink, and fishing. We unloaded the kayaks and the boys turned them over and set to a fierce drumming, six to a boat, building a mellifluous, smoothly syncopated whole. Eduardo played until my fingers hurt for watching him, but the boys pleaded for more.

After an hour or so I walked out to wash myself in the Solimões, then strolled along the duckwalk that connected the six houses. The drumming and Eduardo's earnest crooning filled the cool night air. *This,* I thought, *is Brazil.*

Joe Kane's writing about the Amazon for The New Yorker *earned him the Overseas Press Club Award for best environmental reporting. He was a member of the expedition that made the first complete navigation of the Amazon*

River; his book about that journey, Running the Amazon, *was a* New York Times *bestseller and it is from that book that this story was excerpted. He is also the author of* Savages, *a first-hand account of how one small band of Amazonian warriors defended their territory against hell-bent oil companies, dogged missionaries, and starry-eyed environmentalists.*

✳

When I am asked what the jungle was like, those are the places I first remember—where the river narrowed to 40 feet and the green walls closed off much of the sky—not the openness of the lower river or the big skies of the Rio Negro. I have tried to think of a word or a sentence to pass off as a quick explanation, but the Amazon cannot be distilled, though many try, including me.

The more I thought about it, the more I sensed the Amazon was like the tree that fell the night before and the noise it made. Maybe even the absurdity the philosophers argued about had meaning. The Amazon, and every other point in the universe, was an immense interaction, a composite of everyone's stories, and everyone who had stepped foot in it added to its form, even if a good part of it was lies. The Amazon is a tangle of life fighting for a piece of the sky, a pressure of green that forces you to react. It is a place that, with its bugs and its heat and sun and animals and size and diseases, is always at you. It never lets up until it draws you out, and when you become part of the tangle, then for you, that is the Amazon.

—Paul Zalis, *Who Is the River: Getting Lost in the Amazon and Other Places*

Argentino

An Americana and a stranger move as one
in a samba's embrace.

MARCOS AND MARINHA NASCIMENTO WERE TAKING ME TO A Christmas party. I had arrived in Belo Horizonte the night before, our visit having been arranged by Zé, my host in Rio. True to his promise, they made me warmly welcome.

Laconic Marcos, with his cap of tight black curls and wiry frame, stood in contrast to his copper-haired wife, affectionate and expansive and *gordinha* (a little meat on her bones). The couple's three children shared Marinha's ruddy coloring, especially the toddler Hipolita, a Titian cherub; the kids and their friends watched my every move, this blonde Americana with her inexplicable Rio accent. From the Nascimentos' modest apartment, filled with the creations of painter and craftsmen friends, I took in the rolling emerald expanse of Belo, capital of the mountainous interior state of Minas Gerais.

As we arrived at the party at the home of the Passarinhos that perfect summer evening, I felt the gears in my brain start grinding in preparation for social chatter. My Portuguese served me well enough one-on-one but tended to stall when required to produce quick banter in large groups. Marinha was my safe harbor while I sized up this gathering.

I found the refreshments and helped myself to a cold *chopinho,* then walked outside for some air. Typically, the Passarinhos' house was enclosed by a high solid wall that afforded security and privacy from the street. Partygoers were thus mingling in the front and side yards, the sultry air perfumed by jasmine and the flamboyant trees in flagrant, scarlet bloom.

Strings of tiny lights illuminated the yard as darkness finally fell and the music rose from background to main event. The irresistible sounds of samba brought a number of people to their feet, and started mine itching as I sat sipping my beer. It wasn't long before I was invited to dance, by an ardent bear of a man named Tadeu. He was sweaty and sour-smelling and a bit drunk, but I was quite thrilled to be up and moving with the crowd. Tadeu, in fact, was dancing by himself, off in his own sensory world, and so, therefore, was I. But that was fine with me. In a fundamental way, I had traveled thousands of miles to be doing exactly this—seeking some kind of intimate knowledge of the samba, with the body as hierophant and the soul the ecstatic recipient of its gifts.

While conversing with the rhythms on the dance floor in the vicinity of the frenetic Tadeu, I scanned the yard, savoring the styles of the dancing couples. One man in particular was making the samba all his own with movements of wonderful finesse and a captivating swing (or *sue-wing-ghee,* in the local parlance). As soon as the record was over, I bade Tadeu *adeus* with a thank-you-man and wasted no time in approaching the evening's prize dancer.

"Quer dançar?" I proposed, a bit breathless with anticipation.

"Lógico," he smiled, taking my hand. But of course!

His right hand alighted on my blue-draped hip, my left on his shoulder; our remaining hands found each other high in the air, laced loosely, as hips and legs and feet began to respond in unison to the tensile rhythms. It was simple, and sublime.

We introduced ourselves not long into our maiden dance—his name was Argentino, a handsome man of mocha complexion, slender build, and uncommon grace. He described himself as a poet. I was Teresa the *Americana*, as usual the only one present and therefore charged with the burden of explaining American politics. But

Argentino offered instant expiation; like everyone I'd met in Brazil, he brightened at the mention of San Francisco, my home base, and offered the requisite compliments on my Portuguese (*"Você fala muito bem!"*).

Frankly, though, talking got in the way of the purity of the dance. We were a team now. As each record ended, we remained poised for the next, grinning, relishing our glorious calibration.

Doubtless there are men in the world who love to dance and are good at it and who can lead a woman partner through an experience where two are one and aren't even thinking about taking off their clothes. I had just never met such a man. Dancing with men meant dancing near them or at them, as with Tadeu, or leading them, as with my friend Jim, who could expertly follow my every step and spin.

But here with Argentino, it wasn't even a matter of his leading me; it was more like his moves *were* my moves, we were just making them together at precisely the same moment. Moreover, his *suewing-ghee* was of a piece with mine—closer to the pulse of the music, right in it rather than spurting out from it. Peripherally I could see many such gushing dancers in the yard, exhausting themselves after one go-round. Argentino and I, we kept percolating, marveling at the persuasiveness of a hip with intent, exploring the rich dimensions of movement in the smallest possible space. We *were* the heartbeat of samba.

How many hours passed? We hadn't left each other's company all evening, nor had the smiles left our faces. But the music had quieted down, the party was rapidly thinning out, *madrugada* was settling in. Marinha and Marcos were saying their good-byes to the Passarinhos, and that meant I would have to bid farewell to Argentino.

We faced each other with this task, still aglow. *"Você dança como um anjo,"* I said helplessly. You angel you.

Not missing a beat: *"Aprendi esta noite contigo,"* he replied, the picture of serenity. I learned tonight with you.

In English the concept of speaking *with* someone is self-evident, but in Portuguese you also learn with someone, not from them, and you dream with someone, not about them, suggesting that these are not solitary activities. Clearly Argentino and I had both dreamed of a mutual surrender to the music on a tropical Christmas night. As we danced together, we learned how to make our dreams come true.

Born in New York and "actualized" in California, Terri Hinte fell in love with samba and bossa nova many years ago and studied Portuguese in order to travel to Brazil. She has worked as a music business publicist for more than twenty years, and contributed to the Brazilian music section of The All Music Guide. *Whenever she travels, she pines for her garden and her Siamese cat, Eartha.*

*

If you are going to Brazil, be forewarned: when you come back home, if you do, you will have added a few special words to your emotional vocabulary. You will join us in the group that knows the feeling yet cannot explain the meaning of the word…*saudade*. If you can explain it, you've made a poor translation. It has a place of its own, it changes you more than your vocabulary.

If you haven't been somewhere but yearn to see it, you may be getting a glimpse of *saudade*. It means longing for someone or something, more or less in the realm of "I miss you," in English. Yet, it carries more than longing, more than missing. Yearning…a hole carved in one's heart, a feeling which stands on its own as much as it permeates one's whole being…. It simply cannot be translated.

A Brazilian person *has saudade* or *feels saudade. Tenho saudades do Brasil* or *Sinto saudades*…portraits of a melancholic yet sweet longing. It transports me there when I say it.

—Neise Cavini Turchin, "Longing for Brazil"

EDWARD A. RIEDINGER

✦ ✦ ✦

Once Upon a Time in Ipanema

*The author recalls the splendor of Rio's
most enchanted neighborhood.*

FOR SEVERAL YEARS I LIVED IN A NEIGHBORHOOD THAT I CAME to consider the most singular in Rio—if not the world—Ipanema. A middle- to upper-middle-class haven, Ipanema rises on a narrow isthmus between an ocean beach and a lagoon, arched by the mountain peaks of the city. One of these peaks is crowned with the city's emblem, the statue of Christ the Redeemer with out- stretched, benignly protective arms. Indeed, almost in the shadow of that peak, one of the most elegant passageways of Ipanema is tree-shaded Redeemer Street.

Ipanema, which stirs my memories not only of the neighbor- hood but of Rio and of Brazil, recalls a saying associated with one of the most popular Brazilian soccer teams, Flamengo. Its followers assure everyone that *"uma vez Flamengo, sempre Flamengo"*—"once you're for Flamengo, you'll always be for Flamengo." Thus sums up my fondness for Brazil, "once Ipanema, always Ipanema." Since Ipanema—and Brazil—harbor for me the memory of so many magical moments, I find it easy to recall each one beginning with another wonderful phrase: "Once upon a time.... "

Many years have passed since I first strolled into Ipanema. Its unique atmosphere immediately struck me. Its tidy houses, casual cafés, and well-stocked shops gave a sense of comfort and domestic security. At the same time, beautiful scantily-clad bronzed bodies strolled leisurely from the homes to the nearby beach, giving an electric sense of sensuality and serene openness. Never before had I known a place with such a wonderful air of the familial and of the exotic. The beautiful people were often taking toddlers to the sea, trailed by maids and pets.

What for me was then a duality, for Brazilians was a long-standing synthesis. They possessed a sophisticated balance, a *bossa*, between domesticity and pleasure. The signature song of *bossa nova* (the "new beat") was "The Girl from Ipanema" (*"A Garota de Ipanema"*), written at a café-bar in the heart of the neighborhood, the lyricist inspired by a physical beauty that was commonplace in the vicinity. (Though as a young teenager in the American Midwest, first hearing this song and knowing nothing of Brazil and its language of Portuguese, I imagined Ipanema was a city in Mexico!)

Ipanema made me re-examine the words *cosmopolitan* and *sophisticated*. I had always thought of them as virtually synonymous, but I came to see they were actually quite different. Brazil was not generally cosmopolitan in the sense of having a singular variety of cultural institutions, museums, symphonies, and ethnic groups. However, many Brazilians were quite sophisticated. They possessed a variety of liberal perspectives from which they viewed the world.

How certain Brazilians acquired this sophistication without a more cosmopolitan environment puzzled me until I experienced more thoroughly the country's cultural development. Ironically, economic and language limits

Why is it we're comforted to discover certain spots are exactly as promoted? Somehow, dipping my tootsies into this renowned sandbox brings the same Pavlovian response of wonder as stepping into the postcard views of the Taj Mahal or Tiananmen Square. In mankind's symbolic language, there can only be one church called Notre Dame, one skyscraper called the Empire State Building, and one beach, Ipanema's contiguous Copacabana.

—John Krich, *Why is This Country Dancing?: A One-Man Samba to the Beat of Brazil* provoked it. As a country economically dependent for centuries on exporting agricultural products (sugar, cotton, coffee, rubber, etc.), its economic elites always had to divine the outlook of their customers, the foreign buyers. Further, as speakers of a relatively obscure language, Brazilians had to learn the languages of others, particularly English and French, in order to communicate in the world. Learning these languages also meant absorbing the others' cultural perspectives, even assuming some of their postures. Moreover, Rio was an especially liberal city, like many world ports of call and tourist meccas, and Ipanema was its chic core.

Most memorable about Ipanema was the beach, and the fondest memories I have are of lying on it, my head resting in the hand of my upraised arm, looking out over the sand to the sea. It is a late summer afternoon. Sea and sky almost match each other on the faint, aqua line of the horizon. Land's end, paradise begins. There is a breeze; and the rays of the waning sun fall in long, resonant golden shafts. Gray and white doves flutter over the beige sand seeking scraps left over from snacks and picnics. As they land, the edges of their outspread wings are caught translucent by the radiant sun. The mountains, lightly covered in haze, stand as an ethereal backdrop. Those who earlier were strolling by the water's edge, whose eyes then met someone who returned their glance, recline now paired off in conversation—and, who knows, perhaps making arrangements for a later tryst.

Ipanema made me realize two things about Brazil that so contrasted with my memories of American life. I can hardly remember ever hearing, as is so common in the United States, the word *sex* linked to the word *violence.* In Brazil I almost always heard the word *sex* followed by the word *love.* This, of course, did not mean that people drawn together stayed so. Such comings and goings were much the same as anywhere. The association did mean, though, that intimacy was not associated with assertion and taking but with a certain tenderness and warmth.

Warmth also determined time in Brazil. South of the equator seasons were reversed; the year began in warmth, not cold. Seasons had no meaning, were but waxing and waning periods of heat. The months and days passed as subtle variations of light. Very distinct though was the sunlight of May, the peak of "autumn." With the sun's rays falling lower from the sky, the leaves of trees, the stones of walls, and the fruits and vegetables in street markets were bathed in a waning gold luster, an antique glow.

Ultimately, it was in Ipanema that I perceived something about the rhythm of life in Brazil that so differentiated it from other countries. I lay on its beach, strolled in its squares and byways, walked by its lagoon at midnight when the street lamps cast shimmering white banners into the water, chatted in its bars until dawn—then went off to my work. Brazil was life the way one truly wanted to live it.

Other countries, in contrast, came to appear more as life as one had to live it. Compressed into it. For all the comforts of American life, its rhythm was dominated by daily schedules, weekly meetings, monthly bills, conferences, reports, even yearly "retreats." The comforts seemed but lubricants for the treadmill.

The leisure and indulgence Brazilians knew in their lives, so enriching time, came to appear ironic to me. Here was a "Third World" country with a more aristocratic sense of living than any I had ever seen. These aristocrats, moreover, were in no way exclusive. They possessed the essence of nobility, a cordiality and poise, welcoming others to share their lives.

Thinking about time makes me recall a question I once asked a Brazilian friend long before I had ever visited his country. I wanted to know if there were time zones in Brazil. He responded that there were two: one for the eastern half of the country and another for the Amazon. These zones he hastened to add, with that bemused, low-key irony I came to find so enjoyable in Brazilians, had no significance. Why would the Indians use watches?

Ipanema lies at the heart of my Brazilian memories, but from there my mind wanders through Rio. There is Copacabana beach on the first New Year's Eve I spent in Brazil. It is the feast of Iemanjá, goddess of the sea in the Candomblé syncretist religion merging Catholicism and African spiritism. Her colors are white and blue (those also of the Blessed Virgin); and on this night her followers must offer her gifts of perfume, flowers, and mirrors, set in small candle-lit boats launched at midnight. Everyone is in white. More people crowd and jostle here on the beach this night than do sunbathers on any day of the year.

As midnight explodes with fireworks from the windows of the apartments bordering the beach, the jubilant worshipers of the goddess of the sea launch their offerings. They then continue the night with music, dancing, and trances until dawn. The first light reveals sprays of flowers all along the sand, returned with the tide of a beneficent goddess, pleased with the homage of her faithful.

There is Copacabana on cloudy days, not at all depressing. The sky is tinged an elegant, pearl gray. One can gaze at it while listening to piano music and lounging in the tea room of the Copacabana Palace Hotel, a tropical cream replica of the hotels lining the beach esplanade in Nice.

Copacabana and Ipanema are oceanside neighborhoods. However, Rio, similar to San Francisco, is situated on both the ocean and a bay. The Bay of Guanabara harbors the port and downtown areas in one of the most thrilling urban landscapes imaginable.

Rio's sidewalks are made not of concrete, but fist-sized black and white stones arranged in various mosaic designs throughout the city. In Charitas, you stroll on alternating bands of black and white, decorated with white and black ovals. Downtown, it's chains of rounded squares, the white and black fitting together like an M. C. Escher drawing. The sidewalk in Copacabana frames the long, sandy crescent of its famous beach with fat-bellied S's that echo the ocean waves and bare bottoms of the women in fio dental bikinis. Chances are, if you blindfolded a Carioca and drove him around until he was thoroughly confused, it would take only one glance at the sidewalk for him to tell you his location within a few blocks.

—Arthur Dawson,
"One Day in Rio"

A bayside parkway curves through this landscape, hugging the water's edge. From the water on one side rises Sugarloaf (Pão de Açúcar) and other low mounds across the bay. On the other side, behind and within the city, rise towering mountains draped in lush greenery. The highest mountain peak is called Corcovado, the pedestal for Christ the Redeemer.

I took this route almost every day, sometimes several times a day. Always it was a thrilling, dramatically changing sight. It was so extraordinary that there could be such a combination of mountain, water, and verdure in a metropolitan habitat, regularly, subtly transforming itself with the changes in duration, angle, and strength of light. A small, wayward cloud would sometimes wander over the top of Sugarloaf; and a wreath of clouds might cover the top of Corcovado, leaving Christ levitating with outstretched arms over the city. I once actually saw the rainbow end at a stone base behind Sugarloaf.

Sometimes I took this route accompanying former President Juscelino Kubitschek from his home in Copacabana to his office downtown when I worked as his secretary for English correspondence. To remain anonymous, he rode about in a chauffeur-driven Volkswagen beetle. Seated with him in the back seat and with the car ripping along the parkway, its windows open, we shouted over the wind to communicate, endlessly grasping at maddeningly flapping papers.

Moving from the port area of downtown into the heart of the city is a trip through several architectural and historical periods. There is the late colonial and early imperial period, represented chiefly by the old palace and cathedral.

Then there follows narrow blocks of 19th-century houses and shops, some intermixed with new commercial highrises. The older buildings have wedding-cake façades, many freshly painted thanks to an extensive historical restoration and preservation project. Entering some of the stores quickly gives away their age, the wooden floors creaking underneath as one shops for valises here, stationery there, and pastries down the street.

There is also a quite modern, late-20th-century area of downtown, reminiscent of Brasília. Most striking here is the state petroleum company's headquarters, a mammoth glass cube with some floors left as hollowed-out spaces for hanging gardens.

Yet just behind this striking building is the last cable car station

in the city, its route climbing into one of the first residential suburbs built in Rio during the last century, Santa Teresa. Set on a hill,
Santa Teresa offers riders breathtaking vistas. As the car resolutely
winds its way up, you spy beyond the gardens and roofs of ginger-
bread mansions and cottages growing views of the bay lying on one
side and the ocean on the other.

This neighborhood also has one of the most striking museums
in the city, the *Chácara do Céu* (roughly meaning, "Heavenly
Manor"). It was originally the residence of a wealthy industrialist,
built after the Second World War. He decorated it with furnishings
and artworks of an astonishingly pure taste, achieving a spare, elegant balance of Brazilian Baroque, Chinese Classical, and Brazilian
and French Modern. Upon his death, he stipulated that this home
be converted into a museum.

A visit to it proves a cleansing experience. One lingers in its
rooms, absorbing their refined ambiance, and gazes out the wide
windows onto the luxurious grounds of the house. Beyond them
lie the expansive vista of the city and water below. It seems a *primi-
tif* painting, possessing the striking force of elemental images as in
Garcia Lorca's vibrant gypsy ode to "green" nature: *"El barco sobre el
mar / y el caballo en la montaña."*

Never did I meet the museum's founder, but I felt such a kin-
dred spirit with the ambiance of his home that I recall the place as
if it were a tasteful companion of my Brazilian days. The Romans
held that there were gods or spirits of home and hearth, called *lares*.
A Portuguese derivative from this, *lareira*, is the word for fireplace.
A spirit does live on at the Chácara.

All parts of Rio intrigued me, and a small adventure I often
liked to pursue was to get on any bus and stay on it to the end of
the line. Looking out the moving window, I delighted in the parade
of shops and houses. One block held a sequence of barber shop, bar,
shoe repairman, hardware store, pink house, yellow house, green
house; the next was a bakery, fruit store, pharmacy, church, garden,
green house, yellow house; the next.... I enjoyed it like a sequence
of scenes in the toy village of department store windows during the
holidays.

At any point one could alight and refresh oneself. Everywhere one roams in Rio, or any Brazilian city, there appear every few blocks or so *botequins*, café-bars somewhat like Paris bistros that are tropical urban oases. They are usually open-air, like almost all stores in Brazil, with the side fronting the street having a metal screen that rolls up into the ceiling. At the bar, bordered by stools, one can have a drink; at tables along a corridor or in the back, one can order a meal. A coffee urn usually rests at the end of the bar near the street, serving *cafezinho*, the demitasse of strong coffee with sugar Brazilians drink numerous times a day. Near it there is also almost always a case of freshly baked pastry snacks stuffed with chicken, shrimp, or ground beef. Sitting for lunch or taking a quick coffee break, one gazes out on the world strolling by.

Invariably *botequins* are neighborhood watering holes, especially for men. Given the ease with which Brazilians enter into conversation with anyone, I always enjoyed these places for the welcome they gave into the local affairs of the neighborhood or into the average Brazilian's view of the country and the world. It was in one of the myriad *botequins* I frequented that I believe I heard the ultimate Cold War putdown. A stentorian voice near me declared that "if communism were such a good thing, they'd have it in the United States."

One of the most charming places in the Bay of Guanabara was the island Paquetá. Butterfly-shaped and with a small village at the point where the wings met, its charm was due to several factors. Just over an hour by ferry from bustling Rio, it was like some remote, tranquil fishing village far from anywhere. Moreover, no car traffic was allowed on the island so that everyone got about either by walking, riding a bicycle, or in horse-drawn buggies. In summer (December through March—thus, you wore a tan to holiday parties, not overcoats) flamboyant trees blossomed along the beach. They appeared as exotic Christmas flora. The branches were fernlike and had flowers very similar to crimson poinsettias.

At one time the boat trip to Paquetá offered an exceptional scene: dolphins leaping in the water, accompanying the ships. These centuries-long residents of the bay, however, have disappeared in recent years due to oil pollution from tankers. They are remembered though on the seal of the city of Rio, bordered not by pompous lions or impossible unicorns but leaping, delighted dolphins.

Eventually a day came I had not imagined. I had a wrenching decision to make, whether to leave this country that had so enchanted me. I remembered Robert Frost's poem on the fragility of nature and paradise: that "Eden sank to grief" because "nothing gold can stay."

The first culture we come deeply to know outside our own is so memorable because, like first love, it takes away our innocence of the world. It is the first we cherish for having revealed and then lightened our ignorance.

Edward A. "Ted" Riedinger is on the faculty of Ohio State University and has published extensively on Brazilian politics and cultural history. Currently he holds a Fulbright scholar award to complete field research for a book, Renaissance in the Tropics, *an analysis of the achievement of Brazilian culture in the 20th century. He is a founder and the secretary of the Brazilian Studies Association (BRASA), an academic organization that supports Brazilian studies in the humanities and social sciences. The association has a free Internet list, BRASANET: brasa@unmvma.unm.edu.*

★

I'll never forget the first time I met the Carioca spirit face to face. Several years ago, I was sent by a magazine on a dream assignment—to join a samba school in Rio and dance in Carnaval. Since I would be staying on for several months, I rented a small room in Copacabana from *Dona* Vitória, an elderly widow who rose at dawn every day to bake cookies for high-society parties. One night, when we were discussing whether she should leave the door unlocked for me, I muttered something about having found a new boyfriend, and was perhaps—well—not coming home. For a moment she looked confused, then suddenly she threw out her arms and hugged me. "Ah, *querida,* go! Have fun, eat, dance, laugh, make love! Life is so short!" In that brief moment, the joy of her Carioca spirit blazed through me, and, as I shut the door behind me, I felt somehow I'd been blessed.

                    —Pamela Bloom, *Brazil Up Close: The Sensual and Adventurous Guide*

Tambourine Men of Recife

The music they produce reveals
something profound and true
to those who listen.

RECIFE. OK. I WILL WALK ACROSS TOWN AND LOOK FOR A REEF. The town's harbor, lined with rusty freighters and incredibly old coastal steamers, is like a wide river with the reef, now covered in a long, thin line with huge rock chunks, forming the river's far bank. The ocean breakers crashing against this long stone wall throw up spray that shines in the sun where isolated figures of boys in swimming trunks with long cane poles throw lines into the surf. Their poses as they wait are as languorous and studied as Whistler drawings. Everything, even the distant boys, the boats, the docks, the street deep in the shade of mangos, the piled rocks at the reef, has a timeless, frozen look. Something planned by Englishmen, something built to last, a memorial to a decent past, that old vanished world of my grandfather's "where a man's word is his bond."

This section of town where the sailors hang out is a barrio of neglected and seedy one-storied buildings, narrow streets, and old trees. In a way it reminds one of San Francisco's Haight-Ashbury district during the '60s, a place that reflects the passions and vices of another time. The bars are as menacing as opium dens; no movie set could capture the sense of danger and violence that these façades suggest. Looking into their dark entranceways one is surprised at the quiet (it is early afternoon) when one is straining to hear the shrieks of drunken syphilitics in various stages of delirium tremens or the whistle of knives being thrown into careless backs. The skid row section of Recife, what a setting for the last chapter of a sordid novel about moral disintegration. In the last century, Joseph Conrad's bars, by comparison, are as classy as the Raffles Hotel; not even Jim in his moments of most intense self-loathing would have pushed against these swinging doors from which the paint has peeled off in blisters as though boiled away by the heat of the passions and vices inside.

Close to the river some parallel streets have been closed to car traffic. All day and at night until midnight people stroll along these malls or sit on benches enjoying the coolness. There is a flower market at one end of one street, great piles of fruit massed at the other end; when seen from a block away even at night the pure glowing colors—orange, scarlet, apple red, the yellow of marigolds or daisies—are celebrations, great shouts of joy. Hucksters, magicians, kids, or older men or women with trays of cheap jewelry or razor blades or Japanese cassette tapes wander back and forth with small expectations. At ten o'clock at night comes a religious procession of priests and acolytes, and behind them heavy, soberly dressed women all with candles that illuminate the tragic faces they have assumed for the occasion, and behind them people off the street who fall in at the rear until the street is more procession than onlookers. Everyone is singing; everyone is solemn. It is 16th century; very heavy-duty stuff. It is intensely moving to be in a city where *everyone* believes in God, and I consider joining them, not because I believe in God, but because, though the spectacle is depressing for its ritual, I believe in the emotion that has joined them together.

One night, bored with sitting in the park just outside the hotel and bored with establishing half-comical, half-grotesque father-daughter relationships with whores, I wander into the mall, drawn there by the sound of music. On one corner at the center of a small crowd two men are singing songs of their own invention: a highly stylized dialogue between friends, a friendly argument, the purest, most authentic music I have ever heard. The singers are two brothers in their late twenties. The older, one leg shorter than the other, walks with a terrible swooping stagger. They are poorly dressed in stained t-shirts and stiff, cheap trousers. An older man is working with them, an old confidence man in a double-breasted coat, spotty and rumpled, that is many sizes too large for him. His face has the blank, corrupted look of a man who has fooled too many people with cheap tricks. His younger companions also have a blankness growing in their faces, a pitilessness as though they have begun to withdraw from a life that has lost its promise and its challenge. The three of them hold tambourines, and at the end of each verse they tap and shake them in a most subtle and controlled way, drawing from these simple clown's instruments the most precise and delicate sounds.

Each brother sings one verse to the other. I cannot understand the words except for the first sentence of each verse. *"Hermano, tu no sabes nada."* Each one emphasizes the last word, *nada*, in a way that is strong, innocent, and loving and then goes on to comment, correct, expand, or digress. "Brother, you don't understand how things are." The crowd is controlled absolutely by the singers, even the cops, who are mentioned from time to time in satiric ways. The people laugh, sigh, nod their heads wisely, or look vaguely at the ground as though great truths were being revealed to them by this simple and profound music that is coming to them from out of the heart

It has been said that the harsh essence of the sertão—the arid backcountry of the Northeast—gives Brazil its soul, and that the spirit of the sertão pervades works of art that possess a depth not found in works from other regions. What many consider the country's greatest novel (Guimares Rosa's Grande Sertão: Veredas*); its greatest film (Glauber Rocha's* Deus e o Diabo na Terra do Sol*); and its greatest epic (Euclides da Cunha's* Os Sertoes*) are all set in the* sertão.

—AH and SD

of a great country. This is music out of the *sertão*, music made of dust, sticks, rocks, fickle women, mean storekeepers, fate, death, sun.

I listen for twenty minutes, for half an hour, keeping tight control of myself to not break into tears, to keep from dancing, embracing the singers, taking out all my money and laying it at their feet. In some sense that I don't understand, it is the most overpowering music I have ever heard; I want to sob, laugh, clap, and jump around; I want to shake one of the listeners, an old man, who seems unaffected, and yell at him, "But listen, listen, this is incredible."

As they sing, as they lose themselves in the music, their faces beam, transfigured. They are radiant with a pleasure that comes from doing something with flawless skill. It is possible, though I don't notice, that our own faces have changed and now reflect a profound delight, one of the best pleasures in the world: the joy in watching men who are doing something at which they excel.

If there is a sadness in watching the singers, it is one that is grounded in my American sense of values. It is sad to watch great artists wasting their sweetness. They are too great for the streets of Recife; there is an incongruity in their rags and in this little crowd of twenty that is gathered around them rather than at the amphitheater that would hold the thousands they deserve. I would not travel to Madrid to stand before some single Bosch in the Prado, but perhaps one day I will go back to Recife and wander the malls listening for the tapping sound of those tambourines, the glittering sound of those tambourines like a gush of water and those pure, plain voices revealing something profound and true about Brazil.

When the concert is over I give the older man a one hundred cruzeiro bill; he accepts it nicely, modestly proud that someone has recognized the true power of their art. And every night for the four nights more that I stay in Recife, I go out into the mall after dinner and stand in the crowd, stunned by the emotion that the three men create in those country songs that transform their faces and that open up life to those of us who listen.

The late Moritz Thomsen, born in 1915, made his home for many years in Guayaquil, Ecuador. His first book, Living Poor, *chronicles his four-year Peace Corps experience of living in a small fishing village in Ecuador in the*

1960s. He returned to Ecuador after leaving the Peace Corps to become a farmer on the Rio Esmeraldas, an experience he describes in The Farm on the River of Emeralds. *He also wrote* The Saddest Pleasure: A Journey on Two Rivers, *from which this story was excerpted. He continued to travel and live in South America until his death in 1991.*

✳

The traveling *repentista* singers of the marketplace keep alive the memory of the heroic bandits of the *sertão*, Lampião and his Maria Bonita, Antônio Conselheiro of Canudos, and Padre Cícero of Juàzeiro, among other rebel priests, defiant cowhands, and utopian mystics and visionaries of the *Nordestino* backlands. But even as they sing the praises of the traditional folk heroes, the *repentistas* usually strike a note of caution, warning against acts of open defiance. And as for the popular heroes themselves, these generous bandits, passionate visionaries, and charismatic miracle workers imagined at best a new Brazil, a kingdom of God on earth, made up of a multitude of small subsistence-based peasant and herding communities independent of the state and secular authority and free of hunger, money, civil marriage, and the tyranny of landlords, political bosses, bureaucrats, and tax collectors.

—Nancy Scheper-Hughes, *Death Without Weeping:*
The Violence of Everyday Life in Brazil

* ⋆ *

Rio Risqué

In a city brimming with earthly delights,
one's thoughts turn to finding a little romance
before Carnaval ends.

FROM WHERE CHRIST STANDS ON THE MOUNTAINTOP ABOVE
Rio de Janeiro, His arms outstretched, He can take in all of Carnaval. He can watch men reach out and stroke, with total impunity, any flesh that sashays by amid the heat, smoke, and samba. He can watch women respond by clamping their thighs around kneecaps, tossing their heads back and grinding toward Heaven and Hell. Beneath His gaze, foreigners are ordering prostitutes as easily as beers. Health activists are prancing through the streets costumed as condoms, to remind everyone of the raging AIDS epidemic. This is a city where murders are commonplace, where tourists pass graffiti that reads "WHERE THERE IS HUNGER THERE IS NO LAW." A city where soldiers—carrying FAL assault rifles and grenades and wearing ski masks to avoid reprisals—come in tanks, armored cars, and helicopters to combat drug gangs that have taken over entire neighborhoods. This is a city that spends millions on spangles and feathers and parade floats while homeless children scavenge amid the rubble. From high upon that mountaintop, Christ can see one pure man and one pure woman, born thousands of miles apart, heading toward each other. And maybe, above all the crime and lust and fear and violence, that is why His arms remain outstretched.

✳

You don't simply step off the plane at the airport in Rio and explode into sexual shrapnel. No, you're tired, and your neck is a little sore from the all-night flight, and your eyes are blinking away the sun that is suddenly pressing upon your skin and drying your throat, and you just want to reach your hotel on Copacabana Beach so you can change and then relax on the white sand. And once there, as the women pass like a delightful breeze that brings a shiver, you realize that Carnaval lasts for nearly a week and you have to save yourself. So you lean back under the pillowy clouds and sip the syrupy water from a coconut that's been slashed open with a machete by a man in a hut covered with palm fronds, and you imagine the possibilities of the wildest party in the world.

That's when you notice the woman with straight, blunt-clipped brown hair adjusting the two tiny seashells of purple nylon that barely stretch over her breasts. Anna Luiza is her name.

Out of the corner of her eye she's scanning the white sand for skin that is untouched by sun: foreign skin. She's heard that sometimes foreigners are faithful. Not that she wouldn't be happy with an honest Brazilian man. It's just that such a thing is hard to come by in a city where local legend has it that there are seven women for every man. "Is the ratio really seven-to-one?" a distinguished sociologist in Rio once wondered. "But I have only three. I must be inattentive."

It doesn't matter that Anna Luiza is in her own way beautiful. There is so much grace and elegance along this necklace of beach that she is an afterthought. Anna Luiza is not tall, lithe, flirtatious like the others who pass by in a parade of poetic nudity, like the two friends stretched out beside her. Madalena, to her right, is the type who inspires the honey-lyricked songs about Brazil heard around the world, and there is something about the savageness of Soraya's black hair and the daring play in her flaming charcoal eyes that will always lure your gaze before you turn to Anna Luiza's softer, rounder figure.

At 27, Anna Luiza is seeing her friends marry and drift away;

her anxiety is rounding the bend toward desperation. She's living in a city where thugs scissor hair off women's heads and sell it to wigmakers; where fear of theft and attack forces her to spend more and more weekend nights in front of the thirteen-inch Toshiba in her living room. And now that she's at the beach, she's reading a passing man's t-shirt: "IF I WERE YOU, I WOULD GIVE ME A KISS."

Some of the women whose nails she manicures at work, the wealthy ones who've taken trips to Europe and America, have sworn to her that men there are faithful. Not all, but many. Ah, it's absurd, she tells herself. She is shy among Brazilians. What would she possibly say to a foreigner?

And yet, as she lies back under the clouds that caress the mountaintops, Anna Luiza is quietly thrilled. This is her first Carnaval in Rio. She moved here with her mother and sister not long ago from the countryside. Madalena and Soraya have made the trip from their hometown to help her celebrate, allowing her to flip off the Toshiba and head out to taste the sizzle of the night.

In the plastic window of a pocket-size photo album in her apartment, Anna Luiza has pasted a thought balloon above a photo that captures her face in dreamy expression. Words inside the balloon say *"Saia dessa vida,"* which literally means "Leave this life" but really translates as "If only I could find something better.…"

But a faithful man in Rio de Janeiro during Carnaval? Do snowflakes fall upon Copacabana Beach?

As Ken walks along the black and white sidewalk tiles that flow alongside that beach like waves, his head appears to be in a pinball machine—ricocheting each time it's struck by the sight of fresh breasts.

It would be unfair to call Ken by the name on his birth certificate, because just now Ken is not himself. In ordinary life, he never gets lost. He never stands with an open mouth in front of passing women. But this week he is like everyone else. Everybody becomes a different person during Carnaval.

For months he's worked sixteen-hour days in a laboratory. Now, his snow-white skin gives off a scent that widens the nostrils of a barefoot black boy who sleeps on the streets and survives by slicing camera straps off passing shoulders with a knife fashioned from a crushed soda can. Either a German or an American, the boy senses—and both have money.

The boy eyes the glasses sliding down the foreigner's long, sweaty nose, then the back pockets for bulges and the socks for rolled bills. This is the type, the boy is sure, who will hand over everything without a fight if the jagged edges of a broken bottle are held to his neck. The boy must decide if the evening is yet drunk enough for him to get away with that. Carnaval is just starting—the street just beginning to succumb to the rhythm of samba surging from the bare-chested musicians at a sidewalk café.

The pale foreigner walks past a teenager nibbling the earlobe of a girl with heavy-lidded eyes and steps into a beehive of activity— bellhops carting luggage, vendors hawking t-shirts, artists pointing to paintings, taxi drivers and moneychangers hooking tourists by the arm. Chaos is as opportune as desolation. The boy remains ten steps behind.

He glances around and sees a policeman whose muscles swell under his t-shirt, on the back of which are printed words the boy can't read. "I'M LOOKING OUT FOR YOU," they say in English, reassuring foreigners who've heard news reports about invasions by hordes from the *favelas* in the overlooking mountains. *"Arrastão,"* this type of assault is called: a wall of human piranhas, devouring all in their path.

The foreigner stops and spins like the needle on a broken compass. Finally, he heads into a towering hotel, where a bowl of room-service spaghetti costs $20, and leaves the boy standing in the street with a vague grinding in his stomach.

It's in the hotel lobby that I spot him. "There he is," I say to my wife. "See. The blond hair. Coming this way."

"He looks so lost," Docinha says in English that is flavored by her Brazilian accent. It's been two years since she joined me in America. She shakes her head.

"By the end of Carnaval," I say, "he'll have two mulattas on each arm."

"*Him*? No way! Look at that face," she answers with a laugh that makes her hands instinctively calm the jiggle of her pregnant belly. "He's too innocent."

I watch the glasses slide down that long nose. Then Ken's head swivels toward a backside that looks like a perfectly formed apple sliced down the center.

"I'll bet you he makes love before the week is out," I say, feeling my jaw jut out a dare. "It's Carnaval. I'll bet you *anything*."

She extends a hand to make the bet, then pulls it back when she sees me staring at a prostitute. "Oh, no," she says. "Not like that. He's got to do it naturally."

"No problem," I say. "What's your bet?"

"If he gets through Carnaval without making love, I get to name our baby *whatever* I want."

I cringe, for we fought over names during much of the plane ride from New York until we met Ken, and I now imagine my poor son taunted and having the shit beat out of him in a junior high schoolyard because some tall, gawky white chemist didn't get laid.

"And what's yours?" Docinha asks.

My smile raises the ante. "If I win," I say, "I come back to Carnaval next year. Alone."

Relief lights Ken's face when he spots us. Three days earlier, his flight landed. Three days from now his flight will leave. He has decided to let himself go wild for the first time in his life. And all he has to show for it so far is a stiff neck and a slack jaw. He can feel the anxiety building.

As he steps toward us, he nearly bumps into a white V-necked blouse that comes to a point at a creamed-coffee-colored belly button. The treasure trove is richer than he imagined, but because he doesn't know the language he is naturally shy and can't let his body speak, he can't touch what lies at his fingertips.

For years he's been sitting stiff at the spines of his textbooks. In all his 27 years, he's never gotten drunk, never made love to a woman, and if you ask him why, he'll joke, "I'm a geek!"

He recently decided to become a doctor, to work on humans in the real world instead of chemicals in a vacuum, and he's been accepted by one of America's best medical schools. But before he takes on four more years of rigid discipline and $80,000 of debt, he wants to lose himself in feathers and spangles.

There is no choice now. This pregnant Brazilian woman and her American husband, whom he met on the plane, will have to open the doors to this world he cannot enter alone. Ken swallows when we are joined by an immense, silent black man who wears sunglasses even though it is now dark. "This is Valmir," I say. Valmir's hands are large enough to crush him like a beer can. Some of Ken's friends back home had seen the news and warned him about Rio. It is only that little swelling of belly beside him that is getting him through this. A pregnant woman could not possibly be leading him somewhere he might regret for the rest of his life. And then, suddenly, he is tucked into a cab, which veers into the darkness, and there is no escape from his escape.

"You really should dance in the parade with us," Docinha gets Ken's attention by touching him on the wrist. "I was born a thousand miles north of here, and it was always my dream. People in the neighborhoods around Rio spend the whole year making costumes and floats for the competition. It's their life. Fights break out when judges announce the scores. We're trying to arrange costumes with one of the best groups."

*ofa: literally it means soft, fluffy, squeezable. It's mostly used to describe a person (*fofa for female,* fofo for male) who is just adorable, sweet, lovable or simply cute and nice. Lovers all call each other* fofa *or* fofo *for honey or sweety, in English.*

Cafuné: *cuddling, scratching your loved one's head, caressing . . . doing* cafuné *is a gift you give someone for his/her pleasure . . . asking for* cafuné *might mean availability to play, cuddle, make love.*

—Neise Cavini Turchin, "Longing for Brazil"

"But I don't know how to samba," Ken protests. "I wouldn't be losing points for them, would I?"

"Just relax and have a good time," I say, smiling at Docinha, "and they'll love you."

Neon takes over the night. The taxi stops down the street from a huge club with luminous peacock feathers fanning out over its entrance. The door opens on a three-tiered theater of color and cleavage, on women with red fishnet stockings, on strings of pearls dripping from tight black *tangas,* on nipples protruding through lacy bras, on feathery Indian headdresses and devil masks.

I lean toward Ken's ear. "As the poet said, 'There is no sin below the equator.'"

Sparkling high heels samba at twelve beats a second under flashes of sunburst yellows, molten reds and flaming oranges to the music of a trumpet-and-slide-trombone band that blares through speakers the size of monuments. Valmir extends a beer to Ken with a smile. I extend a second and a third. Valmir is good for the fourth and fifth.

Soon the dance floor floods and shirtless men and viola-shaped women take refuge on the tabletops. Women approach Ken to dance, and through the smoky haze he notices the beads of sweat above their upper lips and the moist strands of hair clinging to their temples and their swaying hips and their eyes, which either ask for or promise too much. He dances without connecting, and each woman eventually drifts off and is replaced by another café-au-lait face with moist, gleaming lips.

And then the party begins to heat up.

A group of black teens with shaved heads takes the stage and, pounding drums roped around their necks, sends the crowd into a frenzy, inciting a woman to stand on the table I've reserved and swish her ass only a centimeter from my nose, causing Docinha to grip my chin and yank my gaze back toward her mock smile. Ken floats toward a woman riding a man's thigh as if it were a fire pole, past Valmir, who is being summoned by three gyrating women; past two pudgy men squeezed into taut bathing suits and pressing their genitals together in rhythmic delirium. Ken's eyes close for a minute within the swirl of plume, sparkle, breast, thigh, and ass, and some part of him is up in the smoke.

"You can name our first *ten* children," I yowl over the din at my wife, "if the guy doesn't get laid!"

✴

Of course, from where the 120-foot Christ stands on the mountaintop, it must have been easy to see why it all occurred. From there it would have been perfectly clear why the city below—with its mountains that rise from the ocean like buttocks, its tropical birds twittering, its butterflies shivering with bursts of color, its woozy sun and powdery beaches that make a human feel foolish in clothes—became the global capital of sex.

From here He could have watched, with great relief, the first boats from Europe arrive in 1502. *Relief* because the Portuguese explorers who began the colonization of Brazil preferred to make love to the red-skinned natives, as opposed to the Spanish, who settled much of the rest of the continent and preferred to kill them. Over the next three centuries, Brazil's genetic mix was made even more exotic by the blacks brought in chains from Africa to chop sugarcane in the 16th century, mine gold in the 17th, and work the coffee fields in the 18th.

Though Carnaval dates back to the pre-Lent bacchanalia in Venice in the 11th century, it wasn't until early in the 20th century, after Portugal had given Brazil its independence, that Rio's lust exploded, inflamed by the abandonment of its people, some of whom inherited too much and most of whom were left with nothing at all.

"But how do I know when they like me?" Ken asks. The smoke has evaporated into a clear afternoon—Day Four—and he is riding in a taxi with my wife and me on a raised highway to visit some friends who are arranging costumes for the parade.

"Things will go a lot easier if you just assume that they do," I say.

"But how do I know they're not prostitutes? I don't want that kind of woman. I want it to be natural."

"*Exactly* the way it should be," I say, glancing at Docinha. I still can't believe that Ken went back to his hotel room alone the night before.

The taxi passes a long, open-ended stadium that has a street running through it. The Sambódromo. Alongside it are colossal floats ready for the evening's parade. The taxi descends a ramp, circles and halts. We step out beneath the overpass and stare at shacks nailed together from scrap wood. Electricity has been filched to feed tiny televisions, and water has been diverted from underground pipes to fill washtubs where flabby-breasted black women beat the dirt from clothes. Barefoot, rust-colored boys are playing with homemade bows and arrows amid the squalor. One of them sees the blond foreigner, aims straight for him and, smiling, pulls back the arrow. The other boys laugh. Ken does not even notice.

He walks with us at a steep angle up the mountainside on a brick street. Soon we arrive at a small *bodega* where men are drinking beer, pounding drums, and singing samba. Ken smiles when he sees Valmir, who last night guided him safely back to his hotel—insisting even on paying for the taxi. It amazes him how after only a few hours he can have complete faith in people he doesn't know in a city that has become synonymous with danger. This is what few outsiders understand about Rio. From afar, they hear the news reports about businessmen being kidnapped and the *arrastãos* and the mountaintop slums ruled by drug lords, which police dare not enter, and the local businessmen paying off policemen to kill the street kids who rob their customers with knives fashioned from crushed soda cans. But ask the people who live in Rio if they'd live anywhere else and most look at you as if you are crazy.

A brute man with a thickly whiskered bowling-ball head immediately begins pouring beer. His name is Toco. Like a tour guide, he extols the view of the 120-foot statue of Christ that Ken visited on a package tour two days earlier. Ken is suddenly glad he's no longer on that air-conditioned bus, that he's drinking beer in the heat of the real Rio, that he has taken the risk.

We have attracted a curious crowd, which trails us up to the street and into a neat apartment. Near its front door is a small sculpture of a black hand with the thumb squeezed between the second and third fingers—a symbol of enduring hard times. But this week hard times do not exist. Some of the poorest people in the city devote a quarter of their annual earnings to Carnaval. And the residents of this hilltop, called Santo Cristo, have made sure that every cooler is filled with beer and every grill is covered with meat. Questions come at the chemist as quickly as do fresh bottles of beer. Do people like to play soccer in America? Volleyball? What are the women like? I translate Ken's noncommittal responses over the samba booming from the stereo. It doesn't take long for the natives to size Ken up. "If we were playing a soccer game of books," Toco tells me, "he would beat me 10-to-0. If we were playing a soccer game of life, I would beat him 11-to-0." Yes, it's clear—Toco nods along with me—the *Americano* needs to get laid.

Just then, three women enter the *bodega*. One, with coal-black hair and flaming eyes, has come from the state of Espírito Santo to see the sailor Renaldo, who lives on the hill. But Ken doesn't really notice her—or the smaller, rounder friend on her right. He's hypnotized by the tall one, the song-inspirer, Madalena.

"She…is…my…dream," Ken says through the beer haze. "If I could…if there is any way…if…"

"Relax," I say, patting Ken's knee. "I'll be right back."

"Yes, I guess you could say she is free," the sailor Renaldo tells me. But he adds apologetically that Madalena's boyfriend is expected to arrive the following night. "Maybe a foreigner like you who speaks the language. But Ken? How can he communicate? I don't think he has a chance." His face brightens. "But the shorter one doesn't have a boyfriend. Who knows?"

I walk back to Ken and explain. Ken glances at the shorter girl, at her blunt hair, pretty face, and ample breasts.

"What if she doesn't like me?" Ken whispers. "I don't want to be a thorn in her side."

"Ken says it would be wonderful to be at the side of a beautiful woman during Carnaval," I say in Portuguese, beginning the introductions with a flourish, "for he has been working sixteen hours a day in a laboratory and is about to return to his lonely studies to become a doctor."

Anna Luiza shyly looks him over. Ken is rocking back and forth to the music with a nervousness that she's never seen in a Brazilian man.

I translate questions and answers. When she lists her favorite American pop singers, Ken signals an OK by forming a circle with his index finger and thumb. I smack my forehead. No, winning this bet is not going to be as easy as I thought. "You just told her to fuck herself," I say. But everybody laughs at the gesture's double meaning, and I show Ken how to say "OK" by lifting his thumb straight up.

Under the circumstances, all is going splendidly, this laughter and small talk about music and America and a small-fry Brazilian politician who explained the $51 million in his bank accounts by saying that God helped him win more than 200 lotteries. But suddenly, just as the group is heading out the door to the street party next to the Sambódromo, Docinha explodes at me.

"That's right!" she hisses. "Go with the whores!"

"What?"

"A fair bet is one thing! But what do you know about decency? Corrupting him like that! That little one will take him for everything he has! Everybody sees it!"

I try to calm Docinha, then turn to see Ken disappearing with the others down the steep brick street. I am so preoccupied with fending off my wife's anger that I don't quite take in the gossip coming up the hill about what has just occurred at the street party near the Sambódromo. Some say it is an *arrastão*. Others say it was a war between rival gangs. After a while, it filters through: there is blood on a street Ken is walking toward.

I start down the hill. Toco stops me. "You can't go alone. Relax. Ken's with Renaldo. Renaldo will take care of him as if he were a brother."

I squint down the mountainside, along the overpass, toward the Sambódromo, but cannot find Ken in the darkness.

Coming down off the mountain, Ken, Anna Luiza, Renaldo, and some of the others head for the biggest block party in the world. Tens of thousands of revelers of every shape and tint swarm around stalls where vendors ladle *caldo de mocotó*—cow's hoof soup—to keep the sexual batteries charged. Samba and laughter mix with the scent of cane alcohol and grilled meat. Anna Luiza looks at Ken.

Now they're just two timid people whose translator has vanished. She reaches for his hand, and they start to dance. Sweat pops out of his face, and his legs don't know what to do. But embarrassment is not possible during Carnaval. At that very moment, in fact, the president of the country is in a box overlooking the Sambódromo with his arm around a Brazilian *Playboy* model who's dancing with her hands over her head, wearing only a t-shirt that leaves the full thicket of her crotch exposed not only to the photographers beneath her but also, consequently, to newspaper and magazine readers around the world. "Scandal?" the president will ask in be-wilderment the next day. "What scandal?"

The dance draws Ken and Anna Luiza closer and closer until Ken can no longer feel himself. Their lips graze and then lock in a kiss that Ken refuses to let end.

Hours later, at nearly three in the morning, when Toco, the giant Valmir, my wife and I find them at the heart of the celebration, the two are still entwined.

"God, I'm glad you're all OK," I say to Renaldo the sailor. "We heard about an *arrastão*."

"No problem at all," Renaldo says, pointing to Anna Luiza and Ken. "It was finished by the time we got here. This is Rio. Comes with the party. Just because someone gets AIDS, that doesn't mean the rest of us stop making love."

I glance at Ken and Anna Luiza and manage a smile. After all is said and done, at least there's this: the geek and the girl in a torrid embrace. "So you're set, then?" I say to Ken. "I've got to get my wife back to the hotel."

"What should I do?"

"*What should you do?*" I look toward the mountaintop for divine intervention. "Come back in the cab with us and take her to your hotel."

All eyes—Ken's, mine, and Docinha's—turn toward Anna Luiza.

"Well?" I say, after translating the proposal.

Anna Luiza's lips purse. Her eyes blink.

"Have him call me tomorrow," she finally says.

"Tomorrow?" says Ken.

"*Tomorrow?*" I say.

"Or maybe the day after," says my wife.

Day Five. Ninety-two degrees. I pace the brick street on the mountainside under the heavy sun. I'm in a sweat. I'm in a whirl.

Anna Luiza waiting at home for the phone call to arrange the liaison with Ken. The sailor Renaldo pulling me off to one side, begging me not to call Anna Luiza because if Anna Luiza comes that evening to the samba parade, she'll bring her friend Soraya, to whom he'd made love the night before, which will ruin his chances with Eliza, whom he has lined up to make love to tonight. "You can't do this to me," he cries. "I'm counting on you."

Ken pulling me off to the other side, bewildered that he can't call Anna Luiza. "She's going to think I stood her up. There's no time to explain later. I'm going to be leaving soon."

Docinha pulling me off to yet another side. "You can't call Anna Luiza. That will ruin everything for Renaldo. Remember, he's your host."

I snap. "Now you're the voice of integrity," I say, turning on my wife. "Now you start standing up for the rights of a cheating male."

Docinha shrugs. I turn to Ken and say weakly, "Maybe you'll meet somebody else. It's complicated...."

> *I*n popular Brazilian culture the idioms of food and sex, eating and making love, are interchangeable within a continual word play of mixed metaphors and meanings. Hunger, fome, is commonly used with reference to sexual desire, and intercourse is described as eating, comendo. One thinks immediately of Jorge Amado's novel Gabriela, Clove and Cinnamon, in which the dark, sultry heroine is a temptress of the table as well as the bed, or his Dona Flor and Her Two Husbands, which contains elaborate recipes for heavy Afro-Brazilian dishes redolent with pungent flavors and aromas that can also be read as recipes for Brazilian eroticism and desire.
>
> —Nancy Scheper-Hughes,
> Death Without Weeping: The Violence
> of Everyday Life in Brazil

Time is running out, yet passing so slowly as we travel across the city to pick up the costumes and then return to the apartment. Our silence overwhelms the samba blaring in the distance. I bite my lower lip as I pull over my legs the shiny lime-green pants with lavender tassels that rain from knee to toe. I exhale heavily as I reach for the double-decker blue-and-gold streaming Shriner's fez. Over a heart that feels hollow, Ken puts a red-white-and-yellow court jester's chest piece with tutti-frutti lollipops on each shoulder.

Then comes a miracle. Anna Luiza walks through the door.

Renaldo slaps me on the back, telling me how he'd felt guilty— a true miracle, a pang of guilt from a Brazilian male!—called Soraya and asked Anna Luiza to join them.

I become giddy watching Anna Luiza stroke Ken's cheek while Ken poses for photos costumed like a candied peacock. Even Docinha, perhaps feeling a little remorse for her rash judgment of Anna Luiza, is translating for them. Yes, anyone could sense the chemistry between the geek and the girl.

Beers are poured. Plans are laid. After midnight, we will head down the mountain, cross the raised highway to the Sambódromo and dance with our group. Anna Luiza says she'll stay behind on the mountainside, watch the parade on television and then wait for Ken to return.

Ken drinks and drinks some more, then pauses, a chemist about to announce a groundbreaking discovery. "You know something? Beer tastes great!"

Ken, Docinha, and I descend the hill with Toco, Valmir, and a few others from the neighborhood for protection. Our eyes fill with a kaleidoscope of fireworks, our ears with a primal drumbeat. The road leading into the Sambódromo is a mash of spangles and plumes. Docinha, Ken, and I weave through the confusion of thousands of bodies to find our preordained places in the parade.

"This dwarfs the Rose Bowl," Ken says, gaping. "Hey, don't lose me. If you do, I'll end up dying in Rio de Janeiro with lollipops on my shoulders."

Samba pours over us. Floats power forward. The stadium becomes a roiling sea of color. All sense of time is shattered. The 90-minute reel through the Sambódromo is over in a finger snap. It is four in the morning.

Toco, Valmir, and a few of the others rejoin us at the exit, and, stepping over puddles, trash, and sleeping vendors, we all head for the street party alongside the Sambódromo to drink amid the other dancers.

Docinha nudges me, a glint in her eyes, and nods at Ken's sagging eyelids. "Don't count your chickens."

I look futilely for a vendor selling *caldo de mocotó,* then grab Ken and declare: "I'm taking him to Anna Luiza."

Toco steps between us, peers at the distant lights on the mountainside and says, "Alone? Too dangerous. Wait for the rest of us."

An hour passes. Dawn of Day Six is approaching when we finally head for the long, raised highway that leads to the mountainside. Ken wonders if Anna Luiza is still waiting for him. I wonder whether Ken still has the strength if she is. Our group lazily drifts in twos and threes through thinning streets. The raised highway is nearly empty but for some teens scattered along the edges.

"I'll catch up with you," Toco calls. He walks toward a dark, vacant place to relieve himself.

I feel a shiver up the back of my neck. I glance around, see a human wall forming behind me. Toco, I know, is somewhere under the viaduct. But why can't I see Valmir and Renaldo? *You're imagining things,* I tell myself. *They're just going to pass us.* But the flicker in my wife's eyes tells me she is aware, too.

Toco zips his pants closed, climbs the ramp and sees two columns of teenage boys—one of either side of the highway—closing ranks behind his pale, costumed guests. *Arrastão.* One of the teens walking well behind the wall says to another with a grin, "Lost Germans." There is a security guard at the end of the overpass, nearly a kilometer ahead. But what can one guard do against thirty? Toco slides a camera inside his shirt, holding it so that it bulges like a gun, and begins to run toward his friends.

He alerts Valmir, who'd also stopped, and the two get between the hunters and the hunted.

"You're not going to do anything to them," Toco shouts.

A lanky teen in the center of the human wall eyes the bulge in Toco's shirt. "What are you talking about?"

An argument sparks, then rages back and forth. "Walk as fast as you can without running," I say to Ken. It is the last thing I will remember before I feel arms all around me, my wife's arms. We have passed the security guard on the other side of the overpass. Toco and Valmir are quickly backing toward them. Having lost its momentum to the argument and the bulge in Toco's shirt, the human wall has broken into pieces, which spill to the edges of the highway.

Anna Luiza awakens to hear the story told over and over in Toco's living room.

"They were all so nicely dressed. It was hard to believe.... "

"If I hadn't been holding that camera, you might not be here right now...."

"After all that dancing, I had no legs to run.... "

"Look at the lollipops on Ken's costume. Even they wilted from fear...."

"Valmir, I turned around and saw you in front of them. You never looked so small in your life.... "

"I would have fought to the end.... "

Each retelling somehow wrings out a little more of the threat. In a short time, everyone is smiling and laughing and conjuring the next evening's party. Casually crammed among all the others lying on the floor, Ken holds Anna Luiza's hand as if he'd lived on this mountain in Rio de Janeiro all of his days.

So my child will not be beaten up in a junior high schoolyard on account of a name given to him by his mother. And I will have the chance to return to Rio, alone. For during Carnaval in which more than 50,000 people flaunted their flesh and danced their fantasies in a two-day parade that cost more than $20 million to throw; during a Carnaval in which crowds howled at men dressed garishly in drag as they directed traffic on Copacabana Beach, near pharmacies sold out of aphrodisiacs, across from newsstands where scandal sheets of sexual acts committed at the balls appeared next to the nation's most prominent newspapers; during a Carnaval in which approximately 1,150 people were reported assaulted and 64 were reported killed and several million acts of love were consummated, while 25,000 churchgoers huddled in a stadium to pray for the city's salvation; during this Carnaval, the sun rose softly one morning as a naive, blond-haired foreigner walked palm-in-palm with a sweet Brazilian woman down a mountainside into the heart of the loveliest city in the world.

Cal Fussman has picked grapes in Italy, herded reindeer in Sweden, rolled with mountain gorillas in Rwanda, sparred with world boxing champion Julio Cesar Chavez in Mexico, searched for camel races in the Sahara, and been bitten by an insect in the Amazon rainforest that temporarily turned his tongue green. His work has appeared in GQ, The Washington Post, Life, Sports Illustrated, Esquire, *and* ESPN's Total Sports *magazine. He is now learning to play the accordion at his home in Long Island, New York.*

⋆

HOW TO SAMBA (MEN'S VERSION)

Find yourself a street corner. Practice just standing there. You should feel loose, but pleasantly expectant. Check how much time elapses before you feel the need to look at your watch. When you can complete a two- to three-hour stint without having to know the time, you are ready to start practice.

1. The first thing is attitude. You should look and feel relaxed, yet vigilant, playful, and ready to pounce. A slouching posture is easiest, but some crack *sambistas* manage a straight-backed nonchalance that is highly prized. Practice both and decide which suits you.

2. Put the music on. Listen to the beat. It is the road you will walk on, but whatever flow develops in your movements will come from the little plinking guitar or banjo pegging away just behind the singer. Your task is to follow the drums with your feet and spell out their rhythm by flinging your legs as far away as possible from your torso on every beat. Master this, then practice the same movement with your torso casually thrown back at a 45-degree tilt.

3. As your legs cut circles in the air with your torso planed back away from them, it is critical that your head remain level, as if you were dancing wedged under a shelf. Hopping up and down is tasteless. Also, don't fall down.

4. If you have mastered cakewalking in place, swinging your legs under and over each other as if your were climbing an invisible spiral staircase, and pulling up to a sharp halt after sliding sideways very fast with your feet, you are ready to time your performances. Timing is the difference between dancing to devastating effect and looking like a fool.

5. Remain in your street-corner mode until a woman approaches. Let her walk by. Let a few more women pass. Remember, you're not desperate.

6. Wait until a woman you really like comes along, and let her go just past the point where she can see you out of the corner of her eye. Break into samba. If your energy is strong, she will perceive your movement with her back and turn around. Stop. Smile. (Not at *her*!) Tug your clothes sharply into place. Wait for another woman. Repeat many times. With luck, a woman will eventually walk by who turns your spinal column to jelly and sets your ears on fire. She will stop and look at you and smile and avert her eyes and look at you again and start to walk away and turn and grin and throw caution to the wind and break into samba and you'll move right up and dance a couple of circles around her and shrug up behind her real slow and catch her by the hips and circle her down to the floor and spatter a starstorm of steps around her feet and grab her and carry her home and ride her and catch her screams in your ears and lie back and breathe easy and watch her wash up and sing and cook and ask you for a cigarette and give you the eye. If none of this happens, you can always form a circle with the other men and really dance.

—Alma Guillermoprieto, *Samba*

RICK GEYERMAN

Crappola

*Bewitched by the lure of exotic Rio,
a South Dakota couple decides to get married there.
There's just one hitch....*

RIO DE JANEIRO! EXCITING, EXOTIC, AND ROMANTIC! WE decided to run away to Rio, and get married.

The woman at the Brazilian Consulate in Chicago was helpful, but uncertain of the procedure. She advised us to get our blood tests, marriage license, birth certificates, and proof of prior divorce (we both were) and carry them with us.

She gave us the number of an office to call when we got there.

In Rio, we found that the person we were supposed to see had gone to Brasília, for the installation of a new government. We were informed that our wedding was impossible, however, because we hadn't published our intentions in the local newspaper for 30 days. Apparently, scores of Brazilians attempt illegal multiple marriages. Laws had been passed requiring that the public be notified of the pending nuptials. And laws, they reminded us, are laws.

We decided we wouldn't let it ruin our vacation.

We went to our first topless beach. There aren't many topless beaches in South Dakota, where we live.

We rode the tram up to the giant Jesus statue overlooking the bay.

We waited outside in the rain, while they filmed a popular soap opera in our hotel lobby.

In a fine seafood restaurant one evening, Julie drank her finger bowl. The waiter, graciously, refilled it. We don't have many finger bowls in South Dakota, either.

We found that we could travel nearly anywhere in the city for free. Jewelry stores such as H. Stern will pay the taxi fare to their showrooms. By instructing the driver to take us to a showroom near our intended destination, and spending a few extra minutes in the shop, we rode all week for nothing.

Their ploy was effective. The money we finally spent on Julie's wedding ring would have paid for a lot of cab rides.

One other event remains in my memory, even today, ten years after our trip. On a beautiful, bright afternoon, we walked along the Avenida Atlântica. To our left was the ocean, to our right, and as far behind us as we could see, extended a row of giant tourist hotels.

Three boys, nine or ten years old, approached, held up a scuffed shoeshine kit and a greasy rag, and pointed at my shoes.

I was wearing old, white Keds.

Generally I don't polish my tennis shoes. I gave them my best "*No, gracias,*" shrugged, and kept on walking. The kids let us pass, then curiously, circled the plaza, and once again approached us from the front, but still several yards away.

"Polish your shoes, mister?" the biggest grinned, pointing down at my feet.

On the toe of my right shoe was a lump of dog shit the size of a golf ball.

I never saw it happen.

I couldn't have stepped in it. To get that much goop on my shoe, I'd have had to hold my foot directly under the dog's butt as he squatted.

The kid had planted it there somehow. And now, there he stood with an innocent look on his face—my savior with a grimy rag in his hand.

I knew he'd done it, and he knew I knew, but I couldn't prove a thing. We stood there grinning at each other.

Somehow, I found it hilarious.

I gave him five American dollars, to polish my shoes.

Rick Geyerman and his wife have been locked in a lighthouse on Cozumel, had olives thrown at them in Tangier, and been haunted by ghosts in Deadwood. "I guess when you grow up in a place like Mitchell, South Dakota, the line between 'adventure' and 'stupid' is a little blurry," he says. "Sometimes I fly hot-air balloons, and sometimes I play country-western music. So far, life's been pretty interesting." Geyerman has also written for numerous newspapers and had his work distributed on Internet services.

★

While other travelers may collect masks or spoons or whatnot from the places they visit, my friend Mike "collects" visits to unusual museums. If there's a Leprosy Museum or a Collection of Fossilized Animal Feces, he won't want to miss it. His find in Rio was the Carmen Miranda Museum, a small building in Flamengo Park.

Recordings of Carmen Miranda's staccato singing played at full cha-cha-cha over a stereo. They played only to us and the one attendant who had turned on the music when we entered. Flamboyant costumes constituted the majority of the collection. They are all in trademark two-piece style with bare midriff, a low-cut top, and a long skirt. The famous headdress of tropical fruits was on display with other elaborate and fanciful showstopper toppers. Her platform shoes were so high they could cause acrophobia. Her earrings were huge and gaudy. There were miles of ruffles and sequins.

As we walked out the door, Carmen's song was cut off in mid-lyric. But her legacy is going strong. The rest of the world may forget *That Night in Rio, A Date With Judy, Copacabana,* and the other movies starring the Brazilian Bombshell, but Rio will remember because Rio is a Carmen Miranda kind of place, a place of costumes and Carnaval, a city where the poor may spend more on a single fancy costume than on their entire wardrobe, a city where women can manage to wear spectacular ensembles while wearing next to nothing.

—Mary Gaffney, "Carmen's Place"

JULIA PRESTON

Where the Wild Things Are

*Brazil's wetlands are no less alluring than
a steamy soap opera would have you believe.*

MANY PEOPLE HEAR ABOUT THE PANTANAL, THE IMMENSE WET-
lands of western Brazil, from books about bird-watching. But I
learned about it from a naked woman on television.

I had just moved to Rio de Janeiro and was in the early stages of
learning Portuguese. My method was to study the nighttime soap
operas, known as *novelas,* on Brazil's three major TV networks. At
the time, the viewers' favorite was an 8 p.m. *novela* whose opening
segment, repeated nightly, showed a long-haired nude swimming in
the waters of a clear and tranquil lake. Surrounded by swaying
grasses, the woman fell into an underwater embrace with a man
whose state of undress below the waist was implied but not
revealed by the camera. The *novela* was titled *Pantanal,* after its setting, and was one of several soaps one network said it produced to
portray "the Brazil that Brazil doesn't know."

The opener was the first full female nudity to appear on Brazilian prime time. It ignited a hot public debate about broadcast
ethics, in which the critics by and large concluded that even in
unfettered Brazil things had gone too far. The other two networks
promptly responded by refilming the opening segments of their
new evening soaps to add some naked women.

But the nude dip was not all that made *Pantanal* popular. There was also the lovingly shot aerial footage of curling rivers, pristine forests, multitudes of herons taking flight with glinting wings. There was the tradition-bound ambiance of the big cattle ranches, the *fazendas,* which structure the social life of the Pantanal, a contrast to the collapse of the order in urban Brazil.

I learned a good deal of Portuguese vocabulary by following the *Pantanal* affair in the press, but the show itself was not that helpful. The television *pantaneiros,* the people who live in the marshes, were a laconic lot. Whole scenes would go by with no more than a dozen words spoken. The characters who did talk had regional accents, the Portuguese equivalent of a drawl, and it was hard for my inexpert ear to make out the conversations.

But I did understand that the Pantanal was a lush and remote location even for Brazilians. After seeing it on TV, I never thought of it as being merely one of the most enormous, exuberant, and undamaged tropical ecosystems on Earth, as many do who find out about it from bird books. Even before I went there, I believed that the Pantanal was a place where men had achieved a negotiated settlement with nature.

The name *Pantanal* means "swampland" in Portuguese. Technically it's a misnomer. The Pantanal is the Brazilian portion of a floodplain, part of the system of the Paraguay River, which starts in the uplands of central Brazil and flows into the Paraná River at the southwest corner of Paraguay. Two-thirds of the marshy plain is in the Brazilian states of Mato Grosso and Mato Grosso do Sul, covering 54,000 square miles, an area almost as large as all of Florida. Another third extends into Paraguay and Bolivia. The parts together make up the largest wetlands in the world.

The Pantanal's idiosyncratic trait is its flood cycle. The summer rains, from October to March, fill the plain. It's steamy and hot, often over a hundred degrees Fahrenheit. Then in April the rain lifts, the temperature drops, and the waters begin to recede, leaving behind a residue of incomparably fecund nutrients. Fish eat the bugs, birds and caimans eat the fish, jaguars eat the birds, and so on in a glorious sequence of satiety, death, and resurrection.

Meanwhile, the flooding imposes a limit on what humans can do to bend the Pantanal to their purposes (as distraught homeowners in the Mississippi and Sacramento River floodplains have also learned). Each year the waters return to reassert their overwhelming claim.

So impenetrable was the Pantanal until the mid-19th century that the area was shown on maps as the uncharted Sea of Xarães. Geographers believe it was originally a piece of ocean lopped from the Atlantic by some epochal geological jolt. Eventually river travelers explored the navigable waterways, and by the end of the 19th century settlers from coastal Brazil were sending their cattle out across the marsh to scout the high ground for grazing. Today the entire expanse of the Pantanal, save for the Transpantaneira Highway and one small and curiously inaccessible national park, is privately owned by ranchers. They raise an estimated ten million head of cattle, which pasture freely in the dry season and huddle together on dry islands during the rains.

Why did I care about all this? I'm no naturalist, but I like a handsome bird. I like wild places, up to a point; I do not care to sleep in mud or anywhere where I might wake up with a hirsute spider ambling across my face. I like seeing a creature pop out of the trees, like finding its proper name in a field guide. My tastes are cheap. I prefer gaudy macaws and svelte egrets. When the cognoscenti start talking about flycatchers and antshrikes, I get bored.

I knew that people who go bird-watching in the illustrious rainforests of the Brazilian Amazon often come back with stiff necks. The tree canopies are high overhead, the forests dimly lit, and the birds widely dispersed. In the Pantanal the wildlife roams in wide-open spaces and tends, as the dry season progresses, to gather around the remaining water holes. It's easy.

The Pantanal does not compete with the Amazon rainforest for sheer numbers of animal and bird species. But there are at least six hundred different kinds of birds to be seen there, plenty enough for me. Besides, as an ecosystem the Pantanal has several advantages. Unlike the Amazon Basin in recent decades, the Pantanal was never viewed by Brazil as a strategic frontier that would provide raw materials to thrust the nation into the developed world. It was never convulsed with the manic gold rushes and land grab that devastated so much of Amazônia. The economic life of the Pantanal has been guided mainly by ranching families who have been there for generations, who have learned to live with the rise and fall of its waters and have no urge to burn or export its natural bounties.

This at least was the argument I heard from Orlando Rondon, the owner of Fazenda Rio Negro.

There is no feasible overland route to Rondon's *fazenda.* It takes a damned expensive hour-long Cessna air taxi ride from the city of Campo Grande, southeast of the Pantanal, to get there. But I wanted to visit Rio Negro, because that was where the Manchete network filmed the soap opera. In the Pantanal there are numerous *fazendas* of varying sizes that take in guests. Some are more hotel than *fazenda,* but not Rio Negro. You pay your fee before you get on the plane to go there; then you have the run of the place without any new charges. But *Seu* Orlando explained firmly, over dinner the first night, that "our style is to receive people into our house without changing the family work system of the *fazenda.*" When you stay at the Rio Negro, you rent a patriarchy.

The center of the 37,500-acre ranch is a long, low clapboard house, built in 1920, with ceramic tile floors and a veranda down the front, on a rise above the banks of the Rio Negro. No hasty face-lifts here for the tourists; the white paint peeling under the eaves will be renewed when other chores allow. Wild monk parakeets infest the site the way swallows fill American barns. By the hundreds, they raise a racket in the palm trees in front of the house and snatch the mangoes from the back patio.

Seu Orlando is a stocky, still-powerful man in his seventies, with a bushy mustache and fierce eyes. Over dinner, with a whirring ceiling fan dispersing the heat, he spun his lore. "This is my whole world. It's still here because of our spirit of preservation," he said grandiosely.

Seu Orlando's grandmother, who founded the ranch with her new husband in 1895, was widowed in 1904, when the eldest of her eight children, his father, was fourteen. She taught them all to read and write and expanded the ranch to 130,000 head of cattle.

"When the Pantanal was settled, there was nothing here but brutal nature," *Seu* Orlando said, continuing his discourse. "We had to adapt to its brutality because we needed it. We learned not to put a bullet in a bird or animal unless we were going to use it for something. *Pantaneiros* don't attack animals."

I wasn't sure what to make of this peroration until the following dawn, when *Seu* Orlando took me out in his pickup truck. The scrub woods and marshes around the house were so thickly populated, it was Manhattan for wildlife. We passed a pair of American rheas—tall, ungainly birds very much like ostriches. We saw a couple of foxes, some wild pigs rooting in the mud, and scads of burrowing owls heading for their holes in the ground. Up to the ankles in a water hole was a flock of roseate spoonbills, leggy birds with white wings edged in brightest vermilion. In the trees by the river were nests of jabiru storks, Brazil's biggest flying bird, with a wingspan of more than seven feet. The jabiru has a red collar, like a velvet ribbon, at the nape of its thin black neck. Heads of chicks, like dandelion puffs, were sticking up from the platform nest. In the far

Jabiru stork

trees, howler monkeys proclaimed their turf with their peculiar roar, the sound of a jet bombing wing on distant takeoff.

As a bird-watcher *Seu* Orlando was, you might say, self-taught. He assured me, for example, that the buff-necked ibis, a big bird with a narrow, curving beak and plaintive honk, has a menstrual period. (I have yet to find an ornithologist who could even guess at the basis for this assertion.) At another point, he went on a boisterous chase after a pair of hyacinth macaws we spotted sitting in a leafless tree. The hyacinths are the longest macaws, more than a yard from beak to tail. They are brilliant indigo blue except for their beaks and yellow rims around the eyes. They nest in bare trees, and their squawk can be heard from half a mile. On the black market they are worth up to ten thousand dollars a head. No wonder, then, that they are one of the world's most threatened bird species, with no more than three thousand left in the wild.

But hyacinths are nothing special to *Seu* Orlando. Gaggles of them linger near his house all the time. While I sat in reverent silence, adoring the pair through my binoculars, *Seu* Orlando jumped out of the truck and ran toward them, flapping his hat for my benefit, so I could see them fly—not a performance to repeat for the Audubon Society.

The birds were tame, even those striking and beautiful birds which under man's persecution are so apt to become scarce and shy. The huge jabiru storks, stalking through the water with stately dignity, sometimes refused to fly until we were only a hundred yards off; one of them flew over our heads at a distance of thirty or forty yards. The screamers, crying curu-curu, and the ibises, wailing dolefully, came even closer. The wonderful hyacinth macaws, in twos and threes, accompanied us at times for several hundred yards, hovering over our heads and uttering their rasping screams.

—Theodore Roosevelt,
Through the Brazilian Wilderness
(1926)

Back in the house, I noticed an aging black-and-white photo of a youthful and muscular Orlando kneeling behind an inert jaguar with a shotgun on his knee. Today the Pantanal's jaguar is another endangered species.

"We used to hunt jaguar. It was one of our greatest pleasures," *Seu* Orlando confessed in that accent which I had learned to comprehend. "But then they started to disappear. And we stopped."

Since 1967, hunting wildlife is a serious crime in Brazil, punished with a mandatory jail sentence. But that's not why *pantaneiros* stopped hunting jaguar. Enforcement of such laws is lax, with a federal forestry police grossly understaffed for the huge areas they must patrol. According to *Seu* Orlando, many *pantaneiros* discovered that when they went after jaguar for sport, they also encouraged incursions by lowlife poachers who wanted skins to sell. At the same time, jaguars eat a Pantanal rodent called capybara, essentially a guinea pig the size of a cocker spaniel. When the jaguar population dwindled, the capybara proliferated alarmingly.

"It doesn't work to go against nature in the Pantanal. When you least expect it, you end up paying for it," said *Seu* Orlando soberly. "The Pantanal does not accept aggression."

Almost everywhere else in Brazil the *fazendeiros* are the prime instigators of environmental depredation. In the Pantanal, however, *Seu* Orlando and his colleagues have formed the most effective conservation group in the region. They helped create a state forest police and declared open hostilities against jaguar and caiman poachers. After a decade when jaguars went almost completely out of sight, now they are noticeably on the rebound.

Capybara

At midday, when it is too hot to work, *Seu* Orlando padded about his house with bare feet and a bare belly. He was shadowed by Guta, a bare-faced currasow, sort of a tropical cross between a chicken and a pheasant. Guta had a crest on her head of white-tipped black feathers, which she flared to prove her beauty to any doubters. Toward *Seu* Orlando she was maternal, trotting behind him and cooing to warn of anything she regarded as potential trouble.

One morning six cowboys came in with the last of the *fazenda's* herd, which now numbers 4,000 head, for annual branding and vaccinations. The men and their horses drove cattle toward the corrals with moves as familiar as instinct.

The cowboys drove their needle guns into the ebony flanks and used green disinfectant to kill teeming clusters of fly larvae in the wounds where the new calves' umbilical cords had dropped off. Brands went on rumps and ears. The place of fences in the Pantanal is taken by an honor system. Ranchers must protect and return their neighbors' strays.

Rio Negro cowboys don't get rich, making the equivalent of fifty dollars a month, but theirs is a skilled and respectable calling. They suffered considerable ribbing from their colleagues from other ranches during the filming of *Pantanal,* because they spent days marching the cattle up and down the field in front of the *fazenda* to get just the right panorama for the cameras. Conservative in their customs, they were appalled by the diving nude. But *Seu* Orlando confessed he thought she was wonderful. "It wasn't like the sex of the city," he said. "It was just nature beckoning."

One afternoon at Rio Negro I ran into Jorge Schweizer, a Swiss-educated Brazilian surgeon who owns a ranch downstream on the river from *Seu* Orlando. For the past eleven years Schweizer, who is in his 50s, has all but abandoned the operating room to spend his time cruising the river in an open motorboat looking for giant river otters.

"I had the most wonderful day yesterday," Schweizer said, speaking in English. "I spent eight hours making observations. I saw two otters making love."

Since it was late on a hot, still afternoon, the otters had retreated to the cool of their dens. We didn't see any. But the following morning I took one of *Seu* Orlando's motorboats back down the river to a spot Schweizer recommended. Three of them were at play, plunging and snorting, propelled through the water by broad, flat tails. As Schweizer predicted, they were happily unaware of their proximity to the abyss. When I made them uneasy, they bounded up through the brush along the bank, where they rustled and crashed as loudly as horses. Soon they were back in the water, sneaking glimpses at me. But they couldn't keep their minds on the intruder. One had to dive to catch a fish, and the others couldn't go on without sharing a nuzzle.

It occurred to me that everything I might say about seeing the rare otters would be banal. It was akin to the pleasure I once took in those episodes when my daughter, at the age of one, mastered a new word or managed at last to place a square block in its appointed square hole. My satisfaction was great, but private. I knew I couldn't recount the simple thing I'd witnessed to make it novel for someone else. Yet I was confident that many other people, in my position, would also have been delighted.

Having reconnoitered the southern Pantanal, I took a regular commercial jet from Campo Grande to the main city to its north,

Cuiabá. There I rented a Volkswagen van and headed back into the wetlands to see the northern end.

For visitors, this is the poor man's Pantanal. There are no genteel, high-priced *fazendas* like Rio Negro on this end. South of a raunchy mining town named Poconé, I hit a rippling dirt road, and after paying a toll at a government environmental agency outpost, I was on the Transpantaneira Highway. This violently bumpy thoroughfare goes southward through swamps for 96 miles, ending at the settlement of Porto Jofre on the Cuiabá River. It's not hard to decide what to do in the northern Pantanal: the road is the only event. It requires full attention, however, because it passes over more than 100 wooden bridges, not one of which is adequately constructed to handle the traffic. I often found myself performing *corvée* for the state of Mato Grosso, shoving splintered boards back into position so my wheels could cross.

Although no one planned it that way, the Transpantaneira has a different character than most roads that violate nature sanctuaries. Its builders dug trenches along both sides of the raised road and water holes under each bridge. Instead of fleeing the human movement, all manner of creatures congregate around these reservoirs. So, one's progress down the road goes in spurts. Every few hundred yards there appears some new reason to climb out of the car and train the binoculars.

Hawks, herons, storks, spoonbills, so many of them it's easy to become jaded. *Another* snail kite, that princely raptor with the hooked beak which lives, quite literally, on escargots and is nearly wiped out in its American habitats? *Another* capped heron, exquisite with its powder blue bill, black beret, and pale yellow chest? The falcon known as the *caracara* is the national bird of Mexico, but in the Pantanal it is common trash, scavenging along the road oblivious to passing cars. Toward the end of the Transpantaneira is an open marsh, about a mile wide and as long as the eye can see in either direction, where herons and ibis make rookeries. At this site, one bird-watcher I know who comes often to the Pantanal has seen flocks numbering in the hundreds of thousands.

Along the road, trees come in stands and patches that are

monkey havens. The howlers are big and black, but from what I saw, their early morning warrior chant was all bluff. In the heat of the day they sat dead still on high branches and scowled, as if to remind all comers how mean they were without having to prove it. Some marmosets I saw were the emotional opposite of the howlers, skittling single file along a path through the treetops, which required some showy acrobatics.

Caimans, known locally as *jacarés,* also crowd around the Transpantaneira. By current estimates the Pantanal is home to two million *jacarés,* probably the densest population in the world. For a human being, it is remarkable to observe so many animals of the same species so close together with so little interaction. In the midday torpor they lie motionless side by side at the roadside trenches, with their tails on the mud and the rest of them in the water, except for their triangular eyes and their nostrils, which periscope up. If you watch long enough, you may see one blink, to shoo away a kind of butterfly that lives by drinking the tears from the *jacarés'* eyes.

It was the blackness that made the brilliant eyes so captivating. At the end of my flashlight beam, like glowing embers on a sea of black velvet, the fire-orange eyes of a thousand caimans reflected back at me.

The field stretching out before me mirrored the starry Southern sky. Every sweep of the flashlight lit up scores of eyes, some not twenty yards from where I stood at the end of the Transpantaneira Highway.

—Scott Doggett,
"Lush Life in the Pantanal"

At night, a beam of bright light across the lily pads near a wooden bridge will illuminate a Milky Way of amber *jacaré* eyes. This is, in fact, the technique of Pantanal skin hunters, though they tend to do their bloody business far away from any road. They shine a light and then shoot down the middle between two glowing orbs. The skins, destined for swank First World purses and pumps, are marketed across the border in Paraguay. In the late eighties, poachers took as many as one million *jacarés* each year. It's an indication of the resilience of the tribe that so far this carnage has not caused any permanent decline in its numbers.

By one water hole I saw the mortal remains of one member of another legendary Pantanal family, the anaconda. It was a little fellow—only about ten feet long. The anaconda tends to be nocturnal, and from the looks of the crime scene, this one had slithered into a fisherman on the bank of a water hole in the darkness of the previous night. Whoever it was apparently shot it in self-defense. A strapping anaconda can grow to more than thirty feet. A Pantanal bird guide I know told me he had once seen an anaconda swallow a wood stork, a bird that stands about four feet high.

My last stop on the way back up the Transpantaneira was the ranch created by the late Sebastião Camargo, reportedly one of the richest men in Brazil until his death in 1994. Camargo was the owner of the construction company that built much of Brasília, the futuristic capital, completed in 1960, that was raised from a bare plain. The ranch spans 178,000 acres of the Pantanal. From the front gate of the property to the front door of the main house is a 22-mile drive. The Fazenda São João is not open to tourists. To visit it I had to get written permission from Camargo's company.

Today 25,000 head of cattle pasture on the ranch. The livestock, however, are the product of a two-decade confrontation between Camargo, armed with money and bulldozers, and the Pantanal, which Camargo lost. In the late sixties Camargo embarked on a huge earth-moving exercise to change the course of rivers and build dikes around much of the property, with the idea of planting rice and corn. It was thought that the natural irrigation of the Pantanal would make it spectacularly productive for commercial crops.

It took only three years to abandon the project. "You planted seven thousand acres. Three thousand were for the birds and the animals," remembered a ranch hand named Geraldo who had worked at São João for 23 years. Today the dikes serve only to control the Pantanal's excesses, so the Camargo cattle can at least graze on planted, instead of wild, pasture.

Part of the property is an island, reached only by a ferryboat, on which Camargo built a surprisingly unexceptional modern ranch house, where he liked to fete distinguished visitors. On the outside wall are plaques commemorating notable visits: former Paraguayan dictator Alfredo Stroessner in 1975, a publisher of the French news-paper *Le Monde* in 1987, Prince Michael of Kent in 1990. Apparently Camargo's pride here was not in his house but in the jet airstrip that stretches away from it, the only such landing field in the Pantanal. With this, at least, Camargo prevailed.

The plaques hinted at Camargo's sense of the struggle in which he was engaged. Each one notes that the visitor came "to the deepest heart of the Pantanal." Through a picture window I glimpsed a primitive mural that dominated the living room and appeared to depict the Pantanal. But what it showed was an animal uprising, with a man lying wounded on the ground, his rifle beyond his reach, and a raging marsh deer buck trampling the dirt around him.

To receive the guests he brought in by jet from far away, Camargo had built a wide outdoor patio covered with a conical thatched roof. Scores of bats had nested under the roof and were dropping a downpour of excrement on the patio. In the latest of an endless series of high-, medium-, and low-tech efforts to expel the bats, ranch hands had tied about two dozen champagne bottles upside-down around the edges of the roof. They had heard that the sound of the wind passing by the mouths of the open bottles would irritate the bats and drive them away. So far, though, the bats were holding firm.

It seemed clear, however, that wild things were overrunning the Camargo *fazenda* for the simple reason that they were at ease there. On my way out, I came upon a giant anteater sauntering down the road. It stood about as high as a German shepherd but had a long tail with hair that hung to the ground and a very pointed snout. After many dry days, a good rain had fallen the night before, bringing out the bugs. The anteater, another endangered species in Brazil, made its way among the legs of grazing cattle, plunging its stringlike tongue into anthills and termite mounds, licking up a feast.

During my first flight into the Pantanal, I had flown over the Taquari River, one of the tributaries that traverse it. In an old aerial photograph, the Taquari looked translucent black, like most of the wetlands. But now it had turned a dull ocher. It was fouled with tons of sediment from nearby plains that had been farmed carelessly, with no regard for erosion. As a result, I was told, the food chain in the Taquari had come unlinked: fish couldn't swim upstream through the muck to spawn, and without the fish, the caimans starved or moved. And so on.

The farming on its perimeter is only one of the threats to the Pantanal's overall balance. There are plots to carve a waterway for commercial freighters through one corner. Callous day-tripping tourism is degrading another.

As I left the wetlands at dusk that day, I remembered my talk with Guilherme Mourão, an alligator expert who was leading the first ever census of Pantanal wildlife. Guilherme and his team had been flying for days in a small plane at 250 feet over the marsh surface, counting head. Although he had been in the Pantanal innumerable times, he returned from this inspection a little dizzy with the beauty and abundance of it.

"The Pantanal is a sturdy environment," he had said. "It resists."

Then, on second thought, he paused and added: "But no one knows for how long."

Julia Preston is a journalist who has been writing about Latin America since 1977. She covered the wars in Central America for The Washington Post *from 1986 to 1989, and was based in Rio de Janeiro for the* Post *from 1990 to 1992. She was the Mexico bureau chief for* The New York Times *from 1995 to 2000, and won a Pulitzer Prize in 1998 for coverage of Mexico's narcotics underworld. She is also a coauthor of* Opening Mexico: The Making of a Democracy.

✳

Cross the seventieth bridge of the Transpantaneira Highway. Large common egrets, wood storks, and cormorants fill the squat bushes surrounding the water. In the short grasses are caimans, and they're all over the place. Maybe a hundred of the two-meter-long reptiles lounge along the water's edge, many with jaws open.

Several float in the water like tiny islands, with only the bumps of the eyes and plated skin showing. One cruises the middle of the pond, exhibiting no bodily movement except the powerful drive of the tail swishing from side to side, snout pushing a bow wave. Yet this is an oddly peaceful scene. These caimans show remarkably little aggression. Is this caiman sunstruck?

In fact, on a finger of land strewn with water plants is a striking demonstration. An eighteen-kilo capybara is resting in the sun, absolutely relaxed, not more than a meter away from an adult caiman, jaws agape. Both are clearly aware of each other; in some other place they would be mortal enemies—predator and prey. But there seems to be an understanding that this afternoon isn't time for a fight.

This isn't the dark and forbidding jungle where it's catch as catch can. Even during the dry season there's plenty to eat for all. That is, as long as there are fish. Maybe I'm getting cooked in this tin can four-wheel drive or being lulled by the endless open landscape that's easy on the eyes and spirit. But the Pantanal seems a garden rather than a wilderness.

—Vic Banks, *The Pantanal: Brazil's Forgotten Wilderness*

STEVEN BERKOFF

✦ ✦ ✦

Whose Vice Is It Anyway?

*A British actor wanders into a Rio sex club
and discovers that depravity varies with country.*

A FEW NIGHTS AFTER A NICE DINNER AND GOOD CHAT WITH
legendary train robber Ronnie Biggs, I wandered into one of those

"sex cabarets" that I had seen
dotted around the Copa. In fact it
was Ronnie Biggs who focused
my mind that way when we
briefly chatted about them. I'd
have never ventured in otherwise
since they seemed the usual tatty,
tired, and slightly dangerous
places I had seen all the world
over. But I was wrong. This
wasn't your average "British" vice
with its built-in con and filthy
Soho hovel. Nothing is worse,
colder, or more depraved than
the taste of your *vice anglaise,* its
tattiness and shabby, *News of the
World*-type thrills. Perhaps a vice
reflects the spirit of the country

*In August 1963, Ronnie
Biggs was one of sixteen
men who held up the Glasgow-to-
London Royal Mail, taking off with
$7.2 million in sterling, or about
$60 million in today's dollars. All
were soon caught, but Biggs later
escaped from prison and beat a path
to Rio, where he lived in a cozy
villa recounting the Great Train
Robbery to paying guests until
2001. It was then, with his health
failing and having spent is $3.3
million (in 2004 dollars) share of
the loot, Biggs gave himself up and
was ordered to serve the rest of his
sentence—about 28 years. He now
spends his days in the Belmarsh
prison in Southeast London.
—AH and SD*

in its true colors. In its entrails so to speak. In Britain, vice seeks to cheat you by offering you the possibilities of an excitement it will never fulfill. It regards vice as something extraordinarily nasty that must be savored in the nastiest way possible—by cheating, stealing the poor tourist's money, and flogging cheap wine for fortunes; by making vice something inordinately horrid. The shadow-life of England—its horrible hovels and perverted sex celebrated in such tacky movies as *Personal Services.* Not so here. You are not conned. You pay your money and you see healthy bodies, or healthy-looking bodies, making love…or making sex.

So I entered the doors to this club and mounted the stairs to a smallish room with a center stage thrust out into the center. On its three sides sat customers, drinking and vaguely watching the show. I was taken in by a waiter and, since I seemed like a tourist, found myself being escorted right to the front in view of the whole audience and the girls on stage. I ordered my compulsory and paid-for beer, and prepared to watch the show.

Six women of moderate attractiveness—which was not a lot— were embracing each other and performing various feats involving much writhing, kissing, and simulated cunnilingus. I had moved swiftly to my table, not wishing to make any dent in the concentration of male faces, but as it was they all seemed to look at the new arrival as if I was an accomplice in the "crime" and wanted to make sure that I knew that they knew. So I sat, not paying much attention to the labyrinthine mass of intertwined bodies until I had ordered my drink and the waiter vanished. When I looked up and my eyes became accustomed to the gloom it was with a shock that I realised I was given a privileged position as a "moneyed" type of tourist, and that from the front I looked part of the show. The lights spilled over and on to my table. I watched for a few seconds as hands, mouths, and legs were congealing into one huge octopus of flesh, and then I decided to move to the back.

The girls were replaced by two couples—male/female this time—who proceeded to perform in public, conjugal acts. I had never before seen this, but having heard of such things imagined that the acts were simulated, much as actors these days are forced to do in "serious" movies. I was prepared for the kind of worn-out sex that one might see on the British sex scene. However, here it is quite a different kettle of flesh. For one thing, the price of four dollars to include one drink is not going to deplete the tourist's pocket or make him feel ripped off. It's a show like any other and you'd pay the same or even a great deal more to see a samba show. So the fact that it is a sex show doesn't here automatically mean you pay through the nose and feel privileged to see a peep of nipple. Here it is merely a different type of entertainment. Flesh instead of fowl.

The two couples are reasonably attractive and surprisingly healthy looking with good bodies. The two men look quite athletic and might be going out for a gym display. The music is thumping, the lights are changing, and the two couples move together in perfect synchronicity, just bobbing and weaving, and eventually the men have the ladies' knickers off. The customers are fascinated and watch what is surely the most healthy, nourishing and life-giving act nature has ever devised. The fact that it is public is its lurid fascination, even if they could see monkeys doing this every day in Regent's Park Zoo.

The watching faces are now becoming vocal in their appreciation and making encouraging noises to the two pairs, who seem quite impervious to it. The two men now have erections of considerable merit. Both couples were sleekly built and graceful together, as if they were used to each other and had built up an easy routine. The men now, at the same time like mirror images of each other, penetrated the women, and in time to the music. They resembled a strange, ritualistic dance. It wasn't even very erotic. It was more clinical and remote and, in its austere performance, strangely beautiful. One woman climbed off her man. He was kneeling back on his haunches demonstrating no wilting whatsoever. Like a mini-athletic team the two couples prepared again from a different position.

What was most impressive was the way the first man made himself totally remote from the audience and performed as if they weren't there. His erection was real and non-passionate and the kind of erection that most blokes get without thinking; a kind of unconscious rising when staring out of a window in a bus and relaxing since there is nothing else to do. Such indolent moments can provoke hard-ons. Hard-ons are not always the signal for passion. It's almost a reflex action. I think most blokes get H/Os a couple of dozen times a day without thinking too much about it. However, this man and his friend were supporting giant ones in full view of a drunken, leering audience, with full lights on and the waiter moving to and fro taking orders for drinks. And yet the performers seemed relaxed in their minds and bodies and were just getting on with the job.

The first couple were investing the coupling with choreographic variety while the couple behind them performed theirs with no less diligence and application in sync! I was more fascinated by the first man since he was nearest to me and was more the "star" of the two couples. His face wore a totally impassive look and could have been playing Hamlet, while his mate seemed more vulnerable to the audience's jibes and had an expression more amused, as if sharing the joke with them. He also had a very sinewy body but his moustache gave him the feeling of being half dressed. The couples appeared to be quite gentle with each other, not to spoil the equilibrium, especially for the male without whose appendage the act would not be working.

The whole event took on a less and less erotic flavor and appeared in a curious way quite ordinary, even admirable. They were an expert team, as their ease with each other revealed more and more, and not only practiced but in some way most tender with each other as if they alone knew that somehow they were made to vilify themselves but were concealing any such feelings from the audience. They had made a wall between us and them and the music continued to provide a kind of blanket for them. The music became a complicit partner and was as guilty, if any were to be guilty of anything.

A "horn" is a most temperamental beast that usually will brook no upstaging by other thoughts. It is likely to leave the stage if threatened by an unwelcome rival and not return until that rival has left. So I admired this man more and more since nature demands in the male a state of mind for its passions and here was a man who was able to control them and summon them up with the aid of an attractive woman in the most hostile circumstances. Here, in spite of the customers baying and waiters talking he was nevertheless an ardent lover. I began to admire his courage and heart to do it, even if habit "hardened" him to his task. I admired them for enduring what most of the world would regard as degrading and humiliating. But they lost no

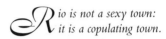

*io is not a sexy town:
it is a copulating town.*

—George Mikes,
*Tango: A Solo Across
South America*

dignity. We, the audience, were the animals, leering, jeering, drunk, fat, greasy, and stupid for a night out of raunchy voyeurism. The performers on the stage were strong and fit and untouched. Here were two couples exposing to the world with ease and dexterity the aesthetics of fucking. Naturally, without perversion or props, just the health and vigor of their own bodies.

Society has clothed the sex act with such awesome mystery and power, invested millions in preserving its myth that it is able to reap millions in profits by titillation and indecent exposure; by hinting, playing with, simulating, glimpses of pubic hair, sexist mags—how daring, etc., etc. And movies do not hesitate to push willing and unwilling actors into the buff for a touch of fake box office passion. Except that the movie actors fake it for a lot of money and in Rio they do it for real for a pittance. Is there a difference? I am not sure that the performers in Rio are not more honest. They are poor and poverty has driven them into this situation. Apart from hard-core porn movies the actors in your serious quality movies are not poor, but oblige the stomachs of film producers.

In fact what the two couples did was less harmful to themselves than yobs getting drunk and vomiting all over Leicester Square. The iniquity of massive unemployment plus a callously indifferent regime has created a market in human flesh for the rich tourist who wants to see what Rio is famous for apart from the samba. However evil the circumstances that created this situation where people could exploit the young bodies of men and women, there was nothing that these people did which humiliated themselves. Rather they stripped away the total hypocrisy surrounding the act and made it as natural and wholesome as playing tennis. It was their achievement that was awesome. That the audience had paid to see images of their own dirty minds exposed had no relation to these four people. Ultimately I felt that the actors and theater on British stages, with their thin, fakey emotions and watery, expensive productions, were more degrading and far less honest than what I was witnessing here. All that drippy West End howling and screeching about F. A.—how vacuous they seem before the real event of these four young men and women who stripped themselves bare! The real sin is poverty.

anny Adams, or F.A., is a British euphemism understood as "fuck all" or "nothing at all."

—AH and SD

They finished their act and left the stage. I felt like cheering their performance. After, in the Boulevard Copacabana, I saw the first couple on their way home. They looked like two serious actors after a heavy workout. Their faces were clean and I could not identify them as anything less than great performers.

Actor-director-writer Steven Berkoff is the author of I Am Hamlet, Steven Berkoff's America, Tough Acts, Shopping in the Santa Monica Mall and Other Surreal Adventures, *and* A Prisoner in Rio, *from which this story was excerpted. Though most of his work is in the theater and is political in nature, he has also made a memorable movie villain in a diverse variety of films. He is probably best known for his roles as the war-mongering Russian General Orlov in* Octopussy, *the nefarious art/drug dealer in* Beverly Hills Cop, *and the sadistic Russian Lieutenant Colonel Podovsky in* Rambo: First Blood, Part II. *He has also appeared in* A Clockwork Orange, Outland, *and* Nicholas and Alexandra, *and numerous television movies. He was born in London in 1937 and continues to live there.*

✦

RIO DE JANEIRO

Too good to be true—a city that empties
its populace, a hundred shades of brown,
upon its miles of beach in morning's low light
and takes the bodies back when darkness quells
the last long volleyball game; even then,
the sands are lit for the soccer of homeless children.

A city that exults in nakedness:
"The ass," hissed to us a man of the élite,
"the ass has become the symbol of Rio."
Set off by suits of "dental floss," girls' buttocks
possess a meaty staring solemnness
that has us see sex as it is: a brainless act

performed by lumpy monkeys, mostly hairless.
Still, the herd vibrates, a loom of joy
threaded by vendors—a tree of suntan lotion
or of hats, or fried snacks roofed in cardboard—
whose monotonous cries in Portuguese
make the same carnival mock of human need.

Elsewhere, chaste squares preserve Machado's world
of understated tragedy, and churches
honored in their abandonment suspend
the blackened bliss of gold. Life to the living,
while politicians dazzling in their polish,
far off in Brasília's cubes, feign impotence.

                    —John Updike, *Collected Poems, 1953-1993*

ALEXANDER SHANKLAND

✦

Soul of the *Sertão*

*Many years ago the dream of a holy community
in the desert was brutally put down,
but the dream lives on.*

"AH, THE *SERTÃO* FRIGHTENS ME—THE *SERTÃO* AND THE THINGS
that can come out of it." Professor José Calasans suddenly fell silent
and sat back, his eyes fixed on the invisible horizon of the past of
blood and suffering that had been his object of study for more than
40 years. We were sitting in his austere office in the Banco
Econômico Cultural Center, a formerly crumbling colonial building in the Pelourinho district of Salvador that had recently been restored as part of the drive to smarten up the city's image. Outside
the window, the colorful street life of coastal Brazil went on its
merry and chaotic way. But as Professor Calasans paused, the room
suddenly seemed filled with the mysterious and somewhat sinister
presence of a very different Brazil—the *sertão*.

The *sertão* is the hidden Brazil, a vast expanse of semiarid backlands almost four times the size of Great Britain. It is a forgotten
anti-Amazônia of dry riverbeds and twisted scrub, which begins a
few miles behind the beaches of the Northeast and stretches almost
to the eastern fringes of the rainforest. Periodically racked by
drought and famine, its existence is rarely recognized by the Brazilian authorities. Until the last decade, information on the *sertão* was
considered an issue of national security.

Few know the *sertão* better than Professor Calasans, a historian acknowledged as the greatest living expert on the bloodiest conflict ever to sweep the Brazilian backlands: the Canudos Revolt. That was why we had come to talk to him; my friend Mark and I were at the start of a journey into the interior to find out what remained of Canudos. Just as the parched *sertão* gave the lie to Brazil's image of a land consisting entirely of beaches and forests, so the story of Canudos seemed to explode the myth of an easygoing country free of the revolutionary bloodshed that marks the past and present of the rest of Latin America. To a journalist obsessed with Brazil and its contradictions the time seemed right for an attempt to uncover the soul of the *sertão* and of its people, the *sertanejos,* a century since the founding of Canudos, and the government's failure to ease the suffering caused by a devastating drought was leading to rumors of a new revolt in the backlands.

The Canudos story had fascinated and inspired many people before us. It reached a worldwide audience in semi-fictionalized form in *The War of the End of the World,* the 1981 best-seller by Peruvian novelist Mario Vargas Llosa. Like all the other accounts of the conflict, Llosa's has been questioned. No two historians have the same vision of how Canudos came about or what it represented. Some facts, however, are clear. The sequence of events that was to culminate in the greatest tragedy of the Brazilian republic began in 1893, with the founding of a religious community in the heart of the scorched *sertão* of Bahia. Its founder was a charismatic wandering preacher known as Antônio Conselheiro, the "Counselor." His followers were the dispossessed of the backlands: landless peasants, escaped slaves, even a few surviving Indians. They all came in search of the *sertão*'s own version of a land flowing with milk and honey. "Among the *sertanejos,* the legend ran that in Canudos the river flowed with goat's milk between banks of cornmeal," said Professor Calasans. With them came the *jagunços,* the feared bandits of the backlands, some seeking to save their souls and others in search of a convenient hideout.

Flourishing on a curious mixture of communist-style collective agriculture and astute commercial exploitation of its position on one of the *sertão's* main trade routes, Canudos became a state within a state, and Conselheiro's flock a church within a church. Neither church nor state could tolerate its existence for long. Between 1896 and 1897 first a company, then a battalion, then a brigade marched against Canudos. The fanatical courage of Conselheiro's followers and the guerrilla expertise of the *jagunços* combined to inflict a series of humiliating defeats. Finally, a fourth expedition consisting of almost half the Republican Army annihilated the settlement after a three-month siege. Five thousand soldiers and up to twenty-five thousand defenders died.

A taxi ride took us past the beach and its gaggle of new hotels, and up into the leafy middle-class district of Rio Vermelho. We had arranged to meet Pola Ribeiro, director of a documentary about memory and resistance in the Canudos region, which we had seen in São Paulo before leaving. We were looking to him for clues to the links between today's *sertão* and the desert that had witnessed the epic of Conselheiro and his followers. He was friendly and helpful, and gave us addresses and telephone numbers for locating Padre Enoque de Oliveira, the radical priest who was among the subjects of his documentary. I asked Ribeiro about the looting incidents that had recently been reported in towns across the *sertão,* with peasants who had lost their crops to the drought forcing their way past armed guards to sack government food deposits. "The people of the *sertão* are slaves to the weather, but they'd sooner die by the bullet than of hunger," he said. I thought of another film by a Bahian director, which Mark and I had watched as we prepared for our journey: the masterpiece of the 1960s *cinema novo,* Glauber Rocha's *Deus e o Diabo na Terra do Sol.* Before he sets off to meet his fate at the hands of vigilante Antônio das Mortes in a duel at the film's climax, the bandit Corisco sums up the philosophy of generations of *jagunços* in the *sertão*: "In this land, a man's worth nothing unless he takes up arms to change his own destiny."

Pola had told us that Padre Enoque's main base was in Euclides da Cunha, between the more accessible Baixo Sertão and the stony desert known as the Raso da Catarina. We had asked if this would be a good place to hire mules for the trek into the Raso da

Catarina and he laughed and dispelled our illusions: almost every town in the *sertão* was now served by buses, and the mule trains that had stopped to water in Canudos in Conselheiro's day had been replaced by trucks and four-wheel-drive Toyotas. The politicians may have done next to nothing to alleviate the scourge of drought, but they had built roads. Roads guaranteed their kickbacks from construction companies, and once the village bar was on the delivery route of a Coca-Cola distribution truck it was easy to convince the *sertanejos* that their votes had taken them into the modern age.

The night bus ride from Salvador into the interior was a procession of garishly lit *rodoviárias,* brand-new bus stations whose soaring concrete shapes seemed to dwarf the huddled buildings of the towns they served: more monuments to the politicians' idea of modernity. On the bus to Euclides da Cunha, I read Euclides da Cunha: the soldier-journalist whose positivist ideals had collided with his human sensitivity to produce *Os Sertões,* his testimony of the Canudos campaign. Though it is da Cunha's style rather than his bitter description of tragedies born of mutual incomprehension among Brazilians that has won him an enduring place in literary reading lists in the country, *Os Sertões* is universally recognized as Brazil's national epic. I had bought a copy, a 1920s edition, in a secondhand bookstore in Montevideo. I had looked in vain for *Os Sertões* in São Paulo; it had proved hard to find copies of Brazil's national epic in Brazil's own bookstores.

> *D*a Cunha has been held up in recent writing on the Amazon as an early ecologist. His text rings with powerful denunciations of the manhandling of the Brazilian environment. "We have been a disastrous ecological agent, an antagonistic and barbarous element against the very nature that surrounds us," he wrote. He decried the wanton practitioners of plantation agriculture, who promoted "the impoverishment and the sterilization of the earth. They fill up the land by emptying it out."
>
> —Mac Margolis, *The Last New World: The Conquest of the Amazon Frontier*

The town of Euclides da Cunha got its name in 1933, three decades after the publication of *Os Sertões,* in which it gets a few

passing mentions under its old name of Cumbe. The renaming was
little more than politicians' opportunism, a cashing-in on the
posthumous fame of the author, who was killed in a duel with his
wife's lover a couple of years after the book was published. Cumbe
was a rear-area supply dump for the Republican regiments that
marched against Canudos, not the scene of any epic struggles. Perhaps acting as a supply base for struggles taking place deeper in the
sertão is the town's vocation, for it was in Euclides da Cunha that
Padre Enoque had chosen to establish the main safe house for his
"Popular Church of Canudos."

We were welcomed there by Maurinda Ribeiro da Silva, who
cheerfully asked us to call her by her nickname Nega, or "Blackie."
Though in Afro-Brazilian Salvador skin color is about roots and
race, in the *sertão* it is merely a distinguishing feature, like stature or
hair color. Whether it is Portuguese, African, or indigenous
Amerindian blood that predominates in their makeup, *sertanejos* see
themselves as belonging to a race apart.

A small, pleasant person, Nega lost no time in bustling us round
the house for which she was proudly responsible, most of which
felt more like a country inn than the nerve center of a rural revolt.
At the end of the tour, she showed us reverentially into its inner
sanctum, a long room where the whitewashed walls were covered
with roughly painted images of the martyrs of Canudos and with
columns of epic verse in their honor. The poems' author was Padre
Enoque, and their style left no doubt as to the extent to which he
saw himself as Conselheiro's heir. "I have brought Canudos up from
the depths of the waters…seeking to build a New Canudos for the
People," ran one. Suitably inspired, we turned to Nega and asked
when we might be able to meet the great man himself. Would we
have to trek out into the desert and interrupt 40 days
of wandering and fasting? "Oh no, you can see him tomorrow if
you want," came the reply. "He'll be in Monte Santo then. Just take
the bus."

Monte Santo is known as the "Altar of the *Sertão*," and its spectacular setting provides the ideal backdrop for the theater of faith
in which the Catholic Church excels. Huddled at the foot of a

dramatic bluff topped by a shrine whose reputation for miracle-working has made it one of the most important pilgrimage sites in the Brazilian backlands, the town has done well out of the *sertane-jos'* passionate and sometimes desperate faith. Monte Santo is famed for its Easter processions, during which hundreds of penitents make the arduous journey up the hill to the shrine on their knees, stopping along the way to pray at each of the chapels representing the Stations of the Cross.

In the 1980s Monte Santo's Holy Week commemorations began to receive an injection of fiery oratory and Liberation Theology from a new master of ceremonies. The town's recently appointed parish priest was a young man who, like Antônio Conselheiro himself, had been born farther north in the *sertão* of Ceará: Padre Enoque de Oliveira. Nega had told us how, until the Church expelled him in 1986, Enoque had used the weight of his position as priest in charge of the holy site to challenge the violent land-grabbing of the local ranchers who were driving peasants off their small holdings, and to denounce the corrupt political system, which sanctioned this banditry. The peasants had organized resistance, usually passive but occasionally violent, and the ranchers had been temporarily faced down. The glimpse of a more just world that this had offered the people of Monte Santo provided fertile soil for Enoque's preaching of a link between the "Altar of the *Sertão*" and the *sertão's* own blood sacrifice: the slaughter of the faithful in Canudos.

Nega had got word to the "friends of the movement" with whom Padre Enoque was staying in Monte Santo, and he was there to meet us off the bus. We had seen his face in Pola's film, but film distorts and we did not immediately recognize him. We had unconsciously assumed that Conselheiro's self-appointed heir would have an imposing physical presence, but Enoque did not. He was short, stocky, and bearded, and wore a faded red t-shirt. He was undoubtedly possessed of considerable energy but his abrupt movements seemed more fussy than decisive.

We were obviously not the first journalists Padre Enoque had met, and he began to talk about his work and his vision almost immediately, mixing stock catchphrases of the Brazilian Left with parochial sideswipes at the local Catholic Church and generous use of the pronoun "I." Gesturing at local points of interest on the way ("That building over there is the town hall, where the destruction of Canudos was planned"), he led us up some steep cobbled streets to a comfortable house where the "friends of the movement," Vanda Santana, Nildo Souza, and José de Jésus, awaited us. Enoque had some more people to meet in a town farther down the road, and after a while he concluded his introductory spiel and left with a promise to meet us the following day for a trip around the remains of Canudos.

Vanda, an intelligent and sensitive local schoolteacher who had been working with Padre Enoque since his days as parish priest of Monte Santo, took up the tale. She brought the conversation down to earth from Enoque's rhetoric of popular revolt against the collusion between church and state, and spoke frankly about the current situation of the "Popular Church of Canudos." It was clear that the founding of a second Canudos inspired by Enoque's preaching was growing less likely. The movement had shrunk to only a shadow of its former self, as Enoque had lost his pulpit and the novelty of transforming Canudos from a shamefully taboo subject into a monument to the faith and courage of the *sertanejos* had worn off.

Despite the fact that Padre Enoque's followers were clearly a diminishing band, their talk had little of the resentment-fueled defiance of their leader. It was as if the fact that they still counted themselves as part of a movement was enough, even if the revolutionary vision that had once fueled that movement was fading. The *sertanejo's* strength has always been resistance, not revolution. I was reminded of what Pola Ribeiro had said: "People talk about 'the Canudos Revolt' but Canudos wasn't a revolt, it was a community." The community had only been defending itself, even if its very existence had been treated as a mortal threat by the Brazilian republic. And when it came down to it, the *sertão* certainly knew how to defend itself. Professor Calasans had cast his penetrating eye over Brazil's history of bloodless coups and halfhearted revolutions and concluded that "this is a country where things fall easily." Yet the community of Canudos, which only wanted to be left in peace, had fought the army of the largest state in South America to a standstill. Crushing Conselheiro's vision of a New Jerusalem had taken two years and cost up to 30,000 lives.

The afternoon was drawing on, and Mark and I had little more than an hour before the bus back to Euclides da Cunha, from where we would be setting out to rendezvous with Enoque and the remains of Canudos. The young and earnest José de Jésus escorted us to the foot of the pilgrimage trail that led up the hill to the shrine. On the way, he treated us to some of the Canudos lore that, as Monte Santo's librarian and amateur historian, he had made it his business to collect from the *sertão's* rich store of oral history. Shyly, he offered to read us the poems he had composed in honor of Conselheiro's slaughtered followers. They were unpolished but heartfelt and genuinely stirring. He was a peaceful, book-loving young man, but somehow it was not hard to imagine him choosing to die in the ruins of Canudos rather than abandon his faith, had he been born a century earlier.

The hike up the hill, a race against the dying of the light, proved to be tiring even for impenitent foreigners not making the climb on their knees. Mark, a keener sportsman than I, made better time and was rewarded by catching a glimpse of the sun's last rays on the stark, simply built shrine and the extraordinary pile of offerings that lay beside it. This pile consisted of dozens of artificial limbs, left by grateful pilgrims to represent the members healed through the shrine's miraculous intervention. It looked like someone had reenacted the Republican Army's grisly massacre of the survivors taken prisoner at the fall of Canudos, with life-size wax effigies for victims. We made our way to the parapet and looked over. The *sertão* lay spread out below us, impressively vast but monotonous in its various shades of brown, and no less inscrutable for being examined from such a privileged vantage point.

We looked toward Canudos as the sun set, half-hoping that our climb would be rewarded by the clichéd drama of seeing the site of the massacre bathed in bloody fire. But we were facing the wrong way: it was in the west that the dust hanging in the dry air had tinged the sun red as freshly spilled blood. To the east, the low hills that marked the location of Canudos were ochre. If they were the color of blood, it was blood spilled a very long time ago.

The boy who did nightwatch duty at our shabby hotel in Euclides da Cunha had promised us a four a.m. alarm call for the bus to Nova Canudos, which left at five a.m. He was still snoring beside the desk when the bus woke us at five by hooting its horn to announce its departure, and he shrugged in response to the Anglo-Saxon expletives with which we woke him in turn. We set off to find a man with a car we could hire to get us to Bendegó, the hamlet where we were due to rendezvous with Padre Enoque. We eventually located João, the mustachioed owner of a battered Ford, and he condescended to do the run after insisting on a price that would have been sufficient to pay for the bus tickets of two entire *sertanejo* families and all their goats. João had the worldly air shared by many *sertanejos* who had made the 2,000-mile trek south to São Paulo and stuck it out on the production lines and building sites long enough to amass the modest capital that passed for a fortune in the backlands. He probably regarded overcharging tourists as a sophisticated technique worthy of a big city, and the fact that his fellow *sertanejos* did not practice it as a sign of their ignorance.

When people ask me why I keep wanting to go to Brazil, part of the answer is that it's because the country is so vast and so raw and sometimes so monstrously beautiful; but it's mostly because I find it easy to get along with the people.

—John Dos Passos,
Brazil on the Move (1963)

The trip to Bendegó in his car was a suspension-scraping ride over dirt roads, through country that became harsher and stonier as we moved farther into the Raso da Catarina. The streambeds we crossed were invariably dry, and the tall, gaunt *mandacaru* cactus increasingly dominated the landscape. Here and there we would pass the ruins of a wattle-and-daub hut, homes abandoned by the *sertanejo* families driven by land-grabbers or drought to join the exodus heading toward the city slums.

When we arrived, Padre Enoque was not there. We located our

contact, the venerable "friend of the movement" Maria Cardoso Souza. *Dona* Maria, a redoubtable lady of 70, told us that the Padre's bus had been delayed. She needed little prompting to fill the wait with stories of Canudos, crowned with a vivid account of how her grandfather, Joaquim Macambira, a prominent figure in Euclides da Cunha's narrative of the struggle, had died in an attempt to spike the giant cannon known as *A Matadeira* ("The Slaughterer") by charging at it armed only with a wooden pestle. She was posing for heroic photographs with her own pestle when the bus finally rolled in and deposited Padre Enoque.

Nearer to the site of the events that had been the source of his inspiration, Enoque seemed more at ease, and his rhetoric flowed free. Even the bad state of the road that had delayed him was denounced as part of a plot against the memory of Antônio Conselheiro: "When the government came to pave a road into the interior, they deliberately didn't choose this one because it might lead to the Canudos question spreading into the rest of Brazil." Other accusations seemed more credible, such as the assertion that the benefit of the waters of the huge reservoir that came into view as we pulled out of Bendegó was reaped not by the smallholders and their thirsty livestock but by the giant seed company Agroceres, which had bought up all the arable land around the lake.

This lake in the desert was more than the dubious result of yet another wasteful government project, however. It was the Cocorobó Reservoir, and its waters had covered the site of Canudos. Conselheiro had prophesied that the *sertão* would become a sea, and now his bones lay under 60 feet of water.

When Padre Enoque led us to the house of Eulina Alcântara de Oliveira, it was clear that the memory of the Conselheiro's time remained alive and bitter in Nova Canudos. *Dona* Eulina had tears in her eyes and her voice faltered as she retold what her late husband had heard from his survivor grandfather—how soldiers slit their prisoners' throats after making them dig their own graves. "I'm sorry," she said, "thinking of it makes me so angry." Her granddaughter Carla, a bright and pretty 21-year-old, had been listening quietly at the edge of the conversation until then. Suddenly, she flared up. "When you think of what Canudos was, what it was they destroyed, it's enough to put you in a rage," she declared. She paused, then went on more quietly. "The spirit of Canudos is not dead, though…its strength will not go away."

We progress at night while the politicians sleep.
—Brazilian saying

As João drove us back toward Bendegó, Enoque told him to turn down a rutted side road. We stopped and got out of the car on the crest of a low rise overlooking the placid surface of the reservoir. "You're standing on Alto da Favela," Enoque said. "Does that mean anything to you?" It did, doubly. In *Os Sertões,* I had read Euclides da Cunha's description of the terrible struggles for control of this strategic height, from which the army's cannon had an unimpeded line of fire into the heart of Conselheiro's mud-brick citadel. After the campaign, the memory of the hill led to a new term entering Brazil's vocabulary. A group of soldiers, veterans of the hand-to-hand fighting on Alto da Favela, returned to Rio de Janeiro only to find themselves cheated by the government of the housing promised before the campaign. They settled on a hill above the city's center that they rechristened Favela after the site of their suffering. It was Rio's first slum; today, the shantytowns that crowd every major city in Brazil are collectively known as *favelas*—and many of their inhabitants are migrants from the *sertão.*

With half its slope hidden by the water of Cocorobó, Alto da Favela did not look much like a commanding height. The hill's appearance was deceptive, like so much else in the *sertão*—including the plant for which it was named. The *favela* trees that dotted the landscape looked like inoffensive overgrown shrubs, but when we stopped to examine one Enoque pointed out the poisonous thorns that its attractive white blossoms concealed.

At the point of the lakeshore that is closest to the site of the Canudos, we found a fishing village. By stocking this lake in the middle of the desert with fish and moving a few families of unemployed fisherfolk there from the coast, the government had come a step nearer to fulfilling Conselheiro's prophecy that the *sertão* would become a sea. "Conselheiro understood the need to transform the *sertão*," Enoque had said. Prophecy or no prophecy, I wondered whether this was really the transformation the Conselheiro had had in mind. In his day, the *sertão* had been harsh but habitable, in need of social rather than ecological transformation despite the periodic scourge of drought. The River Vaza-Barris, which was dammed to form the Cocorobó Reservoir, had flowed all year round when Conselheiro founded Canudos. The years of the campaign were drought years, yet the besieged community never ran out of water. Even before the dam was built in 1968, however, the Vaza-Barris had shrunk to a stream and ran dry for years at a time. The reason was the advance into the interior of what Euclides da Cunha called "the centuries-old martyrdom of the land." The peasants' goats could live off the native vegetation, which their grazing seemed not to harm, but the ranchers' cattle needed grass. As the thorny *caatinga* scrub, which attracted and retained precious moisture, was burned off and grubbed up for pasture, so the land became more and more arid. The *sertão* had always been dry, but it was only now becoming a desert.

We wandered down to the edge of the reservoir, searching the taciturn surface of the water for clues as to what lay beneath it. We searched in vain: it was impossible even to guess the location of the river bend that marked the heart of Canudos, where heavy-caliber shells had finally blown apart the community's dream of flourishing in peace. Padre Enoque's words echoed in our ears: "This dam was built by a guilty government to drown the memory of Canudos forever." It was only later, when we had dropped Enoque off with more "friends of the movement" and were heading away from the water toward Bendegó, that João the driver turned to us with his worldly air and put paid to one more illusion. "The dam wasn't meant to be built here at all, you know," he said. "They didn't want to shift the people who had come back to live on the site of Canudos, but they ended up having to because the original dam site proved to be no good. The Cocorobó Reservoir was intended to supply Canudos, not to drown it."

We took rooms behind a bar in Bendegó for the night, and went to bed exhausted. Our host proved better at early morning alarm calls than the boy in Euclides da Cunha, and the next day we were up well before the bus arrived at six o'clock. As we bumped along the dirt road out of the Raso da Catarina and onto the metalled highway heading north to Juazeiro and the mighty Rio São Francisco, I thought about the *sertão's* many illusions. Outside the bus window, the *caatinga* was suddenly vivid green, dotted with white-blossomed *barriguda* trees. It had rained here, but the sense that the drought was over was itself an illusion. The water holes had not filled up, and the cattle were dying at the edges of the muddy puddles that remained. Professor Calasans's words came back to me: "the *sertanejos* are like their land—just as the *caatinga* flowers at the first sign of rain, so they endlessly renew their hope." The hope was an illusion—but the resistance was real. Conselheiro's dream of a holy community in the desert had been viciously shattered, but for those who had chosen to live in Canudos it was an illusion worth dying for. Or maybe no illusion at all. We had failed to walk among the rubble of Conselheiro's New Jerusalem, but the intensity of the memories we had encountered had left a greater sense of its reality than any amount of amateur archaeology could have done. Plenty of fantasies had been built on the ruins of Canudos, the greatest of which was the belief that it could be made to rise again. But like all legends, Canudos had reality at its heart, and it was a reality that fire and water had failed to erase.

Alexander Shankland was born and brought up in Southern England, and thought he was destined for an academic career until the experience of studying English at Cambridge University convinced him otherwise. After traveling extensively and working as a journalist, teacher, and translator, he fell in love with Amazônia and now works as manager of a series of health projects with forest-dwelling communities for the British charity Health Unlimited. He divides his time between the Amazon and São Paulo, where he lives with his wife Cristina and two children.

★

Why do peasants from the interior plateau, or workers in the sugar fields or elsewhere, move into Rio with such a rush? The answer could not be simpler. They think that—eventually at least—they will get a better deal in the city, a better standard of life. Conditions may be frightful in the squatter towns but they may well have been even worse in the *sertão,* where the serfs lived like animals, barely managing to survive even on a subsistence level. Once in the towns they have at least a fighting chance to get some kind of job and thus enter a money economy, earn wages, and perhaps see movies, read newspapers if they are literate, and above all have the possibility of education for their children and partake of other social benefits provided city dwellers by the state.

—John Gunther, *Inside South America*

Maracanã Whiz

Nothing brings out Brazilians' passions,
and other primal behavior, quite like soccer.

I'D NEVER PLANNED TO GO TO MARACANÃ. BUT MY HOSTS, ZÉ and Yara, suggested we take in a soccer game after lunch that August afternoon, and I readily agreed. When traveling, what is the point of saying no?

Maracanã, Rio's huge soccer stadium, is located far from the city's tourist beaches in the old working-class district of Mangueira, famed for its prizewinning samba school. Frank Sinatra and other luminaries have appeared at the stadium, packing in as many as 200,000 roaring faithful. But Maracanã's primary role in Carioca life is as a soccer shrine—notably for bouts between Rio's arch-rival teams, Flamengo and Fluminense.

The teams we were about to take in lacked the star power of "Fla" and "Flu": lowly Fortaleza, from the northeastern state of Ceará, was playing hapless Botafogo, the favorite of Claudio, Zé and Yara's eight-year-old son who accompanied us to the game. ("Botafogo never wins," Zé confided to me, chuckling, out of Claudio's earshot.) We were part of a paltry crowd of 15,000—which under certain conditions could constitute a small city—but this mob was not without its fierce partisans, Claudio among them.

The battery of military police, to a man resembling mean whippets, would presumably maintain order.

We took our seats in the rear of the stadium's upper tier, at one end of the field. The concrete slab floor of the uppermost deck formed a stifling roof above us; I felt as though we were trapped in a dank echo chamber. But Yara assured me that ours was a fine location. During especially crowded or hotly contested matches, she informed me, rowdiness reached the point where men in the top deck would urinate on the fans below them. To quell the ardor of those in the lowlands, I wondered? Or just to infuriate them? Quickly I glanced overhead, saw the looming deck, and instead of feeling claustrophobic was flooded with relief.

Down on the field, I noticed, men in shorts were now intently swarming, signaling the start of the match. But I hadn't a clue what they were up to. My only connection with the game had been tenuous, through my former lover Rogerio, back in the San Francisco Bay Area. He was a one-time professional soccer player, and his thighs were unlike any I'd ever seen: massively muscled, built up from hours on end of dancing with the ball, teasing it mercilessly with kicks and blows.

Just a few minutes into the game, a band of about a dozen drummers and percussionists swarmed into our sparsely populated area of Maracanã. They took their places across the aisle from us, ten feet away, and with frightening intensity began to beat, pound, shake, rattle, whistle, and otherwise bedevil their instruments, setting up an intoxicating swirl of rhythms. Then they started to chant *"fogo,"* the Portuguese word for "fire" and apparently their nickname for the Botafogo team. But their bellowing chant sounded like a foghorn from Hades: *Fooohhhhhhhhhh-goooooooo!* I felt my hair stand on end, the blood was pounding in my head. It was an electrifying display, as male as a phallus. I swore I was seeing red!

Suddenly the inexplicable dance out there on the field made some sort of physical sense: I was experiencing it under my skin through the relentless chanting and pounding of my neighbors. This impromptu drum corps/cheerleading squad provided the game's soundtrack and pulse. I was in a state of near-ecstasy as the ritualistic rhythms continued to throb, more insistent than my own heart.

Claudio was likewise entranced, especially since his team had already scored a goal. Dark eyes flashing, he clutched Botafogo's black and white banner to his chest as his mother Yara beamed through her beer. She was chugging away, and offered me a sip, but I declined. Just a couple of hours earlier, we'd consumed large quantities of *feijoada,* the black bean stew that is Rio's traditional Saturday lunch and demands an accompaniment of cold beer. But all this talk of golden showers had turned me off to guzzling. I didn't care to make the acquaintance of Maracanã's pissoirs.

We had gone to Ipanema because we wanted to see the International Beach Volleyball Championships. We weren't sure of game time or any of the particulars, but the beach was a pleasant place to hang out until the action started. As we waited, we watched a surfer catching waves remarkably close to shore. As if to meet him, a well-built gray-haired man walked toward the water, stopped at the water's edge, and began to pee into the bay. When he finished, he shook himself off, rearranged his bathing suit, and sauntered toward the volleyball grandstand.

—Mary Gaffney,
"Carmen's Place"

Dusk was falling as the game drew to a close. Botafogo had indeed won. Yara announced that she had to go *xixi*—not surprising, after all the beer she'd imbibed. She and I set out in search of a restroom, agreeing to meet Zé and Claudio at the stadium entrance. As we wandered through the maze of Maracanã, we saw many bathrooms for men. We found none for the ladies.

Yara grew increasingly panicky, then desperate. Her face was contorted. "I'm going to pee in my pants," she grimly predicted, her teeth clenched. Her entire body, in fact, was clenched as she ran, with me trailing helplessly, so thankful I hadn't been drinking beer.

Finally she lurched into one of the men's lavatories. *"Desculpe,"* she cried, begging their pardon. The men were nonchalant: *"Tudo bem."* I waited just outside, my nose assaulted by the stench of a steaming ocean of piss.

Smiling, breathing deeply, Yara emerged a new woman. We managed to find Zé and Claudio, the boy in a state of transcendental joy over his team's victory. "What a wonderful night for him!" Yara marveled. She wagered that he would never be separated from his team's flag, now wrapped around him like a hero's cape.

It was already dark. The new moon shed little light on us and the seemingly improvised parking arrangements around the stadium. Cars were heaved up on the sidewalk, head first into a wall, like gleaming beached seals. Then one by one they slinked off into the winter night.

As we approached our Volkswagen, one of the few cars remaining, something caught my eye. Even in the dim illumination of the street lamp I could see a long row of dark wet spots staining the wall against which the cars had been parked. Then it dawned on me. Each paterfamilias had not-so-discreetly taken a leak before boarding his chariot for the ride home. Did organized sport provoke this mass outbreak of male marking behavior? Next time, I reminded myself, I would definitely take a seat in the tippy-top deck.

Terri Hinte also contributed "Argentino" in Part I.

✳

Jackie and I are seated at a sidewalk café at the western end of Copacabana on a Sunday afternoon, only hours after our arrival. Four young troubadours are coaxing samba rhythms from drums, bongos, tambourines, even a used soft drink can half-filled with pebbles. Several women are singing, and one of them is dancing. She is a woman of a certain age, tightly encased in a red workout suit several sizes too small. From her look, one would guess that she was not born to good fortune and that her life has been a hard one. But none of that matters now. What matters is Sunday, this Sunday, the beat of those instruments, and the dancing, her body moving sinuously and her feet flying in a manner perfected through the centuries, passed on to her as a child, and practiced through the years. For several minutes she dances, oblivious to everything but the spirit that moves her. Then suddenly her eyes lock with Jackie's. She smiles broadly and beckons Jackie to join her. It's an invitation not simply to dance but to share the understanding that this moment, once passed, is irretrievable.

—Leonard Gross, "Rio: Yes or No?" *Condé Nast Traveler*

.

ERIC SCIGLIANO

Aracaju Surprise

A family connection helps the author
discover the funky charm
of the far Northeast.

IT'S HARDLY A BRACING START TO YOUR TRIP, TO FINALLY FIND
the obscure South American destination you're bound for mentioned in a guidebook—and dismissed as "the Cleveland of the
Northeast." And it's even more discouraging to land in a famously
arid, sunny region, amid hundreds of miles of tropical beach, and be
hammered down by merciless, unending rain. I tried to tell myself
that grim omens and bad beginnings were necessary preludes to
pleasant surprises—and, to my surprise, I was right about a place
called Aracaju.

The Northeast in question is Northeast Brazil, the poorest, most
chaotic, but most heterogeneous and culturally fertile part of that
mind-boggling country.

I was bound for Aracaju, the capital of Sergipe, the smallest and
perhaps the most forgotten state in the country. "A poor capital...visually quite unattractive," said my guidebook, and worked
down from there.

To make matters even less auspicious, we were embarking in
mid-May, just as the rainy season in Northeast Brazil would peak.
But this was a trip too long-awaited and long-delayed, booked after
too many battles with officious Brazilian airline officials, driven by

too many reasons that had nothing to do with guidebooks, to jettison.

Those reasons were supreme: I was accompanying my girlfriend Lucia on her first visit home since she left Brazil four years earlier and wound up broke and stranded in Seattle. As the prodigal daughter's companion, I was the guest of honor: "Whoever loves Lucia, I love," her mom, *Dona* Isabel, said when we arrived, and the welcome never flagged while we were there. A constant parade of sisters, friends, sisters' boyfriends, friends' cousins, cousins' girl-friends, and so on, passed through the modest apartment. All seemed to take a personal stake in my fledgling Portuguese studies; they'd speak slower and slower, repeating things again and again, until I got the jokes. One visitor—Ashton Vital Brasil, the grandson of the great herpetologist Vital Brasil—even volunteered to be my travel guide to other parts of the Northeast.

We gorged on conversation and the best food I had anywhere in Brazil: not just the national favorites, *cozido* and *feijoada,* but the distinctive dishes of the Northeast. These recalled Caribbean and American soul food in many aspects—plentiful beans and rice and greens and okra. I wondered if this was a cuisine, like southern Italian or Greek, that thrives more in homes than restaurant kitchens—or if, as my friend claimed, Mom just happened to be the best cook in the world.

In Brazil, there is a sharp distinction between the concept of food and the concept of a meal. In the language of Brazilian cuisine, these terms express a fundamental semantic opposition between the universal and the particular. Brazilians know that all edible substances are foods but that not every food is necessarily a meal. In transforming food into a meal the preparation is of critical importance, but a degree of ceremony is also required.

—Roberto DaMatta,
"The Meal is the Message:
The Language of the Brazilian
Cuisine," UNESCO *Courier*

The world outside seemed considerably less hospitable, however. Day after night after day, the rain fell in great sheets, whooshing against the walls and rattling the louvers, and at times almost physically pushing us back into the small apartment. Could this be

the Northeast of the desert *sertão* in *Barren Lives,* Graciliano
Ramos' epic of its hungry people's struggle against a parched life?

In fact, as I realized when I later traversed its rolling seas of sugarcane and orchards, the Northeast's coastal region is lush and fertile, a tropical Iowa with cane instead of corn. As dramatically as
they'd descended, the rains burned off and the whole landscape,
from coconut palms to the ubiquitous worn VWs, glistened as
though it had just stepped from the shower. We emerged as if from
a cocoon, our senses whetted by the forced incubation. I promptly
acquired the obligatory *gringo* (yes, the Mexican term carries down
here) sunburn and, in leisurely fashion, came to appreciate Aracaju's
quiet charms.

Those charms do not include colonial grandeur. Most of Aracaju is relatively new—less than 150 years old. It was Brazil's first
planned city, hence the great granddaddy of that colossus of urban
planning, Brasília. In Brazil, or at least in tropical northeastern
Brazil, planning has its limits: the tidy grids of central Aracaju soon
evaporate into the usual jumbled sprawl.

But for its citizens, Aracaju is the Northeast's *City That Works.*
And it is indeed a calm, harmonious sort of place, at least compared
with teeming, picturesque, quasi-African Salvador and the nearby
cities of Recife and Maceió.

In Aracaju, in fact, planning runs to ludicrous overkill. In a
nation where it's every driver for himself and red lights mean
"honk and speed up," Aracaju's planners erected what may be the
world's largest, most nearly impassable speed bumps. Again and
again, in rattling little taxis or my hosts' long-suffering VW bug, I
would grit my teeth and pray to the god of oil pans as the chassis
scraped its slow way across one of these killer bumps. But planning
has its merits. Aracaju's spacious, parklike central plaza, ringed by
the usual cathedral and public buildings and crossed by a splendid,
cooling tunnel of arching trees, made me feel transported to some
grand European capital.

At one end, a small municipal gallery showed a surprisingly
strong selection of local photographers, most projecting edgy
surrealism or angry social commentary. At the other, in a long,

handsome ochre building along Rua de Propria, the state folk arts center held an equally impressive display of Sergipe's crafts, with dozens of practitioners and vendors set up in the surrounding alcoves.

❧ortuguese colonists brought their native tradition of weaving renda, *or lace, to Brazil in the early 17th century. Designs and stitches were influenced by the regular visits of Spanish and French merchants, who distributed models of new kinds of lace popular in Europe. Centuries later Brazilians still sing this folk lyric:* Hey, lace maker / Hey, woman making lace / If you will teach me to make lace, I will / teach you to fall in love.

—Elizabeth Heilman Brooke, "Brazil's Intricate Designs in Thread," *The New York Times*

There also was lots of exquisite Northeast handmade lace, a legacy of colonial times. More unusual were the various villages' wildly varied ceramic sculpture, from expressive, elongated saints from Carrapicho to an even more expressive figure of an emaciated cow from the parched *sertão*—just what El Greco and Soutine might have sculpted if they'd worked in clay.

A family friend named Hunaldo introduced me to another local art, the care and flavoring of *cachaça,* the fiery cane liquor that is the traditional national beverage. Here, as almost everywhere else in the world, beer has supplanted tradition for those who can afford it. But *cachaça* is a much cheaper and, in the Northeast Sugarcane Belt, varied and flavorful potion. It is distilled and infused, in a rainbow of hues, with herbs, roots, and much stranger substances for every sort of gustatory and medicinal purpose. Sometimes snakes are pickled in it, in the belief that repeated sipping lends immunity against their venom.

Hunaldo poured some *cachaça vermelha* (red) he had just made with the root of the *pindaiba* tree, and guaranteed it proof against digestive upset. It was spicy, even peppery, and bittersweet. Hunaldo claimed a yellow *cachaça* called *milone* was much more bitter, and causes lockjaw. "The more you drink, the harder your jaw locks, till you can't talk at all. After 30 minutes it goes out your pores, leaving yellow marks all over your clothing."

"He's just a typical Brazilian," one friend interjected, meaning that he was making it all up.

"No, no, it's true!" another insisted. "I've seen it."

Of course, that friend also claimed to have seen a six-foot rat at the entrance to the city market. The old market—sprawling, picturesque, but fairly clean as such markets go—is the place to investigate exotic *cachaças,* and the equally exotic local fruits, fish, herbal remedies, and other produce. What looks like long, coiled, glistening blood sausages is in fact the sweet-cured local tobacco that country folk smoke in their pipes.

Cachaça around the dinner table is well and good, but when the sun returned it was time to do what any red-blooded Brazilian would: go to the beach and drink beer. Aracaju's beaches will not win any awards in Brazil, though they're fine by North American or European standards. The problem is the rivers that empty into the sea nearby, particularly the wide, deep Rio Sergipe, which once gave Aracaju its reason for being as a port. It now constrains its tourist aspirations by clouding the surrounding waters with fine silt.

In May this was no particular loss, however, since even the famously limpid waters around Maceió and Recife were clouded by the rains. But the rivers also nurture the special delicacy of Aracaju beach life: the succulent *caranguejos* (marsh crabs) that nest in the estuaries' mangrove swamps, climbing the trees and even eating their leaves. We chose the aptly named Caranguejo Bar, at the end of the beach road Avenida Presidente Jose Sarney ("Dog Road" to some disrespectful locals), for our crab feast.

First we savored two delicious and distinctly Aracajuano beach snacks: skewered strips of chewy, slightly tart farm cheese roasted just short of melting on portable braziers, and peanuts boiled in salt water, proffered by hordes of shirtless young boys who traipse through even the tonier beach bars.

The peanut pushers lure customers the way we used to get suckers to start biting by tossing a few bread balls in the creek. Without a word, a kid will drop a nut for each person at your table, then stand back and watch as if to say, "Bet you can't eat just one." One boy simply dumped an entire preemptive canful of nuts on our table and walked off, doubtless to return and collect later. Trouble was, I really wanted some peanuts, and would have obliged, but my companions were determined to resist such extortion. I finally satisfied all of us, though. I confused the poor kid by calling him back, dumping the nuts back in his basket, then ordering a fresh batch.

Brazil's deep class divisions extend even to that most democratic of places, the beach. The close-in beaches served by city buses were populist and crowded, and those that required a car more exclusive. Thus did Rio's beautiful people protest mightily and abandon Ipanema when an extended bus line enabled the *farofeiros,* the "manioc eaters," to get there.

But unlike Ipanema and Copacabana, the Northeast's beaches, both popular and elite, still seem safe and easygoing. Coconut vendors tool along in mule-drawn two-wheel carts, past fashionable bathers dressed, sort of, in the latest *fio dental* (dental floss) bikinis. *Repentistas* (from *repente,* "sudden"), guitar-strumming poets from the interior, improvise verses on any subject desired for anyone who will hire them for a song, a party, a day.

The beaches are named after the bars, which make sure the beer is kept properly *estupidamente gelada* (chilled to a stupor) in Styrofoam sheathes. Along with the beer, I imbibed the surprisingly rich lore of Aracaju—much of it from the town's Jorge Amado, a newspaper columnist and popular historian named Hugo Costa. He had just finished a novel, *João Picadaco* ("John Steelcock"), about a local hero of Amadoesque proportions. He is celebrated as "the father of the city" in ways both figurative and literal—including the fathering of hundreds of its citizens.

Picadaco sounded like the usual sort of ancient figure whom the centuries had turned into fabulist legend, but I was assured that he still lives, and that one of his sons served as a governor of Sergipe. Just so, it's said in Bahia that Amado didn't invent, he merely recorded. But everyone expects Bahia to be full of wild and fabulous tales; who would expect them in the Cleveland of the Northeast?

The road we drove to the beach was called *Avenida dos Naufragos,* "Avenue of the Drowned." No plaque explains the reason, but it was a dramatic one: the only attack on Brazil during World War II, and the incident that drove it to enter the war on the Allied side.

In 1944, two German U-boats sank five Brazilian coastal ships, killing at least 900 people. The bodies washed ashore like jellyfish. The United States was promptly suspected of a provocateur plot, until Radio Berlin boasted of the attack, gave details and mocked Aracaju's defense force, a single airplane.

On my last night in Aracaju, I rode the ferry to Aracaju's better side, Ilha Santa Luzia, which stretches like a Lido across from the city and is its residents' weekend getaway. Its beach, Praia Atalaia Nova, is nearly waveless, but exudes that indefinable but unmistakable mix of languor and wildness that makes a tropical paradise, a town unspoiled even by the proliferation of weekend houses.

Horseback is still the preferred means of transport here; tidal flooding has turned the dirt streets into crab pools nearly impassable for autos. Across the river, Aracaju's skyline twinkles, looking much more metropolitan than it is, a vouchsafe of urban cares left behind.

On the island's other side is a self-contained French resort. But the only lodging on the funky Praia Atalaia Nova is the little Pousada Casa Lavrada, the lovely wood-and-thatch handiwork of a sail bum whom everyone calls "Jorge da Cachaça" because he used to run a distillery. Now Jorge frets over the bar in back, the island's party center, that keeps his guests up till dawn each weekend.

I was pulled from sleep at one a.m. by a throbbing electric beat in one ear and a sweet crooning in the other. It was a local balladeer serenading a few lovers at the sand-floored Bar Olanchão. Everyone else on the island seemed to be up the beach at another bar called Geraldo's, milling about on foot and on horseback, flirting and gossiping, and I joined them there.

Two fellows got into a spat and took a few *capoeira* kicks at each other, the way the performers do for tourists in Salvador. And they danced, with the inimitable Brazilian free-hipped jitter, first to disco, then *lambada,* then the music they really wanted: *forró,* the progenitor of the notorious *lambada,* though you may not spot the resemblance at first.

Forró is a typically Brazilian case of musical syncretism. The name is a transliteration of English "for all," the term used to announce public dances at the old U.S. naval base at Natal, a beach city to the north.

But the sound is much older, a sort of exuberant Brazilian Western swing performed in the distinctive cocked leather hats of the *sertão* cowboys. The simple *forró* trios of accordion, triangle, and drum achieve surprisingly complex and infectious, hip-shaking rhythms.

Their songs build upon outrageously raunchy, boastful, and by turns ingenious and improbable, puns. One begins, "*Vou com meias velhas,*" which means "I'm going wearing old socks" but sounds exactly like "*Vou comer as velhas*"—"I'll eat up the old ladies."

And so on. Thus did backcountry dirty doggerel beget sophisticated dirty dancing.

When I think back to this Northeast, seeking magic in memory, and imagining a chance to make new memories, I long for more days in the quirky tranquility of Ilha de Santa Luzia, watching Aracaju's misleadingly metropolitan skyline twinkle across the Rio Sergipe. Even if it means staying up all night learning to dance *forró.* Cleveland should have it so good.

Despite a childhood spent partly in Vietnam between French and American wars, Eric Scigliano found French, Spanish, Italian, and Portuguese easier to learn than Vietnamese, which he's saving for his old age. He is the author of three books, including Love, War, and Circuses: The Age-Old Relationship Between Elephants and Humans. *He writes regularly for the* Seattle Weekly *and has contributed to* The Washington Post, The New York Times, The Wall Street Journal, The Nation, *and* Outside. *He found the last house in Seattle without a view.*

✳

As we got to the top of Praia da Canoa Quebrada, the rest of the world disappeared. The last leg of the trip, 200 paces up hill, or should I say up dune? Sand white and fine as sugar, a mountain about twenty feet high, only accesible on foot, its *chique-chique* music making the rolling grains slide from under our feet and reality slip from under our memory.

We stopped and I understood the meaning of "breathtaking" as my body seemed to slowly welcome in the new music now embracing us. It had a step of its own, my favorite rhythm, the rocking of water, breaking of bubbles, infinite see-saw of comfort and sweetness, the Atlantic Ocean at the furthermost point of the Brazilian coastline.

Having lived in the south most of my life, and having been abroad for the last four years, I realized then what my brother had meant by "You have to come home and show Curtis [my American husband] that part of Brazil." He meant "remember Paradise and share it a little." I felt lucky, blessed, as if the silver blue ocean were a gift just to me, just because...I had been chosen to be born there.

A couple, an older man and his wife, walked toward us and reached for our luggage, two wornout backpacks, and our sandals in our hands. "*Bom-dia,*" he said, with a smile that made me wonder if we had met before.

We followed him to the *casa,* a 30-foot-square house made of bricks and mud, covered with coconut fronds, a long wooden table with home-made chairs, about eight of them, the only furniture in sight.

The bedrooms I peeked in through the doorless doorways housed a few other backpacks, straw mats, and silence.

Our room had only two hammocks hanging from the walls.... I walked in, slowly into the emptiness, and I knew God was everywhere.

—Neise Cavini Turchin, "Longing for Brazil"

In Search of Miracles

*A skeptic finds that while evangelical sects
may not be performing supernatural acts, they give
dignity to Brazil's slum dwellers.*

PASTOR LAIME, ONE OF MANY PREACHERS WHO PARTICIPATE IN
an all-day schedule of services at the main Rio house of worship
established by the Church of God Is Love, can't keep track anymore
of how many houses of worship his church has. He debated with
the receptionist outside his office whether the total was fifty-two
hundred or fifty-four hundred, and finally settled on "five thousand
and something" in Brazil alone, in addition to about three hundred
temples in other Latin American countries. In his office, separated
from the temple itself by three flights of stairs and four electroni-
cally controlled gates, it was possible to talk quietly: there was only
the sound of air-conditioning and, in the background, the piped-in
voice of the pastor who was conducting the service downstairs, and
whose sermon was being taped on a professional sound system.
Five television screens silently monitored the security gates and the
altar. Downstairs, however, the pastor and a multidecibel sound system had to compete with the racket of incessant hammering as a
construction crew worked around the clock to build extra balconies, where more pews could be fitted. Most of the newcomers
to the church, Pastor Laime said, were fleeing the clutches of Satan.
"Every time I hold a baptism—let's say there are fifteen hundred

people present, six hundred will be former Umbandistas renouncing the Devil."

Fundamentalist evangelical sects like God Is Love, the Assembly of God, and the Universal Church of the Kingdom of God have been operating in Brazil for several decades. The oldest, the Christian Congregation in Brazil, was founded in 1910 by an Italian immigrant who passed through the United States on his way here and liked what he saw of the Pentecostal rituals in the Deep South. All the sects are invariably referred to as "the new sects," though, because their phenomenal growth has taken place only over the last twenty years, and because this period of growth coincides with the development of a new type of ritual, which is probably unlike that of any Protestant cult ever previously known. They rail against the Catholic Church, which they claim is an invention of the Devil, who hides behind every saint in the form of an *orixá*. They call the *orixás* demons, but also address them by name ("Come out, Xangô! Come out, Ogum!"), and the *orixás* growl and curse more richly than they are ever allowed to at an Umbanda temple, but finally quit the bodies of their victims and flee the presence of Jesus Christ. In nearly all the new churches, flasks of oil or water are blessed and used for faith healing. At the Church of God Is Love—which also conducts *orixá* exorcisms—the faithful are encouraged to write letters to Jesus Christ requesting a miracle, and the letters deposited on the altar are prayed over by the preacher and a fervent congregation. The sects have made it easy for converts to renounce a lifelong association with Umbanda: they do not have

In Candomblé the African orixás themselves possess their worshipers; in Umbanda they are usually distant astral figures who are too evolved to descend to Earth. Instead, they send spirit intermediaries, most of whom are pseudohistorical figures from Brazil's distant or recent past. Umbanda is "lighter" than Candomblé, demanding less of its devotees and restricting its scope to socially acceptable forms of desire and benevolent "white" magic. "Candomblé is African," says José Paiva de Oliveira, a pai-de-santos. "Umbanda is Brazilian."

—Peter Winn, Americas: The Changing Face of Latin America and the Caribbean

to admit that the *orixás* do not exist—only that they are the Devil, and that God is stronger. And, in this country that so badly needs miracles, the possibility of supernatural benefits cannot easily be overlooked. The preacher shouts over and over at the Church of God Is Love that the only true miracles, the best miracles, the biggest ones, are performed by Jesus Christ.

At nearly any hour of the day, it is possible to find one's way from President Vargas Avenue—the sixteen-lane slice of modernity that cuts through the run-down heart of colonial Rio—to the main house of worship of the Church of God Is Love by following the sound of chanting through the surrounding narrow streets. The stucco-decorated houses along these streets were once among the most delicate and charming in the city, but now their pink or blue façades are faded and crumbling, and they are occupied by electrical-supply stores, garages, and butcher shops. The main temple—a whitewashed warehouse from which songs issue all day long, at the end of a street barely wide enough for one car—blends easily into its surroundings.

When I arrived there in midafternoon a few days after my conversation with Pastor Laime, a preacher was warming up the congregation by lying on the ground behind the altar, so that only his voice, emerging through the sound system's gigantic speakers, held sway. It was hard to understand what he was shouting from his position, but that didn't seem to make much difference to the crowded house. The women sat to the left and the men to the right of the altar, which stands in front of a wall on which a large rainbow has been painted. To judge by the worshipers' knobby bone structure and threadbare clothing, they were among Rio's very poorest, and, to judge by their manner of praying, they needed a break. Some sat weeping silently. Some stood and prayed loudly, with their palms raised to Heaven. Several were kneeling up against the altar with their arms raised high, and others had flattened themselves against the booming speakers in order to feel the preacher's voice vibrating through their bodies.

Ushers—elderly women wearing uniforms and name tags—patrolled the aisles, taking up collections and handing out slips of paper on which the faithful could write letters to Christ. I noticed that a heavyset woman in a faded skirt and blouse sitting a few rows in front of me kept turning to stare in my direction. Soon she moved closer, struggling to fit herself and an overstuffed plastic supermarket bag she carried in lieu of a handbag into a small space next to me. "I don't know how to write," she said as soon as she sat down. "Will you write my letter for me?" Then she dictated it in rapid bursts, pausing hardly long enough between thoughts for me to get the words down.

"Dear Lord Jesus Christ," she began. "This is from Maria da Conceição. Please help me find a job. And bless my daughter and tell her to stop screaming and yelling at me. I know it's not her but the Devil that's making her do it, but still she just won't listen to sense. Tell her yourself to stop being an Umbandista; you know she never pays any attention to me. And her husband, who's worthless—at least help him find a job, so that both of them can move out, and so he can earn enough money to help feed the kids. And bless João and Gerónimo and Zé Carlos and Zézhino and Nilse and Ilcemar."

When I later asked Pastor Laime, who is a serious, intensely religious young man, what God Is Love could do to improve the lot of its faithful, he answered straightforwardly that that was not the church's task—that God did not want His worshipers to be more interested in material things than they were in Him. He admitted reluctantly, however, that many people's lives do improve when they quit Umbanda and join God Is Love. He cited himself as proof, saying, "Before I joined the church, I was smoking two packs a day. That's money. You save even more when you stop drinking, and it gets easier to hold down a job. And Umbanda costs a lot of money—all those offerings, the costumes, the parties. They add up."

God Is Love costs a lot of money, too. Believers are expected to turn over a tenth of their income to the church, and also to buy Bibles, hymnals, and records of church music. During the services, collections are taken up constantly, and the preacher will often begin by asking those who want to demonstrate their faith to display a large-denomination bill. Maria da Conceição told me

proudly, it was a major sacrifice for her to put the money together
for the suburban train that brought her to the church every day. She
showed me the Bible she was paying for on the installment plan—
one more sacrifice for God. I asked if someone at home read it to
her, and she said the Bible itself talked to her when she prayed to it.

The new evangelicals not only ask for money outright but also
boast of their wealth—which is proof of Christ's support—
by building larger and larger
churches and setting up more and
more elaborate television pro-
gramming, whereas Umbanda
principles state unconditionally
that "blessings aren't paid for." It
is only by charging for "consulta-
tions" and by relying on wealthy
patrons—who will often make a
cash contribution in return for a
miracle—that the head of an
Umbanda temple can make a liv-
ing. But love potions aren't as important as jobs, and if someone
like Maria da Conceição can begrudge the *orixás* the money her
daughter spends for their ritual candles and food offerings, while
herself giving unstintingly to the church from her meager funds, it's
because the *orixás* and the *exus* don't seem to be able to perform
the kinds of miracles that people need these days.

*I n the world's largest
Catholic country, there
are more Protestant preachers than
Catholic priests. Up to 30 million
Brazilians call themselves evangelicals, and the Catholic Church
estimates that 600,000 of their
faithful convert annually.*

—Jack Epstein,
"Evangelical Fervor Stirs Brazil,"
Christian Science Monitor

A self-employed handyman I know says that the help of an evangelical church—the Assembly of God—is what has kept him and
his wife not only married to each other for fifteen years but also
happy about it. In the *favela* of Vidigal, where family life is often violent and chaotic, this is a feat so remarkable as to make some of
Jamin and Maria Tereza Mendonça Merense's neighbors consider
conversion. Jamin, a birdlike, intensely curious and restless man, is
lucky in other ways, too. He is well-off even by the standards of
Vidigal, which is easily the most prosperous and consolidated of all

Rio's *favelas*. He has a car, which serves him well as he makes the rounds of his clients, most of them well-paying foreigners. True, he has to park the car about a half a mile away from where he lives, because that is where the nearest road is, and it takes him about half an hour to coax the aging vehicle out of the steep, hillside chicken yard that serves as a parking lot. Yet there the car is, a venerable American model vast enough to accommodate his entire extended family. He has a house, which he built himself. So do all his neighbors, but Jamin, because he is an exceptionally thoughtful, thrifty, and industrious craftsman, was able to figure out ways of building three stories of fairly stable brick and concrete on top of a one-room brick shack his wife inherited long ago. The house looms skyscraper-like over its neighbors, and from its top story one can see not only the crazy jumble of tilting brick houses, winding alleys, trash dumps, open sewers, and surviving bits of forest which make up Vidigal but also a far more awe-inspiring expanse of beach and ocean than that enjoyed by guests at the Sheraton Hotel, which lies at the foot of Vidigal Hill.

Jamin, whom I have known for years, was happy to take me on a tour of his living room, tiled bathroom, master bedroom with balcony (ocean view), and terraced top-floor work-and-play area, where his wife has her knitting machines, and their children—two girls and a boy—have a rusty seesaw and a swing. From the terrace he pointed out less populated areas farther uphill, where the local drug traffickers have their hideaways, and the nearby neighborhoods of Ipanema and Leblon, where many of Vidigal's residents find jobs as maids or construction workers. Leaning against the railing, one small, bare foot resting on the instep of the other, skinny arms folded against his chest, he reflected again on his luck, and on where he would be today if he and the beautiful Tereza had not found their way years ago to the Church of the Assembly of God.

Tereza, who has a large capacity for introspection and a seeming inability to paper over unpleasant facts, tells the story more precisely. She met Jamin when she was fifteen. He was working as a delivery boy, while she was working in an office, washing dishes and preparing the little cups of coffee that Brazilians drink all day long. She is very black and Jamin is classified as white—a combination that is not unheard of in serious relationships here but isn't common, either. Her friends warned him away: "That girl is insolent. She's going to give you a *bad* time. You're spending too much money on her." She wasn't wild about him, but when she mentioned that she liked to knit he took all his savings and bought her a little knitting machine. They moved in together, but soon Tereza decided that he would drive her crazy with his doglike devotion and suffocating jealousy. She left him, and then she discovered that she was pregnant.

Tereza told me this story while she combed her two lovely daughters' masses of bouncy, ringleted hair and tied it with ribbons. Tereza keeps the girls and the little boy dressed in picture-perfect pastels and sees to it that the children have pleasant manners. There is an orderliness about her—an emotional discipline—that one rarely finds among people in a very poor urban environment, but she told me that she was not always that way. When the first baby was born, she said, she used to keep it locked in the crawl space below the shack, so that she wouldn't have to hear its crying. She would struggle all day to calm her nerves, but when she heard Jamin trudging up the path in the evening, her heart would start beating in anguish. Soon she would be yelling horrible things at him. "She was sarcastic," Jamin recalls. "Whatever plan I came up with, however I tried to please her, she would cut me down. She made me feel worthless." They did not speak to each other except when they were quarreling.

It was because she was in a complete state of despair that Tereza agreed to let a neighbor take her to an Assembly of God church service one afternoon, and although she didn't like the shouting and the chanting that went on there, she was interested in some pamphlets her neighbor gave her which had to do with the family. She read that women should obey their husbands in everything, and not talk back to them; that they should not go to parties where provocative music is played; and that they should dress modestly. There were instructions on child care. In the *favelas,* many children are disciplined through beatings, and it is not uncommon for them to be chained for hours at a time, either as punishment or to keep them safe while the parents are at work. The pamphlets forbade child beating and all other forms of child abuse, along with wife beating and drinking and gambling. They defined a role for each member of the family and provided instructions on how to fill it.

Tereza took Jamin to the Assembly meetings. She began guitar lessons, and she and Jamin practiced hymns together until late at night. She stopped talking back to him, and noticed that his jealous fits eased almost immediately. They discussed child-rearing methods and the homemaking suggestions in the pamphlets, and applied them. They were so excited by all these new ideas and methods that they hardly noticed that their relationship had changed until, sitting up in bed late one night, they suddenly realized that they had been having their first conversation. They were in love.

Umbanda's strength has been the ability to imagine an alternative reality better than the present, dreary one, but to a large extent the evangelical sects' genius is to have helped their followers *change* reality. Never mind that most of the worshipers' most ambitious letters to Jesus remain unanswered; Tereza wears high-cut blouses and below-the-knee skirts and keeps her husband happy, and more and more women in the *favelas* are becoming convinced that doing that is miracle enough. Converts are instructed in the virtues of formality, punctuality, and self-control, and the lesson has proved so successful that many job interviewers will give "believers" preference in hiring, particularly for unskilled jobs. Despite these clear benefits, Protestant sects are unpopular in the media and among many intellectuals, on the basis of their puritanism and what is seen as their Yankee origin. One intellectual who isn't bothered is Darcy Ribeiro, the near-legendary anthropologist and leftist politician, who, despite surgery to remove one cancerous lung nearly a decade ago, continues to spout ideas, articles, and government projects at an undiminished pace.

"The sects are a form of worship that has found a way to dignify the lower-income sectors," he said cheerily the other day, brushing aside objections that the new churches deal in snake oil and siphon money out of the pockets of people who desperately need it. "This is a class of people who want to discover the values that will allow them a stable family life and respectability. It's a class that suffers enormously from the effects of alcoholism: every Friday night, the husband comes home pickled in *cachaça,* he beats his wife, and then he gets on top of her. Umbanda has no religious morality; basically, it's a lumpen ethic and so, of course, it has had to suffer in the face of this new cult, which is so full of family virtues, protects children,

> *The connoisseur of social patterns in Rio will soon become aware of the word* jeito, *which means a way out of a situation, or an unorthodox solution to a problem—a fix. This symbolizes the national desire for accommodation and mild hypocrisy. The word also means favor. If you get an advantage but have to pay for it, it is not true* jeito.
>
> —John Gunther,
> *Inside South America*

and has a very strong notion of sin. There have probably never been so many virgins in Rio as now! The Catholic Church always preached about the family, but the fact is that there has never been much family life in Brazil; in the upper classes, it's all hypocrisy, and what has prevailed among the poor is the model of the heroic mother raising a family that is poorer with every new child. Also, the new churches have a Brazilian *jeito*—a Brazilian way of doing things. That is particularly true of the Assembly of God, but all the others are nonhierarchical and informal, too. They're growing like weeds."

Actually, Assembly of God is not growing at the same exorbitant rate as the God Is Love and the Universal churches, perhaps because its *jeito* isn't quite Brazilian enough. The Assembly combats Umbanda and practices faith healing, but what draws crowds is the rapturous theatrics of its younger competitors. I asked Father Valdelí Carvalho da Costa, a Jesuit priest who wrote a dissertation on Umbanda, why religion in Brazil tends toward the extravagant and the magical, and he answered that this is a reflection of the Brazilian soul. "We live in a mythic universe," he said. "It comes from our African and Indian roots, and it's much more fluid and all-encompassing than Catholicism, which is the official religion. This universe is inhabited by all Brazilians, from the most illiterate slum dweller to a novelist like Jorge Amado, who has been both a member of the Communist Party and a follower of Candomblé. It's as if this mythic mentality were a parallel atmosphere we float in. Everything is always in flux, always changeable. As in the stories about men who turn into jaguars and jaguars who turn into armadillos, transformations are always possible."

"We believe in what we see," I was told by the sociologist Mariza da Costa, who is an initiate in Candomblé. "I believe in the *orixás* because I see them. The Western perception that one should believe in what one can control is the complete opposite of this. People who come from abroad to look at the Afro-Brazilian religions are always asking me, 'Do you really *believe* in this?' I tell them that in those terms one has to make a distinction between belief and faith. I have faith."

Alma Guillermoprieto—award-winning journalist and author of Samba, The Heart That Bleeds: Latin America Now, Looking for History: Dispatches from Latin America, *and* Dancing with Cuba: A Memoir of the Revolution—*was raised in Mexico. A professional dancer from 1962 to 1973, she reported on Central America for* The Guardian *and* The Washington Post, *and later reported on South America for* Newsweek. *Working as a stringer for the* Post *in 1982, she broke the story—along with Raymond Bonner of* The New York Times—*of the El Mozote massacre of unarmed peasants in El Salvador's civil war. In 1995, she received a MacArthur Foundation fellowship, often called the "genius award," for original contributions to journalism. She writes regularly for* The New Yorker *and* The New York Review of Books, *and makes her home in Mexico City.*

*

The huge electronic signboard in the Maracanã stadium announces the imminent miracle as though it were the next feature. On the stands of the giant soccer arena, 200,000 *crentes* are gathered for the start of Easter weekend; crowded, sweating, and mumbling with their eyes shut tight and hands pressed on the top of their heads. There aren't enough pastors to move through the crowds like pickpockets, placing their hands on the heads of their faithful to exorcise the demons, and so the faithful, moved by the reverberating voice of Bishop Edir Macedo, founder of the Universal Church of the Kingdom of God, in white shirt and tie in the center of the field, perform their own auto-exorcisms. When they open their eyes, they will be filled with divine light.

"If you trust in Jesus, you'll be able to see. You won't need your glasses," promises the Bishop. "Throw away your glasses, for He is coming!"

And thousands of pairs of spectacles shower onto the soccer field.

Bishop Edir Macedo, who has "made a pact with Jesus," does not throw away his glasses, however.

—Paul Rambali, *In the Cities and Jungles of Brazil*

* * *

Police Beat

A couple's run-in with the law reveals
a surprising code of enforcement.

WITH OUR MONEY RUNNING OUT AND OUR BRAZILIAN VISAS expired for well over a month, Jill and I walked into the headquarters of the Policia Federal in the coastal town of Maceió. Presenting ourselves to the green-uniformed policeman at the front desk, we explained our situation. He pushed some buttons on a grey mechanical adding machine, then pulled back a lever to get the total.

"Your fine will be three million," he announced, speaking of the amount in the local currency. It was almost double what we'd expected, a quarter of our slim assets.

"But," I protested, "the police in Rio said it would be less than two million."

"Yes, but because of inflation the fine has just increased to fifty-six thousand a day."

I started to tell him we didn't have much money, but his attention had shifted to Jill, who had tears streaming down her cheeks. Drawn by this display of feminine distress, another officer appeared from the back of the office. The two officials conferred in a blur of Portuguese and quickly reached a decision.

"It may be possible that you only pay a portion of your fine…. Or you could pay when you come back to Brazil," they said, anxiously studying Jill's face to see if their words were having any effect.

"Could we really?" she asked, not quite believing it.

"Yes, yes," one of them replied, sounding more decisive.

"That would be good," she said, drying her eyes.

Relieved, the policemen dropped their shoulders. "Come back after lunch and we'll take care of it."

Returning that afternoon, we were directed to a pair of chairs facing a desk presided over by a man in his twenties, who wore a white shirt rather than a uniform. "My name is Pedro Wanderly Vizu," he said in excellent English, grasping our hands warmly and gesturing for us to have a seat. As he pulled official forms from several drawers and file cabinets, piling an impressive stack of paperwork on his desk, I wondered if Pedro might be annoyed with all the work we'd created for him, but his attitude remained light-hearted and friendly.

"Tell me why you did not leave Brazil," he asked, feeding a document into his typewriter.

"Because we like it too much!" said Jill, and all three of us burst out laughing. Getting more serious, the two of us described the events of the past month, while Pedro faithfully recorded them on the form. It was enough to fill a small novel: our desire to stay for Carnaval (any Brazilian would be sympathetic to this); our attempts to find cheap passage to Africa, and finally, how we were booked on a flight to Luxembourg, leaving in seven days.

"May I see your air ticket receipts?" Pedro asked.

Digging out the slip of paper, Jill handed it over. I was curious to see what Pedro's reaction would be when he saw our tickets had cost thirty-seven million, many times the penalty we owed. His only comment was, "If I saved for thirty years I could fly to Europe, look around for ten minutes, and then I'd have to return to Brazil."

The two of us sat quietly as he typed our story in quadruplicate—the office lacked both a copy machine and carbon paper. I was amused by the subtle irony of our situation—here we were, two Americans going into debt to Brazil, one of the biggest debtor nations in the world, much of it owed to the United States. Too bad

Brazil couldn't subtract our fine from its financial obligations.

The typewriter paused its clattering as Pedro fed it another form. "What is your address in Maceió?" he asked.

"Green tent, *sem numero,* Riacho Doce Beach," I answered.

Pedro chuckled as he typed it in. "*Sem numero*" or "without number," is a common address in Brazil, where many buildings are unmarked. Checking off a box near the bottom of the document, he marked our status as one step short of "*Deportaçâo.*"

Noticing a guitar leaning against the windowsill behind Pedro's chair, I asked if he played.

"A little. Do you?"

I nodded.

After a couple of hours of tedious form-filling, broken frequently by off-the-record jokes and conversation, Pedro rose from his chair and led us to another police station a few blocks away, where the local constable took our fingerprints.

"If you were being deported they would have taken your picture also," Pedro informed us with a grin.

On the way back to his office, Jill asked, "What happens when we come back to Brazil? Are they going to make us pay the fine before we can enter the country?"

"Oh, no," Pedro replied. "You can enter with no problem. You will have to go to a Federal Police station to pay it."

"Will they know how much our fine is?"

"Oh no. You'll have to tell them how much it is." After a short silence, he announced, "Since you cannot pay your fine, you will have to play a song when we get back to the station."

Back at his desk, Pedro stapled our fingerprints to one of the forms and had us sign every document—I lost count after the twelfth one. Pedro and three of his office mates put their signatures below ours; every form had to have four witnesses.

When all the dotted lines were full, we opened our passports and received special exit visas stamped in purple ink. If we weren't out of the country in eight days, we'd be shipped by bus to Venezuela.

"It's time to pay your fine," Pedro said. Picking up his guitar, he led us to the door of the police chief's office. Putting a finger to his lips, Pedro warned, "Shhh...don't play anything too loud. This is a Federal Police station and we wouldn't want anyone to get the wrong idea."

Pedro knocked and a deep voice bid us to enter. Middle-aged, with thinning hair and a chest covered with medals and decorations, the chief rose and smiled, shaking our hands as Pedro introduced us. While Jill and I sat on an overstuffed couch, four or five other workers trickled in, quiet and curious. As Pedro handed me the guitar, I realized how long it had been since I'd played, especially in front of an audience. I was nervous. A love song I'd written for Jill was the softest one I knew. Everyone listened attentively as she and I sang in harmony, my fingers fumbling at the chords. As we finished, our audience clapped enthusiastically, calling in English for "More one! More one!" Still singing in a hushed voice, I played another, feeling more relaxed.

I could tell by the way Pedro's fingers were moving restlessly in his lap that he was itching to get the instrument in his hands. Concluding my second number, I passed him the guitar. Until that moment I would have described Pedro as mild mannered. But the instant that guitar touched his palms, he was transformed into a wild man.

"Jojo was a man who thought he was a woman, but he was another man! Get back! Get back! Get back to where you once belonged...." Pedro cut loose with throaty vocals and exaggerated facial gestures, rendering the classic Beatles tune with more emotion than the original. Next he sang a Brazilian song that set the whole office slapping their legs in rhythm. One woman swayed sensuously back and forth beneath her tight dress, dancing around the office.

"Shake-a-shake-shake-a-shake-a,..." the police chief had picked up a matchbox and was jiggling it back and forth like a rattle, his face one broad smile. Even in a Federal Police station it took only the slightest excuse to bring out the fun-loving side of Brazilians, who are always ready to celebrate for any reason or no reason.

Pedro played several more songs, all in Portuguese, the words and music blending together with a smoothness and fluidity that can't be matched in English.

"Well, it is time for us to go home," he said, fingernails strumming the last chord. The clock on the wall read five-thirty.

"Thank you for everything," I said.

"I wish you a good trip."

Everyone gathered to shake our hands before we left, except the police chief, who smiled and snapped to a salute. I saluted him right back and he laughed. Then Jill and I were out the door, Pedro waving as we walked out to the main road, where we caught a bus for Riacho Doce Beach and our green tent, *sem numero.*

Arthur Dawson is the author of A Passport from the Elements, *which chronicles a three-year journey he and his wife made around the world, traveling by sailboat, elephant, dugout canoe, steam train, and at least one bus with no brakes. Since their return home, he's been a little more stationary, teaching poetry to elementary school children and writing in a studio he built near Jack London's former ranch in Glen Ellen, California.*

✳

We become frightened of direct experience, and we will go to elaborate lengths to avoid it.

I found I liked to travel, because it got me out of my routines and my familiar patterns. The more traveling I did, the more organized I became. I kept adding things I liked to have with me on trips. Naturally I took books to read. Then I'd take my Walkman and the tapes I liked to listen to. Pretty soon I'd also take notebooks and colored pens for drawing. Then a portable computer for writing. Then magazines for the airplane trip. And a sweater in case it got cold on the airplane. And hand cream for dry skin.

Before long, traveling became a lot less fun, because now I was staggering onto airplanes, loaded down with all this stuff that I felt I had to take with me. I had made a new routine instead of escaping the old one. I wasn't getting away from the office any more: I was just carrying most of the contents of my desk on my shoulders.

So one day I decided I would get on the plane and carry nothing at all. Nothing to entertain me, nothing to save me from boredom. I stepped on the plane in a state of panic—none of my familiar stuff! What was I going to do?

It turned out I had a fine time. I read the magazines that were on the plane. I talked to people. I stared out the window. I thought about things.

It turned out I didn't need any of that stuff I thought I needed. In fact, I felt a lot more alive without it.

—Michael Crichton, *Travels*

BILL MCKIBBEN

A Place for Living

*An environmentalist finds
that the greenest place in Brazil
is not necessarily the Amazon rainforest.*

THE FIRST TIME I WENT THERE, I HAD NEVER HEARD OF
Curitiba. I had no idea that its bus system was the best on Earth,
that it had largely solved the problem of street children that plagues
the rest of South America, or that a municipal shepherd and his
flock of 30 sheep trimmed the grass in its vast parks. It was just a
midsize Brazilian city where an airline schedule forced me to spend
the night midway through a long South American reporting trip. I
reached my hotel, took a nap, and then went out in the early
evening for a walk—warily, because I had just come from crime-
soaked Rio. But the street in front of the hotel was cobbled, closed
to cars, and strung with lights. It opened onto another such street,
which in turn opened into a broad leafy plaza, with more shop-
lined streets stretching off in all directions. Though the night was
frosty—Brazil stretches well south of the tropics, and Curitiba is in
the mountains—people strolled and shopped, butcher to baker to
bookstore. There were almost no cars, but at one of the squares a
steady line of buses rolled off, full, every few seconds. I walked for
an hour, and then another; I felt my shoulders, hunched from the
tension of Rio (and probably New York as well), straightening.

Though I flew out the next day as scheduled, I never forgot the city.

From time to time over the next few years, I would see Curitiba mentioned in planning magazines or come across a short newspaper account of it winning various awards from the United Nations. Its success seemed demographically unlikely. For one thing, it's relatively poor—average per capita income is about twenty-five hundred dollars. Worse, a flood of displaced peasants has tripled its population to a million and a half in the last 25 years. It should resemble a small-scale version of urban nightmares like São Paulo or Mexico City. But I knew, from my evening's stroll, it wasn't like that, and I wondered why.

It was more than idle curiosity. The longer I thought about my home place, the more I knew that its natural recovery was mostly a matter of luck and timing—that it could easily deteriorate again because people had not changed the economic habits or attitudes of mind that laid it to waste in the first place. We in the U.S. still cherish notions of extreme individualism; if anything, our sense of community weakens more each year. Our politics is ever more firmly in the hands of those who exalt the private, those who write off whole swaths of people and places.

Although I no longer live an urban life, I knew that the key to many of these mysteries involved cities—and not simply because of their potential for environmental efficiency. More because they had long been the places where we worked out our most important accommodations. Where we built our most important links, however tenuously, between different kinds of people. Where sheer crowdedness made compromise essential. The erosion of the sense of community in the cities I knew—most essentially New York, but in fact any place ringed with suburbs—seems to me to have signaled the erosion of politics as something useful, to have turned it from a source of togetherness and common feeling into a reflection of apartness and self-interest.

If any of my hopes for the small and lonely places I love best are ever to bear fruit, that cynical divisiveness has to be reversed. Maybe an effort to convince myself that such a decay in public life was not inevitable was why I went back to Curitiba to spend some real time, to see if its charms extend beyond the lovely downtown. For a month my wife and baby and I lived in a small apartment near the city center. Morning after morning I interviewed cops, merchants, urban foresters, civil engineers, novelists, planners; in the afternoons we pushed the stroller around the town, learning its rhythms and habits.

And we decided, with great delight, that Curitiba is among the world's great cities.

Not for its physical location: there are no beaches, no broad bridge-spanned rivers. Not in terms of culture or glamour: it's a fairly provinicial place. But measured for "livability"—a weak coinage expressing some optimum mix of pleasures provided and drawbacks avoided—I have never been any place like it. In a recent survey, 60 percent of New Yorkers wanted to leave their rich and cosmopolitan city; 99 percent of Curitibans told pollsters that they were happy with their town; and 70 percent of Paulistas, residents of the mobbed megalopolis to the north, said they thought life would be better in Curitiba. It has slums: some of the same *favelas* that dominate most Third World cities have sprouted on the edge of town as the population has rocketed. But even they are different, hopeful in palpable ways. They are clean, for instance—under a city program a slum dweller who collects a sack of garbage gets a sack of food from the city in return.

And Curitiba is the classic example of decent lives helping produce a decent environment. One statistic should underline the importance of this place to the world: because of its fine transit system, and because its inhabitants are attracted toward the city center instead of repelled out to a sprawl of suburbs, Curitibans use 25 percent less fuel per capita than other Brazilians, even though they are actually more likely to own cars. Twenty-five percent is a large enough number to matter; in the United States, we are battling, unsuccessfully, merely to hold our much-higher fossil fuel use steady. And this 25 percent came before anyone redesigned cars or changed energy prices or did any of the other things only a federal government or an international treaty can do. It came not from preaching at folks about waste or ranting about global warming. It came from designing a city that actually meets people's desires, a city that is as much an example for the sprawling, decaying cities of the First World as for the crowded, booming cities of the Third World. A place that, at the very least, undercuts the despair that dominates every discussion of the world's cities, where half of human souls now reside.

It is a place, most of all, that helps redeem the idea of politics. If there's one lesson that Ronald Reagan and Newt Gingrich have successfully hammered home to Americans, it's that "public"—education or transit or broadcasting or health care—is necessarily shabby and cumbersome, while "private" is shiny and efficient. Until that notion (which all too often reflects the present truth) changes, nothing will alter the basic momentum of our predicament. If Curitiba seems at first far removed from the forests and villages and suburbs of my home in the rural East, it came to seem an absolutely essential first stop on my journey.

At 900 meters above sea level, Curitiba is atop the great escarpment along the route from Rio Grande do Sul to São Paulo. Due to this location, it flourished briefly as a pit stop for gauchos and their cattle until a better road was built on an alternative route. Curitiba quickly went back to sleep.

—Andrew Draffen, Robert Strauss, and Deanna Swaney, *Brazil - a travel survival kit*

The Portuguese arrived on the Planalto, the first plateau above the Atlantic, in the middle of the 17th century. They were looking for gold, which was gone by 1660; a few stayed on to found a backwater town, Curitiba, which was known as the "sleeping city," a good stopover on the route to São Paulo. But the coffee farms of Paraná state drew a steady stream of European immigrants—especially Italians, Poles, and Germans—many of whom eventually settled in Curitiba, the state's capital. By 1940 there were 125,000 residents. By 1950 the number had jumped to 180,000, and by 1960 doubled to 361,000—the explosive, confident growth that marked the entire country was under way in Curitiba as well. And with many of the same effects: traffic downtown started to snarl, and the air was growing thick with exhaust. It was clear that the time had come to plan; and as in almost every other city, planning meant planning for automobiles.

Curitiba's official scheme called for widening the main streets of the city to add more lanes, which would have meant knocking down the turn-of-the-century buildings that lined the downtown, and for building an overpass that would link two of the city's main squares by going over the top of Rua Quinze de Novembro, the main shopping street. Any American living in a city that has undergone urban renewal or been cut off from its waterfront by a belt of highway would recognize the plan in an instant; in one form or another, it's how urban areas around the globe have been reconfigured for the auto age.

But in Curitiba, resistance to the plan was unexpectedly fierce. Opposition was centered in the architecture and planning departments of the local branch of the federal university, and the loudest voice belonged to Jaime Lerner.

Jaime Lerner is a chubby man with a large, friendly, and open face. He also looks silly stuffed into a suit; so even though he's been mayor of Curitiba on and off for the last two decades, he normally wears a blue polo shirt. He has an abiding interest in almost everything. His press secretary says that quite often, answering a question on television, Lerner "starts in about this city here that he's just visited, and this movie he was thinking about, and this book he just read. And I tell him, 'No, No, No—you need *shock asterisks*'"—what we in the States call sound bites.

In the late 1960s, however, he was just a young planner and architect who had grown up in the city, working in his Polish father's dry goods store. And he organized the drive against the overpass, out of what might almost be called nostalgia. "They were trying to throw away the story of the city," he recalls; they were trying to emulate, on a much smaller scale, the *tabula rasa* "miracle" of Brasília—the capital city that was still being completed in the country's interior—perhaps the grandest stab at designing a city from the ground up in the world's history. Brasília was the buzz of architects and planners everywhere, and the country's greatest claim to modernity. Its site was chosen from aerial photographs of various scrublands and turned over to Oscar Niemeyer, the foremost Brazilian disciple of Le Corbusier; as Alex Shoumatoff, in his history of the city, writes: "Most of the young intellectuals in Latin America at that time were eager to break with the past and take a long leap forward." Their plan was for a rational grid of buildings precisely the same size, with a giant "Sector of Diversion" in the center. Functions were strictly separated—work in one area, shop in another, play in a third—and the regions were linked mainly by road. It was a "speedway city," to be built entirely without intersections; anyone walking between the monumental buildings would have to use overpasses. Construction drowned the richest forest on the central plateau, and the glass buildings baked like ovens in the sun—it is a city inconceivable without the air-conditioner and the car. But never mind. Astronaut Yuri Gagarin visited. "I feel as if I have just disembarked on another planet, not Earth," he said, meaning it as a compliment. France's Minister of Culture André Malraux, speaking for European modernity, told a crowd that "a murmur of glory accompanies the pounding of the anvils that salute your audacity, your faith, and the destiny of Brazil, as the Capital of Hope surges on!" Frank Capra thought it was the eighth wonder of the world.

With all that exaltation in the air, it was a good thing that Jaime Lerner had visited Paris as a young student and especially that he had grown up loving the mix of people in Curitiba. Because Lerner, through a chain of political flukes, found himself the mayor of Curitiba at the age of 33. Brazil in the early 1970s was ruled by the military, and the local governor was not interested in appointing anyone who might turn out to be a political rival. He picked Lerner, who took the job despite his repugnance for the army. All of a sudden his friends and colleagues were pulling their plans out of the cupboards. All of a sudden they were going to get their chance to remake Curitiba—not for cars but for people. "I was born on the street of the central railroad station," says Lerner. "My father—he had a shop in this street, and we lived in the back of the business. I used, since six, to play in the street. Since my childhood

I had everything from the street. Peasants, they came each day. We had big factories so I knew all kind of workers. We had the state assembly. The old streetcars. We had circus, newspapers. The whole life—hotels. So I could have an idea about the whole society. I was playing, and just watching. I never could forget this street, which was a street like other streets that everyone has in his life. But a street is the synthesis of the whole city, the whole society."

And so the story of Curitiba begins with its central street, Rua Quinze—the one that the old plan wanted to obliterate with an overpass. Lerner insisted instead that it should become a pedestrian mall, an emblem of his drive for a human-scale city. "I knew we'd have a big fight," he says. "I had no way to convince the store owners a pedestrian mall would be good for them, because there was no other pedestrian mall in Brazil. No other in the world, really, except maybe Munich. But I knew if they had a chance to actually see it, everyone would love it." To prevent opposition, he planned carefully. "I told my staff, 'This is like a war.' My secretary of public works said the job would take two months. I got him down to one month. Maybe one week, he said, but that's final. I said, 'Let's start Friday night, and we have to finish by Monday morning.'" And they did—jackhammering up the pavement, putting down cobblestones, erecting streetlights and kiosks, and putting in tens of thousands of flowers.

"It was a horrible risk—he could easily have been fired," says Oswaldo Alves, who helped with the work. But by midday Monday the same store owners who had been threatening legal action were petitioning the mayor to extend the mall. The next weekend, when offended members of the local automobile club threatened to "reclaim" the street by driving their cars down it, Lerner didn't call the police. Instead, he had city workers lay down strips of paper the length of the mall. When the auto club arrived, its members found dozens of children sitting in the former street painting pictures. The transformation of Curitiba had begun.

But this was not some romantic revolution, a cultural protest of the sort so common in the wake of the '60s and so evanescent. Even this small victory was possible only because Lerner and his architect friends had thought so carefully about the future of the city. They had, among other things, carefully replotted the city's

Jaime Lerner served three terms as mayor of Curitiba, and two terms as governor of Paraná state.

—AH and SD

traffic flow, not only to make the downtown function without cars on its main street, but also to direct growth throughout the city. Instead of buying up buildings and tearing them down to widen streets, planners stared at the maps long enough to see that the existing streets would do just fine—as long as they were considered in groups of three parallel avenues. Traffic on the first avenue would flow one way, into town. The middle street would be devoted to buses, driving in dedicated lanes so they could move more quickly. A block over you'd find motorists heading out of town. No highways in the city—three streets still scaled to human beings. And more important, once the planners had designated five of these "structural axes" leading out from the center of town like spokes in a wheel, they could begin to tinker with zoning. Along these main routes, high-density buildings were permitted—the apartments that would hold the commuters eager to ride the buses. Farther from the main roads, density decreases.

From the observation deck on the top of the city's television tower, you can see the results spread out below you: not a ring of high-rises choking the downtown, but orderly lines of big buildings shading off into neighborhoods along each of the axes; a city growing on linear lines that removed congestion from the center, and kept a mix of housing—and hence, of incomes—throughout the city. "Every city has its hidden designs—old roads, old streetcar ways," says Lerner. "You're not going to invent a new city. Instead, you're doing a strange archaeology, trying to enhance the old, hidden design. You can't go wrong if the city is growing along the trail of memory and of transport. Memory is the identity of the city, and transport is the future."

Transport in the case of Curitiba means buses. Though larger Brazilian cities were investing in subways and though "there were always people trying to sell them to us as the modern way," Lerner and his team decided the subways were too expensive—that they were stuck with buses. They also decided that buses needn't be stuck in traffic. They quickly designed the system of express lanes that sped travel to and from the downtown, and ridership began to take off. In 1974 the system carried 25,000 passengers a day; by 1993 the number was 1.5 million—or more than ride the buses in New York City each day. The route network looks like a model of the human brain. Orange feeder buses and green buses traveling in constant loops through the outer neighborhoods deliver passengers to terminals, where they catch red express buses heading downtown or out to the factories on the city's edge.

In an effort to increase speed even further, the red express buses were replaced in the late 1980s by silver "direct line" buses on the busiest streets. The buses move faster not because they have bigger motors but because they were designed by smarter people. Sitting at a bus stop one day, Lerner noticed that the biggest time drag on his fleet was how long it took passengers to climb the stairs and pay the fare. He sketched a plan for a glass "tube station," a bus shelter raised off the ground and with an attendant to collect fares. When the bus pulls in, its doors open like a subway's, and people walk right on (or, in the case of wheelchairs, roll right on). A year after the "speedybuses" went into service, the city did a survey: 28 percent of the passengers were new to the system, commuters who had parked their cars because of the new convenience. In 1993 Curitiba added another Lerner innovation—extra-long buses, hinged in two spots to snake around corners and able to accommodate 300 passengers. Five doors open and close at each stop, and on busy routes at rush hour one of these behemoths arrives every minute or so; 20,000 passengers an hour can move in one direction. There is a word for this kind of service: subway.

Amazingly, the city doesn't need to subsidize its bus service. The fleet is purchased and owned by private companies; the government assigns routes, sets fares, and pays each contractor by kilometer traveled. For about 30 cents, you can transfer as often as you want; and the whole network turns a profit. A few years ago, to help celebrate Earth Day, Curitiba lent New York several of its loading tubes and special buses. Brazilians installed the system in five days, and for a couple months the buses plied a loop from the Battery to South Street Seaport and back. The *Daily News* reported "looks of bewilderment" at the "space age pod" donated by the Third World to the absolute epicenter of world finance, but by all accounts passengers loved the system. Still, it seems to have disappeared into some bureaucratic maw. The New York City bus system has seen ridership fall 42 percent in the last twenty years and is only now beginning to experiment with "innovations" like stopping every third block instead of every second one. The "realistic hope," according to a Transit Authority report, is that ridership will fall only seven percent in the 1990s. I understand why; I never rode the buses when I lived in New York. I could walk faster than a rush-hour bus in midtown, and the rest of the day they rarely came; the windows were so scratched that once you were on board you had to peer owl-eyed to see if your stop was approaching. But in Curitiba I rode every day, pushing my daughter's stroller onto the bus, finding my way more easily than in Manhattan despite my pidgin Portuguese. The *bus* serves *you,* and not the other way around; you feel in control of the city, not a victim of its tie-ups and bottlenecks and ancient everyday-repeated traffic jams.

I set out one day on the bike path that ran by my apartment, intent on compiling a sensory catalogue of a little of the urban pleasure Curitiba offered. On this sunny afternoon, the path was crowded with cyclists, but most were just noodling along; and it was no problem to push my baby daughter in her stroller. The path ran beside the Rio Belém; the water was dirty and carried some trash, but even two blocks from downtown, flowering trees were growing wild out over the banks. We walked by a sandy soccer field jammed with eight-year-old boys (not a parent in sight) and then across a street and into the Bosque do Papa, a small park dedicated to Pope John Paul II, who visited Curitiba in 1991. Cobbled paths wound through the park to a small cluster of wood-plank buildings: a replica of a Polish immigrant village that was moved here when the park was commissioned. One building, a chapel with

four rows of pews, holds a beautiful icon of the black virgin of
Czechostowa. Outside, older women sat on benches watching their
grandchildren play. The path left the park and moved into a residential neighborhood of big and small houses, running past a concrete municipal skateboard ramp that would shake the heart of any
city attorney in the United States. Young trees grew all along the
edge of the sidewalk, carefully staked out by city workers—it's easy
to see there will be a corridor of shade in another decade. Past a
Bavarian beer house and a bike-rental stand, the path reached the
Parque São Lourenço, whose big lake was one of the original
flood-control projects. On the right a municipal go-cart ramp
plummeted down from the highest hill. On the left a shepherd
gathered the municipal herd of sheep, which were done trimming
the grass for the day. Swans and geese floated on the lake; at its head
sat the former glue factory, now a municipal Creativity Center,
with a ceramics studio, a sculpture garden, and a giant chess set
with pieces the size of children. The *ciclovia*—bike path—connects
everything with the other parks—Parque Barrigui, for instance,
where today Ziggy Marley was giving an outdoor concert, the
Third Age center (for seniors) was holding quiet yoga sessions, and
remote-control planes whizzing around the municipal remote-
control airplane range.

The next morning I headed downtown toward the pedestrian
mall, stopping at the Passeio Público, the city's original park, to eat
a big meal for a couple of dollars at the outdoor restaurant. This is
no Tavern-on-the-Green: a raucous samba band was performing at
one end of the open restaurant, and I could hear its music even
after I'd finished my lunch and left on a stroll down the middle of
the Rua Quinze. Ritzy stores sit next to cheap and crowded
lanchonetes on this pedestrian mall, and hardware stores with a thousand pots hanging from the ceiling stand next to booksellers. A
parade of chanting Evangelicals suddenly appeared at one end of
the street; they had dressed one of their number as Jesus and were
carrying him on a sedan chair down the street. There was a volleyball court in one of the central plazas, half a dozen playgrounds, and
lottery salesmen bellowing on every corner. One of the roving

markets had taken root near a bus terminal, and I recognized many of the handicrafts from my tour of the adult education centers. People wandering out of the main cathedral after noontime Mass blinked to be back in the sun. A man dressed as a giant molar gave a lecture on oral hygiene from a stage while dozens of dental assistants in their white uniforms handed out leaflets and demonstrated proper brushing. In a military tent set up under some flowering *ipê* trees, an army doctor showed a video about AIDS. Waiters in uniforms—old men—served lunch at the Scheffer deli, an establishment so beloved that when it burned a few years ago the city subsidized its restoration. Card tables from several political parties offered competing anticorruption publications; around every new kiosk, knots of people stood reading the posted front pages. The jacarandas shaded the toucans in the small zoo, and off on one corner a little amusement park offered a Ferris wheel and a merry-go-round.

It is a true place, a place full of serendipity. It is not dangerous or dirty; if it was, people would go to the shopping mall instead. It is as alive as any urban district in the world: poems pasted on telephone poles, babies everywhere. The downtown, though a shopping district, is not a money-making machine. It is a habitat, a place for *living*—the exact and exciting opposite of a mall. A rich and diverse and *actual* place that makes the American imitations—the South Street Seaports and Faneuil Hall Marketplaces—seem like the wan and controlled re-creations that they are.

I had to remind myself, wandering through Curitiba, that all this spontaneity didn't happen by itself—that without the planning and the risky gambles that created the conditions for it to evolve, the center would likely be dangerous and dying. There is one subtle reminder every Saturday morning. Municipal workers roll out huge sheets of paper down the middle of one of the central blocks of the pedestrian mall and set out pots of paints so that hundreds of kids can—without knowing what they're doing—re-create the sit-in that drove away the cars and launched this pleasure-filled street at the beginning of Lerner's first term. Some of these children are undoubtedly the offspring of children who were brought here that first dramatic Saturday, and their presence raises a question of the first importance: can you, by changing the conditions under which people live, slowly change the character of the people? It's a key question; any long-term hope for dealing with the massive problems of the environment involves changing people around the world. Or no—not *changing* them. Bringing out the *part* of them that responds to nonmaterial pleasures like painting on the sidewalk and walking in a crowd and gossiping on a bench and drinking a beer at a bar. And slowly de-emphasizing the side that we know all too well: the private, muffled grabbiness, the devotion to comfort, the fear of contact that resides in each of us, side by side with the qualities we need to muster.

To learn from Curitiba, the rest of the world would have to break some long-standing habits—the habit of finding answers in the rich countries, for instance. "People can't imagine there's a city in Brazil with all the facilities," says the director of the city's housing authority. "When I visit America, people are convinced that when I come home, I have to take a jeep from the airport through the jungle, like Tarzan. Residents of the First World say, 'Curitiba is a Third World city, what can it teach us?'" sighs Lerner. "People in the Third World say, 'We're a First World city.'"

The hardest habit to break, in fact, may be what Lerner calls the "syndrome of tragedy, of feeling like we're terminal patients." Many cities have "a lot of people who are specialists in proving change is not possible. What I try to explain to them when I go to visit is that it takes the same energy to say why something can't be done as to figure out how to do it." Curitiba, he says, is "not a model but a reference," more important as a reservoir of directions and of hope. "I'm sure of one thing. When people come to visit, they won't forget. Because it's a very strong place. I realize there's very few examples in the world. It's hard to make it happen, and that's why it's so strong. For those who make their living selling complexity, it's very strong. For those who want a small sign that it's possible, it's very strong, too."

I was rushing to catch a flight back home when I talked with

Lerner for the last time, and I thought to myself that I would miss this city greatly—not only because of its buses and parks, but because in weeks of doing interviews I'd met very few cynics. The resigned weariness of Westerners about government, which leaves only fanatics and hustlers running for office, had lifted from this place. I came of age during Watergate, and so I needed a reminder that politics in its largest sense can actually be a noble and useful profession, can actually change a place and its people. I needed a reminder that "public" is not a notion consigned to the trash heap of history. I needed this month in the middle of a city to think clearly about the villages and forests of my home.

As I was gathering up my papers to leave for the airport, Lerner talked about his most recent trip to New York, where his daughter is a dancer. Though he was attending a conference, he managed to go to ten movies in ten days, not to mention concerts, bars, restaurants. He behaves, apparently, as if every city was a Curitiba; and it is hard not to think that he might be able to create them wholesale by sheer force of exuberant personality. He is, among other things, a passionate devotee of klezmer music, and spent several hours at an outdoor band shell on the Lower East Side waiting through rock bands to hear a performance by the Klezmatics. (He later invited them to Curitiba, where they were a big hit.) I asked him again about the example Curitiba offers the rest of the world. "The more you study your own condition, the deeper you get in your own reality, the more universal you are," he answered. "Tolstoy said, 'If you want to be universal, sing your village.' This is true in literature, it's true in music—if you know klezmer, you know all of music. And it's true in cities, too. You have to know your village and you have to love it."

Bill McKibben is the author of several books and scores of articles for The New Yorker *and other major U.S. publications. His first book, the best-selling* The End of Nature, *caused an international stir with its portrait of the harm American society has done to the planet. His book,* Hope, Human and Wild: True Stories of Living Lightly on the Earth, *from which this story was excerpted, is a confirmation of hope for the future of our species.*

Experts in the field of sustainable resources rave about him; Rush Limbaugh, characteristically, calls him "an environmental wacko." He lives in the Adirondacks with his wife, writer Sue Halpern, and their daughter, Sophie.

✳

What impresses me most about Curitiba cannot be reduced to cold statistics. Among the people here, there is a palpable enthusiasm, a brightness and zest. I see it in the teenagers bunched over a table at a city-sponsored class, their hands dipping into rich, black earth as they pot seedlings. The students notice me and suddenly turn in my direction, flashing smiles, their faces open and innocent. I think of scenes from Mexico, Ecuador, Vietnam, and other Third World nations I've visited—the grinding poverty and sullen, resentful glances—and ask myself again "what has set Curitiba apart?" Jaime Lerner's words echo in my mind: "Government should respect the people."

—Curtis Moore, "Greenest City in the World!,"
International Wildlife

PART TWO

SOME THINGS TO DO

ALMA GUILLERMOPRIETO

* * *

Opium of the People

*In joining a samba school the author learns
more than just how to dance.*

THE HEAT BLOOMED IN DECEMBER AS THE CARNAVAL SEASON
kicked into gear. Nearly helpless with sun and glare, I avoided Rio's
brilliant sidewalks and glittering beaches, panting in dark corners
and waiting out the inverted southern summer. Nevertheless, certain rhythms, an unmistakable urgency in the air got through to
me. Although there were still three months left to the Carnaval celebrations that would close down Rio for nearly a week in March,
the momentum was already building. The groups of men who
normally gathered for coffee or beer in front of the tiny grocery
stores that dot Rio were now adding a percussion backup to their
usual excited conversation. They beat a drum, clapped their hands
in counterpoint and toyed with a stray verse of song before letting
the rhythm die out again.

There was a faster, more imposing beat to the sambas on the
radio. I made tentative inquiries: Carnaval? Boring. Vulgar. Noisy,
some people said, and recommended that I leave town for that horrible weekend. Samba schools? Tacky, some said. Highly original,
said others, and volunteered that the "schools" were in reality orga-
nizations that compete on Carnaval weekend with floats and songs
and extravagant costumes, each group dressed entirely in its official

137

colors. But was it true that Carnaval was something that happened principally in the slums? Why? There were shrugs, raised eyebrows. Who knows. Opium of the people. Blacks are like that. We Brazilians are like that. You know: on the day of the coup, back in 1964, people were happy because it meant they had the day off and could go to the beach. Opium, yes, probably. But surely it was fun? In March, I ended up on Carnaval weekend with a ticket for the first of two all-night samba school parades.

In the official parade grounds—the Sambódromo—I thought the silence eerie until I realized it was in fact a solid wall of sound, a percussive din that did not sound like music and advanced gradually toward the spectators on an elaborate loudspeaker system set up on either side of the central "avenue," or parade space. At the head of the noise was a gigantic waggling lion's head that floated down the avenue and overtook us, giving way to dazzling hordes in red and gold. A marmalade-thick river of people swept past; outlandish dancers in feathers and capes, ball gowns and G-strings, hundreds of drummers, thousands of leaping princes singing at the top of their lungs. Drowning in red and gold, I struggled to focus. In the ocean of feathers and banners faces emerged: brown, white, pink, tan, olive. Young black men bopping in sweat-drenched suits; old women in cascades of flounces whirling ecstatically; middle-aged

> *Dense rhythms cross and dance with each other, each grabbing hold of the crowd in a different way. By now, the sound is deafening and conversations are out of the question. Everyone is dancing, the sweat flows, and the balmy night air carries more than a hint of eroticism with all the men and women wearing so little and drinking so much. The festive atmosphere is euphoric, as worries and cares are sent flying. There's no doubt in anyone's mind: samba is what it's all about.*
>
> —Chris McGowan and Ricardo Pessanha, *The Brazilian Sound: Samba, Bossa Nova, and the Popular Music of Brazil*

men and women with paunches and eyeglasses bouncing happily in their headdresses and bikinis. What kinds of jobs did they have in everyday life? How much had their costumes cost? Why, in Brazil's pervasively segregated society, had all the colors decided to mix?

Four Styrofoam elephants trundled past on golden platforms, followed by gigantic Balinese dancers in red and gold. There were acrobatic dancers with tambourines; more spinning old women; a flag-bearing couple, who should have been paralyzed by the weight of their glittering costumes, twirling and curtsying instead through a dance that looked like a samba-minuet. Nothing was familiar or logical, and I was reduced to the simplest questions. How could that large woman over there in the sequined bikini be so unconcerned about her cellulite? Why was everyone singing a song about the Mexican *chicle* tree, and who had come up with the idea? Why were a spectacularly beautiful woman dressed only in a few feathers and a little boy in a formal suit pretending to have sex with each other for the audience's benefit, and why was everyone involved so cheerful? Were all these people from the slums? And if they were, how could they look so happy when their lives were so awful?

It was well after dawn when I left the crowd of ever more enthusiastic spectators, as the seventh samba school was about to begin its slow progress. Beyond the Sambódromo were the squalid last alleyways of the moribund red-light district, and beyond that the *favelas*—the slums, perched on their outcrops of rock. Back home, the Ipanema universe of orderly tree-lined streets and air-conditioned buildings seemed remote and barren when compared with the *favelas* I knew only from my maid's descriptions, now suddenly come alive in my mind as the magical enclaves where Carnaval could be imagined and then made flesh. The peopled hills were everywhere—there was one only three blocks from my apartment building—and I spent months staring at the jumble of shacks pitched so artlessly across the steep slopes, imagining the hot, crazy life within. But it was a long time before I could find an excuse to get close.

I went to a North Zone *favela* for my first visit to a samba school. It was springtime in Brazil, when the weather in Rio is loveliest: washed clear of rains, the sky turns a cool and peaceful blue. The nights, too, are soothing, spattered with clean bright stars and edged with promise. Spring signals the beginning of the Carnaval season, which starts up in September with nightlong rehearsals designed to set the festive sap running for the real event. Year-round planning for the parade also shifts into full gear with weekly meetings at which samba school directorates define their strategies and assign tasks.

The taxi crossed the tunnel under Corcovado hill, which links Ipanema and Copacabana to the North Zone; skimmed past the massive shadow of Maracanã Stadium and the concrete wastelands of the state university; and stopped at the edge of a *favela* that chunnels precipitously from one particularly tall hill right down to the pavement itself. This was Mangueira.

The directors of the First Station of Mangueira Recreational Association and Samba School were holding one of their weekly planning meetings, chaired by the school president, Carlos Dória.

Like other schools, Mangueira had already begun its samba harvest; a process of winnowing out competing sambas composed around the official parade theme, until one is selected to be sung in the Sambódromo by the school's 5,300 members. There was general enthusiasm for the theme, and agreement that the competing sambas offered a rich crop, but some members of the directorate were unsatisfied with the costumes and the floats: they were too frilly, and they did not convey enough about the present situation of blacks in Brazil or about their past hardships.

I hung around the edges of the meeting and at the end spoke briefly with Dória, a burly man in his mid-40s with a paunch, thick gold jewelry, a mustache and an unfriendly air. I told him I was a reporter and said I would like to follow Mangueira through its process of making Carnaval. Roughly, he told me I was wasting my time. I was persistent, but he was mean; he was a member of the state military police, and the hostility in his manner was both professional and frightening.

After we had reached an impasse, a young woman listening to our conversation interceded and took me aside. Nilsemar was very pretty, with the modest, precise gestures of a skillful nurse. She had been sitting at the directorate table with other women to whom she now introduced me: her grandmother *Dona* Zica, widow of Cartola, one of the founders and outstanding composers of the

Mangueira samba school; her friend Marilia, a white sociologist; *Dona* Neuma, daughter of a founder of the school and an all-time *sambista*; and Neuma's daughter, Guezinha. The women were as friendly as Dória was brusque. They listened to my questions and invited me to attend the harvest dance the following Saturday. "Don't worry," Nilsemar said softly, when I said Dória might not approve of my presence. "He's gruff, but we'll convince him to let you see what you want to see."

Dona Neuma was the daughter of a school founder who had died of tuberculosis and poverty many years before. Her husband had worked as a carpenter until his death, and *Dona* Neuma and her family had almost always lived in a brick-and-wood shack on the same spot where their

𝓜angueira was the first samba school, founded in 1928. Many more schools were started, but at that time they had no direct connection with the Carnaval. Products of the poorer quarters with high black populations, they played no part in the festival, which took place in the center of Rio and was celebrated by the middle class. Poor people who wanted to take part in the Carnaval did so virtually in secret; they were even chased away by the police when they attempted to sing and dance in the center of the city. This continued until 1935, when Rio authorities officially recognized Carnaval in its popular form.

—Sergio Alves Teixeira, "Samba Time!" UNESCO *Courier*

house now stood. One of the daughters, Chininha, had married well, to an airline attendant. Another, Ceci, had a government job with which to support herself, her daughter and granddaughter, while Guezinha, married to a car salesman, also worked off and on at a store or at other clerical jobs. The family's combined incomes and a little money from Carnaval-related activities had built the house, which was magnificent by hill standards. Its retaining wall climbed straight up off the viaduct to a concrete porch and beyond that to a two-story edifice with an outside staircase leading to a veranda and the suite of rooms where Ceci and Guezinha lived. A floating population of family friends shared the sisters' rooms or, as space grew scarce and the heat rose around Carnaval time, slept on the cool tile floors of the front room or even camped out on the porch. "There's always more room, child," Guezinha liked to say. "There's the veranda upstairs, there's the roof.... You put a little more water in the soup and it's ready for company." The house had been the first on the hill to acquire a telephone—a still scarce commodity—and this was an additional cause of traffic, with Mangueirenses perpetually bursting into the house with urgent pleas to use the phone to call a doctor, or a sick relative, or someone rumored to be looking for a servant or a bricklayer.

Dona Neuma presided over the household and the female divisions of the school with similar style. Irascible and autocratic, she was also completely vulnerable to pleas for help, which is why so many temporarily homeless people ended up at her doorstep, and why all complaints of injustice and wrongdoing in the school were eventually addressed to her. No one was turned away, the same price being extracted from all: unswerving loyalty and wide-eyed attention when *Dona* Neuma spoke.

The household was always bustling. Half a dozen people sprawled on a couple of worn, fake-leather sofas, watching television. New family members constantly emerged from back bedrooms and joined others on the couch. Someone made coffee. Beers were poured. Guezinha stored the week's shopping—beans, rice, macaroni, detergent, toilet paper, and gallons of cooking oil— in a carved wood highboy that matched the rest of the fancy and uncomfortable dining room furniture. I fidgeted, feeling both out of place and eager to linger in the household's chaotic warmth. Guezinha gave me an amused look. "You're here to learn, aren't you? Come here, I'll show you something." She led me to the huge kitchen, where an excited group of women was studying a sketch of a woman in a feather-topped turban, sequined bra, and ankle-length, below-the-navel skirt, seductively draped and slit thigh-high up the front. The outfit looked like something the chorus girls at the Crazy Horse in Paris might wear for their presentation walk-on, but Guezinha said it was supposed to be a parade costume representing an *orixá*, or African goddess. Looking at the sketch I understood why the Portuguese word for costume is *fantasia*—fantasy: all my life, I had wanted to look like that, if only for a few minutes, a few seconds.

"It's for my wing," Guezinha explained. "I have an all-woman wing, 50 of us, and this is the costume we'll wear. Do you like it?" I said I did. She gave me a sidelong glance, then looked around at other women. "Well, how would you like to join my wing and parade with us at Carnaval time?" I said I would like that very much indeed. "But first," Guezinha said, with hardly the shadow of a smile, "you have to learn to samba."

One of the subtler forms of amusement for blacks at Carnaval time is watching whites try to samba. White people have had nearly the whole century to try to samba, and most of them still can't quite get it right. It's not that blacks mind; that whites look clumsy while they're trying to have fun is a misfortune too great to be compounded by mockery, but it's also a fact that can't be denied. Whites are certainly given points for trying, though, and in the Sambódromo the ones who got up to dance seemed to be much more warmly regarded than those who tried to maintain their dignity. But I was terrified of what I might look like, and in the weeks before Carnaval, after lurking in the corners of the *quadra* at almost every rehearsal, I went home and practiced samba grimly and in secret.

HOW TO SAMBA (WOMEN'S VERSION)

1. Start before a mirror, with no music. You may prefer to practice with a pair of very high heels. Though samba is a dance that started out barefoot, and can still be danced that way, high heels will throw your spinal column out of whack and give your pelvis the appearance of greater flexibility. Platform shoes with relatively wide heels provide the best combination of stability and shock absorption.

2. Stand with feet parallel, close together. Step and hop in place on your right foot as you brush your left foot quickly across. Step in quick succession onto your left, then your right foot. Although your hips will swivel to the right as far as possi-

ble for this sequence, your head and shoulders should remain strictly forward. Otherwise you'll start looking like you're doing the *hora*. Practice this sequence right and left until you can do it without counting.

3. Test yourself: Are your lips moving? Are your shoulders scrunched? No? Are you able to manage one complete left-right sequence per second? Good! Now that you've mastered the basic samba step, you're ready to add music. Choose Zeca Pagodinho, Jovelina the Black Pearl, Neguinho of the Hummingbird, or any other *sambista* you like and start practicing. The key thing at this stage is speed: when you are up to two complete sequences per second you are well on your way to samba. Aim for four.

4. A samba secret: add hips. They're probably moving already, but if you are trying to hit required minimum speed they may be a little out of control. You want to move them, but purposefully. When you step on your right foot your hips switch left-right. When you step on your left they switch again, right-left. Two hip beats per foot beat, or about twelve beats per second, if you can manage.

5. Stop hopping! Keep your shoulders down! Face front! The magic of samba lies in the illusion that somebody is moving like crazy from the waist down while an entirely different person is observing the proceedings from the waist up. Keep your torso detached from your hips, and facing where you're looking, and practice with a book on your head until you can stay at full speed.

You've mastered the mechanics of samba. Now you're ready to start dancing. If the following essentials seem a little daunting, don't be discouraged. Remember, you've come a long way from your beginning days. Dress appropriately for this next stage. Preferably something that emphasizes the waist, so that hip movement is maximized. Go for shine. Twelve hip beats per second will look like a hundred if you're wearing sequins.

Arms: if you are up to two to four sequences per second with a book on your head and your hips swiveling at least 45 degrees in each direction away from the wall you're facing, you're ready to ornament your dance by holding your arms out and ruffling your shoulders as you move. Think of a fine-plumed bird rearranging its wings. Keep the movement flexible and easy. Reach out with your fingertips. If you can't shimmy without looking scrunched or panicky, drop it.

Smile: the key rule is, don't make it sexy. You will look arch, coy, or, if you are working really hard, terribly American. Your smile should be the full-tilt cheer of someone watching her favorite team hit a home run. Or it should imitate the serene curve of a Hindu deity's. The other key rule: there is no point to samba if it doesn't make you smile.

Sweat: obviously, you will produce lots of it. You will soon discover that it looks wrong when it is dripping off the tip of your nose. Don't let this upset you. Perseverance and practice got you this far; keep at it. Practice. When you find that your body is moving below you in a whirlpool frenzy and your mind is floating above it all in benign accompaniment; when your torso grows curiously light and your legs feel like carving little arabesques in the air on their own for the sheer fun of it; when everything around you seems to slow for the rush that's carrying you through the music, you'll probably discover that sweat is clothing your body in one glorious, uniform, scintillating sheet, flying around you in a magic halo of drops, and you'll know that you have arrived at samba.

Alma Guillermoprieto also contributed "In Search of Miracles" in Part I. This story was excerpted from her book, Samba.

*

The samba is nothing less than Rio's oral history and ongoing rap, one big rolling tune to which new verses can be added forever. Only in Brazil the blues come out of such sadness that there is no room for it to sound sad at all. Compared to our my-man-done-me-wrongs, the language is more satiric and biting. In Brazil, we get less of the moan and howl. Instead, we get the *grito de Carnaval*. The cry of the release! But the emotion is always a pain that hurts good, the evocation of that indefinable longing inherited from the Portuguese through their favorite catchword, *saudade*. Call it homesickness, nostalgia for happier days, suffering over love lost and dreams squandered, and, ultimately, a confrontation with every man's inherent state of solitude.

—John Krich, *Why Is This Country Dancing?:*
A One-Man Samba to the Beat of Brazil

DIANE ACKERMAN

Where the Sun Dines

*On an Amazon journey, every sense
is opened and filled.*

BY EARLY MORNING LIGHT, WE SET OUT IN OUR ZODIACS, AND soon we pass a woman sitting on a caustic-sapped log, *açacú,* loosely translated as "that which burns the asshole," to wash her clothes in the river in the ancient way, though she uses a 20th-century plastic scrub brush, which she has probably bought from one of the itinerant peddlers who travel up and down the river, selling salt (used for drying fish) and other staples and household goods. A praying mantis flutters into the boat. It is a small brown-and-white insect with protruding eyes, horns on its back, and long waving antennae in front. Its jagged poise is beautiful as it preens its long legs and makes slow and purposeful gestures. Fish leap from the water, fleeing predators. What a perfect getaway: hurl yourself straight into another dimension of reality, as flying fish do, and suddenly appear elsewhere and elsewhen. Three little girls row out in a bark canoe, flash hundred-watt grins, stand up suddenly, and jump into the water. One man on shore holds up a pair of binoculars and watches us, the exotic primitive tribe madly unfolding colored ponchos from their packs and squirming into them because rain has begun to fall like a wall of rubber. Children go on playing in the shallows; adults continue to swim, wash clothes, mend their boats and nets. It

147

is only rain. This is a rainforest. Holes in the banks, carved by walking catfish in April or May, when the water level rises as much as 30 feet, make the mud look like a condominium of birdhouses. On some of the lighter trees you can see the dark waterline, and many trees have large, exposed root systems to grab nutrients directly from the seasonal flood.

In a tall, bushy-topped tree, a dozen hanging nests belong to oropendolas, birds that have a symbiotic relationship with a number of animals. They like to build their nests in trees where there are hornet nests so that the hornets, which attack parasitic botflies, will keep them from the chicks. The oropendolas also allow cowbirds to lay eggs in their nests so that the cowbird chicks, which are born with their eyes open, will eat botflies, too. The siren song of the oropendola is so complex and willowy that river people often build their houses under an oropendola-inhabited tree. The song begins with a wet, two-stage warble, a liquid undulating smooch, part throb, part Moog synthesizer, and ends with the sound of a debutante throwing kisses underwater. *Birds of Colombia,* by Steven Hilty and William Brown, scans it as "EEE-eee-D'D'Clock-agoogoo," but there is a mellow swoon in the final stages of the call that's seductive and magical.

Behind the Zodiac, the wake makes a perfect whitewater butterfly, wings outstretched and outlined in spray. The 40-horsepower engine gnaws like a buzzsaw, and its blade cuts through the reflection of trees in the opaque brown water as we scout the shore for birds, mammals, unusual plants. Along the bank lie logs waiting for high water and their trip to the mills, when they will be laced together in a large raft. A gash of light splits the water about ten yards away, as if a window sash has been thrown open, and then a pink dolphin surfaces and dives back through its window. *Oh!* I say: like the dolphin, I take a small gasp of air. Suddenly four more pink dolphins arc out of the water in front of us, and one surfaces right next to the boat with a small, explosive breath. Close to the ancestral whale, these dolphins and their platanistid relatives are frequenters of the Amazon, Ganges, Yangtze. On their snouts they have short, tactile whiskers to feel for food. At the riverbank a striated heron

stands with its back to the sun so it can hunt in its own shade. A brown sphinx moth with a bright orange body planes low at eye level, followed by a heron, float-
ing pterodactyl-slow with long rippling neck: a stately white ap-parition. We spot a tassel-topped tree, *triplaris,* which has hollow stems inhabited by stinging ants whose venom feels like hot wires. Lianas drip from the trees, anchoring in so many places that it is hard to fathom where the vines begin and end. The brown river bubbles gently; fish leap up, mouths open. We hear the sound of a trigger cocking, then the low mournful call of a patoo, a bird that can mimic dead sticks. A sun bittern flashes the big false eyes of its wings. Trees, swaddled in leafy vines, look like the feathered feet of huge owls. A kingfisher

he pink bôto *and the gray* tucuxi *are pro-tected by the numerous superstitions that surround them, and by the tough-ness and oily blandness of their flesh.* Caboclos *believe the ani-mals are almost human and that they lure women to the water to have intercourse with them. Their dried skin is used as a fumigant for snakebite or ray sting. Children wear porpoise teeth around their necks to cure diarrhea; a* bôto's *ear, worn around the wrist, will guarantee a large and lasting erection, and a grated left eye is an aphrodisiac powder.*

—Alex Shoumatoff,
The Rivers Amazon

sounds like a child's rubber squeaky toy. It is early morning on the Amazon, and the birds sing their territorial anthems. They do not mean to be beautiful. They cannot help themselves. A capuchin (organ grinder) monkey moves through the top of a tree, sampling fruit and dropping what doesn't appeal to it, like someone testing chocolate bonbons. The sound of fingers dragged across a rubber inner tube comes from a bird. When we drift near a fisherman and his son in a bark canoe, my companion David calls in Portuguese: "Good morning, sir. How's it going? Catch much today?"

The man smiles, gestures to the bottom of the boat, where freshly caught fish lie in a pool of water. "Good morning," he says.

"The people would like to have a look at the fish, if that would be possible," David asks in a respectful and polite subjunctive, on be-half of the collective desire of our boat, "the people," as he puts it.

The man grins and maneuvers his tippy boat next to ours.

"You've done well this morning, eh? *Aruaná, peixe cascudo, curi-matão,* piranha. Would it be possible to see the bony-tongued fish there?"

The man lifts the long, glistening fish in his hands. How Himalayan his lined face looks, a reminder that he shares genes with Mongols and many other peoples.

"I'm obliged," David says, and opens the complex and fascinating mouth of the fish, whose tongue is a thin bone. Bony-tongued fish like to eat monkey feces and often wait under a tree where monkeys live. Then David picks up an armored catfish, which has a shovel nose, strange upside-down omegas for pupils, long sensory barbel appendages on its face, and beautiful black stripes. Next David takes a reddish piranha from the old man, opens up its stomach with a machete, and smears the contents onto his finger to reveal that it holds mainly fish scales. The piranha nips at other fish to feed. It is not by choice the voracious carnivore of gothic stories and monster movies; unless it is cut off from its usual food supply and is famished, as it might be in an isolated swamp or lake, it is happy enough nibbling scales from fish. David hands the fish back to the fisherman, who generously offers us some to take back with us, if we like.

"No, thank you. That is kind of you," David insists. "We are glad to look at them, and learn about the life of the river. But, if it wouldn't be too much trouble, I know we'd enjoy seeing how you use your net to fish."

The man's face lights with the pride of shared craft, and he picks up the net as if it were a hemp skirt hung with lead weights, secures one end in his mouth, and tosses it in an arcing spiderweb over the water, then watches it sink down into the shallows where fish wait. There is wonderment in the shape the net takes through the air, its calm descent, how it vanishes into darkness. And the man watches our faces, smiles, drags the net back, and tosses it again and again. A small bird with a bright yellow belly like a dollop of lemon pudding perches on a branch and calls, *Bem ti ví!* ("Good to see you"), its name in Portuguese. In English, the bird's name is onomatopoeic, too: Kiskadee!

Later, at a peddler's boat, we stop to chat. Inside there are stacks of bananas and bagel-shaped bread; large fillets of salted fish are drying on the roof, swarmed over by flies. He offers us the hospitality of his house, just up the hill, behind which there is a large lake; his wife shows us her turtles, parakeets, and two hives of African killer bees, which she keeps for honey (each hive is locked inside a log that opens and closes like a sea chest). Digging at the base of one of the manioc plants in a field, she exposes the root to show us its long white fingers. Painted on the front of her house are the words CASA FEEM DEUS. I ask her what *feem* means, and she looks puzzled, laughs, struggles to explain. After an awkward moment, we laugh,

It is a day of blue sky and a thousand pale lavender-shadowed white blobs of cloud. The greens of the trees which stand knee-deep out of the dark water are incredibly varied. Palms of different shapes sprout out of all sorts of angles. There are misty thickets of bamboo and huge broad-leaved arboreal monsters and spindly saplings with fine pale-green foliage. One of the characteristics of the Amazon forest is the fantastic number of different species to be found in any patch of woodland. You hardly see the same tree twice.

—John Dos Passos,
Brazil on the Move (1963)

too. *Feem* is a contraction of the words *fé* (faith) and *em* (in). I have come from the wilds of North America to ask her what faith is, and I should not be surprised if she marvels at my question. Before we go, she notices how we admire a large green calabash hanging on a tree in her front yard. The only calabash on the tree, it is about the size and weight of a bowling ball and will be dried and carved to use as a bowl. When she offers it to us, we must accept. It is so generous of her; it would be rude to refuse.

Back on the river, we see a large pod of pink dolphins, so we cut our motor and drift right into the center of it. With a snuffle and snort, the dolphins breathe through blowholes as they surface. What a range of pinks—some look like erasers, others are luminous or dusky. We are close enough to be able to recognize individuals. I lean over the side of the boat and put my head in the water to listen for the rapid clicks of their sonar. *Whoosh! Whew!* they blow as they surface. In pairs and threes they gallop through the river. When the rain starts, we head for shore and climb up a bank to a house on stilts. Inside there are shards of American culture: a Mickey Mouse towel, a photo of Lassie, six light bulbs for when the house gets electricity, magically shiny pots and pans (one, with a funnel center, looks like an angel-cake pan). The man who lives there pulls out two long benches, the way one puts an extra leaf in the table when company arrives, and invites us to sit. It is simply assumed that we are welcome and may hang up our hammocks in his house if we wish to.

Instead, when the rain stops, we stroll through his backyard and see a mother sloth cradling her baby up in a tree. About once a week, the sloth climbs down the tree, digs a pit, and defecates into it. This exposes the sloth to predators, but by putting its feces at the base of the tree, not dropping them at random, it invests in the future of its home. Algae live in its fur, which gives it a greenish tint. Moths live there too, as well as beetles and ticks. For long minutes, I stand and watch the mother sloth, who is completely immobile until, struck by a ravishing thought, she gently lifts her head.

When the other Zodiacs have joined up with ours, our guide Iain leads us through the rainforest he knows so well. There is much to see: the pau roxo (*Peltogyne*) tree from whose deep purple wood beautiful bowls are made; the lyre-shaped leaf of *dioscorea,* a vine used as raw material for birth-control medicine because it mimics estrogen; a young kapok tree covered in sharp gooseflesh spines so that rodents can't climb or woodpeckers peck. At first, it seems such a tree must have bounty overflowing that it needs to protect, but perhaps not—there were Renaissance fortress cities supremely well protected, but not because they contained more treasures than other towns. The botanists test trees by making a small slash, looking for latex, noticing the smell, the stigmata of the cambium, a certain readable oozing. As Iain makes a tiny slash in the bark of a strangler fig, white latex tears well up. How old is that tree? I wonder. It is hard to tell the age of a jungle tree because they don't lay down one ring a year. In areas that flood, like this one, many trees have flying buttresses and sprawling, shallow root systems to clutch at the ground. This is not a temperate forest, where sunlight is plentiful, the loam thick and rich, and predictable trees have predictable needs. As we float down the river, we occasionally smell smoke in the air. Though we are miles away from the sites, we are smelling the devastation of the rainforest, smelling the burning of huge tracts of forest. If the destruction continues at its current pace, all of the rainforest will disappear forever in about 40 years. Mining projects, rubber plantations, massive ill-fated cattle-growing projects, hydroelectric dams, highways, and an attempt to burn and dominate the land just because it is frontier and human beings can't abide an unowned space—all have contributed to the destruction of entire ecosystems. Species are going extinct in the rainforest that have not even been named yet. As Iain points out, "We are probably the last generation to have the opportunity to conserve the species of the Amazon forest.… Today we stand at the brink of disaster in Amazonia…a mass extinction of species—one even greater than when the world lost its dinosaurs."

As the day fades, we return to our Zodiacs and start back down the river, which smells different in the evening. In the morning the oxygen is low and the air lightly perfumed. But in the evening, the air sizzles with oxygen and smells of sedge and damp amber. Pink auroras gush across the sky as darkness falls. With a lantern aimed low at the shore, we search for the eyes of caimans, Amazonian relatives of alligators. To get their attention, we make a mating or juvenile distress call, a syncopated grunting: *Uh! Uh! Uh!* Then we float quietly and wait. To see nature you must be willing to cut the motor and drift, to follow wherever the current leads. But this is tough for goal-oriented people. Some people in my boat chat compulsively, polluting the silent grandeur of the forest. At first I thought they were ignoring the wild, rich sounds of bird, leaf fall, river, animal, and the august silence, but in time I began to think that it might be the opposite. Talk makes such small shapes in the teeming wilderness of Nature, small shapes in the formless clamor

of the universe, but they are shapes for those who need them. They
are planks to the shore. "Sshh. Listen," someone says gently, and
everyone quiets down for a few minutes, letting the sounds of night
wash over them. The steady beat of a frog sounds like someone
rubbing a taut balloon. "*Corrusha,*" a bird called *coruja* calls, a samba
in the word. The shore flashes with fireflies, and then a click beetle
with two headlights flies over the boat. Our flashlight is reflected in
the small revolving campfires of an owl's eyes. At night, there are
many mysterious, coal-burning eyes. The reason they seem to shine
so eerily is that just behind the retina of nocturnal animals there is
a reflective membrane called the tapetum, which helps these creatures see in the dark. Light bounces off its shiny surface. These live,
burning embers in the forest remind us that we are burning, too,
from the distant chaos of the sun. An osprey catches a fish and then
tilts its beak up so it will be more streamlined when it flies. Cormorants feed near the shore; each has a sort of mousetrap in its
throat, the better to stalk fish underwater. Terns swoop down in
front of us, gliding, then diving in an accelerated stall, careening up
into a chandelle, an aerobatic half-loop that ends with the tern
rolling over on one shoulder, gaining speed, climbing, and diving
again in a bout of aerial sighing and swooning. Bony-tongued fish,
aruaná, jump to feed. *Caboclo* fishermen still ply the water in bark
canoes, which they steer from the front. Their black paddles are ex-
clamation points dipping into the river.

Fifteen yellow butterflies dogfight and gambol in the green,
sedgelike grass of the shore. An Amazon dove whistles. Then a fork
strikes a crystal goblet, as if someone were earnestly calling the jungle to order. A flock of parakeets sounds like wet rope twisting into
a chirpy screech. Toucans yap like distant dogs. Here and there a
low, shallow bark canoe sits on the shore, awaiting its paddler, on
business somewhere in the forest. A hawk with bright yellow feet
and beak perches on a dead tree branch. Water splashes down a
bank from an oxbow lake nearby. When a Brazil nut tree loses two
leaves, they fall gently and hit the ground with a hollow clatter.
Wheee!, a hawk calls like a child with a kazoo. *Wheee!* Soon the rest
of the kindergarten band joins in with sandblocks, bottles, tin pans,

bells, as different birds take over and the crickets begin to throb and itch with song. An Amazon bird related to the chicken makes a quaking buzz. A trogon calls, *You! You!* We float past a hematanthus tree with bold white flowers, whose alkaloids are used in heart medicine. Tinkling wind chimes fill the air; then comes a howling trill. A spring door slapping and creaking on its frame is a frog.

The new moon makes a slender white canoe above the darkening trees. Bats scout overhead. Iain, knowing of my fondness for bats, tells me that once he saw a bat-eating fish that leaped out of the water, grabbed a bat, and dragged it under. Now the bottle band includes yowling and banshee moans. A white planet, southeast of the moon, floats low over the forest like a shard of ice. In the surging darkness, lights bloom on the river: a single yellow lightbulb from a house; the whiter light of a Zodiac's lantern; the distant flash of a camera where the others are fishing; the twittering greenish-yellow light of fireflies, our ship lying at anchor downstream, lit like a miracle play. In my cabin, deliciously exhausted from the sheer sensory whelm of the day and eager for the days to come, I brew a pot of *casca preciosa* and sip its sweet-scented tonic as the ship rocks gently on the ancient river. Then I fall into the well of sleep. For once, dream is the same as the waking world: there I again snorkel in the river by moonlight, hear the muttering of monkeys, and follow a trail of leaf-cutter ants hauling home their small burdens along corridors of scent.

Diane Ackerman is a nature lover and award-winning author whose work has appeared in America's finest travel, literary, and natural history magazines. She is the author of numerous books, including A Natural History of the Senses, A Natural History of Love, The Moon by Whale Light, *and* The Rarest of the Rare: Vanishing Animals, Timeless Worlds, *from which this story was taken.*

✳

It was dusk by the time we reached Pedro. A full moon had risen. He climbed aboard and took the tiller and motored through the night. Overhead one star after another popped out from behind the sky's black curtain to take a bow, and, in the water, the small stars of caiman eyes peered at us from the forest's edge. The moonlight reflected off the river. Pedro shut off the engine and we drifted, saying nothing.

I realized suddenly why jungles always made me feel so good. Why the tonic worked. Why I had spent so much time looking for something in them. It was the impossible luck of it all. There was no ultimate design, no meaning, no wisdom written in the trees. This forest, this scene, this moment was just a zany roll of the cosmic dice as if the Gothic builders had heaved the stone blocks and flying buttresses and gold leaf into the air and it had all come down as Chartres. In fact, if there were a God, He would spend His tough days visiting the man-made cathedrals and mosques and temples, where people believed in Him and asked favors and prayed for victories over the other guys who called Him by other names. And then He would come here into his green cathedral. He would crack open a beer, walk around in His boxers, put His hands on His hips and mutter, "How about that?" at the miracle of all this being thrown together out of the dust of the Big Bang. He would shake His head at the wild stroke of luck.

Meanwhile, people disillusioned with the world they had made in other places came and knelt and prayed in the green cathedrals, supplicants seeking a momentary respite from complexity, an end to the grayness where life and meaning are undefined. But all the jungles could offer were moments, glimpses.

The green cathedrals were accidents and even more precious for that, but that was their only lesson. Accidents happen. Sometimes they could be good. Now, for crying out loud, put your clothes back on and go home. Get on with life.

It took the Amazon to finally make me see it. Miriam saw it, too.

She was stealing moments here, moments like those I had been stealing when life seems in sharp focus through nature's lens; but in the end, she knew the dilemmas were still there—the diarrhea, the poverty, the social progress—and the green cathedrals were coming down. The jungles were going, and a handful of scientists and a fistful of dollars were not going to stop it. Still, if the universe had gambled and come up with the *várzea,* well, you never knew, did ya?

Two dolphins surfaced and breathed and dipped under the water. I looked at Miriam, who was smiling.

"Is this enough?" I whispered.

"Yeah," she answered. "This is enough."

—Brian Alexander, *Green Cathedrals: A Wayward Traveler in the Rain Forest*

SCOTT DOGGETT

* * *

High on Iguaçu

A helicopter ride over the falls
transports the author to thoughts
of the ultimate destination.

ON FURLOUGH FROM LOS ANGELES, A CITY SYNONYMOUS WITH the worst of urban ugly, I found it impossible to hover high above the mocha swirls and the luminescent spray plume of Iguaçu Falls and *not* stare, stare, stare, bug-eyed and slack-jawed.

Just a few minutes earlier, as the roar of the cataracts drowned the roar of the idling helicopter, I could only think of the ride's $35 ticket and the uneasy feeling I always get inside aircraft—aware of how often flights unexpectedly terminate, along with their passengers. Even as the copter lifted off and buzzed toward the sky, I couldn't help but ponder the odds of survival if the fuel caught fire or the motor flew apart. The crash won't kill me, I thought; it'll be those long black blades that'll do *that* job. I pictured the rotors slicing me into chunks.

But something wonderfully positive came over me at about 500 feet, as the faces of the tourists below disappeared and the horizon became a sliver between a baby-blue sky and a carpet of the greenest forest. It was a childlike feeling, not unlike the euphoria I felt the first time I extended a finger to a groping caterpillar and let him crawl on.

Then it occurred to me: a masterpiece was appearing before my eyes. The higher we flew the more of the sky and the falls and the jungle we took in, until the horizon bent and the mighty Rio Iguaçu became a brown ribbon on a sea of felt.

Words can't rightly describe the majestic mist that rises from the monster plunge of the river that drains the continent's vast floodplain. The Caigangue tribe calls the site "the place where clouds are born," but the expression does little to convey the image of a hundred billion airborne droplets, each catching the sun's rays like a diamond. Clearly the work of God.

From my perspective, it was the place where an ever-evolving cloud embraced two spectacular rainbows and held them for the world to behold. Here I was, in a kind of floating bubble, the unfettered sky above and the lush forest below—and a never-ending river of *café au lait* passing beneath me—and before my own eyes Earth's breath. All that was missing were blossoms of great variety. But then, they were there—down below, bromeliads and orchids decorating trees for miles around and passion flowers, heliconias, and water-hyacinths posing for the bumble bees and butterflies that call on them.

The rainbow-striped plume undoubtedly would not have been so breathtaking—would not have been so marvelously astounding—had it not been the product of some diabolical idea of the Creator. Perhaps *diabolical* is incorrect, but in fact the hellish geological phenomenon to which I refer is named *Garganta do Diabo*—Devil's Throat.

From the air, Garganta do Diabo resembles a jagged horseshoe, out of the center of which rises the radiant cloud. The water leading to the ghastly pit is soil-rich and flows deep and fast but surprisingly smooth—until it reaches the edge, where it becomes furious and streaks, brownish-white, toward impact at the base of hidden cliffs.

A catwalk used to extend from river's edge to the rim of the semicircular precipice over which most of the Rio Iguaçu pours, but the year before my visit the concrete walkway succumbed to the force of Nature—and the tourists on it were promptly swallowed.

It's been several years since I sat in the front seat of that whirly-bird, my mind set aflame by the grandeur of the scene. As I think about it now I'm struck by the notion that one could do far worse than plunge down Devil's Throat.

Scott Doggett's largely normal fascination with death stems from his work as a journalist in El Salvador, Afghanistan, and other war-wracked countries. He is the author of several Lonely Planet books, an editor at the Los Angeles Times, *and coeditor of* Travelers' Tales Brazil.

✳

Like an overture before the main show begins, we could hear the howling waters before we could see them. Moving toward the roar, which one might more reasonably want to escape were the source unknown, we walked into the woods. Beneath our feet the path was paved, but our ears told us we were in a wild place. Surrounded by sound so primordial, pre-historic, powerful, we might have left without ever seeing a drop of water and still have described the falls as awesome. It was strange, months later, to see slides of the falls without the symphony of crashes and splashes.

—Mary Gaffney, "A Spectacular Falls"

CHRISTOPHER HALL

My Night of Candomblé

Attending an African-Brazilian religious ritual,
the author fulfills a dream of twenty years
and experiences a sense of awakening.

THE HEAVY, JUNGLE SMELL OF THAT AIRLESS ROOM IS WHAT I
remember most vividly. That and the glowing, brown face of the
Brazilian woman who stood before me, in a deep trance, howling as
she thrust the remnants of a floral bouquet toward my uncomprehending eyes. What did she want me to do?

This was my night of Candomblé, the centuries-old ritual in
honor of spirits carried to the shores of the New World in the
hearts of enslaved West Africans. For twenty years I had dreamed of
visiting Brazil and experiencing this rite firsthand. Finally, in a
country town fifteen miles outside Salvador, my night of Candomblé was unfolding. And despite those years of accumulated expectations, the night was proving far more fascinating—and puz-
zling—than I ever imagined.

The evening had not begun auspiciously. While still at the hotel,
carefully dressing in the outfit of long pants and white shirt suggested by the tourism official who'd located the ceremony for me,
I'd had a sudden attack of nerves. How was I going to find the *terreiro,* the house of worship where the Candomblé was to be held? I
had only the name of the town and my rudimentary Portuguese to
help me. Once I found the place, what was going to happen?

Would I know what to do? And could I find a taxi or bus to take me back when the dancing and chanting stopped in the early hours of the morning? I continued to worry as I walked the few minutes to the bus stop. Sporadic, fat drops of warm rain fell from the starless sky and hit my clothes with a soft thud, leaving a pattern of blotchy dots. I found a jitney marked with the name of the town and joined a few silent locals already seated inside. We took off, plunging into the deep, humid night of the Brazilian countryside.

The jitney arrived at its destination a half-hour later, and with the help of a fellow passenger I located the *terreiro*—a tin-roofed, cinder-block building set at the far end of a walled yard. Light poured from the doorless entry and its flanking pair of unglazed windows, illuminating rectangular patches of packed earth and scrubby plants. The sound of a few voices and a solitary drum drifted across the yard. I sidled up to a window and peered in.

The room had obviously been prepared for a celebration of some kind, but there was no one to be seen except four small boys. One of them stood on a drum-filled dais across the room, intently playing a conga almost as tall as himself, while the others ran between rows of wooden benches placed against the side walls. The empty concrete floor in the center of the room was strewn with hundreds of fresh leaves; overhead, zigzagging strings of white tissue-paper cutouts hung limp in the still air. The boy with the conga glanced up, spotted me,

orty years ago, it would have been more appropriate to inquire [about Candomblé] at the police station than at the tourist office. At that time the African-Brazilian religions were highly illegal and subject to a great deal of police persecution, as Joge Amado describes quite vividly in his novel Tent of Miracles. *The white propertied class nevertheless respected and feared the African priests and priestesses. That attitude probably dates back to the earliest days of colonialism, when the Portuguese traders are said to have bowed before the great West African kings as they did other foreign dignitaries. Today, the mixture of respect and fear has taken a new turn as the temples of Candomblé have become part of the tourist industry.*

—David J. Hess, *Samba in the Night: Spiritism in Brazil*

and stopped playing. A bewildered, startled look came across his face, a look that made me question whether I'd be as welcome at the ceremony as my contact had promised.

I wandered the town's one haphazardly paved street for the next hour, enduring the open stares of children and periodically checking the *terreiro*. Small groups of people, some dressed in their Sunday best, slowly gathered in the street outside the *terreiro* and quietly chatted among themselves. Eventually—as if on some cue that to me was imperceptible—they filtered through the dark yard and into the building. I followed them, and once inside saw that women and children were moving toward benches on the left. I headed to the right, with the men, and squeezed into a spot on a back bench. No one seemed to notice me.

Almost immediately, the drumming began. Staccato reports shot from the dais and electrified the room. Conversation stopped as we all locked our eyes on the five men beating out intricate, syncopated rhythms on throaty congas and high-pitched bongos. Outside, a crowd collected, craning their necks to get a view through the door and windows, while next to the dais a gravel-voiced man in dashiki and matching cap started to chant in an African dialect. There was a jostling at the doorway and the crowd parted. Then, one after another, thirteen hoop-skirted women slowly entered, swaying in time to the music and singing in high, nasal tones. Their dresses and elaborately tied head scarves were made of starchy, white lace, and as the women dipped and turned in their slow, undulating dance around the center of the room, a vegetal aroma rose from the carpet of leaves being ground underfoot. I could hear the hard, metallic clink of shiny bangles and amulets on the women's arms and the rustling of the innumerable strings of multicolored beads that hung from their necks. The oldest dancer—a rail-thin woman of perhaps 80 years, whose blue-black skin hung from her face in great folds—passed in front of me. My eyes met hers, and she smiled.

The drumming, chanting, and dancing went on for several hours. The smell of the leaves grew increasingly pungent, until it seemed I was breathing the jungle itself. My skin glistened, on the verge of a full sweat, while streams of perspiration ran down the faces of the dancers. Still the drumming continued, its sinuous pattern of constantly shifting rhythms lulling me into a comfortable state of dreamy awareness.

It was then that I noticed a plump, brown-skinned woman begin to tremble as she danced no more than ten feet from where I sat. At first, her trembling didn't really register with me, but as it grew and she ultimately sank to the floor, twitching and writhing, my heart raced. It was a trance, I realized. The woman, dancing herself into a hypnotic state, would receive, and be animated by, one of the African spirits in whose honor the ceremony is held. Several dancers carried the stricken woman from the room, and for the next hour other women—mostly dancers, but also congregants— were struck by a trance and either led or carried away. Many of them lurched back into the room a few minutes later, still in a trance, dressed in costumes indicative of the particular spirit inhabiting them. With eyes half closed, they repeated a lumbering version of their earlier dance. One woman returned with a giant, wooden bowl balanced on her head. The bowl was filled with little fried balls of spiced bean paste, called *acarajé,* which I'd already seen being sold on street corners in Salvador. The *acarajé* was distributed to everyone in the room, and I waited until I saw the others eating theirs before I did the same. The *acarajé* was flavorful but dry, and like a sponge it sucked the little remaining moisture from my mouth. I suddenly craved one of the tall, ice-cold Brazilian beers I'd grown so fond of during the previous two weeks.

Finally, the plump woman herself returned, resplendent in a flowing, pink satin dress, a veil of beads covering her face and a bouquet of blood-red roses in her arms. She moved in a swaying stupor around the room, repeatedly distributing a single rose to obviously important personages until nothing was left of her bouquet but the palm frond trim, a crackly cellophane wrapper, and a ribbon tying the two together. I watched with ever-widening eyes as she rounded the end of the room, approached the spot where I sat, and came to a stop right in front of me. She grunted and shook the bouquet. I froze, and she grunted again.

What did she want me to do? Through the beads of her veil, I saw eyes rolled halfway back in their sockets. The overwhelming smell of crushed leaves seemed to have displaced all oxygen in the *terreiro*. In desperation, I bowed toward the woman, hoping to appease her. She howled, thrust the bouquet at me like a weapon, and held it close to my body. In a panic, feeling the gaze of 200 believers on me, I slowly reached out and took the bouquet from her. The woman immediately stopped her howling, grunted once, and moved on. The appreciative looks from my neighbors led me to believe that, starting then and there, I became an honorary member of the *terreiro*.

As the Candomblé ceremony wound down, I joined a trickle of congregants slipping out of the *terreiro* through a back door, which led to the rear garden. There, to my astonishment, I found a large party in full swing. The garden air was fresh and sweet, and overhead the cloud cover was breaking up. The leader of the *terreiro*, the *pai-de-santo*, or medium, touched my arm and smiled as he walked by. A few minutes later, one of his assistants came up and handed me a plastic cup of icy beer and a plate of food—grilled chicken, beans, rice, manioc. I thanked him and asked how I might return to my hotel. He told me not to worry, that he'd call for a radio taxi from the airport for me and the few others who'd come on the bus. First, he said, I should eat.

> *Translated literally,* terreiro *means "open ground," but it has come to refer to the house of worship of Candomblé.*
>
> —AH and SD

So, at three in the morning, under an emerging canopy of Southern stars, I joined the others. We laughed, talked, ate, and drank together for the next hour until, finally, the party broke up and the garden emptied.

As I prepared to leave the *terreiro*, one of the dancers—now fully recovered from her trance—told me I should return the following Saturday when the ceremony would be even more beautiful. She looked genuinely disappointed when I told her I'd be back home in the States by then. Rallying quickly, she made me promise to return the next time I was in Brazil.

She had no way of knowing, of course, that it was a promise I'd already made to myself.

San Francisco-based writer Christopher Hall exhibited a penchant for travel as early as age nine, when he started a neighborhood travel club and roped a couple of other kids into joining. Club members took Saturday bike trips to local points of interest and sent away for every brochure advertised in the back of National Geographic. *More recently, he has traveled extensively in Europe and Asia, and he is a regular contributor to* The New York Times.

⁕

Ogum, like the other Yoruba *orixás,* is a demanding god. He requires devotion, veneration, prayer, and celebration with music, dance, and food. The Candomblé religion has maintained within its oral traditions the ritual recipes of the gods from West Africa and even today the dishes are prepared with what can only be described as religious fervor. Ogum's day of celebration began in the syncretized manner of Candomblé with a mass at Our Lady of the Rosary Church in Salvador. From there it progressed back to the *terreiro* where worshipers were served an after-church breakfast which resembled so many that I had eaten growing up: tiny cups of dark coffee—this was, after all, Brazil—accompanied by sweet rolls and cakes. However, instead of the meal taking place in the church basement to the music of an organ postlude, this was eaten to the accompaniment of African drums playing complex rhythms celebrating Ogum's glory.

As the day progressed, working up to the crescendo of the evening ceremony, preparations began again for another of Ogum's meals, this time for the black bean and smoked meat *feijoada* that is his ritual dish. The slave dish has become the national dish of his adopted country. This *feijoada* was served with great festivity at the midday meal and consumed by the votaries of the African gods who ate with gusto during the pause in the daylong ceremony. It was a simple meal, one that has its origin in a dish prepared by the slaves from the leftovers that they were given. It is a preparation that still constitutes a celebration dish for many of the people in this complex country where poverty and riches live side by side. It consisted of well-seasoned black beans and a side dish of various fatty but oh-so-savory pieces of smoked and sun-dried pork and beef. It was also accompanied by a dish filled to the brim with sand-colored toasted manioc flour, called *farinha,* which was sprinkled on the beans and meat to give consistency and add texture. There was chili in the form of *malagueta* pepper for those who wanted a little heat.

As we sat around the simple dining room table, I looked at my neighbors to the left and right. One was an old woman who was the granddaughter of slaves, on the other side was a youngster who had just been initiated into the religion and was still dressed in her ritual white. Each in turn spoke of the history of the religion. The elder was a living witness to the persecutions that it had survived; the younger one represented its continuation and growth at the end of the 20th century.

—Jessica B. Harris, *Tasting Brazil: Regional Recipes and Reminiscences*

JOHN KRICH

* * *

Simply Irresistible

Crashing the gates of Salvador's Carnaval,
the world's biggest party pooper finds it hard
to say no to the conga line.

NOW THERE IS NO ESCAPING THE MUSIC. IT'S TOO LATE FOR finking out on the bacchanal. Looking up, every stacked balcony, colonial and peeling or concrete and flimsy, has been turned into a vertical danceathon. The heat of bodies has replaced the day's tropical furnace and the cobblestone boulevards have turned to trampolines for an aerobic populace. Bouncing on the balls of my sneakered feet, I periscope above the bobbing heads crowned in Indian feathers and Portuguese admirals' caps, the arms upraised in an exultant vanquishing of inhibition, the hands clapping like metronomes for copulation. *Pulando* is the term locals use for what everyone's doing, but it means far more than jumping up and down—it implies a leap to Heaven, or, at least, the irrational. Grab hold of that slinky waist up ahead if you can, grip a passing set of female haunches if you dare. Sweat is the natural lubricant for our grinding parts. The sole way to make progress through this orange-and-yellow tinsel-draped orgy is to join the boa-length conga line snaking and shoving its way to nowhere. In this human gridlock, there are no handy exits from a slow surging pack whose only destination is dawn. Nothing can move and everybody is moving. On all sides, I'm pinned down by pleasure, hopelessly enmeshed in unleashed mirth.

"There is a law of physics that says that two bodies cannot occupy the same space," goes one of the oft-repeated homilies by which this multitude defines its particular brand of frenzy, "but that law does not operate in Brazil." Only *carne vale!* Just flesh counts, though the derivation of "Carnaval" is translated to mean a farewell to meat, which Catholics can't eat once the wild weekend gives way to next Wednesday's Lent. *"Alegria!"*—roughly, "Oh, rapture!"—shout the newspaper headlines each February, by fortunate coincidence the height of the Southern Hemisphere's summer holidays. *"Rei Momo"*—a rotating and rotund Dionysian figure appointed to reign over the madness—"Commands His Subjects to Joy!" This good news is hardly news at all, merely the summons to dust off old costumes. *"Folia* Animates the Streets!"—and just because it's folly, that doesn't mean you shouldn't join in! *"Brincar!"* goes the command, that most Brazilian of verbs which takes "play" into multiple innuendoes, all of them saucy! The press and TV make it sound like this outburst isn't planned or scheduled, orchestrated down to its last toot. With annual mock astonishment, they trumpet the return of the party.

What is the world's biggest party pooper doing in the midst of the world's rowdiest, lengthiest, bring-your-own-bottle affair? Crashing the gates of Brazilian Carnaval, I can hardly send an RSVP with polite regrets to 150 million hosts. At this most social of engagements, there is no room for small talk. Stripped down for action in sneakers and shorts, a whole country's "in" crowd is out in the streets, along with the outs. But what made me think I could saunter in without an invite? Or expect that an abject beginner would qualify for this advanced seminar on pelvic poly-rhythms, this five-day workshop in overcoming claustrophobia?

Why, on my very first trip to Brazil, have I plunged straight into the action at Salvador da Bahia? Blame it on the bossa nova. Blame it on all the staccato guitar pluckers who whispered their onomatopoeic call to "By-eee-aaah!" Oh, Bahia, sounding like a sigh at pleasures sated! Unwittingly, I succumbed to the call contained in the most sophisticated sambas as well as the ceremonial dirges of transplanted African cults. Bahia, destination disguised as exhalation! Its proper name, Salvador of the Bay of All Saints, was bestowed in 1512 by Pedro Alvares Cabral, Brazil's first Portuguese conqueror, making this the second-oldest continuous settlement in the New World. Abbreviated as Salvador, never to be confused with unhappy El Salvador, Bahia is also know as *A Velha Mulata*—that ancient octoroon gal. Historic center of the trade in sugar and cocoa, requiring ten times the number of slaves ever brought to Virginia, Bahia is the axis of the Afro-to-anyfro fulcrum, font of all things Brazilian!

It makes sense that the country's founding capital should also be the No. 1 venue for participatory merrymaking. Ground Zero for all Brazil's annual emotional detonation is the Praça Castro Alves, Salvador's catchall square. Hell's ballroom on an ocean bluff. The Campo Grande, a sedate square full of palms and tiled mosaics, has been commandeered as the lifting pad for this town of a million's collective leap. A seedy shopping street called the Sete de Setembro—the date of Brazilian independence—has become one long flume of half-naked dervishes flowing toward the Bay of All Saints. From the opposite direction, up the cobblestone slopes of the crumbling Pelourinho, once the cruel heart of colonial Brazil and now the pacemaker of the culture brought here by the colony's African slaves, come the Afro-*blocos,* black nationalist dancing groups modeling the portable upholstery of splashy tribal wraps. Black and white merge in a combustible mix where everyone turns colorful, anything but gray.

Were I able to beat a retreat to my hotel room, I'd just have to put up with a loudspeaker rigged up outside my window that pours out bouncy tunes 24 hours a day. Even if I could part the waves of people, I'd remain trapped by sound. Fore and aft in the rocking processional are huge wheeled ships, their black prows all amplifiers, sending out heart-speeding sounds at a volume that curdles eardrums. An entire citizenry yields up its nervous system to the fervent command of the Bahian institution known as the *trio elétrico*—once three mandolin strummers but now full bands with rock drummers and beauteous backup singers. As their motorized stages lumber down the street as slow as they can go, the bands outrace each other by jacking up the volume and speeding up the frenetic rhythm of *marcha*. Locals claim the electric guitar itself was invented here in the mid-forties by a part-time musician and full-time electrician. The town has certainly perfected the art of turning a flatbed truck into a rolling bandstand built from balanced stacks of loudspeakers. Never has so little horsepower hauled so much amplification.

> *The blocos are a recent musical sensation of Bahia, a neighborhood drum choir. Forty drummers are lined in rows, with the deepest drums, the size of oil cans, slung around the necks of those at the back. They take small steps back and forth in rhythmic formation to the beat of the drums, so loud and low that the ground seems to rock. The pop musicologist Paul Simon came here to record their martial syncopations for one of his albums, and later took them to perform with him in New York City's Central Park. He says he was going back to the source, looking for inspiration in the West African roots of rock and roll.*
>
> —Paul Rambali, *In the Cities and Jungles of Brazil*

With a splash of neon on the side of its truck, this year's most popular trio advertises itself as *Cheiro de Amor,* the "smell of love." I think I'm picking up a whiff of that, along with the more cloying scent of *lança perfume,* an ether-like inhalant sprayed onto handkerchiefs dangling from many carousers' mouths. Organized *blocos* shake pom-poms and hippity-hop through the night in matching sleeveless togas which identify whimsical Carnaval groups like Ecologia or Sympathy Is Almost Love, Habeas Copos, as in cups of Brahma beer, and Hypertensão, which refers to libidinal tensions. "Next Year Will Be Better" is the pledge made by one habitually disorganized bunch of street prancers. Another playful contingent offers ideological debate by calling itself "Next Year Will Be Worse!"

To my right, a distinguished and decidedly muscular black gentleman is dressed up as an outsized all-American high school drum majorette in blond wig, miniskirt, and go-go boots. In fact, if you can call anything in this town a fact, on a designated day of the festivities, there are thousands such transsexualized cheerleaders. The girl to my left is Batman, or Batlady. Charming mermaids slither past, rubbing their fins against eager fishermen. Some of these sirens flash gold-toothed smiles. Others make their interest known by suggestively lifting a corner of my shirttail, as if they're trying to X-ray my pants. In the local argot, freelance fantasists like these are known as the *pipoca* (popcorn). Around me, the action's getting hot enough to burst all kernels of logic.

I've fallen in line behind the Apaches, a typically mirthful and mixed-up Bahian mélange of blacks dressed as Indians out of Hollywood's West. In a wild, wild send-up of their Amazonian brethren, they strut their feathers and string their arrows in time. What animates them is a tribal beat emanating from the wrong continent. Ranting into a raspy microphone, their single singing chief pays tribute to ancestral African gods. The drumming corps is a marching band out of its straitjacket. Their martial rhythm is internationalist in inspiration, too—something they call samba-reggae. The beat that makes the old churches quake is repetitive to the point of inducing the infinite. But one kind of Indian is soon overtaken by another. I'm lost in the turbaned waves of the *Filhos de Gandhi*—Sons of Gandhi—the oldest and largest of the black associations, which appropriated the pacifist saint as a symbol of both peaceful coexistence and racial rebellion. Thousands get civilly disobedient in matching white turbans, sandals, and shocking blue socks, their holy headdresses looking like bowling towels.

I doubt if the Mahatma would approve of all this surplus carnality. The face of this *festa* is sometimes leering, unshaven, and, more often, clown-like, painted, and giddy. Through four nonstop nights that are just another snoozy weekend to the rest of the world, moods are getting meaner. It's already past the time when all of these folks should be safely in bed. In quieter spots, the roads turn to rocky mattresses for entwined couples, cushioned with an accumulating down of confetti and discarded beer cups. The better side streets are pissoirs. With streetlights shattered or burned out, I end up in dark alleys surrounded by more than a few types I'd never want to meet there. In this return to childhood, there are lots of problem kids with raging hormones, taking their innocence to the point where it becomes indistinguishable from mayhem. There are many guests who've overstayed their welcome.

I haven't been properly introduced to the grinning lady who finds enjoyment in rubbing her hands against my hamstrings, the drunk gent who has planted an elbow in my lower back, the groping stranger who is using the opportunity of our enforced coziness to dig his claws deep inside my front pockets. With an extra set of hands down my pants, it feels for a moment that I've grown tentacles, Vishnu-like, or that the khaki shorts I'm wearing are no longer my own. But I've taken the precaution of storing my spare change in the sole of one smelly sneaker. There's no space for me to bend over and claim my wad.

My best protection is to merge with the mob and accept that I'm no better or worse than any other biped succumbing to the stimuli of snare-drum cadences, group hysteria, and unlimited cheap beer. Before I know it, I, too, am pulling an all-nighter so I can sing the sacred and profane praises of this wondrously polyglot place.

Bahia, my eyes are shining / My heart is palpitating / From so much happiness! goes one time-honored samba tribute. *You're the queen of universal beauty / My dear Bahia / Long before the Empire / She was the first capital / Her history, her glory / Her name is tradition!*

After 500 years, this town hasn't begun to exhaust the possibilities inherent in its potent mix of peoples and beliefs. On its privileged perch between ocean and desert, this little Lisbon and compact Luanda grinds its cultural engines to make a mighty noise. We dance in discovery of Bahia's bright shortcut to the dark continent! Strut to savor Salvador's unhinged, nonpuritan version of America! All hail Oxum and Jesus, Mary and Iemanjá! Blessings to Mother Africa, Father Portugal, and especially their bastard child, Brazil!

Now I raise both hands skyward in pagan hosannas. There's no longer any room for two arms at my side. I can't tell whose legs are carrying my rump along. My one moment of glory comes when I tire of bouncing up and down like some stork attempting a takeoff.

Throwing all caution and complexes aside, I break into "the jerk," a dance I've been perfecting ever since I began imitating James Brown in junior high. Within moments, I'm surrounded by a circle of brown Bahian teens doing their best to imitate my too-cool *Americano* moves. *"Tá legal!"* they all cry, adding the thumbs-up sign, which means not only that something is legal but that everything is OK, totally permissible. Their appreciative grins remind me that Carnaval has no stylebook, dress code, or etiquette. *"Ótimo!"* a few murmur, "ultimate" being the most common compliment in a land that tends toward the heights of every experience. Perhaps the surest way to escape assault and battery is by yielding to one's *fantasia,* that doubly rich word for a costume.

What sort of masquerade am I using anyway, not so much the accidental tourist as an inadvertent dancer? Personally, I'm no fan of excessive unsolicited body contact. I've rarely seen the point of contorting various anatomical parts before others in a manner that I wouldn't attempt while alone. I can do without intoxicated strangers seeking a grip on my attention span or a shortcut to my soul. Just when polite conversation turns to a din, when the carpet gets rolled up and everyone kicks up his heels, that's usually the time you'll see me sneaking out. That I've been moved to come here—to the veritable belly button of body-land—shows just how far some of us will go to find our own body. In my case, I've added around eight thousand frequent-flier miles when all I have to do is travel a few inches, migrate to that steamy realm just down south of my neck!

"Below the equator," goes another of those tired homilies that Brazilians trot out before newcomers, "there is no sin." Though I see more innocence on display than anything else—flesh displayed is flesh divested—my resistant Northern mind recoils with a set of judgmental questions: Don't these people ever seek out silence? Shimmy their way toward an inner life? To what purpose have I cast my lot with these sweaty unshod? This giving in to primal forces must indeed be quite an achievement, since I'm having such trouble doing it. There must be some lesson I've got to learn by taking my place amid the profusion of anonymous torsos, through applying for citizenship in this dictatorship of the beautiful.

And I, too, am attempting to become *sem medo de ser feliz*. Unafraid to be happy—that's the fearless slogan that animates this city, this country, this night.

Award-winning writer John Krich is the author of two widely praised non-fiction books, Music in Every Room *and* El Beisbol, *as well as a novel about the private life of Fidel Castro,* A Totally Free Man. *This story was excerpted from his book,* Won Ton Lust: Adventures in Search of the World's Best Chinese Restaurant. *His travel and sports writing, reportage and fiction, have appeared in* Mother Jones, Vogue, Sports Illustrated, Village Voice, Image, Commentary, California, The New York Times, *and many other publications.*

★

Carnaval players spin on an axis of inversions and reversals of high and low, order and disorder, male and female, inside and outside, public and private, freedom and repression, life and death. Carnaval dissolves order and rationality into chaos and nonsense; it tumbles the lofty as it celebrates the humble, absurd, and grotesque. Both the erotic and the maudlin, sexuality and death, are present in Carnaval, so that destruction and regeneration are merged in the absurd Carnaval cry, *"Viva a morte!* Long live death!"

—Nancy Scheper-Hughes, *Death Without Weeping: The Violence of Everyday Life in Brazil*

✦ ✦ ✦

Patience, Patience

The mysteries of the tropical woodlands
do not respond to "Showtime!"

THERE IS A CHICKEN-SIZED BIRD IN THE AMAZON CALLED THE
jacú that squeals, the locals say, just like a pig. Another is the *bis-
cateiro,* Portuguese slang for a masher, so named for its wolf whistle.
A tree with a green velvety trunk and slippery as nylons is dubbed,
fittingly, "the lady's leg." Then there is the *fel de paca,* whose wood is
hard as steel and sends off sparks when struck with a honed
machete blade. Still another, the *formigueiro,* the ant tree, is a sort of
botanical condominium: sever one of its hollow branches, and it
foams with the ants that are its habitual tenants.

A walk in the dark woods along the Cristalino River, in the
west-central Amazon River Basin, where the dense forests of Mato
Grosso meet the tall rainforests of Amazonas, is a trip through a
frustrating and wondrous landscape: wondrous because of the
wealth of plant and animal life harbored in this "rich realm of nature," as the Portuguese reveled when they first set eyes upon the
Brazilian hinterlands; frustrating because for those uninitiated in
the mysteries of the tropical woodlands, such a walk can be nothing
but a passage through a damp green chaos.

Fortunately there was Sebastião, the lithe and agile woodsman, and his father-in-law, Luiz, who had trekked Brazil from the arid northeast to the dripping rainforest, to help us grope our way through the Braille of the Cristalino River's forest. In fact, their knowledge and delight in imparting that knowledge were the best assets any traveler in search of an ecology tour could have wanted. The hotel, the Floresta Amazônica, had indeed provided a proper biologist, a young graduate imported from the best university of São Paulo, fluent in English and French, as well as the more arcane languages of botany, ornithology, and primatology. But a 30-minute walk along a Brazil nut gathering path was a painful demonstration of the shortcomings of classroom diplomas when their bearers are transported suddenly to the rough outdoors. Luiz, with maybe a grade-school education and the nasal, twangy northeastern accent that is said in Brazil to be the emblem of ignorance, relished every moment of the tour.

He was there officially merely to steer the motorboat and walk us along the forest trail, while the biologist performed. But he soon started a prolonged game. Stopping by a tree with rough bark, as indistinguishable to me as any other in the sour light of the forest, Luiz would ask: what is this tree called?

The eager biologist's brow would crease, a forefinger would adjust his horn-rims, and after a moment's silence, he would blurt out a name. Wrong, Luiz would laugh.

And this tree?

Silence. A guess.

You sure?

The biologist would sweat.

The quiz went on relentlessly for the entire 30-minute walk. The biologist clambered back into the boat and spoke quietly about how his assignment at the forest camp was drawing, mercifully, to a close. Luiz wore a large and self-satisfied smile, and later that evening, over barbecued beef and beer, he started up the woodsmen's tales. There was the one about the anaconda, longer than a stretch limousine, its middle as thick as a man's torso, that Luiz had wrestled into submission. The trick, he said, is to get your thumbs behind his eyes, and then he goes all limp. For a visual aid, he then unrolled an enormous, dried snakeskin, presumably the victim's. Then there was the *jaú,* a giant-jawed fish that lurks in the bottom of rivers and had swallowed more than one of his *campanheiros.* He had similar stories of jaguars and probably a few about alligators, too, though we didn't get that far. This was the delightful hyperbole of the woods that many chagrined classroom biologists probably have had to swallow in silence at the day's end around the evening campfire.

Indeed, without a Luiz or a Sebastião to guide, narrate, and perhaps fib a bit, the initial encounter with Amazon rainforest can be a fairly disillusioning experience. "Nevertheless, on the whole, I was disappointed," confesses Alfred Russell Wallace, the renowned naturalist, as he is about to start the fabulous journey that produced his classic *A Narrative of Travels on the Amazon and Rio Negro.* "The weather was not so hot, the people were not so peculiar, the vegetation was not so striking, as the glowing picture I had conjured up in my imagination...." Though he was eventually seduced by the subtler enchantments of this landscape, Wallace humbugged the magnificent forest even miles into his epic passage. "The depths of the virgin forest are solemn and grand, but there is nothing to surpass the beauty of our rivers and woodland scenery," the Englishman declared.

Though most film and adventure writing has, in the name of economy and entertainment, edited out the tedium of tropical wilderness, it is finally time and patience that are required to appreciate fully and then revel in the hidden marvels of the Amazon forest. "Indians and forests and palms cannot be compelled. They come in their turn. They are mixed with litter and dead stuff, like prizes in a bran tub," writes H. M. Tomlinson, in his classic traveler's tale, *The Sea and the Jungle,* remarking on the forests of Pará. Teddy Roosevelt, the great white hunter, had his most disappointing safari in the Amazon, taking precious few jaguars and alligators and a host of less noble beasts, like monkeys and parrots. It was not the splendid mammals but the ants that really impressed the ambassador of the strenuous life.

"It is only in time that the various peculiarities, the costume of the people, the strange forms of vegetation, and the novelty of the animal world will present themselves," Wallace finally allowed. The anthropologist Claude Lévi-Strauss, who walked through much of the Brazilian backlands, spoke about the necessity of calibrating one's expectations in the Amazon. "One universe gives place to another," he writes, "less agreeable to look at, but rich in rewards for senses nearer to the spirit: hearing, I mean, and smell. Good things one had thought never to experience again are restored to one: silence, coolness, peace. In our intimacy with the vegetable world, we enjoy those things which the sea can no longer give us and for which the mountains exact too high a price."

Mac Margolis went to Brazil for the first time in 1981, with his Portuguese language class from the Cambridge, Massachusetts YMCA. A year later, he flew down to Rio for a second look and simply never left. For the last two decades, working as a reporter for Newsweek *and other publications, he has traveled widely through South America. In 2003 he was awarded the Maria Moors Cabot Prize, the oldest international award in journalism, for outstanding coverage of the Western Hemisphere reinforcing freedom of the press and inter-American understanding. He is the author of* The Last New World: The Conquest of the Amazon Frontier, *from which this story was excerpted. He is currently a special correspondent for* Newsweek, *based in Rio de Janeiro.*

★

In New England one walks quite gradually into a wood, but not so in the jungle. One steps through the wall of the tropic forest, as Alice stepped through the looking glass; a few steps, and the wall closes behind. The first impression of the dark, soft atmosphere, an atmosphere that might be described as "hanging," for in the great tangle of leaves and fronds and boles it is difficult to perceive any one plant as a unit; there are only these hanging shapes draped by lianas in the heavy air, as if they had lost contact with the earth. And this feeling is increased by the character of the earth itself, which is quite unlike the thrifty woodland floor at home; here the tree boles erupt out of heaped-up masses of decay, as if the ground might be almost any distance beneath. The trees themselves are so tumultuous and strange that one sees them as a totality, a cumulative effect, scarcely noticing details; there is a strange, evilly spined palm trunk, though, and a crouching plant with gigantic fronds, and a fantastic parasite, like a bundle of long red pipe cleaners studded with olive nuts, fastened here and there to the high branches, and the looming trunk of a silk-cotton, seen only when one is right on top of it; it soars off through the leathery green canopy overhead.

—Peter Matthiessen, *The Cloud Forest*

Costa Verde Magic

*A cruise around an uncrowded bay
becomes an enchanted journey through the land
of slow clocks and Jorge Amado novels.*

I HAVE ALWAYS BEEN A SUCKER FOR RUINS, SO FROM THE MOMENT we sailed into a remote cove on Brazil's Ilha Grande and discovered what looked like a deserted palace, I knew I had to have a closer look. As I surveyed the hacienda, nearly overrun by the mountain jungle that pressed to the edge of the beach, I wondered: What kind of person would build or live in such a monument amid this island wilderness?

Later, as I crossed the beach, I heard a noise. Branches in the surrounding vegetation cracked, the leaves parted and a white horse pranced into view.

It stopped, stared at me and snorted. Then, with a flash of its tail, the animal bolted past me onto the beach. It charged for a quarter mile, then returned to face off with me.

I grasped for the first Portuguese phrase that came to mind.

"Este é um lugar de sonhos!" I shouted, stamping my foot. "This is a place of dreams!" It was a slogan I'd read on a brochure describing this region, called *Angra dos Reis,* the Cove of Kings.

I heard an outburst of laughter behind me and, turning, stood face to face with a boy who reminded me of nothing so much as myself at age fourteen.

"Don't worry," he said in Portuguese. "The horse only wants someone to swim with him."

That said, he peeled out of his shirt, raced down the beach and leaped into the water. The horse followed right behind.

Within seconds, four other boys appeared out of nowhere. Their shouts echoed off the cliffs on either side of the cove. I felt as if I had stumbled into the refuge of Peter Pan and the Lost Boys.

Before my wife, Marilyn, and I began our trip to Brazil, we'd heard rumors of a place 100 miles south of Rio where you could hire a sailboat, book a yacht, or board a schooner to explore hundreds of islands and coves.

On maps, this region bears the label Costa Verde, but the locals call this sanctuary Angra dos Reis, after the centrally located seaport of that name.

"It is almost virgin," a Brazilian friend told us. "They say the clocks in Angra are ruled by turtles. Go to Angra if you want to see how Brazil used to be."

So we did, and, like most people who come to explore Angra, we set up base at a small beach hotel on the mainland. From there we could have rented a small open sloop or a pair of kayaks and headed for one of half a dozen islands that lay just a mile or two offshore. Or we could

or most visitors to Brazil, the only glimpse of the landmass between Rio de Janeiro and São Paulo comes as a bright green blur from the window of an airplane, en route from one city to another. The area is known as Costa Verde, or Green Coast, and even from an altitude of 23,000 feet there is no mistaking why. The aquamarine sea and the emerald forests rising up from the shore are the region's two dominating features, and at ground level they become even more imposing.

—Larry Rohter, "Villages and Beaches of Brazil's Costa Verde," *The New York Times*

have signed aboard one of the 70-foot *saveiros*, trading schooners that have been converted to passenger carriers—complete with samba bands, seafood buffets, and bars—for one- to three-day trips to remote islands and coves.

We arranged to charter a 36-foot boat we could sail ourselves. After a weather and navigation briefing that prepared us for gentle southwest breezes, temperatures in the nineties and clear, deep water, we headed to sea for four days—just the two of us, hoping to find the land of slow clocks and the villages portrayed in novels like *Gabriela, Clove and Cinnamon* by Jorge Amado. As *Tridente* spread its blue, yellow, and white genoa jib before the breeze and we slipped by countless little islands, I thought about Amado's Gabriela, a poor Brazilian girl who flees the interior of her country to find a new life in a small seaport early in this century. In those days, a handful of wealthy landowners ruled the coast from the sugarcane plantations and palaces they erected throughout the islands, overlooking the mainland coves. Into this world stepped women like Gabriela, to add a little tenderness to the coastal frontier.

Looking at the coves and islands of Angra from *Tridente,* it seemed that little had changed since Gabriela's day. In the glare of sea and sun, I could barely make out the fishermen's tiny homes, clustered on the shores in the shadows of a villa or two.

Our tentative plan was to head about twenty miles offshore to the largest and most remote of the islands, Ilha Grande, about twenty-two miles long and eight miles wide. Awaiting us there were countless protected anchorages, great snorkeling, empty beaches, mountain waterfalls, and settlements that had not changed for a century.

On *Ilha Grande* (Large Island), they say, pirate José Grego lived incestuously with one of his two daughters and brought a curse to the island that will keep it forever wild. Ilha Grande, it's said, is a place of lost souls and treasure.

It took us a while to get there. On the first day of our cruise, as *Tridente* sailed close along the west coast of an island called Gipoia, we rounded a headland and came upon a village nestled between two mountains. Fishermen stretched out their nets on the beach, as women in *fio dental* swimwear waded through the clear shallows. Among the whitewashed façades of the houses stood a bright blue chapel and a long terrace shaded with a palm-leaf roof.

"Can you believe it?" said my wife, pointing to the terrace. "There's a restaurant out here."

Drifting down to us on the offshore breeze, the smell of shrimp, squid, and grouper simmering in cayenne pepper was enticing, and within a minute we had anchored *Tridente* just off the beach. I don't know how long we lingered at the Bar do Luis, but it was sufficient time for us to feast on a seafood stew and to get to know Luis, as well as several men carving a dugout canoe on the terrace.

Ready to board our inflatable dinghy for the return to *Tridente,* we found the boat wilted like a flat tire. The sun must have overheated it and popped a chamber, I explained to one of the dugout builders.

"Não," he said. *"Iemanjá!"* He was sure the goddess of the sea— the Mother of Waters from West Africa, called Iemanjá by Brazilian believers of Macumba and Candomblé—had been sporting with us.

The islander gave us—and our deflated dinghy—a ride back out to *Tridente* aboard a fishing boat. On the way, the skipper asked me if I had any money. I guessed he wanted a tip—and it was well deserved—so I handed over a few dollars' worth of Brazilian currency. Instantly, the man tossed the money into the sea.

"Para Iemanjá," he said. "Now you will have good luck."

I'm still not sure that what followed during our cruise can be credited to Iemanjá, but I know what our Brazilian friends think. They think that our trip was charmed, shaped by the forces that rule Angra's clocks. We were "meant" to stop at Bar do Luis, "meant" to see the palace on Ilha Grande with its boys and white horse, "meant" to end up in a certain café in Parati.

This last event still seems a little spooky. On one of our last days in Angra, we visited the port of Parati, at the west end of the Baia da Ilha Grande. With its docks, cobblestone lanes, and flowering patios, it is considered one of the world's richest preserves of 18th-century architecture. Once a booming harbor for the shipping of gold and gemstones from Brazil's interior, Parati fell into dormancy when entrepreneurs opened a road from the mines to Rio in 1723.

For more than two centuries, almost nobody traveled to or from Parati. Then, in the 1950s, improved roads made it more accessible. During recent years the place has flourished as a national historic site, complete with dozens of tiny inns, restaurants, and cafés.

It was at one of these cafés, called Vesuvius, that we stopped for a sandwich and a glass of *chopp* (draft beer). As we sat eating and listening to the small talk of the old men at an adjoining table, I experienced a sense of déjà vu. I felt as if I had sat in this café before and knew the old men's story.

When you see a white horse running on the beach, they said, you have come to a place where time moves like a turtle. The horse is a soul searching for its freedom, and those who spot the animal will see the land of the white horse in their dreams.

Suddenly I realized where I had heard the story before—in a Jorge Amado novel. Was it *Gabriela?* Then I had to laugh: as I looked up at the painting of an erupting volcano behind the bar, I realized why Vesuvius seemed so familiar to me. The film version of *Gabriela* had been made in Parati—much of it shot right in this café.

In the movie, Vesuvius, Parati, the bays and the distant islands—all of Angra—had the rosy, soft-focus look of Never-Never Land. In my dreams, the place still does.

Randall Peffer took off through the Appalachian Mountains on a freight train at age nine and hasn't stopped. He has written about subjects as diverse as the King of the Hobos for Reader's Digest, *monkeys trained to harvest coconuts in Malaysia for* Smithsonian, *and the renaissance of Catalonia for* National Geographic. *His book* Watermen, *a documentary of the lives of Chesapeake fishermen, won* The Baltimore Sun's *Critic's Choice Award. He teaches writing and literature at Phillips Academy in Andover, Massachusetts.*

*

Nowhere in Brazil is there such intimacy between land and sea.
—Brazilian writer Rubem Braga on Costa Verde

DWIGHT V. GAST

On Track

Cruising Brazil's countryside aboard a train
is a many-splendored thing.

AN HOUR AND A HALF BY PLANE FROM BUSTLING RIO DE JANEIRO waits a rail ride through what many consider a Brazilian paradise. Or just Paradise, period.

The *Gralha Azul* ("Blue Chatterbox") is a historic train that climbs and dips through mountains and gorges that are lushly covered with green forests, spotted with pink and yellow tropical flowers, and graced by cascades of white waterfalls. Traveling between the inland city of Curitiba and the seaport of Paranaguá, which is in the southern state of Paraná, the *Gralha Azul* offers a short—three and one-half hours each way—yet undeniably breathtaking interlude.

When I arrived at the station at six a.m. on a chilly Monday morning in November, the half dozen cars of the *Gralha Azul*—a bright blue streak beneath rolled-pewter skies—were already waiting at the platform. I bought my ticket in the station, then went outside and climbed aboard. The train was virtually deserted at that hour, but gradually its rickety leather seats became the stage for an experience in itself as the other passengers took their places.

My fellow travelers turned out to be an amicable mix of all backgrounds and ages. American college kids sat blow-dried and bleary-eyed from last night's escapades in the city. Well-groomed Brazilian tourists, fueled by their strong morning coffee, chatted away about yesterday's soccer games. Retired couples, who brought breakfast rolls from their hotels, unfolded maps and polished binoculars. Indigenous Indians who live in the coastal highlands through which we were about to pass watched stony-faced (for them the *Gralha Azul* is a commuter train) while their children ran gleefully up and down the aisles, racing from car to car.

At just past seven a.m., the *Gralha Azul* jerked to a start, a few minutes late in deference to the Brazilian way. In no time we were out of Curitiba, riding through the open plateau that surrounds the city, passing the umbrella pines and bamboo so characteristic of Paraná. Right on schedule, Attílio A. Gasparini, a tall, gray-haired local entrepreneur, made his way through the aisles in his soiled white hat and jacket describing the wonders we were about to see.

There are about 18,000 miles of railway in Brazil, though much of it is used for cargo, not passenger, transport. During the 1990s, the rail network was turned over to private operators after decades of government control.

—AH and SD

Behind him followed a barrage of soft drink and snack vendors. Meanwhile, the *Gralha Azul* climbed slowly to Roça Nova, at over 1,010 meters the highest point along the route. By about eight a.m., we were near the top of the Serra do Mar mountain range, which separates the plateau from the Atlantic.

Better weather awaited us at the end of a long tunnel beyond Roça Nova. Suddenly the sun was shining, the birds were twittering, and we began our descent to Paranaguá. Over the din of the excited passengers, we heard the rush of falling water known as the *Véu da Noiva* (Bridal Veil) cascading 80 meters into a gorge.

Blissfully ignoring the signs proclaiming "E PROBIDO VIAJAR NAS PLATAFORMAS" *("It is forbidden to ride between cars"),* we dangled outside the train taking in the view. We felt the cool mountain breezes, heard the rush of streams and smelled the scent of orchids and orange, palm and fig trees everywhere. Many of the passengers

snapped pictures and expressed amazement at the soaring mountains, dizzying drop-offs, changing vistas, waterfalls, and lush vegetation. We seemed to be passing through without time to catch our
breath. The Blue Chatterbox was living up to its name, and to add
to the noisy excitement, I couldn't help humming Heitor Villa-
Lobos's *Bachianas Brasileiras No. 2,* a lively little suite he composed
to give "the impression of a trip in a little train in the interior of
Brazil."

Threading in and out of tunnels through the mountains of
Marumbi National Park and over deep gorges lined with gushing
torrents, we caught our first glimpse of the Atlantic coast in the distance. Next, we crossed the 1,000-meter-high Carvalho viaduct,
where the tracks took a sharp 45-degree turn, seeming to leave us
suspended over sheer space. A chorus of voices raised a spontaneous "Ahh!" in a multitude of languages.

A half hour later, a stop at the Marumbi station gave us time to
marvel at the lofty contours of Marumbi Peak—over 1,500 meters
high—as we made out the tiny figures of local mountain climbers
testing its ridges. From then on, the terrain was more gentle, and
the pink and yellow tropical flowers and banana trees, squat with
shiny leaves shaped like serrated machetes, became more numerous
as we approached sea level. After brief stops in Saquarema and
Alexandra to let off several local residents, the *Gralha Azul's* so-
journers stopped once more, for our first head-on look at
Paranaguá Bay, an inlet of the Atlantic, before coasting into the seaport itself. We were nearing the end of the line.

In contrast to modern Curitiba, Paranaguá, with its population
of 95,000, is a sleepy port town—the local inhabitants apparently
dazed by the pungent soybean smell that hangs in the musty air.
But there was much to hold my interest during the six-hour wait
for the return trip to Curitiba.

A leisurely twenty-minute walk from the Paranaguá train station
took me to the old part of town, where people go shopping for
crafts—everything from roughly hewn wooden bowls to rustic
red-clay pottery. Then there was the Museu de Arqueologia e Artes
Populares, which displays artifacts from indigenous, colonial, and

slave cultures in an 18th-century Jesuit monastery covered with bright bursts of bougainvillea. Just up the street from the museum, the restaurant Danúbio Azul served seafood in an open-air setting that overlooked the water. I took advantage of a boat-tour concession near the restaurant and was able to visit the lovely islands that dotted the bay.

But even in this lovely harbor setting, I couldn't help looking back toward the mountains, up to Curitiba. Not that I was in a rush to return to civilization. Quite the contrary. I couldn't wait to get back on the train for the repeat performance, or rather the spectacular last movement, of my own little Brazilian symphony.

The late Dwight V. Gast, a frequent visitor to Brazil, wrote about that country for Art in America, Travel & Leisure, *and other national publications.*

★

The train used during the Rubber Boom to carry *borracha* from the far reaches of Rondônia, Mato Grosso, and Amazonas to civilization had a heroic-comic look. It was the sort of train you see in old American Westerns. It looked like the trains that once brought the Yankee pioneers across the great plains and the Rocky Mountains on the Pacific Railway of olden days—indeed, it was bought from old stock in America. Outmoded grandeur. There it all was, the engine with its wooden furnace belching black smoke through a wide conical chimney, and a bell clanging to warn goodness-knows-what creatures. On its front hung the big lantern to explore the way. It was a train in a world where nightmares were simple daily realities which could break the little train like a toy. And there, in front of the wheels, was the iron cow-catcher, the metal broom that, instead of being used against the buffaloes, swept away pythons and alligators.

—Lucien Bodard, *Green Hell: Massacre of the Brazilian Indians*

MARÍA CRISTINA JURADO

Brasília the Beautiful

*A Brazilian leader's crowning achievement
is hailed by some as a utopian masterpiece,
by others as a sterile work of art.*

BRASÍLIA. ITS CONTROVERSIAL ARCHITECT, OSCAR NIEMEYER, a disciple of the great Le Corbusier, first imagined this Utopia. Its urban theorist, Lucio Costa, saw it as being born of "two axes crossing at a right angle, like the sign of the cross." In Brasília, the Creation is nearby. You lift up your eyes anywhere in this enormous green esplanade and know that if God did not exist, the Brazilians would have invented him.

Brasília seems more a work of art than a nation's capital. Amid the vast miles of heaven and grass, there are more than 1,000 square feet of green space per inhabitant. With an estimated population of 1.8 million, Brasília has no sidewalks or street names. It is beautiful, tall, and elegant like a Russian princess, as French philosopher and writer André Malraux once said. There is something otherworldly about this city. It puts its enormous footprint in the jungle and proves the unbelieving wrong.

Just the task of walking its almost 2,315 square miles demands incredible willpower. This city is not made to human dimensions. To see it, you need the legs of a Goliath, the skill of a David, and seven-league boots. And, of course, a taxi. The streets are so wide, the traffic so fast, that even the most daring mortals are soon dismayed.

Brasília encompasses an entire nation: its politics, national identity, people, and history. The principal impulse came from Juscelino Kubitschek, a French-trained surgeon who was elected president of Brazil in the 1950s. J. K., as he was known, made building Brasília the major goal of his administration. With political force and charisma, he inspired the *candangos,* the pioneers who came from every corner of the country ready to work. They built Brasília in just two and half years.

I sought the curved and sensual line. The curve that I see in the Brazilian hills, in the body of a loved one, in the clouds in the sky and in the ocean waves.

—Oscar Niemeyer

The capital was built in 1960. In 1987, the U.N. Educational, Scientific, and Cultural Organization (UNESCO) declared it part of the world's cultural patrimony and added Brasília to its World Heritage list of protected sites.

Planned by communist skeptics, the city is a focus for intense religious activity. It has the highest concentration of sects and pseudoreligious groups in the whole country. The Valley of Dawn, in northern Brasília, is a colorful example. This movement, founded by a charismatic female truck driver, has 10,000 adherents in this region. Its members, with their elaborate costumes, stand out amid the dry, unpaved streets of the slums.

You cannot find the Carnaval or beaches of Rio de Janeiro here, or the get-ahead pace of São Paulo. The streets of Brasília are as sober and static as a Finnish fjord, only hotter. Brasília is a place to work. Diplomacy, affairs of state, and governmental decisions take place here.

From the air, Brasília looks like an airplane with its nose pointed toward Lake Paranoá, the site of weekend pleasures with its many water-sports facilities. The long fuselage points from east to west. Here are all the symbols of the urban plan: the cross used in the first Mass, celebrated in 1957; the Kubitschek Memorial, which preserves even his car; the television tower, with its viewing deck and crafts market; the cathedral; the history museum; and the Plaza of the Three Powers. In the plaza's center is Planalto Palace, the residence of the Brazilian president. There are no distractions—no noise or neon. One tour not to miss is the one of embassy row. Its buildings are jewels of architecture, with enormous yards donated by Brazil to each nation.

The wings of the plane represent the residential areas. Although residents insist that finding our way is easy here, at first glance addresses are a giant maze. The "superblocks," an idea of the city's founders, are housing units on a super-human scale, situated on the roads running from north to south. No superblock has any building taller than six stories, and each contains its own kindergarten, supermarkets, schools, and plazas. The streets have no names, only numbers.

The best solution is to let others drive—easy enough, because Brasília is not inundated with tourists. Have an adventure. Get out of your car and feel the grass of the esplanades beneath your feet. Stand in the middle of the Plaza of the Three Powers as the sun sets and becomes pure opal. Or watch over Brasília from on high.

It works. There is no Carnaval, but this dream of a handful of crazy men, this piece of history torn out of the jungle, is Brazil as well.

María Cristina Jurado is a reporter for the Sunday magazine of El Mercurio, *Chile's largest daily newspaper. She began her journalism career in 1973 while still in college, and to this day has reported from five continents. In addition to* El Mercurio, *she has worked for* The Irish Times, Agence France-Presse, *and* Deutsche Presse Agentur. *Fluent in four languages, Jurado lives in Santiago with her daughter, Stephanie Marie.*

✳

Brasília must have looked good on paper and still looks good in photos. But in the flesh, forget it. The world's great planned city of the 20th century is built for automobiles and air-conditioners, not people. Distances are enormous and no one walks. The sun blazes, but there are no trees for shelter.

It's a lousy place to visit and no one wanted to live there. Bureaucrats and politicians, who live in the model "pilot plan" part of the city, were lured to Brasília by 100 percent salary hikes and big apartments. Still, as soon as the weekend comes they get out of the city as fast as possible to Rio, to São Paulo, to their private clubs in the country—anywhere that's less sterile, less organized, less vapid. Brasília is also one of the most expensive cities in Brazil.

The poor have to get out—they have no choice. Mostly from the Northeast, these *candangos* (pioneers) work in the construction and service industries. They live in *favelas,* which they call "anti-Brasílias," as far as 30 kilometers from the center. The physical gulf between the haves and have-nots is reminiscent of South Africa's township system.

All this is the doing of three famous Brazilians: an urban planner (Lucio Costa), an architect (Oscar Niemeyer) and a landscape architect (Burle Marx), all three the leading figures in their field. They were commissioned by President Juscelino Kubitschek to plan a new inland capital, a city that would catalyze the economic development of Brazil's vast interior. With millions of dirt-poor peasants from the Northeast working around the clock, Brasília was built in an incredible three years—it wasn't exactly finished but it was ready to be the capital (Niemeyer admits today that it was all done too quickly). On April 21, 1960, the capital was moved from Rio to Brasília and thousands of public servants fell into a deep depression.

An inland capital was an old Brazilian dream that had always been dismissed as expensive folly. What possessed Kubitschek to actually do it? Politics. He made the building of Brasília a symbol of the country's determination and ability to become a great economic power. He successfully appealed to all Brazilians to put aside their differences and rally to the cause. In doing so he distracted attention from the country's social and economic problems, gained enormous personal popularity and borrowed heavily from international banks. His legacy to the country was rampant inflation.

—Andrew Draffen, Robert Strauss, and Deanna Swaney,
Brazil - a travel survival kit

Where Life Comes in Slices

Leave the crêpes to the French;
it's the meat house that gets
Brazilian juices flowing.

A WAY OF COOKING MEAT ON CHARCOAL; BARBECUED. A MEAT house like no other. Here in Brazil everyone who can afford it eats meat with a vengeance. It is the staff of life. It represents the wealth of Brazil: the vast ranches and endless tons of meat that go through the stomach. Not for Brazilians the lean or *nouvelle cuisine,* or culinary pampering for neurotic, water-drinking designer vegetarians. Here meat is ubiquitous like the smog: wherever you go you will smell the tang of roasting meat in the air: in the cafés, bars, butchers; at street stalls sold on sticks and dipped in hot sauces, in snack bars, on the beach, in pasta, as an *aperitivo* in a bar where a group of people will share a dish of finely sliced fillet cooked with spring onions and spear it with toothpicks, in pubs sliced in sandwiches, and finally, the king of them all, the *churrascarias.*

Here you sit and the waiter brings to your table every kind of meat from all parts of the animal. First he comes and dulls the edge of your appetite slightly by offering you a salad plate, which includes the delicious heart of palm, soft and textured like marble. Then along comes the waiter with the meat; like heralds bearing scrolls they enter with these long skewers of meat that have been

193

charcoaled and burnt fiercely on the outside and when sliced reveal the pink flesh beneath. So it has also a slightly erotic undertone, as if the delights were "revealed" by the slicing off of the overgarment. It's only salted on the outside; no other flavor is used in the charcoaling except its own juices.

The waiter carries the skewer of sizzling meat in both hands while simultaneously bearing in his lower hand a little silver bowl in which to catch the fat; not always successfully it would seem, since the floor of this particular café is like a skating rink. One waiter may again offer you a starter, like sausages or chicken, and if you demur another waiter is speeding swiftly toward you with the giant stick from which he will slice off a section of the prepared meat and swiftly return the shaved skewers of meat to the burning coals for sealing. You've hardly finished your slice when the waiter glides back with his sizzling rump or sirloin on its iron skewer, holding the other end in its metal cup. With a razor-sharp knife he slices it slowly from the top and it falls gradually away, but before it reaches the end of its journey onto your plate you are invited to spear the meat with your fork to prevent it slapping inelegantly down. A thin slice, darkly barbecued on one side and virgin on the other. Another waiter will come by, offering kidney, liver, and other delicacies, but you will safely remain with fillet or rump. It tastes unlike any other meat. It tastes supremely good.

I am plummeted back to my heady old meat-eating days, before conscience, ecology, and additives diminished my desire for the red flesh…when meat was wholesome to a growing child, like the slice of bread Mum dipped into the stewpot, held it out sopping and tasting more wonderful than anything on Earth. In later years, living with and knowing vegetarians has opened all the doors of the most divine world of taste. The meat sitting in the fridge on a white plate onto which blood had oozed out was a thing of the past. That slightly sick feeling when you slice a steak and it's just too raw and you are inevitably reminded that it is blood which is leaking out of that piece of meat, however much it is decorated with sauce and peppercorns and surrounded by innocent little sprigs of parsley, as if to help you reduce the slaughter on your plate. Here meat is and feels like sin, and makes no pretense of avoiding its role and decor. Just plain meat.

The white-jacketed waiter approaches. You never tasted meat so good, whose only flavoring is salt. And you don't have to send it back since it comes as raw or as well done as you wish. Offerings are now coming more quickly, before you've even had time to denude your plate—roast beef, turkey wrapped in bacon. The waiter skews off a couple and you get back into the act, washing it down with a good *caipirinha*. A chunk of mignon. The knife flashes and the meat slaps down onto your plate, with you obeying the ritual with your fork, guiding it gently down to land. The slices are not too thick—just sufficient each time to have you wanting more. It's heady stuff. The pork's declined. No more chicken or sausage. This is certainly a place for serious indulgence and it needn't cost a fortune. Sometimes there is in all of us a desperate need to pig out, to indulge in some carnal offering, be it flesh, eaten or desired.

Just as James Bond prefers his martinis "shaken, not stirred," most Brazilians like their caipirinhas *crushed, not squeezed. The national cocktail is a delicious blend of* cachaça—*Brazil's own sugarcane rum—sugar and limes, crushed limes that is. Quarter a lime and place two sections in a gimlet glass. With a pestle or wooden spoon, crush the fruit until all juice is extracted. Remove any seeds.*

Add one teaspoon of sugar and four shots of cachaça *and blend. If you are enjoying your* caipirinha *in Brazil, it's probably best to hold the ice.*

—Annette Haddad,
"Bottoms Up!"

The knife again slashes through, and there is no inclined eyebrow by any waiter since this is what you are here for. The meat sizzles and the fires roar in the distant open kitchen. The smell is good, and now I feel my waist pushing against my belt and relax from the kill and look around at the other carnivores. They don't actually look too healthy, I force myself to admit. A man on the next table is so obsessed with his piece of meat that he is trying to swallow the whole slice and the meat that remains outside his mouth hangs down like some disgusting tongue.... I turn away promptly from the hideous sight... I glance at the other customers and see some solitary eaters like myself, but older, rich-looking men with yellow faces for whom company is a piece of dead meat being brought smoking to their plate. I begin to feel as if I am at a debauched gathering...carnal desire here takes on a new meaning. It's easy to eat since you never see a giant fillet steak on your plate, but only a slice at a time, and when it comes to your plate it almost looks like a piece of burnished wood. It looks too good to refuse.

You forget just how many slices you have had...six, eight, ten, twenty? The offering continues to dance in and out of your vision and you begin to decline and slow down and yet meat is the one thing you can still eat after real hunger has long abated. It longs for your bite and the taste clings to your teeth and I suspect you must be fulfilling or awaking atavistic longings...you feel bestial as you disturb some primitive appetite. I glance at myself in the mirror on the wall to check myself. Do I look evil yet? Gloating? Wolfish? I imagine that I would start to reveal signs of the sweaty, yellow demeanor of the compulsive meat eater. But I am disappointed to see I look more or less the same as when I walked in. Obviously it hasn't taken its toll yet. I pay the bill. I have feasted, if not with panthers, as least like a panther. But a small puritanical streak in me makes me feel as if I have been to a brothel.

Steven Berkoff also contributed "Whose Vice Is It Anyway?" in Part I.

★

When in Brazil, while drinking your *caipirinha* and eating your *mandio-quinha frita,* you may also find yourself singing along with those you are with. It is then you may find yourself in need of São Brás, the saint who will help you get your food down the food pipe while allowing the singing to come out of the air pipe.

Did Brazilians get their patron saint of choking because choking hap-pens all the time when singing during a meal, or is their favorite pastime finding a saint to bail them out of *any* trouble?

Whatever the reason, you are protected! You choke, somebody yells, "São Brás, São Brás, *no copo* (or, *no prato) tem mais!"* You look up to the sky with your red, coughing face, barking noises and pleading eyes and, *pronto!,* miracle accomplished! Solid with liquid take one path, samba comes out clear and dry, and the Brazilians you are with rev up the celebration in religious thankfulness. São Brás comes through once again.

—Neise Cavini Turchin, "Longing for Brazil"

BLAISE SIMPSON

City of Black Gold

The beautiful mountain hideaway of Ouro Prêto
is a living monument to Brazil's colonial heritage—
and an open-air bazaar for precious gems.

AWAKENING TO A CHORUS OF CHURCH BELLS, I OPENED THE
shutters at my window, took a deep breath of sweet mountain air
and watched the colonial village materialize gradually out of the
morning fog. Ghostly processions of pastel buildings crept up the
steep cobblestone streets as a pink sun rose, highlighting the thick,
whipped-cream curves of the stone churches that seemed to crown
every hill.

It took me a moment to remember that I was in Brazil. The
place, a town called Ouro Prêto, seemed so European and so different from the heat and bustle of Rio de Janeiro, a mere 300 miles
away, where I'd been the day before. It was as if I'd stepped abruptly
into the 18th century.

Even the very name of the village, which means "Black Gold,"
evokes the past. The black gold isn't oil: about 300 years ago, a force
of *bandeirantes*—the Portuguese equivalent of Spain's *conquistado-*
res—came through here searching for gold. A servant in their party
found some dark nuggets while drinking from a stream that runs
near what is now the center of town.

At first, nobody realized what they were, but when they were
presented to the governor of Rio, it was discovered that they were

gold covered with a black layer of the mineral palladium. It took the *bandeirantes* years to find the same stream again, but when a subsequent expedition rediscovered the place in 1698 and started mining there, they tapped into what turned out to be the richest single gold deposit yet discovered in the New World. A thriving mining camp grew up around the place, and in 1711, the town of *Vila Rica de Ouro Prêto*—the Rich City of Black Gold—was founded.

Shipped back to Portugal, gold from Ouro Prêto financed the building of much of Lisbon—and later, through Portuguese trade agreements with England, helped fuel the Industrial Revolution. Ouro Prêto also benefited from the gold, becoming the showplace of Brazil. The most talented craftsmen in the country were hired to transform the original mining camp into an architectural jewel. The first municipal theater in Brazil and one of its earliest universities were built here, as were countless grand houses and numerous churches. In 1721, the town became the capital of the state of *Minas Gerais* (General Mines). In its heyday, around 1750, Ouro Prêto thrived with more than 100,000 people—at a time when New York City had only 50,000 and Rio 20,000.

The main vein of gold ran out in Ouro Prêto late in the 18th century, but rich loads of gemstones had also been discovered in the region, and it remained an important city for a time. In 1822, when Brazil gained its independence from Portugal, the Brazilian emperor, Dom Pedro I, declared it the Imperial City of Ouro Prêto, and a short time later, Emperor Dom Pedro II built the National School of Mines here. By the late 19th century, though, the provincial capital had been moved to Belo Horizonte, where it remains, and the town had become something of a backwater, its days of glory all but forgotten.

Ouro Prêto began to be rediscovered only in the early 1930s, when the Brazilian government named the town a protected National Monument, thus saving it from the ravages of "progress." In 1981, the United Nations declared it a World Cultural Heritage Site, and judging from the range of guests staying at my hotel, the Pousada do Mondego, at least some of the world is interested in claiming its share. As I loaded my plate at the sumptuous buffet that is typical of Brazilian breakfasts—complete with platters of cold cuts, cheeses, fruit, and a variety of breads—I heard French, Spanish, Portuguese, and German. I sat with an amiable Brazilian couple who had come to spend a long weekend in the mountains. They told me that although few Americans come to Ouro Prêto, it is becoming a popular vacation spot for Europeans and for tycoons from São Paulo and Belo Horizonte, who have restored many of the old houses in town.

Like the rest of this protected place, the Pousada do Mondego reflects an extraordinary respect for the past. Located on a small square in the heart of town, it was once the mansion of an 18th-century merchant. There are twenty carefully restored guest rooms in the *pousada,* furnished with Brazilian antiques. All the modern conveniences are there, too, from elegant marble bathrooms to TVs, but what I loved most about it were the original wide-plank mahogany floors, the tall windows with panes of old, wavy glass, and the whitewashed walls, constructed from wood and mud held together with leather ties. A sense of history was palpable.

On our first morning in Ouro Prêto, when my husband, Tom, and I went out to explore, we immediately encountered another reminder of the town's mining heritage—a cluster of gem dealers who had set up stalls in the square outside the *pousada.* "Come here, *senhor,*" the dealers cried to my husband, opening small white paper packets to display glittering emeralds, diamonds, aquamarines, tourmalines, citrines, and amethysts. The rarest stone of all, one of them told us, was the pale, sherry-colored imperial topaz, found only in two places on Earth: the former Soviet Union and Ouro Prêto.

I left Tom to bargain while I went to look at the beautiful old church across the square. This was the church of São Francisco de Assis, a masterpiece of Brazilian baroque art, designed by the greatest sculptor of colonial Brazil, Antonio Francisco Lisboa, in the 1770s. Lisboa was a fascinating figure—a great, self-taught artist who was crippled by leprosy at an early age but continued to work with his tools strapped to his arms. The Brazilians affectionately call him *Aleijadinho*—"The Little Cripple"—and revere him for his talent and his courage. He has been called the Brazilian Michelangelo.

Lisboa's round-cheeked stone cherubs beam down from the façade above the entrance to the church, like children spying on a party from a balcony. The main altar, also carved by Aleijadinho, presents a multitude of images—angels and stars, nuns and conquerors, golden crosses and abstract curlicues, all piled into a kind of pyramid on top of which stands a Madonna, wearing a wig and fabric robes. In front of her is a statue of St. Francis himself, carrying a skull and a cross in his outstretched hands and looking considerably more serious than the lover of birds and animals I remembered from Sunday school.

The wooden ceiling is colored with soft pastel paintings of another Madonna, attended by cherubs playing flutes, horns, and violins, by Manuel da Costa Ataíde. He is considered Brazil's second-greatest colonial artist, after Aleijadinho. Ataíde's Virgin and angels are black- or brown-skinned—as are most Brazilians. Ataíde and Aleijadinho were *mulatos,* the sons of Portuguese men and black women, and because they were among the first to accurately portray the mixed racial heritage of their country, they are a source of great pride to the people of Brazil.

When I rejoined my husband—he had resisted the temptation to buy any gems—it was time for lunch. We decided to try a place a few blocks away that had been recommended by one of the gem dealers—the Casa do Ouvidor, a handsome restaurant with wrought-iron balconies overlooking one of the main streets in town. The specialties of the house were local dishes that looked quite different from the food we'd had in Rio, and we chose something called *tutu a mineira*—beans Minas style—mostly because I liked the sound of the name. This turned out to be a delicious plate of black beans served with pork chops and sausage, a kind of cabbage called *couve* and a fried egg. After washing it all down with cold draft beer, we practically rolled out of the restaurant.

Few citizens of Ouro Prêto speak English, but that afternoon we met a gem dealer who did, and she recommended the services of her English-speaking husband, Pedro Paulo Pinto, as a guide to the city. An aspiring travel agent who studied history at the university, Pinto showed us around for the rest of the day. We started in the main square, the Praca Tiradentes, where stands a statue of the great Brazilian revolutionary, Joaquim Jose da Silva Xavier. *Tiradentes,* meaning "Tooth Puller," is Xavier's nickname (he was a dentist). Though born in the village now called Tiradentes, between Ouro Prêto and Rio, Xavier was a member of the *Inconfidentes,* a group of 18th-century intellectuals and poets in Ouro Prêto that launched one of Brazil's first revolts against the Portuguese.

uyer beware: rubies, sapphires, and aquamarine can be heated to darken a light stone or lighten a dark one; emeralds can be "enhanced" with green oil; and lavender jadeite, lapis lazuli, onyx, and sardonyx is often dyed. Turquoise is waxed or treated with plastic. Worse, synthetic versions of gemstones are available worldwide. Gem dealers know their merchandise; if a deal looks too good to be true, it probably is.

—AH and SD

Unfortunately for Tiradentes, the revolt was quickly put down. His co-conspirators were jailed or exiled, and he was imprisoned and later drawn and quartered and decapitated. In the Museu da Inconfidencia, just across the square from his statue, we saw the pike on which Tiradentes' head was displayed as a warning to other would-be rebels. Not everything in the museum was so grisly, though. There were also exhibits of furniture from the time of the *Inconfidentes* and many architectural drawings and sculptures by Aleijadinho and Ataíde. Later, we visited a graceful, arched bridge, famous all over Brazil, called the Marilia. It is named after the girlfriend of Tomas Antonio Gonzaga, the *Inconfidentes'* leading poet, who immortalized her and the bridge in verse.

The cultural community in Ouro Prêto today remains vital. Well-known Brazilian painter Carlos Bracher lives in the city, as do whole families of more anonymous artists, who sculpt the same soapstone that Aleijadinho carved and who set up displays of their wares in the square outside the Pousada do Mondego. Poets are still held in high esteem, too, and it's not uncommon for local residents to use the phrase *meu poeta,* "my poet," as a term of endearment.

For the next four days we explored the city on our own. Ouro Prêto boasts thirteen churches, and we visited every one. All were constructed in the 18th century, and they are considered to be the finest examples of baroque architecture in the country. Brazilian baroque is different from the European version—simpler, and to my eye more beautiful. The churches of Ouro Prêto were built by "brotherhoods" similar to medieval trade guilds—groups made up not just of architects and artists but also of miners, shopkeepers, musicians, and so on. Their magnificence reflects the rivalry between the different brotherhoods, each of which wished to be seen as more pious than its competitors.

Along with São Francisco de Assis, my favorite church was that of Santa Efigenia dos Pretos, built by the local black slave community in 1742 and financed by money from the mine of Chico Rey, Brazil's first abolitionist. Rey was an African chieftain who was sold into slavery along with his tribe and shipped to Ouro Prêto to work in the mines. According to local lore, slaves here were allowed to keep a tiny percentage of the gold they dug, and Chico Rey and his tribe eventually managed to buy not only their freedom, but the entire mine. In thanksgiving, they built the church and dedicated it to St. Efigenia, who was the queen of Nubia.

Larger than the church of São Francisco, Santa Efigenia commands a high hill, its height accentuated by tall, angular bell towers. In the mid-1800s, it is said that ghosts emanated from the walls of the church, and some locals still believe it to be haunted. Perhaps to placate the spirits, the faithful leave offerings of candles, food, and flowers on the ornate central altar in front of statues of the black saints Benedito and Antônio de Nolo.

We missed Ouro Prêto's two main citywide celebrations. One is the annual Congado festival on May 13, the anniversary of the abolition of slavery in 1888. In the old days, freed slaves would elect a king and queen and wear silk and velvet costumes. According to our guide Pinto, it's still a good party. The other special occasion is *Semana Santa,* or Holy Week, the week before Easter, when the main streets of the town are decorated with what look like patterned carpets but are actually a combination of flower petals and colored sawdust. Children dress as angels and their mothers hang homemade lace from their balconies, as processions of holy relics make their way down the flowered streets.

Night life in Ouro Prêto is civilized and rather conversational in tone. There are no blaring discos or packed bars. Instead, the streets are filled with strolling couples or small groups of friends, and it is not uncommon to see people reading or sketching on the steps outside some well-lighted pizzeria. Most of the younger citizens seem to spend their evenings sitting in cafés discussing the day's events.

On one moonlit stroll, we heard music coming from a nearby hill and, following its sound, came upon the old Teatro Municipal, in which a rehearsal for a concert of baroque chamber music was in progress. We were invited in, and as we sat in the red velvet seats, listening to the delicate sound of flutes and violins surround us, I found myself thinking that this must have been what an evening's entertainment was like when the theater first opened in 1769.

On our last morning in Ouro Prêto, before we took a bus back to Belo Horizonte, I realized that I wanted to buy a keepsake. Since we hadn't bought any gems, we went into Brazil Gemas, a shop on the Praca Tiradentes, for one more look. Among a vast assortment of loose stones, a pair of perfectly matched aquamarines and another of imperial topazes caught my eye.

"We can set them in gold for you," the manager told me when he noticed my interest. "You can draw us a picture of what you want." I replied that, unfortunately, I had waited too long, and we were due to leave town in three hours. "No problem," he answered. So I drew a simple sketch, and when I came back almost three hours later, an exquisitely fashioned pair of aquamarine-and-topaz earrings awaited me. Remarkably, I was charged only for the gold and the gems—the workmanship was gratis. The cost was about $475 for four carats of good-quality aquamarine and seven carats of imperial topaz in a beautiful custom-made setting. When I went to the back room to thank the craftsman who had made the earrings, he showed me his handmade tools. The fact that they were so basic made me appreciate his artistry even more.

We made the bus with time to spare. The road from Ouro Prêto to Belo Horizonte is narrow, and the bus stops frequently to pick up or discharge passengers. But it was a comfortable, air-conditioned trip—and as the bus rumbled quietly along, I drifted off to sleep and dreamed about a lost city of gold and the riches we had found there.

In Sri Lanka, a much-traveled expatriate Englishwoman told Blaise Simpson of the endless fascination she had found in "the drama of the village." That has been the theme repeating itself in her travels ever since—she likes discovering out-of-the-way places that time and fashion have forgotten. A former editor at W *magazine and a contributor to* Vanity Fair *and the* Los Angeles Times, *Simpson lives on a houseboat in Sausalito, California, where she and her husband spend time sailing a historic sailboat, surfing the Internet, and plotting their next adventure—an extensive exploration of the Indonesian archipelago.*

✳

Despite the crime problems that trouble other parts of Brazil, and despite the thousands of dollars' worth of gemstones circulating in the town plaza and around it, no one looks over his shoulders for muggers in Ouro Prêto. All stone papers are unfolded openly, and there is little chicanery on the square. Although the dealers drive hard bargains, for the most part they are honest. Dishonest dealers hurt business and are quickly routed by the "stonies" who make their living selling their wares in the plaza. I was traveling with a group of American gem dealers when two members of my party bought what they believed to be blue tourmaline. Our tour guide thought different, took the pieces to a dealer she knew, and learned they were glass. She then approached a group of street vendors she knew to be Ouro Prêto fixtures, explained what had happened, and said, "It's up to you to find the seller. It's your reputation that is on the line." Within two hours the honest vendors had found the culprit and turned him over to the police, who made him return the Americans' money before they carted him off to jail. Later, the street vendors met our group as we were leaving a restaurant. They crowded around us but this time they were not selling. They wanted to know if everything was OK, if they were still in the Americans' good books. We gave them a heartfelt thumbs-up.

—Sharon Elaine Thompson, "The Roving
Stone Dealers of Minas Gerais"

Fishing for Peacocks

An angler goes to great lengths in his
quest to hook a prized river fish.

I FLEW ALMOST 3,000 MILES FROM MIAMI TO MANAUS, BRAZIL, in the middle of the night via an airline named after a prominent Bolivian drug dealer. I was up before dawn to fly four more hours in a single-engine floatplane over an endless canopy of primordial jungle. Finally I was dropped off on an obscure river hundreds of miles from the nearest human settlement somewhere in the Amazon Basin.

Adding to our concern were the impending torrential rains and, in the back of my head, all those amazing Amazonian horror stories I heard as a kid: man-eating jaguars, parasitic *candirú,* electric eels, freshwater stingrays, giant spiders, swarms of ants, killer bees; scores of poisonous snakes, and non-poisonous snakes the size of telephone poles; malaria, dengue, chagas, yellow fever, schistosomiasis, hemmorhagic fever; fungus, heat rash, infection, and inch-long botfly larvae crawling under your skin.

Why? Why would anybody do this? We hopelessly addicted fishing bums are always looking for a justification to experience exotic angling, nature, and cultures far from the so-called civilized world. The epitome of this ideal is the Amazon and its extensive list of gamefish—as exotic as the land itself. Depending upon the watershed, there are as many as twenty different gamefish—all with fantastic names to match their peculiar appearances: *pirapitinga, tambaqui, aruanã, pirarucú, pirapucu, bicuda, jancundá, traida, pirarara, matrincha, peixe cachorra, pescada, arapá,* and *surubim* just to name a few. Of all the great Amazonian gamefish, though, the one that truly stands out is the giant peacock bass: what the Brazilians call *tucunaré azul.*

Tucunaré are not bass at all, but members of the *Cichlid* family— a group of highly aggressive tropical fishes that have adapted to the Amazon's harsh environment. The *tucunaré's* striking beauty starts with blazing fluorescent-red eyes set into a backdrop of green, yellow, red, orange, and black. Top it all off with a brilliant black and yellow eye spot at the base of the tail—an adaptation evolved to distract attacking schools of piranhas, who immobilize their prey by first biting their eyes out.

Concentrations of giant *tucunaré* exist nowhere else in the world except specific locations throughout the Amazon Basin. The trick is to find one of those secret rivers with the exact environmental conditions conducive to holding big fish. It often takes months of searching an area almost the size of the U.S. (with ten tributaries as large as or larger than the Mississippi) to find a worthwhile fishery.

Two years ago I spent two intensive weeks scouting northern Brazil with a local outfitter, Luis Brown, floatplane pilot Bennie DeMerchant, and my jungle-wise guide, Sidenei DePassos. So here I am again, ready to embark upon a second adventure.

The plan is simple. Luis and Bennie drop Sidenei and me off on the upper Preto River, an unexplored basin that Luis thinks is promising. While they go on to scout several other rivers, we assess the Preto as a possible site for a future fishing camp. Two days later, they pick us up for more exploring.

After a three-hour flight from Manaus, the Preto appears in the distance like a copper-colored snake cutting its way through brilliant emerald surroundings. Bennie circles a likely looking spot, cuts power, and descends onto the river.

The plane, a Cessna 185 Skywagon, is so loaded with fuel that supplies are kept to a minimum. A ten-foot folding boat is strapped to the pontoons; our other gear consists of a five-horse outboard, a six-watt radio, two hammocks, one small tarp, one bag of *farinha* (cassava flour), one small loaf of bread, and a battered old aluminum pot for boiling water. Luis tosses me a small bag of black Brazilian coffee—he makes it seem like a real concession. We quickly assemble the boat and then unload our supplies. With that he bids me luck and safe travels, then shoves us off and climbs into the plane, which taxis into the center of the river, and roars off in a blast of water and exhaust, leaving behind an eerie silence.

Slowly the jungle comes back to life. A *guan,* the Amazon's version of a turkey, starts its jazzy syncopated call—*buh-ba-bah-bah-boom…boom!* A lone katydid answers with a series of high-pitched chirps from a nearby palm, and a whistling toucan joins the singalong. Two squawking macaws land atop an *abacaba* palm, while a yellow-rumped weaver bird returns to its intricate nest with an array of warbled notes. The whole jungle is soon an overwhelming chorus of booms, squeaks, roars, bellows, chirps, squawks, and cries.

Within the hour we've boated some thirty fish between three and five pounds. Unfortunately, they are all an assortment of the Amazon's smaller gamefish. Most of them are the *barboleta tucunaré*—a small species of peacock bass that seldom grows much larger than eight pounds. We also catch and release few *traida.* Sidenei calls them "*sabonete com dentes*"—fanged bars of soap.

By five o'clock or so in the afternoon I've landed well over 100 *barboleta tucunaré,* but still no sign of the larger *paca* or *azul* variety. By now the monsoon clouds have formed not far to the south of us, swirling and rising. Soon the rains will arrive, descending like a tidal wave, and ending all fishing until next year's dry season.

We paddle out to the mouth of the lagoon, within casting distance of a small cluster of boulders. On the first cast, my fly is taken by a fairly large *tucunaré.* The frantic fish rushes to the surface in a thrashing boil of blood and glistening silver, surrounded by a frenzied school of white piranha. Now I know why the river holds so few big *tucunaré.*

Within seconds the piranhas disembowel their victim, removing much of its flesh in a froth of blood and water. The snapping jaws are audible some 30 yards away, but the melee doesn't last long. What little remains slowly descends into the tannin-stained gloom.

One of the piranha grabs the fly. After a brief struggle the fish grudgingly comes to the boat with a dozen more of its companions greedily nipping at the protruding bucktail. Sidenei reaches down and carefully grasps the four-pound fish behind the gills, heedlessly singing an off-tune rendition of *"Besame Muito"* to the fish. He looks away for only a split second while attempting to remove the streamer fly, and the hook pops loose.

The piranha snaps its jaws closed, neatly removing the tip of Sidenei's pinkie and a sizable piece of fingernail. The teeth are so sharp that Sidenei feels no pain whatsoever, but the white bone and spurting blood make him wince in disgust. The piranha's jaw make a sick popping sound every time they snap shut on the remains of the finger. Sidenei buries the blade of the screwdriver between the startled piranha's eyes. "We'll eat that one," he says in Portuguese, plucking

In the afternoon, the job was to bring in the catch from the gill nets, and I estimate we had over 80 kilos of fish, which we cleaned on the river bank. All the entrails, heads and muck were tossed into the slow current in front of us. When we had finished, one fellow announced he was going for a swim. We all did our best to dissuade him, after all we had just dumped 20 kilos of blood and guts right there and the water must be swarming with piranha. He paid us no heed so I gave up trying and furtively got out my camera. I was not going to miss the scoop of the century, the first authentic piranha attack. In he went, and I followed him through the viewfinder as we all held our breath. Well, the bastard swam for ten minutes and nothing happened. Nothing. Not even when, in my disappointment, I suggested he go out farther and try swimming downstream.

—John Harrison, *Up the Creek: An Amazon Adventure*

the mangled fingertip from the fish's twitching jaws. Sidenei inspects the finger meat and then tosses it into the water like some useless piece of trash. It is eaten before it can settle out of sight.

We take the piranha incident as an omen, and decide to end the day's fishing. Camp is set on a sweeping white beach void of caiman and jaguar tracks. Sidenei dresses his wound while I clean and cook the piranha over a small fire. The fish seems to be staring at me with a hellish cooked-in grin.

Dinner consists solely of fish and *farinha,* and somehow that seems enough. There is something ironic about eating the finger-eater, but at this point we are both so hungry it really doesn't matter. We sit without speaking, watching the river and the thunder-heads that still loom on the southern horizon.

After dinner, we pitch our hammocks and tarp, then settle in for the night. The river's high acidity prevents mosquitoes from hatching, so we need no netting.

A small band of howler monkeys moves into the nearby, trees to get a close look at us. The alpha male begins his horrid territorial roaring—a clamor somewhere between King Kong and a 500-pound German shepherd—which is audible as far as ten miles away. The roaring suddenly stops, and from somewhere far back in the blackness a jaguar moans its deep guttural call, like a demonic cello player sawing the same notes over and over. Sidenei builds up the fire and restlessly settles back into his hammock, cradling a single-barrel 12-gauge shotgun he calls *boca quent*—"hot mouth."

At dawn the howlers again commence their roaring. The jaguar has decided not to dine on *gringo* and all is well. Sidenei brews a stout pot of jungle coffee. We share a stale crust of bread, then head downriver toward the pickup location.

By noon we reach the confluence of the east and west branches of the Preto River. On the far shore a small campfire smolders next to a primitive structure of several palm fronds stacked atop a skeletal foundation of thin sticks.

We boat over to the campsite and wade ashore to see if anyone is about, stopping to inspect an assortment of charred animal parts atop a crudely built grill made of green sticks. A few are recognizable: the shell and a single clenched claw of an armadillo; the torso, head still intact, of an unlucky woolly monkey. Sidenei looks about warily.

From well inside the jungle a male voice calls out in an indiscernible language. It is soon answered by another man, and then several more people join in until the surrounding trees are full of clamoring voices. One by one they appear from the forest—tiny, stoutly built people, the largest no taller than five feet. Most have little or no clothing, though they all wear intricate necklaces strung with black and red seeds of the *tento* tree, bones, feathers, and jaguar, peccary, and freshwater dolphin teeth. Sidenei says they are Pan-rá (pronounced *pan-ha*) Indians, a nomadic hunter-gatherer tribe who still lead the exact lives of their ancient ancestors.

Bows in hand, the men of the group timidly approach the river bank, bellowing at each other in their rapid dialect. The women and children remain close to the jungle's edge, nervously chattering like a clutch of scared chickens.

It is my clothing, and especially my sunglasses, that scare them the most. I must appear to them like some giant white-skinned apparition from another planet. I take off my hat and glasses and try to look as *friendly* as possible. Soon their curiosity gets the better of them, and before long the whole boat is surrounded. Just as they're starting to calm down, the floatplane comes roaring around the bend in the river, only five feet off the water, flying full throttle. When Bennie spots us he instantly cuts power and puts down, throwing up a great rooster tail. The Pan-rá bolt for the jungle in terror.

We quickly load our gear while Luis interrogates me about the river. I explain the apparent piranha infestation as we pile into the scorching cockpit. Bennie taxis us into position and we roar up over the tree line toward our next stop, the Rio Alegria, the "river of happiness." Luis has heard rumors of that river's giant *tucunaré*, but it's all speculative and sketchy at best. Bennie gains as much altitude as possible, to give him "…more time to pray if the engine quits."

At 3,000 feet the jungle looks like an endless green ocean. There is not a single landmark as far as the eye can see. Luis pulls out his hand-held GPS and takes a reading: 63 degrees 50 minutes west, 00 degrees 07 minutes north. We're right on the equator. To the west is the setting sun and to the south the massive cloud bank, as thick and imposing as ever, gold and salmon in the fading light. Bennie is becoming increasingly edgy, nervously glancing down at several Operational Navigation Charts (ONCs), the GPS, and finally out the window. The river is nowhere in sight.

After several panicky minutes, the outline of a river appears barely discernible on the darkening horizon. We head straight for the nearest bend in the river where, by sheer luck, a small boat sits moored along the bank. The chances of running into people are wildly unlikely, but somehow we've managed to blunder right on top of them. Bennie idles back and we float down onto the river's surface. Another five minutes and it would have been too dark to land.

An old man suddenly comes madly paddling out of a nearby lagoon in his tiny dugout. He heads straight for his little boat; surely he's seen a floatplane before. Luis scrambles out on the float and explains that we're sport fishermen from Manaus looking for *tucunaré*. The man stops his crazed paddling and looks back at the floatplane as if he's just seen a ghost. He waves us over without saying a word, quickly docking his canoe alongside his little junk. Several worried faces peer out of the boat's open window.

Luis rows the plane over to the boat and we exchange formal greetings. The man's name is Euodio Pizzerra de Araujo. He and his small family have boated two straight weeks from Manaus to collect *piasaba*—a type of palm frond used as bristles in industrial brushes. He tells us he plans to return to Manaus and sell his harvest when the rains make the lower part of the river navigable.

Bennie hands Euodio a picture of himself with a nine-kilo *tucunaré,* asking him if he's seen any such fish in the Alegria. Euodio laughs, telling us that he speared and ate a *tucunaré* last night that was much larger than the one pictured. He says the river is full of big fish but wants to know why we've come so far from Manaus to fish for them when they sell them in the city market. Luis explains that we want to catch them for fun and release them unharmed. A slow smile spreads across Euodio's face. "Sport fishing" in the Amazon is an oxymoron—you catch a fish and you kill it, no exceptions. Our explanations are useless. Euodio looks at me in a pitying manner and offers me a bowl of macaw stew. I've never eaten macaw, so I ask him how they taste.

He grins his wide, toothless, smile. "My son, much like parrot, but there's more meat." Euodio takes out an ancient aluminum bowl and piles various macaw parts atop a mound of cassava flour. A drumstick, with clenched claw still attached, rolls off the top of the heap. To refuse the meal would be an unforgivable insult, so with a forced smile, I accept it. The macaw is delicious.

At sunrise, Euodio and his eldest son are ready to fish. Their little dugouts are only large enough for two people, so I go with Euodio while Euodio's son takes Bennie. Together we paddle up-river into a huge lagoon rimmed with towering kapok trees. Large schools of tilapia, silver dollar, and discus fish skitter nervously along the shoreline. From somewhere out of sight comes the terrific splash of a feeding peacock bass.

Euodio laughs hysterically when I pull out my fly rod and begin casting. He wants to know what on earth I plan to accomplish with the *xicote da agau*—water whip—I'm using. I do my best to make him understand, but he can't see why I won't just use live bait. The *tucunaré* always "…swallow the bait deep in their stomachs; they never escape."

From the center of the lagoon comes a great commotion. It looks like children thrashing in a pool on a hot summer day. The giant *tucunaré* have surfaced to feed.

Panicked baitfish, some twenty inches long, desperately skip across the water's surface. Three tremendous wakes follow in hot pursuit. The stampede heads straight for Bennie's boat. He flips his fly into the chaos and the water explodes where it lands. One of the peacocks engulfs the streamer, then races away, dragging the canoe along like a toy boat. Euodio paddles us over so we can get a good look at the fish. The *tucunaré* surfaces like a green crocodile with the 4/0 bucktail looking insignificant in its huge mouth. The fish doesn't even know it's hooked.

Suddenly two others appear out of nowhere and attack the hooked fish, trying to get at the protruding fly. Water shoots ten feet in all directions. I quickly cast my fly toward the shock wave, while Euodio struggles to steady us. A *tucunaré* pounces on the fly and races toward a fallen tree. Line peels off my reel and the fish instantly snaps my 50-pound tippet under a submerged log.

Bennie's fish stays out in open water, making several deep, powerful runs before coming to the boat. It surfaces as if to get a good look at its antagonist and then boils off again, easily towing the boat another 100 yards or so before stopping. After fifteen minutes of struggle, the fish finally comes up on its side. Bennie carefully tails the giant *tucunaré* and gently lays it on the gunwale of the dugout.

The fish is one of the largest *tunucaré* I've ever seen. I lay my tape measure across it. Thirty-seven inches. My scale says 24 pounds exactly. Bennie carefully lifts it up, places it in the water, and rocks it back and forth. Euodio shrieks in protest. With a powerful sweep of its tail the fish disappears into the depths.

Bennie glances up and his smile suddenly disappears. A curtain of rain is bearing down on us like a Biblical catastrophe. We must return to the plane immediately or there will be no way out.

We race back to the plane. The wind has already started to pickup. Luis hastily pays Euodio with an assortment of flies, lures, hooks, and fishing line, which has more value to him than money.

Bennie taxis us out into the main river, full power, flaps down. He crosses himself and we roar up over the canopy, circling around once to wave good-bye to Euodio and his family. The river slips from sight behind the first layer of clouds. Rain blasting the windshield, we are enshrouded in a nightmarish wall of water. With any luck we'll be back in Manaus before nightfall. I sit back, close my eyes, and think about Bennie's monstrous *tucunaré*. The psychedelic fish has captured my soul.

Born and raised in Santa Fe, New Mexico, Garrett VeneKlasen spends much of his time trying to quell his obsessive angling addiction—an endeavor that continues to lead him to some of the most obscure corners of the "uncivilized" world. His work has appeared in such publications as Field & Stream, Men's Journal, Fly Fisherman, The Angling Report, *and* The Orvis News. *His television credits include host/writer of ESPN's* Fly Fishing America *and writer/producer of TNN's* North American Sportsman.

Fishing for Peacocks 215

He now freelance writes and operates a specialized angler's international travel and information research service out of Angel Fire, New Mexico.

✻

My favorite Amazon fish is the *tucunaré*—a beautiful yellow-green fish with a marking like an eye on its flank. It reminds me of the European perch in shape, and by its dorsal fin that becomes erect when angry or frightened. It is also a fine fighter. When filleted, coated in flour and fried, it is delicious. We also caught a brown, scaly fish with pink eyes that I had never seen before. I later learned it was a *trairão,* but for a few weeks we scientifically named it "the bony bastard," and we were to catch many of them.

—John Harrison, *Up the Creek: An Amazon Adventure*

PART THREE

GOING YOUR OWN WAY

JIM LO SCALZO

✦ ✦ ✦

Upriver Chapter

A 2,100-mile boat journey west on the Amazon fills
pages in the author's book of global understanding.

FROM THE ROOF OF MY HOTEL IN BELÉM, AT THE MOUTH OF THE
Amazon River, I see nothing but forest reaching the horizon in all
directions but east.

Situated just one degree below the equator, Belém is the
Amazon's link with the Atlantic. It is the largest port on the river,
where oversized freighters fill their hulls with Amazonian com-
modities before filing back to sea. But for those wishing to head
the other way, into the wild heart of the deepest jungle on Earth,
the city offers a far more ambitious opportunity. From here it is
possible to run the river like a highway across the entire width of
the Amazon rainforest, leapfrogging from village to village on small
fruit and cargo boats until finally reaching Iquitos, Peru, 2,100
miles to the west.

Cargo boats, two-tiered relics of the rubber boom, offer a life-
line to frontier towns along the river, supplying them with everything from bananas to building supplies. Packed in as tightly as
cargo, passengers fill the upper decks—first come, first serve. On
these boats, *capacity* is not a popular word. Nor is *speed*—most chug
along at a stately four miles per hour. But I've got more time on
my hands than money, and in the Amazon there's no cheaper way

to travel. To reach Iquitos, I figure it will take $200 (for boat fare, which includes three meals a day) and six weeks, with a few exploratory detours along the way.

This journey depends on the commerce of the Amazon River, and searching Belém's floating market for the next boat headed upstream, I get my first glimpse of the river's bounty. Hundreds of fishermen are scurrying around their boats unloading baskets of crab and shrimp and turtle. The pride of their catch— the sharks, sawfish, and *pirarucú*, the world's largest freshwater fish—sway from great hooks at the entrance to the docks. I browse past gray river eels, coiled like sausage, and giant stingrays flipped on their backs, bellies glistening white in the sun; past bushels of clams and oysters, and caimans with hammock cords tied around their snouts; past hundreds of piranhas, thousands of sardines, and giant catfish, some more than seven feet long, stacked like logs in a cord. There are more species of fish in this river than the entire Atlantic Ocean. When I ask a vendor the name of the peculiar mixture of fish in the market's largest display, he points to a wooden sign that reads *desconhecidos*, Portuguese for "unknowns."

The king of the river is the pirarucú. Pea green with large, gritty, saw-edged scales that make excellent fingernail files, the pirarucú grows to ten feet and 250 pounds. For a fish it is remarkably mammalian, caring for its young until they reach four months. Up to 160 fry have been seen following around the mother, who secretes from pores in her head a milky fluid to which they home. The pirarucú has gills, but it also has one lung, and come up for air every three minutes.

—Alex Shoumatoff,
The Rivers Amazon

I board a small cargo boat, its lower deck loaded with bushels of onions. Within seconds, a wire-thin man with the name Raimundo stitched on a worn red baseball cap hops from the pilothouse. "Captain, captain," he says, pointing to himself. I ask him how much to Santarém, the next major port, about 500 miles upriver. "I think maybe $200," he says. I stare at him expressionless. "Or maybe $30," he says. I give him the thumbs-up sign, and he gives me a toothless smile and steers me to the upper deck.

Though the boat doesn't leave until morning, the passenger deck upstairs is already crammed with 30 Brazilians, swaying back and forth in brightly colored hammocks. It's a hard-core crowd—mostly shirtless men with unlit cigarettes dangling from their lips. All eyes are on me as I weave through the congestion, and suddenly I feel queasy with intimidation. I catch glimpses of lewd tattoos, long diagonal scars, and the tip of a machete gleaming from a passenger's rucksack. I store my gear on a ceiling rack, sling my hammock at the edge of the deck, and read away the last hours before sleep.

We ship out before dawn, but our departure is so smooth I don't wake up. Only when another passenger's hammock bumps into mine do I realize that Belém has been replaced with jungle—a tight, knotted weave of vegetation slipping beautifully by in different shades of green. The river is wider than I imagined. Our boat is small enough to ply close to shore, and I can barely see the forest on the other side.

The jungle's edge is sprinkled with bird life, and I continually inspect it through my binoculars, checking off various species of parrot, macaw, and toucan in my *Amazonian Field Guide*. Occasionally we pass the stilt homes of *caboclos*, the mixed-race descendants of Indians and Portuguese. Hearing our engine, children paddle out in dugout canoes and try to hitch a ride by grabbing hold of our stern. Passengers and crew cheer them on, but our wake is jarring and most of the young *caboclos* laugh in failure.

Vendors are a bit more persistent, however, and they leech on to our hull with boatloads of caimans, turtles, and river fish. Members of the crew buy their fancy and cook it up with rice and beans. Everyone eats together at a large table on the lower deck, and during the meal we discuss river lore and local politics.

My initial perceptions of the other passengers turn out to be off-base. They're a tough lot for sure, but as friendly and chatty as a group of Girl Scouts. On the river, confinement breeds camaraderie, and many of the passengers become openly protective of me. During lunch, when a crew member hands me a plate that isn't overflowing with food, he endures a scolding from two dozen passengers.

By early afternoon, when the heat is at its most intense, we move our conversation upstairs over a game of dominoes, and in this way pass most of our days—establishing friendships, drinking *cachaça*, and watching pink river dolphins race in the boat's wake.

Like other passengers, I keep my distance from the crew. When night falls, they become a drunken, unruly bunch, and in the mornings, they shovel their beer bottles into the river. The same method of disposal applies to other garbage, spent fuel drums, and one unlucky passenger short on fare.

We arrive in Santarém under the blaze of a midday sun. It is a dumpy little town with lots of mosquitoes and little culture, and I stay only long enough to find another vessel heading upriver: a banana boat. It's much smaller than the first, and I sling my hammock next to a talkative *caboclo* named Edilson. He's a handsome old man who, minus the cigarette, instantly calls to mind the molded portrait on the Indian-head penny: the long braided hair, the steep nose, the omniscient expression. His voice is equally enduring, straining out word after word; a rickety talking machine filling my journey with stories of a richer Amazônia, the one from his youth. He says river travel reminds him of being young and carefree.

Only much later, when we sit alone at the rear of the boat watching a storm gather in the eastern sky, does he admit that his longing for youth isn't as much out of fondness as from years of living with shame. Twenty years ago, when demand for his artistry of handmade wooden carvings began to wane, Edilson accepted work on the controversial Transamazonian Highway, Brazil's early-1970s attempt to alleviate coastal population pressures. The military government hired thousands of workers to clear a 1,900-mile highway across the rainforest, from Belém to Cruzeiro do Sul, on the Peruvian border. Hearing promises of cheap land and future urban development, thousands of families quickly migrated via the highway into the interior, only to be devastated by disease, infertile land, and hostile Indians. Funding for the highway quickly evaporated and most of the road was left unpaved.

When the Transamazonian went under, Edilson and another *caboclo* turned to poaching. "For twelve years we moved cat and otter skins in Rio Branco," he says. "Then in one week I figure the jungle had had enough. My partner was shot in the neck by a Kanamari's arrow—and I got this." He lifts his pant leg to show where a highly feared Amazonian disease called leishmaniasis has blackened his shins and thighs. Transmitted by sandflies, leishmaniasis is a parasite that invades the lymphatic system and, like leprosy, causes lesions on the victim's arms, legs, and face.

Barely able to walk, Edilson now lives with his daughter in Santarém, selling the carvings that once before earned his living. He claims not to be a religious man, but every time we pass a missionary church, which is surprisingly often, he removes his hat and bows his head.

At the end of the third day the forest grows eerily silent. Then the water swirls with foam, and the trees are shadowed by steel; an unlikely modern sprawl called Manaus appears. It's an obnoxious sight so deep in the jungle; a damp, dilapidated city with a rare urban history. A century ago Manaus was just another backwater community. Then a young Scotsman named John Dunlop invented the car tire, rubber demand skyrocketed, and local plantation owners leaned back and grinned. They grew the only source in the world. In just a few years, Manaus became one of the wealthiest cities in the Western Hemisphere. Newfound rubber barons reveled in their opulence. They imported their homes from Europe in prefabricated blocks. They sent their clothes to Paris to be laundered and built a lavish opera house to pass the long summer nights. But while the barons were toasting their success, a British botanist named Henry Wickham managed to smuggle some rubber seeds out of Amazônia, grow them into saplings in London's Kew Gardens, and successfully replant them in the British colonies of Ceylon and Malaysia. The Asian rubber trees flourished, and Brazil's rubber boom came to a screeching halt.

Today, tourism is the boom industry. Hundreds of guides roam the streets offering alligator hunts and jungle hikes. I finally give in to a two-week trek with a fast-talking guide named Assad.

We take a small boat 80 miles up the Rio Negro before entering the forest. Our only provisions are a bag of rice and a bag of salt. "The rest," Assad promises, "will come to us." We walk long and hard but in the dense vegetation only cover a few miles a day. It is virtually impossible to keep dry. In some areas the forest is completely submerged, and we wade through shoulder-high water with our packs held over our heads. In other areas the forest just sweats, dampening everything with a sticky white mist. At night, rain showers tear through the jungle canopy, and through our lean-tos. I'm not a fan of sleeping in wet clothes and on more than one occasion bitch at Assad for telling me to leave my tent behind.

During the days, we have good fortune with wildlife, spotting numerous species of monkey and bird, encountering only nonpoisonous snakes and no injured animals. Insects are hardly more than an annoyance, until one night, when I follow the beam of Assad's flashlight onto the back of my hand, where two rose-colored bites have achieved a peculiar size. I show him a third, more irritating bite under my right foot and he nods in a silent, self-confirming way. "You've got botflies," he says. "They're a parasitic insect. Nothing to worry about." With admirable ease he quickly, painlessly, lances all three, pinching from each a thick, milky larvae. He says that the larvae are completely benign, though had they been left to themselves, they would have eaten quite a hole before growing to size and worming out from under my skin.

> *I*t is significant that the fascination of outsiders with Amazonian life forms centers on those species which have highly charged implications for humanity's self-image as king of the global campus: piranha and caimans because they can eat people; parrots because they "speak;" bôto because they are pink, warm, and fetal; candiru because they are attention-grabbing genital parasites; electric eels because they pre-date the age of Duracell; monkeys because we covet their prehensile tails; pythons because, like electric eels, their eyes are bigger than their stomachs.*
>
> —Stephen Nugent, *Big Mouth: The Amazon Speaks*

Our afternoons are spent fishing for piranha in the flooded forest areas called *igapós*; we pull in twenty an hour with ease. They are thin but tasty little carnivores, not nearly as ferocious as their reputation. We also eat tortoise, palm hearts, Brazil nuts, and a tart Amazonian fruit called *cupuaçu*. Late on the twelfth day we reach a *caboclo* farm on the Rio Negro where the residents serve us tapir with pineapple slices and coconut milk.

After dinner I notice Assad hurriedly packing his rucksack. "I think I'm going back to Manaus," he says without looking up.

"You're leaving right now?"

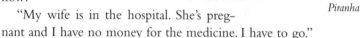

Piranha

"My wife is in the hospital. She's pregnant and I have no money for the medicine. I have to go."

"For what medicine?" I ask, but Assad doesn't answer. "Do you mind if I stay?"

"I don't mind," he says. "Boats go by all the time. Have the *caboclos* paddle you out to one. That's what I'm gonna do."

Though I figure his story is bogus, just meant to fatten his tip, it still works on me. After two weeks in the jungle with Assad I'm sad to lose his company. I tip him well and watch two children paddle him to a passing boat on the far end of the river.

I borrow a hammock from the farm's owner, a bony 50-year-old named Ery. I sling it outside, under what looks like a straw gazebo, and fall asleep instantly. The next morning Ery awakens me before dawn. He is eager to give me a tour of his fields before beginning the day's work. In a lingering blue darkness, he shows me where he has labored to turn twelve acres of forest into a thriving manioc plantation. With his son translating, Ery tells me the soil is infertile and unforgiving. "I burned all this forest to help the soil. Still I can only farm for four years before it turns barren. Then I have to start over."

Out here, Ery's agricultural efforts seem quite harmless, even admirable, but similar farms keep adding up. At the end of World War II, tropical rainforest covered fourteen percent of the Earth's land surface. Now only half of that remains.

Only one boat a week makes the six-day trip upriver from
Manaus to the Colombian border. Last week's boat didn't run, so
I have to travel with twice as many passengers crammed above
twice as much freight. I am in good company though, with a
Swedish couple on their way across South America and an eigh-
teen-year-old sociology student named Cleo, returning from a
field study in Manaus. From her features—flat nose, full lips, and
black, almond-shaped eyes—I would have guessed she was
Polynesian. But she's a member of the Yagua tribe in western
Amazônia.

The Swedes and I bombard Cleo with questions about the
Yagua lifestyle: What clothes do your people wear? What do their
homes look like? What do they think of outsiders?

"Maybe I should just take you there," Cleo answers.

When we reach Leticia, on the Brazil-Colombia border, Cleo
borrows a motor canoe from a Yagua living in town. Leticia is
more populous than I expected. The town's narrow streets are
filled with cafés, bars, and bicyclists. On the river bank is a large,
open-air fruit market. The Swedes and I buy some bananas and
passion fruit, jump aboard the motor canoe, and ride with Cleo
one hour north to the Yagua village of clay adobes with thatched
roofs. Though I am pleased to see that such proximity to Leticia
has not overrun the Yagua's tribal architecture, I am completely
surprised when I meet Cleo's son, both because I didn't know she
had one and because he wears a t-shirt that reads, "I'm Bart
Simpson. Who the hell are you?" However, some of the Yagua wear
their traditional dress, and we spend the day watching them weave
baskets, spear catfish, and smoke Marlboro Lights.

Late in the afternoon, I slip out for a swim and am already
waist deep in the water when two Yagua, walking parallel to the
shore line, casually call to me that the water is infested with *candiru*. I stare at them surprised for a moment and then quickly run
out. The Yagua find this particularly amusing. The *candiru*, a tooth-
pick-sized species of catfish, is one of the most highly feared creatures in Amazônia. Attracted to the scent of uric acid, this
remarkable little menace has adopted the nasty habit of swimming

into a person's urethra and lodging itself there at the painful expense of its host.

In the evening, Cleo and several other Yagua express their enthusiasm for having outsiders visit their community. Contrary to what I expect, they feel that attempts to shelter their community are completely self-serving. "For twelve years I walked barefoot," says Cleo. "Then a man from Leticia boated to our bank and sold me a pair of shoes, and I couldn't believe how they felt. Why should others be denied such a basic comfort? What's right for the Yanomamo isn't right for all of us."

The semi-nomadic Yanomamo is considered one of the most primitive tribes in Amazônia. In order to preserve its culture, Brazil permits visitation by outsiders only for health or sociologic reasons—and only after the visitors undergo rigorous physical examinations to make sure they're free from diseases that could infect the tribe.

Cleo's philosophy seems to be the right balance for the less isolated tribes. "Everyone wants to see how we live," says Cleo. "They want to hear our folklore and buy our crafts and all this interest helps us. It gives incentive to adapt without forgetting tradition."

Cleo helps me find a boat named the *Juliana* for the last 500 miles to Iquitos. A regal oak beauty, the *Juliana* is quite possibly the most idyllic boat on the river. With his boat full of ripening bananas, the captain has no choice but to leave right away. He charges me only $20 for the final leg of my trip, bringing the total to $130—well within my budget.

With only six other passengers on the *Juliana*, I look forward to an uncommonly peaceful voyage. We ship out at noon, and within a half hour all signs of civilization are behind us. The river is much narrower now—the Amazon of my dreams. Vegetation swarms with prehistoric fury: it drapes over the water's edge and across the river itself, enshrouding like fog around our every movement. I scan the treetops, the sandbanks, the brown waters, searching for some movement, any movement. And just when I think I can make out that shadowed figure in the trees, that circling something in the river, there is a slap of water, or a thrash of leaves, and the beast retreats unseen. In the fierce midday sun, caiman show less concern for stealth, basking by the hundreds along narrow, bone-white beaches. Occasionally the captain pulls a .22 from his belt and, with one hand still on the wheel, fires several rounds through the pilothouse window, sending the silver giants waddling back into the darkness. "They bother me," he says.

For some reason the captain only laughs when I ask his name. He's a real river character, an unshaven, tattooed mess. He's the type of guy who always looks hungover—gut drooping below his shirt, hair flat on one side and ruffled on the other, cheeks pinched to keep from belching. His demeanor is friendly, though, and at night, over glasses of *cachaça*, he shows me black-and-white photos of his boat when it was used in Werner Herzog's film *Fitzcarraldo*. "This one's my favorite," he says, pulling out an eight-by-ten of himself on the bow of the *Juliana*. Dozens of Campas Indians, used as extras in the film, surround the captain and aim their arrows into the camera. "This is the way I used to look, before fifteen years on the river gave me this." He slaps his gut and jiggles it up and down. In the photograph, he looks like a film star himself. His shirtsleeves are rolled up and his arms are taut and tan. His hair is wet and combed back, as if he just came in from a swim, and he is wearing a smug, assertive smile. It's a romantic image, and the captain raises his glass to toast its memory.

A bottle and a half later, when the captain dons a clean shirt and, to much applause, proclaims his feared entry into the passengers' card game, I climb the bow ladder and sling my hammock on the roof of the boat. Swaying there in light drunken rhythm, watching the jungle pass below the Southern Cross, Iquitos seems impossibly far away. And yet in two days we are there, plying along the crest of its banks, looking for a place to dock. It's a quiet little city, notable only for being the end of the line. From here the Amazon goes up, way up to its source on Mt. Misti, high in the Peruvian Andes.

I weave through thousands of bananas and disembark with the other passengers. The captain and crew wave good-bye from the *Juliana's* upper deck. I climb the hundred or so steps leading from the docks to the town, make an uncertain left, and search for a place to stay. An outdoor café overlooking the port catches my attention instead. I have a seat at the edge of its large wooden porch and sip through the first bottle of wine I've seen in nearly two months. The docks below me are especially calm. All the boats have already been moored for the night, and the last of the vendors are enjoying a lazy game of cards, the great river unwinding behind them like a thick brown ribbon. I watch them for some time, laughing and carrying on like old friends.

"The Earth is a book," said St. Augustine, "and those who do not travel read only one page." Indeed, travel is a most profound educator. It awakens us to the persistent lure of our past, to the thrill of entering a foreign land, eager to experience and savor, like a breath held in our lungs, life. And so I decide to hang on in Iquitos, maybe read a few books and try the local food, and wait for the same hopeful curiosity that took hold of our ancestors, when they gazed across the broad plains of Africa and felt the urge to move on.

The chance to see wild macaws and toucans drew Jim Lo Scalzo, an amateur birder, to the Amazon. Had he foreseen encounters with botflies, tarantulas, and a twenty-foot anaconda, he may have just gone to the zoo. After his journey up the Amazon, Lo Scalzo left behind riverboats for a rent-a-car. In the fall of 1995 he drove 19,600 miles across 47 U.S. states (he missed Nevada) photographing a book for Random House entitled Letters to Our Children. *He works as a staff photographer for* U.S. News & World Report *in Washington, D.C. and now is content to spot blue herons over the Potomac.*

*

Before it was home to a thousand and one cultures, Amazônia was a desert. A limbo of tree limbs. A distant planet, shimmering and rotting, where no human had ever set foot. Only a child could imagine it, because this forest reflected his mind, wild and melancholy. Truly, a supernature.

—Jacques Meunier and A. M. Savarin, *The Amazonian Chronicles*

ALAN D. EAMES

✦ ✦ ✦

He'll Have Another

A man's quest for the rarest beers on Earth takes him
to Amazônia, where Indians have been brewing
the stuff for a couple of thousand years.

TIED TO A TREE, HANS STADEN SIPPED BEER AND WATCHED IN horror as the Tupinambas clubbed, disemboweled, and roasted their captives during a 16th-century beer and barbecue ritual.

Held prisoner by Brazilian cannibals for nine months, the German gunner Staden, in 1557, wrote one of the first accounts of beer brewing in the jungles of South America. "Now it is their [the Indians'] custom when they are about to kill a man, for the people to brew a beer from roots called Kawi, and after they have drunk this they kill their victim," wrote Staden. In his memoirs,

H̶ans Staden, taken pris-
oner soon after the
Conquest, saved himself by using
"White God" magic to cure a
chief. In his memoirs, he described
many cannibal feasts, which often
lasted for days.

—Carleton Beals, *Nomads and*
Empire Builders: Native Peoples and
Cultures of South America

Staden noted that no Indian captive could be killed until this special beer had been readied, and it was further customary to make sure that the intended meal got his share of the brew before he was dispatched to the grill.

Earlier explorers also mentioned native beers. In 1500,

Pedro Carvajal of Spain located a cache of beer in an abandoned Amazonian village:"Here was found a great quantity of corn and oats from which the Indians make bread and very good beer…and this beer is to be had in great plenty. There was found a dispensing place for this beer…our men were not a little delighted…."

In quest of the rarest beers on Earth, I retraced Staden's trail through Brazil's jungles. In 1985, 400 years after Staden's death, I was approached by a group of Vermonters who had decided to enter the specialty beer business. These discriminating women preferred full-bodied, dark beers and stouts and deplored the fact that most of the 700 beers imported into America at the time were of the lager-pilsner types. Pooling their capital and incorporating under the name Amazon, Inc., they determined to import the richest dark beer available anywhere.

"From where in the world does the best dark beer come?" these ladies asked me, and my thoughts immediately turned to a black beer that has remained in my memory as the best of the hundreds I have sampled. Sadly, the tiny Brazilian brewery that concocted this black ambrosia (called *Ingleshna*) was later leveled to provide parking space for a giant lager beer factory. Nonetheless, logic dictated that somewhere in Brazil, if not in the cities, then perhaps deep within the frontier regions, there must be a beer producer brewing a *preta* or *negra* beer of equal splendor.

Bankrolled by Amazon, Inc., I soon found myself on a plane for the first of many long flights to Brazil to find the brew that lived up to my still-vivid memory of black beer perfection.

Brazil is enormous. Getting from place to place, I traveled by large jet and one-engine bush planes from city to settlement. A land of incredible beauty and varied landscape, Brazil is unique— and beer is queen. And throughout, from deep jungle outposts to the cosmopolitan beaches of Rio, beer is everywhere with tall pint *tulipa* glasses of cool draft beer or *chopp* at less than 50 cents.

The downside of this beer paradise is that the lager giants— Brahmah, Antarctica, and Kaiser—have forced the small, regional breweries—those that made the obscure, native styles of beer—out of business. Still, I found that many of the vanished brands had evolved from Indian beers, and some of these were still brewed by tribes living on the Amazon and Xingu rivers.

Beginning at the University Museum in São Paulo, I identified the names and approximate locations of remaining beer-brewing Indians. Many of these tribes inhabited the Xingu Basin—a vast, partially unmapped and not easily accessible region south of the Amazon. Then, flying to Manaus, a river port, I hired two guides, bought provisions, and set out on my first journey on the Amazon to look for black beer.

Xingu beer label

It is estimated that Amazonian Indians have brewed beer for at least 2,000 years. The type and quality of beer depend on the grain and other available ingredients. The two most common varieties are manioc, or *masato*, beer brewed from starchy manioc root and *chicha*, or corn beer, which is brewed from maize. Other less popular styles include *algaroba* beer, brewed from the seeds of the carob tree by tribes in Argentina and Paraguay. Still other tribes brew beer from sweet potatoes, pumpkins, pears, apples, quince, strawberries, melons, and papaya. These fruits and vegetables often supplement the basic corn or manioc beer recipes.

Fermentation requires contact of sugar with airborne "ambient" yeasts. A source of fermentable sugar, honey is almost always used in Indian-brewed beer. In primitive societies, women are the keepers of the brewhouse secrets. From the journals of Hans Staden comes this account of brewing, which along the Amazon continues unchanged:

> The women make the beer. They take manioc roots and cook them in huge pans. They take the manioc from the pans…and let it cool. Young girls…chew the manioc and put it into containers. After the roots have been chewed, [they] put the paste into a pan and put water in and heat…containers are

buried in the floor and are considered vats for beer. Pour…the manioc and cover the vats tightly. It will ferment on its own and like this will become strong. Leave it buried for two days. Drink it and you'll get drunk. It's thick and tastes good. Each of the huts prepares its own beer when the village wants to have a celebration…they sit around the containers that they're drinking from, some on pieces of logs, some on the bare floor. The women serve the beer as custom demands. They drink all night long. They also dance, at times around the burning bonfires, they shout and play their instruments, and they make a terrible noise once they are really drunk.

By chewing grain, the ptyalin present in human saliva converts the cereal starches into fermentable sugars. Bolivian Indians employ more sophisticated methods in malting—after soaking and sprouting barley, they dry and roast the grain, adding additional moist, chewed mash to the fermenting vats. Indian beers, drunk everyday as a dietary staple, are lagered two to four days. They contain about 2.2 percent to 3.2 percent alcohol by volume. Ceremonial brews, on the other hand, are lagered for much longer periods and often have considerably greater strength.

Fermentation occurs in earthen jars. Some of these vessels hold up to 30 gallons. They are buried until the brew is deemed ready. Other methods call for the beer to be fermented uncovered in hollowed out logs. Some Indians add leaves or fern stems to impart bitterness, flavor, and strength to ceremonial brews. The Lencas of Central America employ perhaps the strangest additive of all. These Indians are fond of adding sheep or goat droppings to beer while it is brewing.

Taste and color of Indian beer varies across regions. Manioc beers tend to be milky white. *Chichas* are pale to dark yellow and taste varies from tart to downright sour. Beer color depends on how long the malt is roasted. The darkest beers are most often found to the north of the Amazon.

Among all South American Indians, beer drinking has deep social and religious significance. Hunting and fishing expeditions, harvests, gatherings to discuss war and peace, and weddings, births, and funerals all call for beer drinking by the entire tribe. The western Brazilian Remos and the north-central Amazonian Tapajos mix cremated human bones into their beer, thereby ensuring that the spirits of the departed are absorbed back into the living.

As nossas boas qua lidades que não são poucas.

To our good qualities, which are not few.

—Brazilian toast

Indian beer festivals are joyous occasions lasting from a few hours to many days—and always until the last drop of beer has been imbibed. The resulting intoxication can range from a mild buzz to alcoholic coma as the celebrants move from house to house, finishing off all the beer in each hut before shuffling on. Beer drinking is always done in groups; the solitary drinker is unknown.

On the lower Xingu, drinking bouts last for days without violence or discord. Elsewhere, beer festivals often lead to fatal encounters. In these more aggressive tribes, the women brewsters may themselves refrain from more than a few beers, ever alert and prepared to hide the men's weapons at the first sign of trouble. The men will continue to drink to oblivion, often thrusting a paddle or "vomit stick" down the throat. Thus, they induce vomiting, making room for ever more beer. Battles within the tribe ignite from resentments among those who have used beer fests as an occasion for romantic encounters with each other's wives. Sociologists believe that beer orgies have a cathartic effect, and that "clearing the air" helps ensure the stability of the group.

Above all, beer is an important dietary staple providing critical nutrition for all. As a daily food supplement, the Jívaros of southern Ecuador drink three to four gallons of mild beer per person per day.

Indians offer varied explanations of the value of beer in their lives. The Urubus of Brazil call beer *Kau-I*, meaning "crazy water," in the belief that a spirit in the beer makes the drinker crazy. Ecuadorian Indians say that beer is a gift from spirits to "rejoice the heart" and to lend courage in asking favors from a friend. Peruvian tribes feel that beer enhances bravery before battle; they also trust in a concept called *Aymara*—a system of beer medicine. Mato Grosso tribes think beer drinking important for witch doctor training, owing to the spiritual insights gained while drunk. Numerous tribes worship plant spirits, praying that fermentation be quick and the brew strong.

Two years of travel in Brazil's wilderness regions eventually yielded a clear understanding of Indian beer brewing. *Negra*, or black beers, result from pan-roasting grain over the acrid smoke of wood fires—a process similar to the smoked beer brewing of Bamberg, Germany. Using ambient yeasts and fermenting at high ale-like temperatures for long periods, the resulting beer is spectacular.

In Rio, a Brazilian association of Amazon, Inc. reached agreement with the Cacador brewery of Santa Catarina to brew black beer on a commercial basis for distribution in the United States and Brazil. Early in 1988, the first production of Xingu Black Beer was made from pan-roasted barley, hops, water, and yeast. Fermentation took place in shallow, open porcelain fermentation tanks—all the malting and brewing steps carried out by hand labor. Cacador's wood-fired boilers and German three-tiered brewhouse—all very medieval in aspect—managed to do full justice to the jungle brews of the Amazon River. Xingu Black Beer is a true lager, not an ale or stout. Jet black, with color so dense that light will not pass through it, this black Brazilian, with its craggy brown head of foam, tastes remarkably light and fruity, with a flavor *The New York Times* found "slightly smoky." The rest is beer history.

Xingu received rave reviews in both America and Europe. And best of all, South America is no longer a forgotten chapter in the literature of beer.

Alternately called "The Indiana Jones of Beer" and "The Beer King" by the press, Alan Eames is an internationally known beer historian, consultant, and beer anthropologist. He has written many articles and several books on beer, including The Secret Life of Beer, A Beer Drinkers Companion, Blood, Sweat and Beers, *and* Oldenberg Beer Drinkers Bible. *Eames is also a founding director of the American Museum of Brewing History and Fine Arts in Fort Mitchell, Kentucky. He lives with his family in Brattleboro, Vermont.*

★

As a seasoned jungle hand with several days in the steamy dark heart of Brazil's Amazon Basin under my webbed Eddie Bauer expedition belt, I herewith offer my Top Ten Tips for anyone with a hankering to check out this remarkable region before it's slashed and burned into oblivion:

1. Monkeys may jump enthusiastically onto your head, but odds are they won't tear off your ears.

2. Tarantulas like to loll on handrails.

3. That bizarre genetic mishap you may just find snoozing lazily on your couch—the one that looks like something like a pig-pony and nuzzles like a lap dog—is a tapir. Don't worry; it's harmless.

4. Those frightening killer bees are wusses compared with some of the other insects you'll find in this jungle.

5. Piranhas are vicious little buggers, but they're far from the most dangerous critters in the river.

6. Yes, you can swim in the Amazon. (See Number 5)

7. The mosquitoes are not as big as hummingbirds.

8. Sweat is good—the more you produce, the better.

9. The narrow dugout canoes in which you do your exploring can tip over pretty easily. (See Number 5)

And last—but not least....

10. The local Cerveja Antarctica will very rapidly become your best friend. Cerveja Antarctica is beer—beer that comes in huge half-liter-plus bottles and usually stays nice and chilled for the entire five minutes it takes to consume one. That's one thing about Brazil: the country may be a shambles, its money hyperinflated to such a point of overload that a dinner can easily cost millions of whatever the stuff is now called, but the beer is always cold.

—Richard J. Pietschmann, "Jungle Fever"

RACHEL CHRISTMAS DERRICK

✦ ✦ ✦

Benin via Bahia

An African-American senses her roots in Brazil's
former slave capital.

SOME PEOPLE RETURN FROM SALVADOR, THE CAPITAL OF THE STATE of Bahia in northeast Brazil, raving about the gorgeous beaches, the elaborate baroque churches, the weathered pastel houses with red tile roofs and delicate wrought-iron balconies. But what impressed me most was Bahia's unmistakable African flavor.

I had traveled to Brazil with friends, all of us African-Americans eager to see what had become of others who were part of the African diaspora. Growing up in the United States, we had been taught by an educational system that said black history began with slavery. By visiting Bahia, we hoped to learn something more about ourselves.

For three centuries, beginning in the mid-1500s, Africans were wrenched from their homes by Portuguese colonists and forced to work on Brazilian sugarcane plantations. These slaves and their descendants refused to relinquish many aspects of their old ways of life. While this African heritage is apparent throughout the country, it is most celebrated in Bahia, where the predominantly black population has kept its past in its present. Overall, Brazil's population is estimated to be 44 percent black or mixed race. The state of Bahia is more than 80 percent black.

Today, Brazil's best-known music and dance, and its mystical spirituality—part of the lives of blacks and whites alike—can only be described as African. Yorubas from what is today Nigeria and Benin even left their mark on the language of the colonizers: the Portuguese spoken in Bahia today sings with a pronounced Yoruban accent and is often peppered with Yoruban words.

More than one hundred years after the abolition of slavery—Brazil was the last nation in the Western Hemisphere to end this institution, in 1888—black Brazilians still have little economic or political power, and racial discrimination is alive and well. Illiteracy is twice as common among African-Brazilians as whites. Census figures also show that even when black people are able to become doctors, teachers, and engineers, they earn 20 percent to 25 percent less than their white counterparts. As an American, I found this scenario hauntingly familiar. Yet there was something wonderfully refreshing and uplifting in the way Bahians are still so firmly connected to our common roots.

A two-hour flight north of Rio, Salvador is a collage of contrasts. The architectural legacy of the Portuguese, who arrived in 1500, is strongest in the *Cidade Alta,* Upper City, perched at the top of a cliff. The newer *Cidade Baixa,* Lower City, sprawls along the glistening Bay of All Saints. Steep roads and an elevator that has been packing people in since 1873 connect the two sections of the country's original capital.

As we wandered along Salvador's narrow, cobblestone streets, we witnessed an intriguing cultural mélange. Decked out in African-style turbans and white, 18th-century European dresses over layers of petticoats, young women framed in doorways beckoned us to browse in lace and gem shops. Samba, indistinguishable from the music of Angola, pulsed from radios in bars near handsome colonial houses and old churches with extravagant façades.

> *The sights, smells, noises of Bahia seem to have crossed directly from the bulge of one continent to that of another.*
>
> —John Gunther,
> *Inside South America*

At the Largo do Pelourínho, the square where slaves were once sold, artists were busy creating and selling paintings and wood carvings of Yoruban gods. I asked about a statue that bore an uncanny resemblance to hirsute Cousin It of the popular American TV show *The Addams Family*. The sculptor explained that this figure, covered with straw from head to toe, was Omolú, the god who protected against disease.

Stirring bubbling pots, older women sat on many a street corner tempting us with aromatic *acarajé*, known as *acará* in Nigeria, Benin, and Togo. These dumplings—made from mashed beans and dried shrimp and spread with a sauce of onions, peppers, ginger, and more shrimp—are fried in dark orange *dendê* (palm oil), which is widely used in both African and Bahian cooking.

In a tree-shaded plaza, we stopped to watch pairs of men practicing *capoeira*, clearly an ancestor of break dancing. With fast and furious flips, kicks, and cartwheels, the highly skilled dancers came dangerously close without touching. Briefly transforming their bodies into abstract sculpture while standing on their hands, they would freeze their legs in one position, then another.

This martial art was brought from Angola by slaves. Forbidden by their masters to fight, it is said they disguised this form of self-defense as art. Periodically, the dancers traded places with musicians playing drums or plucking the *berimbau*, made from a gourd attached to a tall bow.

We relaxed for a while in Castro Alves Plaza, where bronze statues and clusters of trees surrounded a fountain. Here the country's largest street fair erupts during Carnaval. To prepare for the festivities, black nationalist musical groups called Afro-*blocos* study a particular African country or theme and incorporate it into their dance and costumes for the massive annual procession.

As we admired the stark white, domed church that dominated the plaza, persistent children tried to sell us colorful ribbons, or *lembranças do Bonfim*. They instructed us to tie them around our wrists with three knots as we made three wishes. When the ribbons wear off naturally, we were told, our wishes would come true, just as with the West Indian "wish bracelets" I'd seen in the Caribbean.

Bahia's highly seasoned food is made with nuts, ginger, coconut milk, and other ingredients also used in West African cuisine. One afternoon we ate lunch at Casa da Gamboa, which several Bahians had insisted we try for local specialties. Two members of our group were delighted to discover that the delicious *carurú*, a spicy shrimp dish with okra, cashew nuts, and peanuts, tasted just like a stew they had eaten in Benin.

As in many African cultures, in Brazil the spiritual is at least as important as the concrete. Reality is imaginatively fashioned into scores of shapes and forms. In Igrejá Nossa Senhora do Bonfim, one of the city's most important churches, reproductions of arms, legs, and other body parts hang on walls and from the ceiling as an expression of thanks for cures of ailments.

We were awed by the painstaking detail of the interiors of Bahia's many ornate churches, such as Salvador's São Francisco, where hand-carved walls are covered in gold leaf. But at the same time, we were filled with disgust by the barren anterooms we saw in several churches where slaves were forced to worship—if they were allowed inside at all. In response to these restrictions, slaves built Our Lady of the Rosary of Blacks, an 18th-century church that stands in Largo do Pelourinho. Only black saints decorate the altar.

Quite unintentionally, the Catholic Church played a major role in allowing African beliefs and customs to be inextricably woven into the fabric of Brazilian society. Prohibited from worshiping their *orixás*, or gods, slaves simply outwitted their masters: they continued to pray to the *orixás* by pretending to worship Catholic saints with similar traits. Rooted in Yoruban traditions and known as Candomblé, this mystical religion is practiced today by many Brazilians, most of whom also consider themselves devout Catholics.

There may be a church on nearly every corner in Salvador, but Candomblé houses, where *orixás* are honored in riveting ceremonies, are even more numerous. First at the Afro-Brazilian Museum and then at the Museum of the City, we examined the musical instruments, weapons, and elaborate costumes associated with the powerful gods. Each *orixá* represents a different set of natural and spiritual forces. Oxalá, god of the land, is the symbol of purity, and Iemanjá is the goddess of the sea and motherhood. They are the offspring of Oloram, creator of the world.

One night, a woman we befriended invited us to a ceremony at the home of a relative. The men sat crowded on benches on one side of the room, the women on the other. Wearing flowing layered garments and long strings of tiny, colored beads, participants danced in a circle to thunderous drums.

Periodically, people would suddenly fall to the floor and flail around in a trance-like state, exhibiting characteristics of *orixás* as the gods manifested themselves. Except for the drums and the fact that the ceremony was conducted in Yoruba, we might have been in a black American Baptist church watching parishioners "get the spirit."

Another day, we saw an example of Brazil's classic religious syncretism during a visit to Bahia's 17th-century town of Cachoeira, about 70 miles outside of Salvador. We had come for the festival held each August by the *Irmandade Nossa Senhora da Boa*

A big river runs through resplendent Cachoeira, the jewel of fertile Recôncavo region. So concerned were the elected officials that the river would overrun its banks (as had repeatedly happened) that in the early 1980s they rallied and built a colossal dam at enormous taxpayer expense. The jewel of Recôncavo was safe, the politicians boasted, forever protected from the big bad river.

The sexy owner of a restaurant in downtown Cachoeira told me the story of the dam as I stared appreciatively at the wall beside my table. Painted black lines signified the high-water mark for floods since the restaurant opened twenty years earlier. The most recent high-water mark practically reached the ceiling. The date beside it: 1987.

"But what about the dam?" I said, recognizing that the dam had been completed by then.

"We were told its operator was asleep and didn't notice the water rising," the owner replied with a smile and a shrug.

"Bummer," I said.

Bummer, she nodded, and we both looked at the highest high-water mark in wonder.

—Scott Doggett, "Wet Again in Cachoeira"

Morte (Sisterhood of Our Lady of the Good Death). The story goes that the original members of this Catholic order were freed from slavery after their leader prayed for emancipation and died, hence the "good death." The church service was followed by a solemn procession of men and women in white, draped in black–and–red robes, and holding tall staffs.

Then, as samba and Brazilian reggae began blaring from loud-speakers, the streets filled with sensuous, fluid hip action and light-ning–speed footwork. In the center of it all, a woman in a long, full skirt appeared carrying a huge bowl of popcorn on her tur-baned head. As part of this festival for a Catholic order, this woman was paying homage to an African *orixá*—Omolú, the god whose statue I'd asked about in Salvador. The popcorn, which the woman showered into the outstretched hands of the crowd, sym-bolized a skin disease.

Three little girls were tapping my arm, asking me something in Portuguese. Not able to speak the language, I tried both in Spanish and in English to find out what they were saying. They took a few steps back, eyes wide, hands covering giggles. Their surprised faces seemed to ask, "Why are you making such strange sounds when you look just like everyone else here?"

It occurred to me that if my ancestors had been dropped off in Bahia instead of North Carolina, not only would I be speaking Portuguese instead of English, but my tongue might know its way around Yoruba as well.

Rachel Christmas Derrick discovered her passion for travel at a young age. Books, museum visits, and a vivid imagination enabled her to persuade her nursery school teacher that she had been to Africa before she had ever left the United States. Once she did start vacationing abroad with her family, she began writing about her adventures. Her work was first published at the age of fourteen in a national periodical. Since then, freelance assignments for many major newspapers and magazines have sent her to more than thirty countries.

★

In Rio, Our Lady of the Rosary Church is the site of the city's only black museum.… I visited the church often.… Every time I went I discovered another spot in it that Rio's blacks had made sacred. There was the dark room on the ground floor dedicated to the Archangel Michael and made hellishly hot by hundreds of votive candles, so many that gigantic vats covered with grids had been provided for them to drip into. I was told there that St. Michael is associated with the cult of the dead in Umbanda, but it took several visits before I realized that the statue was placed directly on a largish pile of bones, prayerfully described by one of the men in the crowded room as "the bones of unburied slaves...." Eventually I realized that almost every one of the objects in the Black Museum had been sacralized.... A massive carving of a black man's head, labeled "The Unknown Slave," always had a bouquet of roses on the ground before it, and often people would stop to whisper secrets into its ear....

The unknown slave of the unknown history of Brazil's unknown blacks. Seedy and corrupt as it was, the Black Museum was the only place in Rio where the descendants of slaves could have the sensation of physically, directly, being in touch with their own history. Lacking a Wailing Wall, a memorial, any official testimony to their suffering, they had turned the Black Museum into a shrine.

—Alma Guillermoprieto, *Samba*

PETRU POPESCU

★ ★ ★

Alone and Unarmed

A writer recounts the harrowing jungle misadventure
of photographer Loren McIntyre, abandoned by members
of the Mayoruna tribe deep in the Amazonian rainforest.

I WISH I COULD WALK IN A SPIRAL PATTERN, A "RETIRING SEARCH curve," as they call it in the Navy when they try to locate a sea-man fallen overboard and drifting away. Walk in a circle with an ever-increasing radius, alert for human refuse, for human smells or sounds, for anything that could be a clue to where Barnacle, the tribal leader, and his people are. But that's practically impossible: you can't follow a curved line in the forest any more than you can keep a straight one, because of buttresses, elevated roots, sec-ondary trunks, lianas shooting down and sprouting little legs and sticking them in the ground, under your very eyes sometimes.

L oren McIntyre, a longtime National Geographic *photographer and writer, spent 40 years exploring the Amazon forest and other parts of South America and, in 1971, located the Amazon River's source in the Andes. He died in May of 2003 at the age of 86.*

—AH and SD

All I can hope for is to find a rivulet and follow it until it merges with the main stream. I might stumble upon Barnacle en route, or if I reach the main stream I might find the camp I left on the beach, marked by that lupuna tree.

244

My other chance lies with Barnacle himself. He was friendly to me. It was other members of the tribe that abandoned me, that left me to die out here. It's not inconceivable that Barnacle would send a search party after me.

Barnacle. Amazing how much a part of my life he has become. He and his bunch of Protopanoans with spines in their lips.

I walk.

Between 6 a.m. and 8:30 a.m. (give or take half an hour), the temperature is bearable. I almost froze last night. I'm all right now. In an hour I'll be sweating and choking.

But I can't afford to stop, for fear that the tribe might weigh anchor again and move out of range. I have to budget my strength, move as fast as possible, and hope for some luck.

I see light ahead: the canopy is punctured. Sunlight pours into a clearing, making the air in it boil with humidity and higher temperature. I step into the clearing, look up, and glimpse, like the top of the Empire State Building fighting the clouds, a huge emergent tree, in bloom: masses of pink flowers float against sunlit strands of mist, at least 30 feet higher than the rest of the forest.

At this time, the air is still resonating with morning calls. Before the first sun ray, the howlers, the macaws, the orapendolas take up their instruments and go to it, *molto vivace*. There's a spasm of excitement in my heart as I notice that the clearing is littered with hacked-off branches: technological man was here with his buzzsaw, starting to clear a landing site.

I can't climb that huge tree without a rope or some other gear (the canopy is still the least-explored part of the rainforest; lately, biologists have used crossbows to shoot lines up over high branches, then pull up bigger lines fitted with pulleys and all sorts of other equipment, to climb to the canopy and watch it on a more continuous basis). But a man-made clearing encourages me. It looks like it was abandoned just days ago. I'm close to my fellow modern man, the rapacious developer. As objectionable as he may be, I welcome the proof of his presence. He can't be far. I can survive on jungle liquids till I find him. I've torn vines before to wring water out of them. Most leaves that look at all fleshy store

water, and most lianas do, too. The toxicity of the juices some of
them contain is a chance I have to take.

The area I'm in is the limit of how far the Incas journeyed out
of their mountains to explore the jungle.

I leave the clearing, walk back into the trees, stop to consider a
snack of fruits that look almost like blackberries. But they are sour
and their nutritional value must be minimal, so I move on. Five
minutes later, I glimpse another mass of light pouring through the
torn roof of foliage. Out here, prospecting teams are lowered from
hovering helicopters and *macheteiros* start hacking at branches, cutting a shaft downward through the many-storied foliage till they
reach the ground; then they fell trees to make helipads. I see a thick
rope stretching on the forest floor, some cable, probably, abandoned. The dusk of the forest floor makes it shine and glitter, as if
alive. I stop, realizing that it's not a cable but a two-lane traffic of
army ants. Thousands of them parade in opposite directions, often
scrambling over each other's backs, driven by an instinct that
knows no confusion. They carry fragments of some unidentified
matter toward a multiple-cone anthill of mud and leaves, its tallest
cone about four feet high. It looks like a busy downtown mall.

I follow the other lane away from the anthill and find a shoe,
reduced to its thick rubber sole and vestiges of its leather part. A
rich crush of ants engulfs it, disintegrating it, carrying away parti-
cles of it. I watch it with almost morbid curiosity, as if I'm seeing
a devoured corpse. Then I understand, but before I can fully artic-
ulate the thought, I start running along the freeway of ants.

And I find four bodies. I can tell they are human by their skulls:
not much tissue is left on their bones. The swarming, teeming shoal
of ants has reduced leather jackets to their zippers and metal buttons, and has shredded shirts, pants, underwear, everything. Piled
on top of each other, the remains look like a gruesome work of
art. The skulls have been cleaned thoroughly, except for patches of
hair and one baseball cap. They show jaws without gums and teeth
stained by tobacco, and they seem in subtle motion, as the ants,
crawling tirelessly over them, give an imperceptible flutter to those
sinister death grins. Little clouds of flies vibrate around the discar-

nate heads, like a film of busy, hungry life, but the ants don't give them much chance to break in.

Watching, morbidly curious, I notice an arrow coming out of a hulk of chest. Then I see another one, lying on the ground, loosened out of flesh that's not there anymore, and another. Their blackened ends could've been dipped in curare. They are whistling arrows; they sport the kind of boar bristles I saw Barnacle use to fasten the feathering onto the lean, graceful shafts.

I notice another column of ants, the leaf-cutting type. They look like hundreds of minuscule green umbrellas on a pilgrimage: en route to their anthill, each carries a piece of leaf, holding it above its head and body. *Sauvas.* Said to be so numerous that "if Brazil doesn't get rid of *sauvas*, *sauvas* will get rid of Brazil." Their vanguard prudently avoids the horde that dispatched the *macheteiros*.

I move around the scene and identify a chain saw, the metal shell over its engine bashed in. Somewhere in this mess might be wallets with the names of these people, but I can't bring myself to grope around with my hands in what's left of them. They probably belonged to some small prospecting operation, rather than to a government project; otherwise helicopters would've come back and evacuated their bodies.

*C*urare is one of the few words in the English language derived from Amazonian Indian dialects. Also called woorari, wourali, urari, *and various other names, curare is actually a blanket term for all arrow poisons prepared by tribal peoples from tropical plants. Most curares function by interfering with the transmission of electrical impulses from the nerves to the muscles. This causes the muscles—including the diaphragm, which controls breathing—to relax and eventually stop working. A curare victim can suffocate within just a few minutes. But new types of curares are still being discovered. While working in northern Brazil in the late 1960s, Harvard University Professor Richard Evans Schultes discovered an arrow poison that, instead of killing its victims outright, apparently stuns them by inducing hallucinations.*

—Mark J. Plotkin, *Tales of a Shaman's Apprentice: An Ethnobotanist Searches for New Medicines in the Amazon Rain Forest*

Yet, out here, that isn't so sure. The most amazing foul-ups happen, because of faulty phone connections, inaccurate maps, or just because of the Brazilian way. Search parties head in the wrong direction. People tire and decide that they've done everything in their power. A letter to the family closes the case, while the bones rot out here, forever part of the wild.

Should I wait here? Will there be a rescue party?

Looking at the condition of the bodies, it seems silly to think so. I sweat heavily; the heat has risen to its highest level for the day, where it will hover till the brief, unsatisfying dusk. I decide to go on. I just can't linger near this hideous exhibit. I hope I won't look like this in a few days.

There's a serial number on the deformed shell of the chainsaw, and I jot it down in my notebook. Maybe by reporting it, the missing men could be traced and identified.

I walk on, wondering if I haven't been moving in a circle. Where is the river? It could not have vanished. This underbrush should be crisscrossed by streams, brooks, subtributaries of all sizes, all pointing toward the main stream. I encounter not a trickle of water.

The itching I've been experiencing on my back, where I can't reach, has grown unbearable. In some sores on my back I feel the under-skin movement of what I'm sure is screw worms. Sometime later, I notice a swelling on my left forearm. I pull out my knife, open the swelling, and pull out a white maggot. The larva of a flesh-eating fly. I remember its scientific name, *Calitroga hominivorax*. *Hominivorax* means "devourer of men." An infestation of *Calitroga* can kill a full-grown steer in a week.

I keep walking, fantasizing every other instant that I hear the murmur of flowing water.

Whether I keep my direction or not, I no longer know. Another thought gets formulated inside me, and when it's whole it howls savagely, and all the ramparts of knowledge I built in 50 years are blown to bits. I was never part of nature! None of us were! Not even the Indians! I, we, always belonged to a vaster space.

This upsets me more than anything. Bushes block my way, but I stagger on, no longer paying attention to branches, thorns, cutting edges. They prick, bite, sting me. I just stagger on; I don't care. Climbing the gentle slope, I begin to hear something. A flow of water.

I step closer to the sound and then, within seconds it seems, I'm on my knees with my face in fresh water, drinking from a clear, narrow brook.

After a minute of drinking, of dousing my face and arms and of drinking again, I know it isn't a hallucination. I stagger up and follow the brook downstream, lose it behind a line of bushes, break through them to find it again, and keep following it.

It becomes a shallow stream. Rather than trying to follow the shore without a machete, I walk in the water or on the shore when it's not too overgrown. There is the danger of stepping on a stingray, so I look mostly down, but I'm aware of sunbeams occasionally penetrating the trees. This is one of the few cloudless days since I've been here. When unexpectedly the stream opens into a river flowing narrowly but clearly, I lift my head, look up a long stretch, and there, at the end of the water, where perspective narrows the two forested banks into a point, there rises, like a green church cupola, a mountain.

Am I seeing things?

The sun sparkles on its slopes and at its bottom, as if it were set with precious stones.

I know that the river is real, for I'm wading in it right this instant, but what about that mountain? I shut my fist loosely, peer through the hole, and what looks like a tumble of jewels becomes two waterfalls, parallel and so close that I wonder if I'm seeing double from fatigue.

I advance while the mirage holds. It is a twin waterfall.

I find a beach of white sand, untainted by forest floor rot. I sit down on it, pick at the swellings on my arms and shoulders, extracting more maggots, and watch the wonder.

This can only be the source of the Javari.

Finding it like this, when I felt lost and exhausted beyond caring, has a wonderful effect. I sit and watch till the colors of the river and the mountain slope start changing, while the sun begins slanting over my right shoulder. So I must be looking south.

I don't know much about the Javari's source, but this elevation, if I'm not dreaming it, must be the end of the Andes' reach into the plain. The last elevation, followed by two thousand miles of flatland. From the Andes to the Atlantic the altitude level drops only seven hundred feet. Some three inches per mile, making all the tributaries meander sluggishly, like giant snakes.

The mountain looks fairly tall, its crest hovering maybe a thousand feet above the forest. Like a twin jet of pearls, the Javari cascades out of it, splashing into the stream that flows right past me.

The beauty of this Shangri-la is absolute, and in no way designed for human visitors. It's been here for thousands of years, seen only by tribal Indians, boundary surveyors, and maybe a rubber tapper or two. The crash of the waterfall blows mist into the heavy air, feeding a dependent cosmos of leaves, aerial roots, and creatures.

Now I can follow the river, staying on its right bank.

But it's hard to leave this place. I finally do, still not sure whether the waterfall is real. I walk down, listening to its roar. I look over my shoulder and glimpse it back there, unchanged. Then the stream takes a turn. I follow it. The twin waterfall disappears. I have no more reason to turn and look back.

It would be untrue to say that I feel grief, but I feel something. A hard-to-define sadness, relating to that sight's perfection.

The hours pass, and I keep walking. Now the right bank is a string of pools and little bogs left after the seasonal lowering of the waters. I pause to rest next to a fallen tree and notice a little jaguar

Exploration is nothing more than a foray into the unknown, and a four-year-old child, wandering about alone in the department store, fits the definition as well as the snow-blind man wandering across the Khyber Pass. The explorer is the person who is lost.

—Tim Cahill,
Jaguars Ripped My Flesh

very occupied with something I can't figure out. It's a baby jaguar, under four feet long and very splattered with mud. He's using the tree trunk to hang above a muddy pool and dip a paw in it. The hair on his head is so frizzed up that I have trouble controlling a chuckle: he looks like some half-grown street urchin, totally in his own world.

I break a branch, betraying my presence. I need it to fight off the baby jaguar's mother, in case she's lurking nearby. He looks up, with yellow eyes bitten in the middle by a dark dash. He has that touch of intrigued attention in his stare, that how-can-I-get-you flicker of interest I've seen in other felines. I may be his first human.

I make no move. The water under him bubbles, recalling his attention, and two gray-green knobs surface, shining like a ceramic sculpture. A caiman's nostrils, followed by the whole snout. Its craggy skin is spotted almost like the jaguar's, and they're about the same size. Before the caiman can rise completely, the jaguar steadies his footing on the trunk, choosing his best angle of attack. Then he throws a foreleg around the caiman's neck, secures his grip, pulls the prey up, and tries to bite it behind the eye, where the neck is thinner and the scales more fragile. The caiman pulls down, and both splash into the water. They fight without any sounds except the thrashing and

Jaguar

splashing. Then the jaguar sinks his teeth deep behind the caiman's neck and starts pulling it out of the water again. The reptile's left eye, wide open, stares straight at me without any expression, of pain or amazement. It knows who will win, and I know, too.

Death in the forest is usually quiet, often undramatic; this time it fills me with an acute sense of loneliness. I feel so utterly alone that solitude's acidic taste cramps my bowels. Even the clammy heat feels like solitude of the saddest type. Forgotten, forgotten. Unneeded, useless.

I make it to the other shore. Suddenly I jackknife forward and fall on my stomach on rotting leaves. I order myself to crawl, but my body refuses to obey.

I remain lying, thinking of what will happen to me if I lose consciousness. There are jaguars in the area; I just sighted one. But jaguars rarely attack humans if unprovoked. Caimans are aggressive in the water, but seldom on land. Wild boars or even white-faced peccaries are what I fear. They're both carnivorous; when in packs of ten to twenty they unhesitatingly attack stragglers and can devour a human in minutes. Despite their prosaic appearance, they are the land piranhas of this region. Still more dangerous are the snakes and bugs, yet somehow I mind them less than the idea of being gobbled by pigs.

Well, I may never know. I manage to raise my face and see a lion marmoset, the smallest of all primates, observing me from a palm frond. With a humid little look in its eyes, as if ready to burst into tears. My last conscious impression is the marmoset's eyes. Death is a bank of klieg lights, being switched off. A vast theater in my head grows dim like a cavern, and then black.

They found me, and brought me back to the village.

I awoke in a hammock, sweating from high fever, under the hands of two shamans, who pulled gently at my limbs; finding no fracture, they turned me over and sucked out with their mouths the maggots and remaining thorns from my back.

Later, over a shaman's naked shoulder, I glimpsed the little pile of my belongings: pants, shirt, and notebook. My only links to the world I came from.

Then one of the shamans pressed his mouth to my forehead and "sucked out the demons." Then both shamans lit cigars of green tobacco and blew the smoke at my face and all over my torso. Then they stood on each side of the hammock and chanted, while I drifted back and forth between dream and reality.

Petru Popescu, a best-selling novelist and moviemaker in his native Romania, defected as dictator Nicolae Ceaucescu was entering his terminal dementia. Resolving to write in English, Popescu settled in Los Angeles, where he authored the scripts of the movies The Last Wave, Death of An Angel *(which he also directed), and* Nobody's Children. *He traveled around the world, visited native tribes, and befriended explorers—as evoked in the true story* Amazon Beaming, *excerpted here. One of Popescu's recurring themes is the re-adjustment of "civilized" heroes to unexplored wilderness, and their ensuing revelations about nature and themselves. He is the author of the novel,* Almost Adam, *and the autobiography,* The Return.

✳

Fortunately, as we've gone from one stopping point to another in the Amazon of northwestern Brazil, we've always had a guide. Otherwise, we would have ended up lost in the forest. That's especially true in this area where leaves cover the ground and you can't see clearly where the trail goes. Besides that, the trails crisscross one another: rubber trails, trails for avoiding rapids, and side trails. It's easy to wander from one to another.

This morning, when I was half impatiently looking for someone to go along with us as a guide, a ten-year-old girl who has lived in the forest her entire life told me, "It's all straight, *Seu* Padre. Just go straight ahead and you'll get there. You can't miss it." I smiled to myself and thought: "My God, how easy it is for her! But for those of us who aren't from here, the forest is as indecipherable as an Egyptian hieroglyph. We're illiterate, or just beginning with our first primer, when it comes to moving and living in the jungle."

—Clodovis Boff, *Feet-on-the-Ground Theology: A Brazilian Journey*

Finding Uncle Will

*An expatriate's grandnephew finds Southern
comfort in learning of the life and death
of* Confederado *William McCann.*

THE TOMB WAS A WHITE MARBLE BOX. A SORROWING ANGEL guarded it, her head turned in perpetual grief from the legend chiseled into the slab at her feet. In Portuguese, it began, "In memory of William Theodore McCann."

For nearly 80 years, Will McCann had rested here in this little cemetery in the small city of Pirassununga in the interior of Brazil's São Paulo state, waiting for me to come and reestablish contact on behalf of the Waco, Texas, kinfolk he left behind more than 120 years ago.

He had been one of hundreds of Texans among about 20,000 Southerners who chose to leave the fallen Confederacy and emigrate to Brazil in the years immediately following the War Between the States.

Some gave up and returned to the United States. But most of the families stayed to farm the famous *terra roxa* soil around the towns of Santa Barbara d'Oeste and Pirassununga. Their homes became the nucleus for the town of Americana, now a textile center with a population of 250,000. Their descendants live there to this day.

Will McCann settled in the village of Pirassununga, about 110 miles north of São Paulo. Twice he returned to Waco, once in

1898, again in 1910. My mother, now in her 90s, remembers his last visit. After that, the family heard nothing more from Will McCann.

My mother yearned to discover what had happened to him. How did he fare in far-off Brazil? Had he remarried? Was there perhaps a family of McCanns in Pirassununga? When and where did he die? I promised my mother I would go to Brazil and learn what became of Uncle Will.

My first stop was São Paulo. In the 1870s, the place had a population of just 30,000. Its French Empire public buildings decorated broad, shady streets of a gracious city on a broad plateau watered by four pretty rivers.

Today, it is home to twelve million people. The industrial heart of Brazil, São Paulo spreads out over an area of 772 square miles.

My first order of business was to learn more about *Los Confederados* and see if Uncle Will had left some kind of paper trail. I called Maria Eugenia Galvão, a reporter with *O Estado de São Paulo,* who had studied at Columbia University. When I told her of my quest and explained my mother's hope, her eyes filled with tears. Like Southerners, Paulistas love sentimental stories about lost causes. Maria put me in touch with Jo Simonetti, an archivist with the São Paulo Bibliotheca do Archivo.

Jo disappeared into the stacks and returned with clippings from *O Municipio,* Pirassununga's turn-of-the-century newspaper, official documents filed by the city fathers, a promotional brochure of 1904 describing the town and its leaders, and a history written in 1975 by M. P. de Godoy, of the National Council of Scientific and Technological Research. Finally, she offered the name and address in Americana of Judith McKnight Jones, the official historian of the Confederate colonists.

Suddenly Will McCann became more than a name. On arriving in Pirassununga in 1880 at the age of 41, he went into the dry goods business in partnership with an Englishman, Frederic George Port. Courthouse files established that he never remarried and died a bachelor.

There were photographs: McCann as a colonel of the Guarda

Nacional de Pirassununga, as a member of the Town Council, as a director of the republican (anti-royalist) party. There was a map indicating that grateful Pirassunungans had named a street after him.

But how to get to Pirassununga?

A call to Vera Marelim, a bilingual secretary at a chemical company whose name had been given to me by friends, helped lead to an answer. She suggested that I call a man by the name of Joe Alves, who worked as a driver and guide. And he spoke English.

On a brilliant October morning with the springtime temperature rising into the upper 80s, Joe and I motored northwest on a six-lane freeway, the Bandeirantes Highway. Its name honors pioneers, the "flag bearers," who broke trail into the interior. Rolling hills so similar to those of central Texas rose and fell in easy slopes. The land was formed from soft, red sandstone 200 million years old that lie atop a lava base. The rocks have decomposed into some of the thickest, richest, reddest topsoil on Earth. Because of it, Brazil leads the world in the production of coffee, sugar, and oranges. When freshly turned by the plow, the color vibrates so palpably that your eyes ache. Green fields of sugarcane and groves of orange trees soften the soil's glare.

Here and there, the slopes fell away in narrow defiles cut by watercourses. Japanese farmers work these valleys, growing vegetables and bananas in lush small farms. Since the turn of the century, Japanese have been immigrating to Brazil in large numbers and now constitute its third-largest ethnic minority. They grow so much of Brazil's produce that the lands around São Paulo are called the Green Belt.

Our destination was Americana, home for many of the Confederates. The city filled a wide valley with buildings roofed with red tile.

Judith McKnight Jones lives in Americana. She is the historian of the Fraternity of American Descendants and the author of a book in Portuguese, *Soldado Descansa!*, about *Los Confederados*. A Brazilian by birth, she is a descendant of the McKnight family from Texas and the widow of the late Dr. James Jones, whose family came from Alabama. I hoped *Dona* Jones could give some direction to my search. Her home, *Chácara Jones*, is located on what was once the outskirts of town. The large walled property shaded with fig and rubber trees now lies well within Americana's burgeoning city limits.

At 71, Judith McKnight Jones still spoke English with a Southern accent and twinkled for company as only a pert Southern belle can do.

In her cool parlor, we spread a genealogical feast, and spent two happy hours among our roots. Will McCann, it seems, was a great friend of the McKnights and stayed with them in Rio de Janeiro during the fatal illness of Emma, one of their daughters. But did McCann go with the rest of the Texans to São Paulo? After a careful search, Judith uncovered a letter listing McCann as one of the São Paulo settlers. Another piece of the puzzle found.

"How shall I proceed?" I asked Judith.

Roughly half of the 20,000 ex-Confederates who emigrated south—the biggest political exodus in U.S. history—settled in the wilderness, partly because Brazil still allowed slavery (until 1888), but mainly because Emperor Pedro II, in hopes of building a cotton kingdom, subsidized their trips, exempted them from his draft, guaranteed them freedom of religion, and sold land for 22 cents an acre. Some Confederates tried to establish plantations along the Amazon. But tropical illnesses and giant cotton-eating ants ended most jungle settlements. One colony prospered—a town called Villa Americana by the settlers, later shortened to Americana. The expatriates produced not only cotton but also watermelons, peaches, and pecans. Today, Americana is a thriving textile center, the only city in Brazil with a Confederate flag in its coat of arms.

—Jack Epstein, "Ancestor Worship in the Deep, Deep South," *U.S. News & World Report*

"Go to Santa Barbara d'Oeste and visit the Immigration Museum there," she advised. "Next, go to the Confederate Cemetery where many of the colonists are buried. Then look up Suzi and Adhemar Franchi in Pirassununga," she said. "They will help you."

The building in which the Immigration Museum is housed was built in 1893 as Santa Barbara's city hall and jail. Handsomely restored, its thick white walls house familiar implements from the 19th-century South. One exhibit contains a cast-iron cornbread mold in the shape of a corn cob, identical to the one my mother still uses in Waco. Along one wall stood a cooking range made in Cleveland. In a display case I beheld a six-shooter, the product of Samuel Colt of Connecticut. A violin rested under glass, and near it, sheet music for "Home, Sweet Home."

A docent gave me directions to the Confederate Cemetery, about eight miles southeast of Santa Barbara. Protestant *Confederados* created their own graveyard because Brazilian Catholics denied them permission to bury their dead in the consecrated ground of church cemeteries.

Road signs pointing to the cemetery led us down dirt roads amid cane fields and orange groves. We found the tombs of the old soldiers and their wives and children on a hilltop shaded by pine, fig and palm trees. Near a small chapel, an obelisk stood. The red field and blue bars of the Confederate battle flag adorned its base. The names of the families of the Lost Colony of the Confederacy were inscribed there, as on the Washington memorial to the dead of the Vietnam War. They evoked the people of England, Scotland, Ireland and Wales who settled the Southern states as colonists in yet an earlier wave of immigration. Now the pioneers rested in a rose-red land, their pioneering done.

Every Fourth of July, several hundred descendants of the Confederate families meet here to commemorate their past and to keep alive a proud tradition. They observe religious ceremonies and picnic on Southern fried chicken and biscuits. Most speak English, although it is becoming rare among the younger generation as they become assimilated into Brazilian culture.

In 1972, while still governor of Georgia, Jimmy Carter and his wife, Rosalynn, came to the Campo Cemitério. She located the grave of a great-uncle, W. S. Wise, who was born in South Carolina and died in Santa Barbara d'Oeste.

"My primary feeling," Carter said in an interview after his return, "was one of appreciation for their preserving in an almost unblemished way in names, inflections, and voices of their ancestors their obvious love for the United States. My most significant feeling was one of great sadness they had foregone for all those generations the enjoyment of being a part of this nation they still revere so deeply. The futility of it all was apparent. None of them looked upon their ancestors as mistaken. They didn't seem to feel any self-pity."

Alone on the hilltop, with the wind rustling the pine needles and birds calling from a nearby citrus grove, I sensed the shades of those doughty old warriors and their loyal wives. In abandoning one life, they had found another of value and quality before death claimed them.

Yet, Will McCann was not among their number. He had settled in Pirassununga, and there, the Franchis awaited to tell me about him. Now retired, Adhemar was once in the lumber business. His wife, Suzi, was born in Brazil. She is a descendant of the Terrells of Texas. Suzi learned English from her mother and grandmother, Susan Speed Smith, of Waco, my ancestral home.

Before getting down to business, Adhemar insisted that we have lunch at Cachoeira do Emas, Pirassununga's most celebrated attraction. We drove down a country road lined with eucalyptus trees to the *cachoeira,* or falls, where the Mogi-Guassu River descends in a series of cataracts. Fish swimming upstream to spawn must leap the falls. For centuries, people have come here to take them for food. The Tupi Indian word *pirassununga* translates loosely as "place where the fish go splash when they jump over the rocks."

Ancient fig trees lined the riverbanks. Snowy egrets stood in the shallows, on alert for minnows.

Will McCann came here with a group of frolicsome citizens on November 20, 1903. The event was reported in detail on the front page of *O Municipio.* The picnickers arrived in nineteen horse-drawn tilburys and cabriolets, accompanied by ten gentlemen on horseback. They dined on a long table set under "an enormous fig tree." Fish "served in all guises and in all possible sauces" was washed down with beer, red wine, and port wine. Dr. Oliveira thanked the picnickers on behalf of the organizers for coming to the outing. Mr. Pinto thanked the organizers on behalf of his stomach. The "gay outing to Cachoeira" gave them all "joy beyond price."

The spot remains as popular as ever. The restaurant's deeply recessed rooms opened directly onto the riverbanks. From high ceilings electric fans stirred the air. Bench-legged tables draped with white linen were set with heavy tableware. Courtly waiters served us. The cold beer was delicious. The fish—broiled, baked, fried, and steamed—was superb. The food came family style, with each dish brought to the table on a platter and passed around for diners to help themselves.

The Franchis showed me the street that now bears the name of Guilermo MacCan. It is a quiet residential lane paved with basalt cobblestones. A horse-drawn taxicab clopped by, taking home a family and a load of groceries. Passersby nodded in greeting. *Ipé* trees raised cones of golden blossoms toward the springtime sky.

Will McCann chose well. His hometown of choice today is prosperous and clean, its people courteous and welcoming. Even though Pirassunungans now number 80,000, they continue to use the solid brick-and-stone buildings that have served them for 150 years. "This is the real Brazil," I thought. "This is what *Los Confederados* had in mind."

Finally, the Franchis took me to the city's cemetery. They led me down a shady walk to Will McCann's tomb. "Born February 26, 1839; died November 30, 1918," the inscription read. His life had ended at home and among friends.

I placed a hand on the sun-warmed stone. "Hello, Uncle." My throat developed a lump. Odd. I never knew him, but I wish I had.

As a student, Downs Matthews discovered he was a dunce when it came to algebra and a weakling when it came to feats of strength. But he could type eighty words a minute! Those discoveries date back more than fifty years, and for nearly as long he's been writing for profit. Hailing from Houston, the fourth-generation Texan has written for dozens of periodicals ranging from Smithsonian *to* Sports Illustrated. *He specializes in science and technology subjects, but prefers natural history and nature travel. He is the author of several books for young readers, including the award-winning* Polar Bear Cubs *and* Arctic Foxes.

❋

A few of the newly freed slaves in the United States emigrated side by side with the Confederates to Brazil. Freedman Steve Watson was administrator to a São Paulo sawmill, one of a string of enterprises owned by Judge Dyer of Texas. Prior to the Civil War Watson was Dyer's slave. Given his freedom at war's end, he chose to remain with Dyer, whom he trusted, rather than take his chances in a risky Southern economy.

Watson was able to learn Portuguese, unlike most of the other colonists. He was an able leader and helped build the sawmill into a profitable enterprise. Dyer's nephew, Columbus Watson, from whom the freed man adopted his name, was the third partner in the enterprises at the New Texas colony. Products from the sawmill were transported by riverboat to Rio, finding a good market there. The enterprise came under severe financial strain, however, when their steamship was wrecked one stormy night at the entrance of the Juquia River. The loss was financially overwhelming and emotionally traumatic. Both Dyer and Columbus Watson soon headed back to the United States. Before leaving, however, they deeded all of the surviving property, the sawmill, and 1,200 acres of land to Steve Watson.

Watson gathered the remains of the business, rebuilt it and became very wealthy, married a Brazilian woman and raised a large family. He was highly admired in the region. In the area of the Juquia valley there are many Brazilian families with the name "Vassão," the Portuguese pronunciation of "Watson."

—Eugene C. Harter, *The Lost Colony of the Confederacy*

⋆ ⋆ ⋆

Amazon Stir-Fry

On a scientific expedition in the várzea, *Brazil's vast
flood plain, a hanger-on finds a way to fit in.*

WILL'S FINGER BECAME PROGRESSIVELY WORSE. IT WAS BLUE AND
swollen, though he insisted it did not hurt. Not much, anyway. The
red bump on the back of my hand had developed a fascinating
white crown. Pete walked out of the bedroom grumpier than
usual.

"The bloody goddamn bat pissed on me all night, the little
bugger."

Will and I laughed. Miriam laughed. Jonas and Antonio, who
did not understand a word of English, laughed.

"Oh yes, quite funny," Pete said smiling. "Try sleeping with a bat
pissing on you all night."

"Finger's worse this morning," Will said, showing Pete his bul-
bous thumb.

"Can't work with that," Pete told him, being a little fatherly.

"But we have a lot to do today sampling the floating meadows."

I swallowed a sip of coffee and said, "Can I help?"

"Would you mind terribly?" asked Pete.

"Of course not. If all you need is labor hauling nets, I think I
can handle that."

"That's all; even you could do it."

"Thanks, Pete."

"Oh, you might want to watch for the occasional anaconda, Brian," Pete said jokingly over his shoulder, referring to the giant water boas living in the *várzea*. They regularly grew to over twenty feet in length. The record was thirty-eight.

"And whatever laid into me," said Will, holding his hand in the air.

"Let's just hope we don't pull in any snakes, which we do one in five times," Pete replied, not kidding at all.

I dressed quickly and joined Pete and Will and Jonas in an outboard canoe. We sped up the Mamirauá to a smaller stream and motored to a grassy meadow floating in the current.

These floating meadows, islands of grass that thrived in the wet months, were an integral part of the *várzea* ecosystem. Manatees grazed on them, and small fish lived among them. Some species of spiders lived atop the grass. We pulled up to the island, a small one, and Pete and I got the net ready. Jonas sliced through the grass with his machete to carve out a section. Pete and I fed the net around the section and waited until the bottom weights had time to stretch the net vertically. Then he pulled on a line that closed off the bottom. We strained to pull in the grass and the net and whatever was inside. Once the net was aboard, we yanked up handfuls of grass, tossing them back in the water. Slowly, we uncovered a variety of life I never would have guessed would be living in the meadow. There were small catfish, water bugs, spiders, but, thankfully, no snakes. There was, however, an electric eel.

"Oh, god, do not touch the eel," Pete warned me.

Electric eels were common in the Amazon, and I had already seen several Will and Pete had brought back to the floating house. One was especially large, and even the *caboclos* avoided it. The jolt from an adult eel could knock a man over.

We sampled three grassy islands and brought the buckets of fish back to the house where

Electric eel

Pete and Will would sit and weigh and cut and describe, and amuse the *caboclos*.

That night, when the door was closed at sunset and the mention of dinner floated in the conversation, I volunteered to cook. Leftovers from the night before and from lunch, a *caldera*, naturally, were available, but I was having a hard time looking forward to more boiled fish and rice; and besides, I was feeling a little useless and wanted to help.

"Sounds good, Brian," Pete said. "You cook, do you?"

"I make the best Spam carbonara you ever tasted," I said.

"You are joking," Will exclaimed, a little horrified.

"Of course," I lied. In fact, I was hoping there might be a can of Spam on the kitchen shelves. There wasn't. There was a can of what I think was corned beef, although I could not be sure since I could not read the Arabic script. The can, a product of Brazil's burgeoning beef industry, had been destined for the Middle Eastern deserts but had somehow escaped to Tefé instead. Finally, I spotted a two-day-old fish, a *tambaqui*, which the *caboclos* had caught. It sat, split in half, on the wood planks of the floor.

I picked it up and sniffed it, fully expecting to smell decay, but it had been salted. More rooting around on the shelves and the floor yielded a potato and an onion. I also found some pepper and corn oil. The cook, I thought, had been holding out on us.

I grabbed a machete off the wall, hacked the poor *tambaqui* into chunks, and heated some oil in the only skillet.

Jonas came into the kitchen and out the back door. Then he came back in the kitchen and stared at me, the skillet, and the oil.

As the oil heated, I sliced the potato and the onion, then tossed them into the skillet. The version of home fries spluttered and spit and filled the house with the smell of frying onion.

Jonas was joined by the woman who had been cooking our delicious *calderas*. She was not happy. I smiled. She stood with her mouth gaping open at the havoc I was wreaking in her kitchen.

I used the machete to scrape the potatoes and onions in the skillet as they browned.

"Smells very good, Brian," Pete shouted from the outer room.

I had attracted a crowd. The *caboclos* stood in the doorway dumbfounded at the sight of frying potatoes. How would popular American TV hostess Martha Stewart handle this? "Yes, entertaining in the Amazon can be easy, and fun, too," I imagined her saying. "And now we will place the potatoes ever so decorously in the giant plastic bowl on the floor—presentation is everything, you know—and add more oil to the skillet to sauté our *tambaqui*.... "

I served the fried *tambaqui* and potatoes and onions. Pete and Will were grateful. There were tears of delight in their eyes because there was no *caldera* in their bellies.

"Oh, God, this is delicious," Pete panted between bites, demonstrating once and for all that a captive audience is the best audience.

I carried my plastic plate into the kitchen, where Jonas stood at the stove explaining to the gathered *caboclos*, all of whom were eating *caldera*, what I had done to the *tambaqui*. I don't think they believed him. The cook sat on the wood planks just outside the back entrance and sloshed river water into the skillet. She gave me a dirty look. I offered the leftover fish and potatoes to the *caboclos*. They thought it was disgusting. The cook threw the food into the river. From this moment on, whenever they were near me, the *caboclos* shook their heads and chuckled. The one *caboclo* who had been sharing my room moved out.

Brian Alexander is a journalist who has had a fascination with jungles since his parents kept telling him to "go outside and play" as a boy. His work has appeared in numerous publications, including the Los Angeles Times, *the* San Diego Tribune, Outside, Details, Science, *and* Glamour. *He is a coeditor of* Travelers' Tales Greece *and the author of* Rapture: How Biotech Became the New Religion *and* Green Cathedrals: A Wayward Traveler in the Rain Forest, *from which this story was excerpted. He lives in San Diego.*

✳

About 2 p.m., we pulled up at a big shaky river house, where a warm-hearted man named Jibuzcio came striding down an elevated walkway to meet us. His wife and six children soon joined him. They invited us to stay, and I sent one of the young sons off in his *casco* to buy nine soft drinks, one for each of us. He returned with five, explaining that he'd bought out the store.

When Dana and I had bathed and shampooed, I asked Jibuzcio if he had a razor. "*Sim*," he said, and he produced a rusty old razor blade fastened with thread to a popsicle stick. Our trip has taken us many thousands of miles, and I've yet to laugh at anyone's misfortune or poverty. But when I saw that old razor blade on the popsicle stick, I couldn't help bursting out laughing. There was no way I could shave with the thing.

"Will you shave me?" I said to Jibuzcio. "*Sim*," he said, and in no time I was seated in the main room of the house with my head back.

For fifteen minutes, Jibuzcio scratched away at my beard, throwing the scratching out the window into the river. At one point I asked him if he'd built his own house and when. He'd built it, he said, but he couldn't remember quite when. "Maybe 25 years ago."

A few minutes later—still with my head back—I happened to glance at a rafter which was deeply inscribed with the numbers "27 4 55." It had to be a date, and, after a few seconds, it dawned on me that it was today's date, but 27 years ago. I waited a minute and said cryptically, "Your house is 27 years old, not 25," and I pointed at the inscription. He peered up at it for a few seconds and excitedly called to his family. All of them rushed in and stood gazing into the rafters at the numbers. The house was 27 years old today, and the whole place instantly took on a birthday atmosphere—and I didn't get so much as a nick from my shave.

—Don Starkell, *Paddle to the Amazon*

Belém Takes Its Time

While the rest of Brazil seems hell-bent on modernizing,
Belém prefers to remain a place of tattered 19th-century gentility.

DAWN WAS BREAKING AS THE *RODRIGUES ALVES* ENTERED THE BAY of Guajará and approached the city of Belém. It had been a cold and windy trip down the Rio Tocantins, the air redolent of diesel fumes and black pepper. The big wooden riverboat was full of passengers, their hammocks looped in two colorful rows, one on either side of the open deck. Bags, suitcases, and cardboard boxes were piled everywhere, down the middle, against stairwells, along the white slat railings. Like some natural traveling alarm clock, a rooster suddenly began to crow in the half-dark.

We passed the floating gas station in Belém's harbor, and soon I could make out the wooden tiers of the Salt Port looming through the early morning mist like an ink sketch still unfinished, the gray sky speckled with circling vultures. Behind a clutter of rusty tin roofs and weather-beaten sheds rose the sheer white wall of the Salesian school; to the left I saw the twin towers of Our Lady of Carmel Church. The boat docked and emptied quickly. In spite of the early hour, the port was busy with men wheeling out loads of black pepper and cacao beans, threading their way through the tired passengers on the wooden boardwalk.

I walked to the square in front of Our Lady of Carmel and caught a bus to the home of my friend Elizete Gaspar. The bus took me past Ver-O-Peso market, through the main square and up Governor Malcher Street. I got off a block from the Nazaré church. Elizete lived in a modern eight-story building on a street lined, like many in the area, with mango and chestnut trees. The area around the basilica used to be the upper-class section of Belém, a gracious district of large, elegant houses, ornate with louvered windows, wide verandas, balustrades, and balconies running beneath a shady fretwork of hibiscus and palms.

I had met Elizete in the gold-prospecting town of Itaituba, on the far side of Pará state, on the Tapajós River. Elizete had grown up in Tapajós region and had recently returned to do research for her master's degree. We quickly became close friends, and her apartment in Belém, which she shared with a younger sister who was expecting her first child, became a second home to me in Brazil.

It was still early when I arrived, and over breakfast I told Elizete about the situation I had seen in Cametá the previous day. Even though Cametá was so close to the city, few people in Belém were aware of the suffering of the river dwellers on the Tocantins. Within a short while, however, my early start and the sleepless night on the boat began to catch up with me. I had a hundred things to do that day, but I was so tired I was almost sick. "Try some of this," said Elizete, who jumped up and got a small jar of *guaraná,* a kind of dried ground berry, out of the cupboard. "I used to use this all the time in university when it was exam time."

She mixed some of the brown powder with honey and water, and I drank it. It was typical of Elizete to have such a remedy. She had lived in the city for years, but in some ways she retained a number of customs of "the interior." The breakfast table, for example, was usually set with powdered milk and tinned butter and hard, dry biscuits, even though there were supermarkets with fresh milk and butter nearby. She and her sister, Beth, also liked to boil up a batch of *pupunha* palm fruits for breakfast when they were in season, another custom of rural Amazônia. The *guaraná* worked wonders. Within minutes, I was feeling full of energy. Elizete told me that the *guaraná* had come from the Indians, who liked to use it to hunt at night, for it kept them wide awake and very alert. "You can go down and get it fresh at any one of those tourist stores in the square," she said. "They have big sticks of it and grate it for you right there with a dried *pirarucú* tongue."

Founded in the early 17th century, Belém do Pará is the oldest city in the Amazon. It is poised strategically at the mouth of the great river and is an important link between the river and the Atlantic Ocean. Its relations with Portugal and Europe were traditionally much stronger than those with the south of Brazil. All the products of the region—rubber, hides, oils, and medicinals—had to pass through its crowded harbors on their way to foreign markets. The early explorers set out from Belém on their voyages of discovery through the maze of Amazonian waterways, and the Jesuits on their "reductions"—their grouping of Indian tribes into large colonies protected by the Catholic Church. Belém was also the headquarters for Portuguese raids against foreign invaders, i.e., the Dutch, the French, the English, and even the Irish, who set up a short-lived colony on the northern bank of the Taurege River.

A number of beverage companies, including Pepsico Inc. and Coca-Cola Co., sell soft drinks made from the caffeinated guaraná *berry that are sold only in Brazil, where such drinks account for 24 percent of the market. The berry, which comes from the* guaraná *tree in the Amazon rainforest, has two and a half times more caffeine per ounce than coffee.*

—AH and SD

More than 350 years later, Belém is still a small provincial city of fewer than a million inhabitants. At a time when the tendency to replace the old with the new seems overwhelming in many other Brazilian cities, Belém remains relatively unscathed. A few modern blocks have broken into its skyline, yet the overall feeling of the place is one of tattered 19th-century gentility; a historic city imperceptibly moldering in the humid tropical air. Nonetheless, there is the feeling there of being in the center. It is the capital of all the riverside communities scattered throughout Pará, the only modern city for hundreds of miles. And as well as being the transition point between the river and sea, it is also the link between the untamed north and the rest of Brazil, between wilderness and civilization, between the realities of the present and the dreams of the future.

Belém feels far more like an ocean port than a river port. In Brazil the Amazon is called the *Riomar*, or "river sea;" to cross from Belém to the northern bank would mean a journey of more than 200 miles, and the island of Marajó, the largest in the Amazon delta, is the size of Switzerland.

The ports extend along the city, and spiny with masts and cranes and booms, they seem to draw it in. The Coal Port, the Salt Port, the Açaí Port: their names indicate what was and still is unloaded there. With constant movement of boats of all sizes in the water and the throngs of people on land, the ports form the heart of Belém's existence. Local newspapers print lists of the big foreign liners and tankers at anchor in the modern harbor, and their ports of origin. Double-decked riverboats clog the smaller wooden wharves, waiting for passengers traveling north to the gold-rich territory of Amapá; or west along the Amazon to Santarém, Manaus and stops along the way; or south down the Tocantins and Araguaia to Cametá, Tucuruí, and Marabá.

It is also down by the waterfront that you find the Ver-O-Peso market, where a public scale once invited shoppers to indeed "see the weight" of whatever they had purchased. As crowded with vendors as it is with shoppers, it snakes along the waterfront, an elongated conglomeration of tiny stalls and cavernous stone buildings, all of it in a constant buzz of activity. Ver-O-Peso is dominated by a grandiose market building of cast iron and glass, imported from Liverpool, England, during the days of the rubber boom, rather resembling the Gare St. Lazare in Paris. Elaborate with scrollwork and filigree, a winding staircase in the middle leading to nowhere in particular, it is now used to sell meat and poultry. Inside, great slabs of red beef hang from metal hooks, while defeathered fowl are laid out in pale rows on the marble counters.

Nearby, in a simple brick building, is the fish market, its white-tiled stalls filled with the myriad freshwater abundance of the Amazon. The air inside is thick with the cries of fishmongers attesting to the freshness of their wares. And there they lay, mouths agape, on the stone counters, brown-and-yellow-spotted *surubim* like piscine jaguars; glistening piles of *tamatá*, their black carapaces split open like fruit to reveal the dense yellow flesh inside; slices of silvery pale *filhote*; big *tucunaré* with black and gold disks on their tails; ugly, catfish-faced *gurujuba*; dozens of small *pescada* slipped onto stakes through their gills; flat, circular *pacu*, like silvery moons; *xareu, curimata,* big-mouthed piranha showing rows of sharp teeth like tiny needles; shrimp and chunks of *pirarucú*, the largest fish in the Amazon, which can grow to the size of an ox. The fishmongers wrap purchases in long green *ravenalia* leaves; little boys weaving through the crowds sell brown paper bags lined with plastic to those who prefer something more hygienic. At either end of the building, vendors hold out baskets of bright green limes, lemons, bouquets of tiny round peppers like red and yellow beads in a nest of green onion, everything necessary to do justice to any fish as it travels, inexorably, toward the cooking pot.

Between the two buildings is another market, a crush of tiny stalls offering what should have no price, but in this case does—health and happiness. Hawking miracle cures, medicinal plants, and good-luck charms, the *curandeiros* stand around all day chatting, importuning the curious with loud cries of *"Diga fregues!"* which more or less translates as "Tell me, customer."

One morning as I was walking by the *curandeiros* an old man offered to sell me the dried eye of a dolphin, specially cured with herbs and incantations, which would, he assured, help me to find love. I replied that I already had, and he said, "Well, you can put it in your purse and you'll attract all kinds of good luck, in business, finance, you name it."

The old man's stall was crammed with bizarre objects, and as he slipped the dolphin's eye into a plastic bag, he told me what the objects were used for. Aside from the eyes, he was also selling the dolphin's sexual organs, dried; I didn't know if people were to carry those around as well, but the organs supposedly attracted love, or maybe just an exciting night on the town. He also had a few jars of what looked like water and leaves, labeled "dolphin preparation," to be used as a perfume or in the bath. And like some archaic dating service, the old man could also provide the lovesick and lonely with an alternative, a piece of bull's horn to immerse with themselves in the bathwater.

To get to Ver-o-Peso we had to slink through a ribbon-wide opening between lines of rickety wooden stalls offering everything from essence of turtle perfume to smoked dolphin vagina, a mythic delicacy in that region. The stalls were so close together they blocked out the sun, and wares were displayed in eerie dimness—dried boa skins, tapir skulls, large rubber monkeys masturbating. How do you bargain for piranha teeth? What is the right price to pay for jaguar's testicles? We strolled and stared and remembered easily that this was the strange Amazon that, long ago in Chicago and Washington, we had expected to see everywhere.

—Brian Kelly and Mark London,
Amazon

Goat's horn was to be put in the backyard, he said, "to keep away evil." A small dried snake's head, called a *panegosso*, brought the businessman good luck in trade or commerce. The *curandeiro's* narrow shelves were filled with bottles of various palm oils and old coffee and mayonnaise jars contained the lard of turtles, snakes, manatees, and caimans. Other jars had small snakes coiled inside, one pale blue, the parrot snake, used as an antidote to snakebites. Strings of hooves and paws and caimans' tails dangled from one corner; the tiny wood-deer hooves were to be rubbed against the legs of a small child who refused to walk, while dried monkeys' paws were for asthma. The old man had some long pink flowers for stomach pains, and hard little oranges, *laranja da terra*, that "were good for any ailment there is." The rest of his space was taken up with bundles of perfumed wood, resins, and crinkly patchouli roots, known as *cheiro do Pará,* or "Pará fragrance."

The old man told me that he was 76 and had run his stall in the market for 50 years. I asked him where he had learned about all these popular cures, many of which were obviously of Indian origin, and he answered, "We are all servants of the Lord. Some people have the gift of singing, or writing, or playing the guitar. This here is my gift." Then he rooted around among his paper bags and jars until he found one of his business cards, a slip of paper with his name and stall number typed on it. Unfortunately, I lost it somewhere on my travels, and only remember his nickname, *Gracas a Deus*, or "Thank the Lord."

Past the fish market, the shore turns up and opens out into a square known as the Açaí Port. There the small boats come in from the Tocantins and its many islands with large baskets of *açai* packed in palm leaves. At night, the vendors haul the baskets out and line them up on the sidewalk, ready for the first early-morning customers. When they have finished, they go to sleep on the curb, presumably oblivious to the radio music blaring from the little palm-thatched bars across the square. And equally oblivious to the *açai* men, customers sit in the light of the street lamps, drinking beer at rickety tin tables and enjoying the gentle bay breeze after a hot, humid day.

Two possible routes take you away from the port and toward Belém's main square, the Praça da Paz. The quick way is to walk along the shore, past the coffee-colored customs building with its green bars, then to turn up Getúlio Vargas Avenue. The slower is a stroll through the crush of narrow cobbled streets of the old town. There you find a hive of shops and several 17th-century churches, their flat white façades, low roofs and trim of narrow molding making them look like sheets of paper burned and curling at the edges. Following the old tram tracks on Rua Santo Antonio, you see various relics of the past: the city library, an imposing structure of indeterminate color, where a chandelier hangs in the lobby, and the elegant Magasin Paris, with its bronze filigree and arched windows.

The Praça da Paz is a wide square of park, the city's tectonic showpiece, and, like the flamboyant theater at its far end, a relic of the rubber boom. Painted in graduated shades of magenta, the theater is Belém's version of the famous opera house in Manaus. A trio of arched doors opens a grand porte cochere surmounted by bronze statues. Low marble balustrades run along the roof. Across from the theater the park unfolds its green lawns, interrupted by fountains, trees, and little Grecian-style gazebos.

In the shade of the mango trees that tower over the square, life seems to move at a lethargic pace. The several souvenir shops that line the square cater to few tourists, but serve a more useful function as places to change American dollars at the black-market rate. Small children beg for change, and adherents of Krishna, their hands sprouting sticks of incense, beg for attention. Uniformed schoolgirls loiter in the shade of newsstand awnings and leaf through the magazines to see pictures of their favorite soap-opera stars. Reserving a park bench or two for their clients to sit on, women stir boiling pots of *tacacá* soup on wooden carts shaded by sheets of plastic. Surrounded by tools and old shoes, cobblers sit on the sidewalk, waiting for new customers. Beside them wait the pot menders and the shoe-shine men, leaning against the little wooden feet at the base of their thronelike chairs.

When I arrived in Belém, the city was in the throes of preparations for its annual *Círio de Nazaré*, Brazil's largest pilgrimage which is held to honor the city's patron, Our Lady of Nazareth. Every October, a small wooden statue in a cloak of gold-embroidered silk is carried from the cathedral to the port in a litter covered with white and yellow flowers. Thousands of people, having applied for a place in the procession sometimes years in advance, follow the statue, clinging to the stout rope attached to its back, in the expectation of some divine intercession from the Virgin. In the harbor, the boats are decorated with paper flags and streamers, and at night fireworks are set off by the stevedores and sailors.

Visitors come to Belém from all over the country, booking all the available hotel space and airplane seats for the region's biggest festival. With the city expecting crowds of at least a million, workmen were putting up bleachers in the park behind the theater and along Getúlio Vargas Avenue and decking the mango trees with strings of lights. Vendors of food, drinks, and all kinds of trinkets were setting up their stalls along Avenida Nazaré and in front of the cathedral. The local newspapers reported, however, that the vendors were upset this year because the usual flocks of wild parakeets that traditionally herald brisk sales had not yet appeared in the mango trees. Some were even demanding the return of the money they had paid for their concessions.

Augusta Dwyer is a Canadian writer, based in Toronto, who claims that her uneventful childhood on a Southern Ontario farm made her want to travel to places as unlike it as possible. To that end, she has traveled in Europe, North Africa, and most parts of Latin America, with Brazil becoming like a second home to her. She is fluent in French, Spanish, and Portuguese, and finds that the more she travels, the more she realizes that people everywhere are essentially the same. This story was excerpted from her book, Into the Amazon: The Struggle for the Rain Forest.

*

Across a street and just behind the harbor in Belém is a little block-square park with a dry fountain and a dry pool in its center and straight paths lined with mangoes cutting the park into eight pieces like a pie. The benches are all occupied by either old men or shoe-shine boys, and I sit on the edge of the pool to change a roll of film. All the trees are heavily loaded with green fruit, tons of pale green pear-shaped mangoes still a month from harvest. As I gaze up at the fruit, from all those millions, a yellow mango, probably the only yellow mango in the city, probably diseased at the stem, suddenly comes sailing out of the sky and plops down in the middle of a path.

Across from me an old man comes to attention at the sound. I watch him as he sits there studying it, looking at it steadily for a full two minutes, staggered, as though he can't believe in a May mango. He gets up finally and goes to it and stares at it with his hands clasped behind his back. He puts on a pair of glasses and looks at it some more and after an interminable time bends, picks it up, and studies it intently, rolling it in his hand, peering into its stem, holding it to his nose. It is obviously rotten, but it is obvious, too, that the old man is consumed with the passion to eat a mango. I sit there imagining that the whole city, living under the promise of this enormous harvest that will soon engulf it, when all the streets and parks and sidewalks will be knee deep in golden fruit, is also waiting in a kind of tension, a citywide lust of anticipation.

The old man throws down the mango and wanders away. Two minutes later a shoe-shine boy has found it, circled it unbelieving, picked it
up, sniffed it with passion, and flung it away.

   —Moritz Thomsen, *The Saddest Pleasure: A Journey on Two Rivers*

A Close Encounter

A skeptic is read by a spirit medium and what he's told defies explanation—unless you believe in Candomblé.

"YOU, *GRINGO*, I'D RATHER NOT TALK TO!" FUSSED THE BABY-faced black man alleged to be a Candomblé priest. He spoke in the lilting Portuguese common to citizens in northeast Brazil, and his green eyes had been casting me a withering look from the moment we had been introduced.

"You think my religion is some kind of amusement," he continued, "but you will see differently: you have a problem with the ancestors. Meet me by the river at two tomorrow afternoon. We will talk to the saints!"

So began my close encounter with a religion brought to Brazil by the slaves of West Africa—an encounter that would rank as perhaps the strangest in all my years peeking into the dusty corners of the world.

While roaming coastal Brazil, some friends had brought me to a private island called Comandatuba. We were in the state of Bahia, where almost everyone has roots in what today is Nigeria. Here the hot ocean breeze blows all the way from Africa, and all manner of people consult dark-skinned mediums with the frequency of true believers. In Bahia I was expecting to meet with a *pai-de-santo* (father-of-the-saints), a man who has the rare distinction of

277

being the head of a Candomblé temple; such positions are usually held by a mother-of-the-saints.

Before this moment when the *pai-de-santo*'s words flew in my face, I had anticipated my friends acquainting me with a Bahian fortune-teller the way they introduced me to *lambreta*, a local soft-shell crab—just so much local color. I had imagined the *pai-de-santo* telling me vague and fanciful things about my life and then relieving me of twenty American dollars. When it comes to fortune-tellers and the spirit world, I've always been skeptical.

But as I approached my meeting with the Candomblé priest, I felt uneasy: this guy had been openly hostile to me, had divined me as a man with a problem, and said he didn't want any money to "read" me. Either I had met a *pai-de-santo* with the world's worst business sense, or this fellow knew something that I didn't.

His name was TiTiTi, which in Brazilian slang means "gossip," and my friends had discovered him cooking in a restaurant on the premises of Comandatuba's only resort, the Transamérica. But at the appointed hour of our meeting, TiTiTi looked nothing like a resort chef. I found him on the bank of an intracoastal river dressed in a white turban and flowing white robes. He sat chanting at a table covered with a batik cloth, burning candles and joss sticks. In the afternoon heat the air smelled of incense and monkey dung.

Without any greeting he commanded me to sit in a chair facing him.

His method for divination was casting a handful of cowrie shells, called *búzios*, on a table as if they were dice, and as soon as we faced off across the table, the shells began to clatter and roll. TiTiTi's green eyes shuttled back and forth between glances at the shells and penetrating looks at my face.

In short order he told me that the African god who ruled my life was named Xangô, the deity of justice and thunder. Then the *pai-de-santo* went on to say that I was a man who only believed in free will, that I earned and spent a lot of money, that for me life was a road. Such vague and ambiguous remarks sounded like the most amateur kind of humbuggery, and behind the mask of earnest concern I had fixed on my face I began to laugh at myself for ever being anxious about this meeting. TiTiTi seemed to have about as much insight into my life as a bedbug.

So what was the big problem, I asked. And waited for the father-of-all-saints to dream up something amusing.

"Your problem is that you don't believe in spirits and one has been trying to contact you," he began. "It spoke to me yesterday. It is stronger than any spirit I have felt for as long as I can remember, and it said I must read you whether I want to or not. The spirit is a woman, and we must try to make contact."

Great. This interlude was becoming more entertaining with every new casting of the shells. I could hardly wait to hear what TiTiTi would tell me next. A female spirit? I thought a mermaid might be nice.

"Did you know a black woman well when you were young?" asked the *pai-de-santo*.

The answer was yes. My mother had continued with her career during the first five years of my life. My caregiver during those years had been a childless, African-American woman.

"Is she dead?" probed TiTiTi after another role of the shells.

She was.

The priest's arm swept up the *búzios* like a casino dealer clearing the table. Then he shook the handful of shells next to each of his cheeks. He took a long time with this and murmured words that sounded African and prayerful. At last, his cupped hands opened and the shells tumbled in a broad pattern across the table. Moments after the last shell had clattered to a stop, TiTiTi sat there with his hands frozen palms up in the act of casting the *búzios*. As the seconds ticked by in silence, I noticed that the priest's soft, black hands had begun to shake.

"Her name is Gertrude," he said at last.

On hearing this name, I felt all of the air in my lungs rush out of my mouth with a horrendous sigh. Tears poured from my eyes, and the hair on my body stood at attention.

"Gertrude is the spirit watching over you," said TiTiTi, "and she has brought you here to learn that she is always with you, protecting you."

As he spoke the *pai-de-santo* began to weep along with me. Minutes passed before either of us could get ourselves together enough to talk. We just stared at the shells lying on the table as if the very face of Gertrude Gaston might show itself in the pattern of the *búzios*.

Finally, TiTiTi gathered up the cowries and cast them several more times. The shells told him many things about my life with great clarity and specificity. But throughout all that he said, I only half-listened. In my mind I heard my voice asking over and over, "How?" How did this man seven thousand miles from my childhood home come up with the name of the long-dead surrogate mother about whom I never spoke?

I still can't answer that question rationally, but something tells me I used good sense—and uncommon restraint—when I turned down TiTiTi's offer to tell me my fortune and put a curse on someone. Gertrude would be proud.

Randall Peffer also contributed "Costa Verde Magic" in Part II.

★

It was New Year's Eve. I was going to go to the beach at midnight, like most of the residents of Copacabana and Ipanema, who, dressed in white, congregate to light a candle in the sand and throw a white flower into the ocean with a prayer for the goddess Iemanjá. I asked my friend *Dona* Jurema how I should pray.

"I would say something like this," she began. "Iemanjá, Our Mother, please make this year a better year than the last. Not that last year was a bad year, don't get me wrong: I received many benefits, many good things happened to me, and I'm not complaining. But now, thinking over everything that's happened, I would like to ask you for something from the bottom of my heart: please bring me twice the amount of good things, and take away half the number of bad."

—Alma Guillermoprieto, *Samba*

Capoeira Rhythm

*The author jumps feet first into the heart
and soul of Salvador.*

INSIDE A DILAPIDATED FORT ON THE WEST END OF SALVADOR'S OLD city, bodies whirl in muscular pairs. They spin to the music of a *berimbau* and, landing softly on the concrete floor with the palms of their hands and the soles of their feet, they create their own rhythms. These rhythms move a neighborhood, a city, move other pairs of bodies continents away. For this is at once the hothouse and the heart of *capoeira*, and all the eyes in this strange art's small world turn here for inspiration. I have come from Connecticut, to meet *Mestre* João Pequeno, to touch the hem of his garment, to play *capoeira*.

This is the Forte do Santo Antônio, a hulking colonial wreck, patched, wired, and outfitted with dubious plumbing, two stories of stone and cement enclosing a weedy cobblestone courtyard. In the 16th century, the city ended here, in manned ramparts over-looking the glistening Bay of All Saints to the south and the gloomy hinterland to the north. Since then, the city has sprawled in all directions, and the fort long ago lost any defensive signifi-cance. The building is a hodgepodge of original structure and half-hearted renovation: it is architecturally unexceptional, and bare as a Franciscan's basement. It squats on the west side of the plaza in the neighborhood of Santo Antônio além do Carmo. On the south side is a modest promenade offering a view of the Lower City and the gentle curve of Bonfim peninsula. On the north is Nossa Senhora do Santo Antônio, probably the plainest of Salvador's colonial churches. The neighborhood itself is similarly unadorned, quiet, friendly but not effusive. Unlike the brash, teeming Pelourinho district directly to the east, it does not boast of its status as one of Brazil's cultural centers.

The unlikely activity of the fort, however, makes it precisely that. Ilê Aiyê, one of the best bands in this musical city, uses the fort as its de facto headquarters, and holds an open rehearsal in the courtyard every Saturday night. These rehearsals—starting around 10 p.m. and finishing anywhere between midnight and 4 a.m., depending on the season—draw a few hundred people every weekend, making this by far the busiest night in Santo Antônio. (Even so, crowds are sparse in comparison with the throngs that pack the Largo do Pelourinho every Tuesday for the rehearsals of Olodum, Salvador's premier band.) Throughout the rest of the week, the fort sees only light traffic, consisting almost entirely of those who come to play *capoeira*.

There are three *academias de capoeira* inside, including those of *Mestre* João Pequeno and *Mestre* Moraes. Prestige is a complicated thing in *capoeira*: it generally attaches to individuals and not to institutions, and wears a mask of humility. Reputation, though, is as much a part of the game as athletic skill, and there are no doubts that these schools are a source and center of prestige. They are therefore completely unassuming in appearance. João Pequeno's academy is on the ground floor in the southwest corner of the fort. It is a single, dingy room, painted aquamarine long ago, divided roughly in half by a series of low stone archways. On one side there is a narrow, curtained changing room, a table, a few water jugs, a collection of old jars. On the other side, several wooden benches enclose a bare patch of cement, roughly three meters on each side. But playing *capoeira* in this space is something like playing violin in Carnegie Hall.

Moraes's academy, directly upstairs, is larger, and somewhat more ambitious in its decoration. It is freshly painted in black and yellow, the academy's colors, and its tile floors are always clean. Like João Pequeno's academy, it is dedicated exclusively to *capoeira angola*. Capoeira is a game originally developed by slaves in colonial Brazil. These slaves combined West and Central African traditions with New World innovations, inventing a combative dance that emphasizes stealth and trickery. Over the last several centuries the game has changed considerably, although absence of documentation and current practitioners' claims of historical authenticity make determining the nature of that change close to impossible. Today, almost everyone divides the sport into two broad styles of play: *angola* and *regional*. Most players concede that this division is superficial and misleading, and then proceed to use it anyway. Roughly, *capoeira angola* is slow, playful, theatrical; *regional* is fast, aggressive, acrobatic. As with all the general rules of *capoeira*, these are fraught with exceptions, which are usually unveiled at the last minute to the disadvantage of the neophyte.

he origins of capoeira *are controversial. Some claim that* capoeira, *born out of a fierce desire for freedom, began as an acrobatic technique developed by slaves who were forced to hide their self-defense practices from their masters. Others claim the techniques derived from an African male puberty rite, or that the name refers to the partridge called a* capoeira, *which fiercely engages in bloody cock fights.*

—Pamela Bloom, *Brazil Up Close: The Sensual and Adventurous Guide*

Many good players claim to be able to play in both styles, a claim that is usually exaggerated. (*Mestre* Nô, also of Salvador, and his students are the most notable exceptions, combining *angola* and *regional* with breathtaking agility.) Moraes and João Pequeno are among the purists—they have no interest in *regional*. Anyone who steps into their academies and vaults into a big, spinning *parafuso*— a roundhouse jumping kick that is a *regional* staple—is likely to meet with uncomprehending disdain. This is precisely the singular devotion I came searching for.

I had been playing *capoeira* for a year and a half, almost all of it in a *regional* academy in the United States. Before arriving in Bahia

I spent six weeks in Rio, where I tested my skills in the local academies. I immediately perceived that playing *regional*, I could get in dangerously over my head. The kicks come hard and fast, and sympathy is not a part of the game. *Regional* also values back flips and back handsprings, skills that elude my fragile spine. I began to despair that I would never be any good. Then I saw *angola* for the first time: here, suddenly, was beautiful *capoeira* played without ever leaving the floor, and where mistakes could lead to humiliation but not concussion. *Angola*, I thought, was *capoeira* my body could handle.

I soon found out how naïve I had been. *Angola* is not as dangerous as *regional*, but is just as physically demanding. There are no flips, but there are many back arches and an unimaginable variety of cartwheels, making a pipe-cleaner spine the most enviable physical attribute, if not an absolute prerequisite. Just as quickly, however, I discovered other reasons for suddenly calling myself an *angoleiro*. The game has a richer emotional palette than *regional*— humor and pantomime, balanced by moments of hypnotic spirituality, play a larger role. And if agility remains indispensable, this emotional nuance does offer possibilities of disguising physical limitations. There are no points in *capoeira*, and no declared winner, but each game is a competition. And in *angola*, forcing the other player to perform more challenging and strenuous moves can be a strange kind of victory. The problem is, these emotional intangibles are far harder to learn than physical skills.

Most important, *angola* is more precise. There is no attack that does not lead directly to defense and counterattack, and there is no wasted motion. Ideally, *regional* play is equally interactive, but *regional* games often degenerate into exhibitionism. *Angola* is more likely to summon the tension between rivalry and participation that gives *capoeira* its energy. This is a dance where you destroy your partner.

Like most young travelers to Salvador these days, I stayed in a youth hostel in the Pelourinho, the center of the old city, a period

shopping mall done up in bright pastels and red tile roofs, a fraternity row of African–Brazilian culture.

Climbing out of the Pelourinho by the steep *Ladeira do Carmo*
(Hillside of Carmel) one passes first the massive Igreja de Nossa
Senhora do Carmo, and then its convent, both of them master-
pieces of the Brazilian baroque. In the midmorning, a *capoeira regional* group often plays on the steps of the convent, passing a hat
through the crowd every now and then. They are clearly more interested in their own workout than in the spectators, but whenever
they see an onlooker holding a souvenir *berimbau*, they know they
have an easy mark. The *berimbau* is the one instrument indispensable to *capoeira* music, and hence, for *capoeira*. It consists of a thin,
sturdy branch, usually about five feet long, curved almost to the
breaking point by a wire stretched from end to end and pulled
taut. About six inches from the bottom, a gourd with a loop of
string through its back ties the wire close to the branch. Striking
the wire with a smaller stick causes the gourd to resonate. Using a
stone or coin to fret the wire, and accompanying themselves with
a rattle, the best players can produce an astonishing range of tim-
bres and rhythms.

Every *capoeirista* also
plays *berimbau*, and most
*mestre*s fashion their own instruments from supple *biriba* wood.
Souvenir *berimbaus*, made with flimsier
wood, are lighter, more fragile, and less sonorous.
In the Pelourinho, they are usually garishly painted in
green, yellow, red, and blue spiraling stripes, with
black and white dots. Buyers of these souvenirs tend
to stand out in a crowd, and the *capoeiristas* at the convent rush up to them, holding out the hat,
flashing a big grin.

*Musician with
a* berimbau

Passing the convent along Rua Direito do Carmo, one immediately leaves behind the crowds, and the freshly painted façades.
Another kilometer ahead stands the Igreja do Pilar (another colo-

nial beauty) and its sloping, cobbled Largo do Boqueirão. Past
Pilar, the street becomes Rua Joaquim Távora. At the end of this
street is the *Praça* (Plaza) *Santo Antônio*, and the fort.

This is the path I followed my first evening in Bahia, a rainy
Thursday in August. Stepping through the tunneled entrance of
the fort's courtyard, I immediately heard the familiar, caustic resonance of a trio of *berimbau*s. The only light spilled from the doorway of João Pequeno's academy: peering in, I could see about
twenty people gathered in a *capoeira roda,* or ring. I had enough experience entering strange academies to know that *capoeiristas*, even
novices, are always welcome, and that the only misstep is to linger
in the doorway. I strode in and sat on one of the benches, and then
looked around.

There were a handful of other spectators seated with me along
the bench closest to the door. The musicians sat across from us,
playing *pandeiro* (tambourine), *agogô* (bells), *atabaque* (drum) and the
three *berimbau*s, each with a different timbre. The middle *berimbau*
player led the *corridos*, the call-and-response songs that accompany
every game. I was familiar with most of these, and quietly joined
in on the chorus. On the other benches, *capoeiristas* waiting to play
sang along, watching the action. Most wore white clothes, but not
all; most wore shoes, but not all. Some academies have strict rules
about clothing and footwear, and I immediately took heart at the
apparent looseness here. In the center of the room, a pair of *angoleiros* were playing the most beautiful *capoeira* I had ever seen.

Regional games tend to be short—often a pair of *capoeiristas* only
gets 30 seconds in the *roda* before another player cuts in. *Angola*
games, on the other hand, are usually allowed to develop, lasting
five minutes or longer before one of the players bows out, or the
lead *berimbau* signals an end to the game with a succession of high
notes. Advanced players tend to stay in longer—there are legends
of games lasting for hours—and the players in front of me were
clearly among the best. They moved with feline grace, effortless,
low to the ground, implacable. One of the players, a man of about
25 wearing a yellow t-shirt and black casual trousers, seemed to be
able to turn himself inside-out at will. He arched backwards from

a squat into a handstand, and, spinning slowly clockwise, touched a foot behind his head. Suddenly, he swung his legs in the other direction, trapping his opponent in the *tesouras*—the scissors. His rival, an older man dressed in white, reversed just as suddenly, sliding between the first player's legs with his chest two inches from the ground, covering his head with one hand.

Exhausted, the first player rose and, stepping backwards, stretched his arms wide in the *chamada de benção*, the call to blessing. The second *capoeirista* crept back to the feet of the lead *berimbau* player, breathing heavily. After tracing the sign of the cross on his chest, he turned a few slow cartwheels around the perimeter of the ring. Rising carefully, he touched the top of his head against his opponent's belly, hands crossed below his face to prevent a sudden knee to the chin. The first player rested his hands lightly on the other's head, smiling, tilting his own head back and singing with the rest of us. In this pose, they stutter-stepped warily back and forth, until the first player spun quickly, bringing his foot into his partner's behind. Only then did I notice *Mestre* João Pequeno, seated at a child's school desk just to the left of the musicians. I recognized him from photographs I had seen in books and articles about *capoeira*—a wiry, brown man in a golf cap, chuckling at the action in the *roda*.

Later, I learned that these players were *Mestre* Beto and *Mestre* Cinza, two of the finest *angoleiros* in Bahia. There were several excellent players at the *roda* that night: Siri, a lanky teenager in designer jeans; Boi Manso, a long-bearded joker who could spin in circles on one hand; Marco, a deceptively stocky scrapper with a sleepy eye and a treacherous foot. There were three women, all of them astonishingly good. One in particular caught my eye: she was no more than five-feet-two, with thick

*R*esidents of Bahia and those who have traveled there are easy to spot in Brazil. Tied around their wrists they wear a colored ribbon with the words, "Remembrance of the Lord of Bonfim of Bahia." Tradition has it that when the band falls off, the wearer's wishes will be granted.

—Kathleen Barrows, "The Church of Our Lord of Bonfim"

dreadlocks and a booming voice. She was the only player who never smiled in the ring—she controlled her games with stone-faced intensity, forcing her opponents into the corners, dismissing their attacks with a skeptical glance. She could sink from a hand-stand to headstand and then push back up again, never leaving a gap in her defense. Twice, I watched her bring an opponent to the floor with a surprise attack. Each time, she feigned exhaustion and began to circle the ring counterclockwise, a common *angola* tech-nique. When her opponent did the same, she held her left hand in the center of the ring. Again, her opponent followed her example. She lingered just long enough to touch his hand, and then spun rapidly in the opposite direction, grazing the top of his head with her right foot.

João Pequeno himself only played once, at the end of the long evening. He is about 70, and as I watched him move with cautious deliberation I began to think that he was a figurehead, a bandleader who had lost his chops. His opponent was some 40 years younger, and appeared to be gently toying with the *mestre*. The younger player swung into a looping *meia lua*, a half-moon kick. He looped too far: João Pequeno lunged, knocking him out of the ring with a head butt. I reconsidered my opinion.

Triumphant, the master closed the *roda*, leading a loose parade around the room, singing "*adeus, adeus*"—good-bye, good-bye. As the younger players dove into the *roda* for a few seconds of ag-gressive play, João Pequeno addressed us, the meager audience. He lifted the gourd of a *berimbau* to his chin and spoke into it as if it were a megaphone: "*Senhoras e Senhores*! Thank you for coming, thank you, for visiting our academy, for watching our beautiful *capoeira*. Remember, our doors are always open...."

As the players began to collect their things and stream into the courtyard, I remained on the bench, rapt, waiting to speak to the master. Before I got the chance the dreadlocked woman ap-proached me, introducing herself as Ritinha. She told me that she taught *capoeira angola* upstairs, every day, from nine to noon. Wear white, bring an extra shirt, see you tomorrow, goodnight. Before I had said much of anything, I found myself enrolled. I got my chance to speak with João Pequeno that night and on several other occasions, and he was always as generous and as sly as he had been in the *roda*. But it was Ritinha who became my teacher.

Foolishly, I showed up the next morning at nine. Even Ritinha, who turned out to be sternly punctilious in matters of *capoeira*, did not arrive at nine for our nine o'clock appointment. I lingered in the courtyard, feeling exposed, self-conscious, out of place. This was good preparation for my classes. For the next five weeks, Ritinha dedicated every weekday morning to my embarrassment. First, I had to unlearn the big, open kicks I had been practicing in *regional* classes. She forced me to the ground, bending my inflexible, clumsy frame into the *angola* positions. She drilled me for hours on sequences of cartwheels, spinning kicks, and *quedas de rin*—collapsed handstands performed with the torso resting on one elbow. Whenever my head came above her knee level, she bellowed "*Não!*" and knocked me in the ear with her foot.

Many times I wondered what I was doing to myself, and dreamed of rest, of revenge, of standing up and quitting. But rapid progress dissuaded me: within a week I could dive into an *aú Santo Amaro*, a cartwheel that finishes in a *queda de rin*. Within two weeks I had learned seven new ways to snap the *tesouras* shut on my opponent's legs. After workouts, Ritinha taught me the rhythms and inflections of the *berimbau*, and even granted my musical errors a bit of indulgence.

Over those five weeks, of course, we became friends. I learned that she had been born in Santo Antônio, and had hardly left the neighborhood, much less the city. I learned that she was only my age, 27, and that she had been João Pequeno's student for ten years. I borrowed her creaking bicycle to ride out to the bakery for lunch, she borrowed two *reais*—about two dollars—to buy a joint from the loafers downstairs. I soon realized that she had been smoking not only after class, but before. This knowledge appalled me: I found it humiliating to think that, even impaired, her reactions so clearly eclipsed my own.

Every Thursday and Sunday evening I attended João Pequeno's *roda*s. I played a few times, but never stayed in for long. Only on the last night did I summon the courage to initiate the *chamada de benção*. This is the most intimate part of the game, a moment when the constant movement of regular play ceases, and both players stand fully exposed, as if awaiting judgment. *Mestre* Curiô, another great *angola* legend, once explained to me that the *capoeira roda* is a court of law. The *berimbau* players are the judges, and the other musicians are the jury. The best an *angoleiro* can hope to do is to plead his case in good faith, and to make a crafty argument. At the end, regardless of what happens in the ring, he can only return to the bench and ask for mercy.

I think I made a good argument before the jury on that last evening. I played with *Mestre* Beto, who overlooked my weakest defenses, and who worked to maintain the flow rather than to make me tumble. I moved as smoothly as I ever had, using the *tesouras* to set up my next attack, keeping my head covered. And when I rose for the *chamada*, Beto responded. I led the odd waltz for a moment or two, relaxed, aware of João Pequeno at his desk in the corner, of Ritinha at the *atabaqué*. And then I spun away, and sank to the floor once again. I soon bowed out, feeling flushed and expansive, and walked out into the courtyard. For a long time I sat there beneath the night sky, listening to the *corridos* drifting through the doorway: "*Devagar, devagar, é angola.*" Slow, slow. This is *angola*.

The center of the redecorated Pelourinho is the Largo Quincas Berro d'Água. It is a tony plaza, surrounded by bars and patrolled by bulky guards. Pastel walls, a thatched-palm gazebo, and the name itself all allude to Bahian folk culture, but the plaza looks more like South Florida than any other part of the new Pelourinho. In the center of the plaza is a telephone booth shaped like an inverted *berimbau*, painted in the same design as the souvenir *berimbau*s sold in the local shops. But it is not only upside-down, it is backwards: the "gourd" sheltering the telephone sits on the concave side of the pole, when it should sit on the convex side. One could easily take this as another sign that the restoration project has been backwards, misguided, and unfaithful to Brazilian culture. And there is some truth to that.

But there is another way to see the *berimbau* phone. The big hood that protects a Brazilian public phone is called the *orelhão*— the giant ear. Every caller knows that this hood does not provide a damn bit of soundproofing or privacy, whether it is painted like a *berimbau* or in standard yellow. But it still makes a brilliant metaphor: as Caetano Veloso, the great poet-composer from Bahia, put it, "Brazil might be absurd but it is not deaf, it has a musical ear that is something more than normal." And the *orelhão/berimbau* doubles the metaphor, embodying two facets of Brazilian cultural vitality: it is both giant ear and folk instrument, both receiver and producer of noise and information. And (as every caller in Brazil knows) a few crossed wires can sometimes make the message more interesting. Salvador will always change its visitors more than the visitors change Salvador. This city makes a rhythm strong enough to move us all. Or at least that is what I think as I happily make my way back from Santo Antônio to my crowded hostel.

Bryan McCann fell for Brazil the first time he heard João Gilberto, in 1987. Since then he has been an avid fan and scholar of Brazilian culture. He is the author of Hello, Hello Brazil: Popular Music in the Making of Modern Brazil, *and is an assistant professor of Latin American history at Georgetown University.*

✳

Capoeira is a dance fight. How the street breeds the dynamic spirit of its people. Street life. Street games. Street improvisation. In the group I was watching, practicing on a street in Rio, there was a child no more than ten years old who took his place and went through his motions like a baby veteran, executing incredibly fast spins, his tiny legs working like pistons. What a training for such a fledgling. No sitting in front of the TV for this one, or crying for his toys or other substitute love accessories, since his parents couldn't afford such absurd junk. His life was fully expressed here and his strong young frame was already glistening, and his rewards were the approval of his peers and the claps of his audience.

—Steven Berkoff, *A Prisoner in Rio*

Sailing Down to Rio

*Eden-like beauty and irresistible Brasileiros greet the
crew of the* Taigun *along Brazil's central coast.*

"IF ONLY WE COULD HAVE CRUISED HERE TWENTY YEARS AGO!"

Jurgen and I heard that lament a lot along our routes; in fact, we usually joined in. But when we spent a few months gunkholing the coast of Brazil from Salvador south to Rio de Janeiro, we finally tasted what it's like to cruise in the right place at the right time. The coastline offers a lush tropical feast of reef islands, spectacular beaches, and jungle rivers that remain unspoiled—and apparently undiscovered by casual sailors.

When we first sailed into Recife aboard *Taigun,* our 35-foot Vindö ketch, after a passage from Gambia, on the western coast of Africa, our plans were to hop south to Salvador for Carnaval and then ride the Southeast Trades north to the Caribbean. Who could have foreseen our infatuation with the country's natural beauty and delightful people? Within days of our landfall, I knew that we were headed for an affair with Brazil that would be much more than a passing fling.

"Say we do sail as far south as Rio," Jurgen said, as we discussed our plans. "That's easy, since the prevailing coastal winds are northeasterly, and we'll have a south-setting current. But are you going to be ready for a 1,100-mile beat north to Recife when it's time to come back?"

"No problem," I assured him, turning to a page in our pilot book. "According to this, during the winter months from June to August, there are increasingly frequent periods of southeasterlies, and the current shifts to the north. If we take our time south, we can wait until winter and then harbor-hop north during the southeasterlies and still make the Caribbean next season."

"Well, why not?" Jurgen said. "We're in no hurry."

Our decision was reinforced by an unlikely source during our three-day cruise down to Salvador. Jurgen was talking by radio with Volker and Rondi, friends who were sailing with us in their ketch, *Sundowner*, when a twangy panhandle drawl broke in.

"Is that a *woman* on the radio?" the voice asked incredulously.

We'd just passed one of several oil rigs along the coast, and within seconds of Rondi's confirmation, the female-starved Brazilian crew, who'd learned their English from Texans on the rig, were clamoring for the mike.

They came from all up and down the coast—Valença, Pôrto Seguro, Vitória, Rio—and when they heard our plans to cruise south, several took turns describing the enticements of their hometowns and insisted we stop for visits. We scribbled down harbor information, directions, out-of-the-way anchorages, and the names of friends, families, and restaurants. The result was a rudimentary cruising guide that dissected the shallow, reef-studded

It is well known that the Bay of All Saints is the doorway to the world…. A flock of islands, each more delightful than the one before, grazes on this sea of dreams, shepherded by the largest island, Itaparica, settled by Portuguese and Dutch soldiers, Indian tribes, and African nations. In the depths of the waters, in the realm of Aioká, lie the hulks of caravels armed for war, Portuguese noblemen, Batavian admirals, colonists, and invaders expelled by dauntless Brazilian patriots.

—Jorge Amado

coastline of our general chart and revealed a much wider range of accessible possibilities than we'd thought existed.

After the incredible madness of Carnaval in Salvador, we recuperated by cruising the islands and mangrove rivers of Baía de Todos os Santos. Then, ambling south on a broad reach, we headed for the beautiful, protected cruising ground at the mouth of the Rio Una. Though an uncharted waterway, it had been recommended by the men on the rig. Despite our entering the shallow river with the tide, shoals were only barely discernible in the murky green water. While Rondi and I manned our respective depth sounders, Volker and Jurgen gingerly held the two boats to a central course five miles to Galeão. *Sundowner* ran aground, but Volker quickly powered her off, and we anchored off the tiny village with the last glowing embers of the sunset.

It had been a long time since Galeãoans had seen a cruising yacht. So the villagers explained as they led us off to the local bar, a minuscule wooden shed lit by a kerosene lamp. As shy children poked their heads through the doorway and eyed us through the chinks in the walls, the proprietor loaded our table with complimentary skewers of sun-dried shrimp and fish fried in palm oil, his efforts hampered by a frantic armadillo that kept popping out of its basket under the bar.

Later that night Francisco, a young fisherman, took us to his father's home, the one house in the village with a generator, and we watched a cancan revue from Rio on TV. While Francisco's neighbors jostled outside along the windowsill for a better view of the spangled, high-kicking girls on the screen and Rondi and I sat chatting amiably, yet unintelligibly, with the women, I was seized in one of those time/distance/culture warps to which travelers are prone: How in the world did I end up watching television in a Brazilian jungle?

Nearly every day on the Rio Una we sounded our way to another faultless anchorage; we could easily have spent months crisscrossing the river from one deserted, palm-framed beach to the next. We found our favorite, though, when we retraced our path to

Morro de São Paulo at the river's entrance and the powdered-sugar beach at Punto do Bicudo.

Two fishermen ashore were deftly husking coconuts with machetes, and by the time we had anchored, bagged the sails, and dinghied across, they were ready with smiles, drinks, and a lunch of boiled crabs, shrimp and mangoes. Afterward, spreading their sails in the shade, they urged us to take a siesta while they set out in dugout canoes to rustle up a little something for dinner.

The days that followed were the kind of idyll you could bolster yourself with during a freezing gale. We set up hammocks, swam, and lounged on the beach; languidly argued over whose turn it was to climb for more coconuts; foraged for breadfruit and papayas; and barbecued snapper on the beach with our newfound friends. Everything we needed to live like kings seemed within arm's reach.

Although we hadn't encountered another sailing yacht since Salvador, we were surprised when none turned up in the large town of Ilhéus, where we stopped for groceries and weathered a three-day rainy spell. Most foreign yachts tend to congregate in the larger ports.

As we continued south, the coastline began to rise, thickly wooded hills replacing palm trees as the backdrop for the unchanging vista of white sandy beach. One isolated peak, Serra Panemosa, was as good a landmark for us as it had been for Pedro Álvares Cabral, who in 1500 was the first European to land in Brazil. Historical buildings from that era have been preserved and are clustered along a hilltop crest that runs parallel to the shore. From the grassy knolls of the village square there's a panoramic view of the reefs offshore and the densely knitted mangroves at the mouth of Rio Burnham.

We could have used the aerial view while navigating our approach to nearby Pôrto Seguro. For up to ten miles offshore, this part of the coast is littered with more shallow reefs than a junkyard has derelict cars. With eyes glued to the chart, log, and depth sounder, we threaded our way among them. Conning at the mast, I was just about to start breathing again when I saw the entrance to Pôrto Seguro itself. A mile-long reef formed a natural break-water a quarter mile offshore, but even at high tide this passage was only two to three meters deep. We were tiptoeing through when a local fishing boat chugged by and led us safely to an anchorage near the river ferry pier.

Pôrto Seguro is mainly a beach resort, and we arrived after the season had ended. The empty, sun-scorched streets were like the stage sets from the movie *High Noon*. As we walked along, we had the creepy feeling that we were being watched from behind the curtained windows.

It was an 80-mile run from Pôrto Seguro to the reef islands of the Arquipélago dos Abrolhos, and as we'd done all down the coast, we poled out the headsails and went winging south in a steady northeasterly breeze. While it was gravy sailing at its best, once again the offshore reefs demanded our constant alertness and the most precise navigation. But we couldn't complain about the weather. We spent night watches in t-shirts, snuggled into our "cockpit berth" with only a sheet to cover us.

The Abrolhos may look like cartoon islands, each one a grassy little mound with a few straggly palm trees and goats, but they offer the best diving in Brazil. We reached around the southwest

> *The land of Brazil is named after the brazil-wood that grows there. This is a fact, though it sometimes seems an improbable one, as if the relationship should have been the other way around. Europeans discovered the country at the very start of the 16th century, and Amerigo Vespucci, the man who unwittingly gave his name to America, was soon chronicling an exploration along 2,000 miles of its coastline. In 1535, the Portuguese sailed up the Amazon from the Atlantic and may have reached as far as the mouth of the Negro, seven years before Francisco de Orellana and his men descended from the west. But in those days nobody cared much about Brazil. First impressions suggested that it was an island, vast and impoverished, with no future, except, of course, for the brazilwood and the possibility that, if it really was an island, there might be a way around it to the spice islands of the East Indies.*
>
> —Stephen Minta, *Aguirre: The Re-Creation of a Sixteenth-Century Journey Across South America*

edge of the largest island, Ilha Barbara, toward its protected bay just as a flaming rim of sun ignited the clouds towering overhead. Shearwaters, petrels and gannets swooped among the few fishing trawlers, whose crews were busily cleaning fish on deck. A row of the crews' gaily colored tents were strung along the beach. "We come here every year around this time," one of the dozen or so *brasileiros* explained. "In two weeks of diving we can bring in close to three tons of fish, which we salt down and sell in Pôrto Seguro during Easter week."

One morning thousands of minnows sought refuge under all our hulls. As we ate breakfast in the cockpit, schools of lightning-fast silver mackerel moved in for the kill, churning the bay into a frenzy. We watched from grandstand seats while minnows sprang in droves from the water, followed by the fleeting gleam of their pursuers. That entire morning our anchorage was the scene of a furious battle for survival, and not ones to let opportunity slip by, the *brasileiros* jumped into the thick of the action, spearing within minutes enough mackerel to satisfy the demands at the human end of the food chain.

Our steady northeasterly disappeared the morning we left the Abrolhos. Nevertheless, we dragged out the spinnaker. I was threading the sheets through the blocks when my attention was galvanized by the edge of a fin jutting above the toerail only inches away. The fin was tangled in a huge knot of blue line and belonged to a mottled brown creature nearly the size of the *Taigun*. Coincidentally, I had recently been reading about whale sharks, so I knew one when I saw one. "Jurgen, get over here!" I screamed. Jacques Cousteau may be blasé about such sightings; I'm not.

"Haul in the sheet!" he yelled back from the foredeck under a billow of spinnaker. Meanwhile, our barely submerged visitor just lay there, letting its pilot fish attend it. We hurriedly got the sail under control, but Jurgen caught only a glimpse of the shark before it made a languid descent. Though I gave Jurgen an inch-by-inch description, I later overheard him reduce the shark's dimensions by half when we talked to *Sundowner* on the radio. For the rest of the 150 miles to Vitória, I searched the seas in vain for the creature to return and restore my credibility. And still I wonder, where did it hook all that anchor line?

"I can't imagine why the guys on the oil rig were so keen about Vitória," I told Jurgen as we closed in on the coast. Dawn had begun to fill in the outlines of the land, but all we could see was industrial blight.

We changed our minds after a few hours of motoring up and down Rio Santa Maria in search of the yacht club. Framed by granite cliffs and wooded slopes that reminded Jurgen of Sweden and me of San Francisco, the river is a natural, protected harbor for the clean, modern city. Although officially we were in Vitória to renew our visas, the Academy Awards had just been presented, and with many of the winning films playing in town, our stay revolved around film schedules. Coming from the Abrolhos, we experienced an acute case of sensory overload.

We stayed but a few days in Búzios, which is a chic resort for the Cariocas from Rio. Just north of Cabo Frio, Búzios has dozens of spectacular bay anchorages. Here, for the first time, we met up with *brasileiros* taking advantage of the day-sailing possibilities. We were excited now, in a hurry to get to Rio.

Our luck had left us, however, and we were bullied by a south-westerly the rest of the way to Rio's Guanabara Bay. During one memorable period, off Cabo Frio, when the wind, waves, and current seemed to hit us from every direction, we spent a night tacking without progress and realized just how spoiled we'd become during the last few months. Our usual stoic resignation to nasty seas and headwinds had all but disappeared.

The Carioca point of view is that "God created the rest of the world in six days, and on the seventh He created Rio," and even the normally dry and reserved pilot book described Baía de Guanabara as "one of the finest...natural harbors in the world." From my point of view, as we motored into the bay, Rio was simply magnificent. Sugar Loaf, Corcovado, Ipanema, Copacabana— the exotic sights I'd heard of all my life were right ahead of us. I could hardly wait to get to the infamous Rio Yacht Club and see the pool where Clare Francis had led a samba line of Whitbread

Round-the-World-Race revelers into the drink. We hadn't been on a round-the-world race, but already I could feel the same kind of mood coming on. After all, half the excitement of reaching a destination such as Rio is in having sailed a long while to get there.

Lori Nelson is a woman difficult to keep up with. When last we heard from her, she was enroute to the Falklands and Antarctica aboard the Sundowner *and was planning to continue her career in New York.*

✶

A major occupation among Brazilian women is trying to pull that tiny lettuce-leaf of cloth out of their asses. You see it on the beach and walking along the promenade, little fingers trying to rescue an inflexible piece of material from obeying the laws of motion. As with the miniskirt, women are constantly and desperately trying to shorten the distance the eye has to travel to what they feel is the fount of their mystery. Women in minis spend fruitless and trying battles of concealment as they sit, stand, cross their legs, revealing in the transition between positions an "accidental" exposure of vast expanses of leg. The thong bikini is no wider than a piece of dental floss and is meant to adhere to the crutch, but the more modest tiny handkerchief is one step away and enables the less bold ones to perform the same game as women did with the miniskirt. But having so little to grip, it quickly slides over the precipice and buries itself. And the sight of those endless pairs of fingers, like busy little worms, stretching out the itsy piece of cloth is another one of those eye-catching pastimes for the tourist in Rio.

—Steven Berkoff, *A Prisoner in Rio*

DAVID GEORGE

* * *

My *Maravilhosa* Career

*Exotic music played at a '60s college party launched
a young man on a romance with Brazil
that endures to this day.*

IT ALL STARTED WITH THE MUSIC. A FRIEND PLAYED SOME JAZZ
samba records at a party in Minneapolis in the 1960s and I was
hooked. The timbre and shifty rhythms of the music, the vocal inflections, and the shape of those crazy nasal vowels felt like inner-
tubing down the Apple River in Wisconsin. I'd studied Spanish and
strained to make out the Portuguese lyrics, skirting the edge of
understanding. Elis Regina crooning "*Samba do Morro*" sounded
like Edith Piaf singing in Castilian. It grew into an obsession: find
the source, get to Brazil. Sure, the place was run by a bunch of generals, but what could that possibly mean to an American student at
the University of Minnesota, whose total experience abroad was
limited to a few short stays in Mexico? So I took up Portuguese.
And sure enough, the dragon of the sea from João Boscols' samba
eventually showed up to fly me to Rio—I received a Fulbright
scholarship to explore Brazilian theater, which I'm still studying all
these years later.

After two weeks of Fulbright orientation in Rio in July 1968,
I signed up at the downtown branch of the University of São
Paulo, which offered courses in Brazilian culture. The university
was located across the street from a conservative private college

called Mackenzie. But instead of culture what I got was a lesson in terror, a narrow escape from getting shot—or worse—when a right-wing paramilitary gang from Mackenzie attacked the students at my school, supposedly for their leftist leanings. The right-wing group had the charming name of *Comando de Caça aos Comunistas*, or Communist Hunting Command. One kid took a bullet in the head, several had acid thrown in their faces. My mind still replays a celluloid face—a boy? a girl?—smoking, melting. The building where I'd studied was firebombed and gutted. The military dictatorship had become a harsh counterpoint to my studies of graceful jazz samba.

A few days after the attack, an American posing as a student at Mackenzie—a Special Forces anti-guerrilla expert who'd traveled to São Paulo via Vietnam—was assassinated. Leaflets scattered at the scene identified the killers as Marxist urban guerrillas, but it was obvious that the whole thing had been a setup, that the Special Forces operative had been slaughtered by the extreme right as part of a massive effort to goad the military into declaring a state of siege, to exterminate the "Red scourge" once and for all. Another American, a graduate student I shared an apartment with, dashed off to a press conference where the American ambassador was to give a briefing, to bolster the official line on the assassination. My roommate began shouting questions about the victim's true identity and the state-of-siege plot. The press, naturally, ignored the ambassador and excitedly grilled my roommate. He made the front page the next day and, unfortunately, our address was included in the write-ups. Well, that turned us into subversives in the eyes of the U.S. Consulate, which administered the Fulbright program and where we had mail privileges. Our one and only friend at the Consulate told us we were being investigated by the CIA and stalked by the very same *Comando*, so we left São Paulo for the soothing beaches of Rio until things cooled down. We settled into life there, reading, listening to music, hanging out at the beach. When December rolled around, the military declared the state of siege my roommate had predicted: no more congress, total censorship, protesters shot on sight, people disappearing into the military dungeons to be tortured, executed, hurled from helicopters into the sea. But nothing grisly happened to us.

Oh sure, a lot of Brazilians thought I was from the CIA. "After all," Cornélia, a student friend told me, "your cover's perfect. You talk good Portuguese, you dress like a typical student. Just the right look for a CIA agent." But the Brazilians, who must be the most tolerant people on Earth, didn't shun me. I'd go to a party and folks would say things like, "How's things with the CIA, *gringo?*" "Fine, thanks," I'd say.

Over the years I spent days, weeks, months sniffing around the library at the University of São Paulo, in the Ministry of Culture archives, in private collections. And there were the requisite interviews with actors, directors, playwrights, and designers. As a producer, I called set designer Flávio Império, explained what I wanted, and he asked, "Are you a *brasilianista?*"

"I guess so," I answered.

"Cool!" he exclaimed. "I've always wanted to meet one. Come right over."

So now I had a new identity: I was a "Brazilianist."

The same year I helped start a new theater group. We rehearsed on weekends, doing long workshops, after which the actors would go out to eat. Initially they never invited me along. A few months passed. I finally invited myself. Sitting around the table in a pizza joint, the normally raucous group was silent. Finally, someone spoke up: "We'd all like to know. Are you from the CIA?"

"Yes, of course," I responded. "The CIA financed my education and provided my theater training so I could come down to Brazil and investigate amateur theater groups."

They got the point. We became friends.

By 1984 the military was on its way out and Brazil's first civilian president in twenty years was being chosen by an electoral commission. A full-fledged bonafide Brazilianist, I was about to spend six months in the country working on a book and teaching a theater course at the University of São Paulo. I worked for free, because I wanted to return something to the country that had given me so much. It was a class in acting methods; surely the best training would be to stage a play, which is what I submitted to the department chairman. The proposal was not embraced rapturously. "Stage a play in three months? Are you joking?" But the project went ahead anyway, the time restraint overcome by eliminating from rehearsals the Brazilian penchant for endless theoretical and ideological discussion.

Byproducts of my heavy-handed method were the labels "censor," "cultural imperialist" and, yes, the old CIA charge was leveled again. But once the students got excited about the possibilities, we forged ahead. It's scary how inventive Brazilians can be and these students were no exception; it was all I could do to harness the torrent of ideas that erupted from their deep reservoirs of imagination. The play opened at the university but soon received an invitation from the Ministry of Culture to go on tour. We performed at theater festivals in and around São Paulo. For the most part, the students were jubilant about their success. But one newspaper review took me to task. The review's title was, "The Mad Gringo's Samba." At least the reviewer didn't accuse anyone of being a CIA agent.

The research? My first book would come out the next year. But something far more momentous happened during the 1984 trip. I met Bia and we fell in love. We would get married in 1985 and in April 1990 Alex, our Brazilian-American co-edition, would be born.

São Paulo is a city of 11 million-plus people and growing. Ringed with mile after mile of *favelas*. Traffic jams that would unnerve New Yorkers. Air pollution that sometimes turns buildings, trees, and passersby into ghosts with sulfurous auras. Water pollution that has transformed the city's two rivers—Tiete on the north side and Pinheiros on the south—into open sewers. São Paulo, my love. Dirty, scuffling megalopolis with its ethnic patchwork of Portuguese, Argentines, Japanese, Italians, Jews, Arabs. São Paulo, with its distinctive neighborhoods: *Liberdade*, home to the world's largest Japanese community outside Japan, where you can order sushi made from fish caught the same day along the coast an hour away. *Bixiga* near downtown with its Italian community—*porca miseria! porca Madonna! porca* this and *porca* that—cantinas where you can enjoy a plate of spaghetti *ao vongole* while the owner serenades you with *E Lucevan le Stelle* or perhaps an aria by Brazil's own Italianate opera composer Carlos Gomes or even a traditional song that celebrates "São Paulo of the cold nights, the verdant meadows covered with frost." (The Paulistas will say—or sing—anything to set themselves apart from the Cariocas of Rio.) São Paulo, a city where people still go in droves to see live theater. On any night—except Mondays, when the theaters are dark—one can see Shakespeare, Molière, an Italian comedy (*ma certo!*), Kabuki, a play by Nelson Rodrigues (Brazil's answer to Eugene O'Neill), maybe an aggressively avant-garde piece by Gerald Thomas and performed not in some tiny off-off space but in the Teatro Municipal, built with coffee money at the turn of the century, with its gold leaf and marble, flamboyant chandeliers, velvet-lined box seats. São Paulo, city of art museums like Museu de Arte de São Paulo, perching on concrete stilts that resemble inverted flying buttresses and looking like a mammoth sarcophagus, where you'll discover the paintings of Modernist greats Di Cavalcanti and Portinari. São Paulo, a South American urban colossus where the 21st century meets the 19th, where chauffeur-driven executives speaking into cellular phones and holding Powerbooks in their laps glance out

> *São Paulo is absolutely fascinating and, for all its New York wanna-be pose, it is as much a part of the Brazilian soul as Rio. São Paulo is a town that isn't trying to cultivate an image, as that wonderful old whore-city Rio is condemned to; it simply sits there and says "Look! Look at my skyscrapers and my slums and my pollution and my traffic jams, and above all, look at my money! My money says I don't have to care a damn about what the rest of Brazil thinks of me! It's because of my money that they come to me, abandoning the clean mountain air of Minas Gerais, the endless beaches of the Northeast, the peerless beauty of Rio—because you can't wear air, drive a beach or eat beauty, and the illusion of my money means everything to those who have nothing but air, beaches and beauty." São Paulo is a mess, but it works.*
>
> —Alexander Shankland, "São Paulo Works"

the window at sprawling *favelas* without running water or electricity.

In December, the vacation month, São Paulo is relatively free of traffic jams and pollution. So-called neo-liberal economic policies have made the city more international, for good and for ill. Shops and restaurants of all stripes have proliferated. While the food still bends to the heavy side, São Paulo cuisine leans increasingly to the light. On the other hand, the city now has a Dunkin' Donuts, Arby's and Pizza Hut. The latter is particularly sad, considering that São Paulo has what many pizza lovers relish as the best in the world.

The latest currency, the *real*, symbolizes a dramatic reduction in inflation—from the thousands to near single digit—monetary stability, and very high prices. Brazil had always been a bargain for those holding dollars, but now São Paulo seems as expensive as New York or Rome. No complaints; if it's good for Brazil, then all power to the *real*.

The country has a new president, Fernando Henrique Cardoso, who was elected on the strength of the "*real* plan," which he authored in his role as finance minister. He is also one of his nation's leading intellectuals. He went into exile when the military took over in 1964, which means that the generation victimized by the generals is now in power.

In spite of the positive trends, Brazilians remain skeptical about their future. There have been too many bright promises that have turned to darkness. Chicanery abounds. Despite, or perhaps because of, so many apparently intractable problems, Brazilian spirits remain luminous. The level of anger remains low; the tribal and ideological hatreds that divide so much of the world, including the United States, seem nonexistent.

And so, I will always return to Brazil when I can. I'm incurably hooked on the place, in spite of incessant complaints about economic problems and crime. It's funny, I've been traveling there all these years, I survived the military dictatorship, I've gone into places and situations I probably shouldn't have, yet I've never been a victim of crime, not even the petty kind. Blind luck? I feel safe when I go there. Naïveté? Passage to the country is always a return home to a sacred haven of human warmth and joy. Illusion? If the answer to those questions is yes, then so be it. Travel to Brazil has changed me permanently, and I have no desire nor even the possibility of returning to whatever I was or might have been.

David George currently teaches at Lake Forest College in Illinois. He writes on Brazilian literature and theater, translates Brazilian fiction, has been a National Endowment for the Humanities fellow, directs occasionally for the theater, and keeps finding Macumba charms in his closets and desk drawers.

★

Há males que vém pra bem. Some evil brings good in the end. This is a very common saying used from childhood on, to aid in the bearing of life's unfairness, disappointments, and frustrations. This expression takes root in every Brazilian who deeply believes that there's a bigger plan than their own. When certain mishaps cannot be avoided or corrected, Brazilians turn to the deeper Truth: there is a God and His plan is always for the good of everyone, in the end. Meanwhile, bear your cross with an open heart.

—Neise Cavini Turchin, "Longing for Brazil"

ALEX SHOUMATOFF

A Walk in the Forest

The author has a chance to follow—briefly—in the footsteps
of slain rubber tapper Chico Mendes.

TWO WEEKS AFTER THE MURDER OF CHICO MENDES, I WAS SIT-
ting in Chico's house in Xapuri in the state of Acre with his 30-
year-old brother-in-law, Raimundo Gadelha; his widow,
Raimundo's younger sister Ilzamar; and a detribalized Indian tapper who was guarding the place.

The Indian told me he was a
Monteiro, from the Rio Iaçu.
"*Eu corto seringa,*" he said, with
solemn pride—"I cut rubber."

Ilza was a tall, poised, striking
woman of 24. She looked
Polynesian, like a Gauguin. She
modeled the towel, now blood-
stained and torn by buckshot,
that Chico had thrown over his
shoulder just before heading out
the kitchen door to take a
shower. It was a relic now.

The Mendeses' four-year-old
daughter, Elenira, who had been

rancisco "Chico"
Mendes, a leader in the
rubber tappers movement in
Brazil, was gunned down in the
doorway of his home on December
22, 1988. He was a valiant
spokesman for the tappers, connect-
ing their plight as workers to the
plight of the rainforest. A local
rancher, Darli Alves da Silva, and
his son, Darci Pereira, were con-
victed of his murder and each sen-
tenced to nineteen years in prison.
In 1992, Alves' conviction was
annulled by a Brazilian court.

—AH and SD

307

watching television in the front room when her father, mortally wounded, staggered back into the kitchen, showed me the blood-stains on the bedroom floor where he had died. She was named after a famous young female guerrilla who was killed by the military government in the '60s. Her two-year-old brother was named Sandino, as in the Sandinistas. Good names for the cause. Chico had been very attached to his children—he would spend hours sitting on the floor and playing with them—and they to him. Whenever they saw a plane now they would ask their mother, "Is that Father?" She would tell them: "Your father is in the sky. He's coming home, but not now."

Raimundo explained how each tapper rises at the crack of dawn to work one of his *estradas*, or trails, and how each *estrada* links about 180 rubber trees. "I've fed and clothed myself my whole life in three *estradas*," he said, and I realized that was where I wanted to be, not here, making Chico's family relive the tragedy, but on a *colocação*, one of the homesteads in the forest where a family of tappers or often several related families live.

The Seringal Cachoeira, where Chico had spent most of his first 30 years, was an eight-hour walk. It was the rainy season, and the road there was too muddy for even a four-wheel-drive vehicle. There wasn't much enthusiasm for the trip. "What about something closer?" I asked Raimundo. He said, "I know a family of tappers that lives not far up the river. But we'll have to find a boat."

So we went to the house of a rich man Raimundo knew and asked if we could borrow his skiff for the afternoon. Soon we were heading upstream, below the juke joints and the stores of Xapuri.

Xapuri is a local Indian word meaning "the place where there didn't used to be a river." According to legend, one day a crack opened in the earth, and water soon found its way along it. The town of Xapuri grew up where the Xapuri River runs into the Acre River. Neither

Our struggle has been to preserve the forest, because it is in this forest that we have our whole survival. There are centuries of existence in this jungle, this forest, in which the man of the forest lives and has never plundered.

—Chico Mendes

river at this point is more than 75 feet wide. Raimundo's friends lived up the Xapuri.

So much of the immediate area around the town had been cleared that we had to travel 50 minutes in the briskly moving outboard-powered skiff to reach the nearest patch of forest. "We are leaving behind the world of lies and dirty dealing," Raimundo said as we passed under the sock-like nests of a colony of crested orapendolas dripping from the branches of a silk-cotton tree. Occasionally a brightly painted shack would appear on the bank, framed by the splayed leaves of cecropia trees. A pair of green parrots with yellow wings flew overhead, followed by a pair of green parrots with red wings. We waved to a boy in a dugout who was pulling in a trapline of thrashing silver fish—probably *piranambú*, larger, less toothy relatives of the piranha. Raimundo reeled off the names of several delicious catfish that swim in the river. I asked if there were any *candiru*. He laughed and said, "Sure. Loads of them."

Soon after passing a stand of twenty-foot-tall plumed reeds, we put ashore and made our way up a steep, slippery bank through a small blizzard of cabbage butterflies to where three men were waiting with their dogs. "*Opa*," Raimundo said, and we shook hands with Antônio Francisco and João Rocco do Nascimento, brothers who had known Chico Mendes all their lives. They were working the same *estradas* their father and grandfather had. We entered their house, which stood in a neatly swept clearing on stilts to keep out insects and vermin. The walls and floors were slats of *jariná* and *aricuri* palm. Next to the house was a tree sagging with huge green gourds, which were halved and used as bowls.

The brothers' mother, an old woman who was working in the kitchen, noticed that I had a cough, a bad one I'd been unable to shake for a week. She picked some leaves of *jambu*, an herb she had planted on the edge of the clearing, and brewed a tea from them. The tea stopped my cough in its tracks for the rest of the day. I recalled the statistics: 25 percent of the medicine on drugstore shelves contains rainforest products, but only one percent of the plants in the rainforests have been analyzed for their medicinal potential. What about the cure for cancer or AIDS? It might be over in that vine.

Francisco picked up a special tool for scoring the rubber trees, and we headed for the forest, passing a homemade press for squeezing the prussic acid out of manioc roots, which are grated and roasted into *farinha*—an Amazonian staple. We stopped at the smoking shed. "We heat the milk from the rubber trees in this

metal basin and keep stirring it with a paddle and pouring it on this slowly turning stick," Antônio explained. Eventually a ball of rubber, known as a *prancha*, weighing usually 30 to 50 kilos—the distillation of maybe five days of tapping—builds up. It's a nasty job: carbonic acid from the fumes gets to your eyes.

João picked up an old biscuit of rubber, squeezed in a press, that bore the stamp of the former owner of the Seringal Floresta, as the place was called. "We never knew who the owner was.

Harvesting a rubber tree

We never met him, only his 'representative,' the *seringalista* [rubber boss] José Ademir, who dominated us and a hundred and eighty other tappers. We had to give José Ademir a hundred and twenty kilos a year as 'rent,' which he said was for the owner, and we had to buy his merchandise at outrageous prices. Twenty years ago we realized there was no owner, and José Ademir left."

We continued through fields of corn reaching far above our heads, of manioc and dry rice, through a nettle-infested thicket, and finally into the forest itself. The brothers had four *estradas* from which they said they tapped 1,000 kilos of rubber during an average year, up to 25 kilos a day when the milk was flowing. They set out before daylight, lighting their way through the forest with helmets, known as *parongas*, that have a wick dipped in kerosene placed in front of a reflective disk.

We stopped at the first rubber tree, which was scored with chevrons of incisions like upside-down sergeant's hash marks, except that one wing of each vee was longer than the other—a pattern known as the flag cut. Other tappers prefer the continuous spiral cut. Francisco cut a new wavy line just under and parallel to the last vee. The milk immediately began to seep down along it, and where the wings converged, at the apex, he placed an empty tin can. Then he went on to the next tree, maybe 30 yards down the trail. "It's like making love to the same woman everyday," he said.

"Are there any dangers?" I asked.

"Plenty," he said. "The *pica de jaca* [bushmaster snake]: it's black and yellow and gets to be twelve palms. The *jararaca* [fer-de-lance]. Its bite affects people differently. Some go blind in ten minutes. Some just swell up. The *tocandeira* [solitary black ant, an inch and a half long, very common on the forest floor, whose sting can put you into anaphylactic shock]. Falling branches. We call them monkeys, *macacos*."

"Where I come from, they're known as widow makers," I said.

"Some trees have been bled so much you have to go up a ladder to get to where the milk will come out, and there's a danger of falling," Francisco went on.

"Two hours later we come back to collect the milk," Antônio explained. "We're back for lunch by eleven. Then, in the afternoon, we do the smoking and take care of our crops. Then the next day, the same thing again." But at this time of year daily deluges made tapping impracticable. "It would take you five days to collect two days' worth of rubber," he said. So the brothers were gathering Brazil nuts, their next important cash crop. The rubber sold for about 50 cents a kilo, bringing in maybe $500 or $600 a year: enough cash, with the income from the Brazil nuts, for their families' needs, since they grew, hunted, gathered and fished almost all of their food.

João picked up a wooden globe the size of a softball from the forest floor—the fruit of a Brazil nut tree, known to botanists as a *pixidium* and locally as a *cengo*—and split it open with his machete.

Inside were a dozen seeds, the Brazil nuts of commerce. The Brazil nut tree, *Bertholletia excelsa*, is one of the monarchs of the forest and grows up to 200 feet. You get beaned by one of these *cengos*, and it's all over.

Where the trail looped back and converged with another *estrada*, I sat on the trunk of a prostrate tree and looked up in the dappled light. High in the canopy a rainbow-billed toucan was gobbling *paxiúba* palm nuts.

Brazil nut

"What about *Curupira*?" I asked—the Amazonian Bigfoot whose feet are said to point backward to throw off trackers.

"No, we haven't seen him," Antônio said. "Here we have the *Caboclinho da Mata*, the Little Man of the Forest. He spirits off your dogs if you shoot more than one deer a week. And there's the Mother of the Waters, who tips your canoe over if you catch more fish than you need."

And what about the *bôto*? "Sure, he's around," said João. The *bôto* is the red freshwater porpoise, widely believed to be able to change into a man and come ashore, where he seduces women— a useful mechanism for explaining embarrassing pregnancies and social diseases.

The brothers showed me the green pods of wild *cacau*—choco-late—sprouted right from the trunk, and the fresh tracks of an ar-madillo. The trunk of this laurel is good to make dugouts from, they explained. The root of this bamboo, steeped in water, reduces swelling. The berries of this big *imbiriba* make a delicious wine....

They showed me where João had met a black panther head-on just last week. They showed me the *copaíba* tree, whose high-octane sap you can supposedly pour into your gas tank and drive off with, and dozens of other marvelous things. We stood and listened to the liquid improvisations of the *uirapuru*, the gray-flanked musician wren. "He is the poet of the forest," Antônio explained. "When he sings, the other birds fall silent. You hear the *uirapuru* and you say to yourself, I'm going to come out here tomorrow and cut another *estrada*." He emphasized how important it was not to tap the trees too often, to let them rest for several days, or the milk would turn to water. "You fall on a forest like this, *senhor*, and it gives you everything."

Alex Shoumatoff is the author of many books, four of which are about Brazil: The Rivers Amazon, The Capital of Hope, In Southern Light, *and* The World Is Burning, *from which this story was excerpted. From 1978 to 1990, he was a staff writer at* The New Yorker *and is a contributing editor at* Vanity Fair. *He has two sons by a Brazilian woman, and lives on a mountaintop in the Adirondacks of upstate New York.*

✳

An empty piece of ground near the customs house was covered in rusting amusement rides. A tiny carousel held little metal bucket seats by chains from the center of the machine. A few brown child-size horses sat on the ground. When the wind came up, it whistled through the miniature rides. A dank urine smell flowed between the rides and the bar next door where a few soldiers and locals drank beer.

Two small, mangy dogs stood fornicating in front of the customs house, mocking the grand designs of empire builders, the civilizers of the Amazon. And, I thought, they were mocking me, my pretensions in going to jungles looking for adventure and definition. The male turned his head and stared at me between thrusts. "Fuck you. Go home."

—Brian Alexander, *Green Cathedrals: A Wayward Traveler in the Rain Forest*

JON CHRISTENSEN

The Ultimate Road Trip

A trip across Amazônia reveals a world transformed by the needs
of its inhabitants—and the struggle of others to preserve it.

POTHOLES BIG ENOUGH TO SWALLOW A JEEP WERE NO MATCH FOR
our desire to keep driving. Nor was the onset of darkness, nor
wandering livestock, nor truckers who preferred to drive without
headlights. We drove as fast as we dared past Ariquemes, a tin-
mining boomtown and the self-proclaimed "malaria capital of the
world."

We reached Porto Velho, capital of the Brazilian state of
Rondônia, after midnight. Bunkhouses and bars spilled their contents onto the sidewalks. In the pools of light, people drank and
laughed. Lambada blared from omnipresent boom boxes. We found
a cheap room in the center of town, closed a curtain against the
neon, and huddled under our mosquito netting.

Welcome to Amazônia, we told ourselves wetly. Our romance
with the rainforest was turning into a sodden road trip.

My wife—photographer Kit Miller—and I had bought a well-
used, four-wheel-drive Toyota to travel across the Amazon as part
of a year-long stint working as journalists in Brazil. In two weeks
we covered 2,150 miles.

We were in our fifth day traveling into the rainforest down a
highway with the unlovely moniker of BR-364. We had started

314

from the futuristic city of Brasília. Brasília is laid out like a drawn bow. The highway begins there under the name of BR-60, like an arrow pointed straight at the heart of the Amazon. Indeed, it had come to symbolize everything at stake in the battle for the rainforest. On maps, it traverses more than 2,000 miles through the jungle to the western frontier.

A few days after we had left Brasília's monuments to modernity behind us, we dropped down from the high plains into the emerald Amazon Basin. The pattern of deforestation, by now familiar to people from pictures and TV documentaries, was obvious: a thin line of dark green on the horizon marked the forest's retreat.

Kit looked at the sparse herds of white zebu cattle that roamed under the bleached skeletons of Brazil nut trees stranded in the cleared pastures. She said it reminded her of home. Cutting Brazil nut trees is illegal, but when the protective forest around them is slashed and burned, the trees die anyway. It is a lesson in the inadequacy of facile legal prescriptions to save the rainforest. We soon learned of another one: the law allows landowners to clear only half of their property. The popular dodge: sell the other half to a relative, who can then clear half of that. And so on.

Compra-se Ouro ("We Buy Gold") screamed the sidewalk signs on Porto Velho's main street. Ragged and muddy miners, looking like characters from

We hadn't planned on going to Porto Velho. We had heard that it was a hub where garimpeiros—*wildcat gold miners—came to gather supplies before heading into the forest, and we had no desire to see it. But en route to Manaus from Cuiabá our flight was delayed when a tire on the plane's landing gear blew out upon landing for a stopover. Stepping onto the tarmac under a dusky sky, there was no doubt we were in the rainforest zone; the humidity cleaved to the skin.*

Perched on the edge of the rainforest, Porto Velho has an exotic feel, in a prurient way. This was ground zero of all the environmental degradation chipping away at the life of the rainforest. This was where modernity came barreling over one of the last patches of primeval Earth, and it wasn't pretty.

—Annette Haddad,
"Rainforest Journey"

a Western, tramped into ramshackle storefronts, plunking down bags of gold to be weighed. They are the latest wave of immigrants to town, lured by gold flakes scattered in the mud on the bottom of the Madeira River. From southern Brazil have come farmers and businessmen, former lawyers and stockbrokers, and international adventurers with enough capital—around $50,000—to build a floating dredge to suck mud laced with gold from the riverbed. From the dry northeast, the slums of Rio de Janeiro, and the failed farms of Rondônia come the hired hands—diesel mechanics, divers, cooks, and prostitutes—for the river's 4,000 gold dredges. These newcomers have swelled the town's population to nearly half a million.

If gold has been the devil's bargain that has kept Porto Velho alive, it has not been the only one. The Samuel Dam on the nearby Jamari River was built to supply electricity for Porto Velho and other Rondônia boomtowns. Although it has flooded 200 square miles and required 30 miles of dikes because of the area's flatness, the dam provides barely enough power for Porto Velho alone. Rainforest activists and environmentalists have vehemently opposed such dams, as well as roads in the Amazon. The paving of BR-364 was stopped halfway between Porto Velho and Rio Branco, the capital of Acre, after environmental groups put enough pressure on the World Bank. The bank has since given new "environmental loans" to shore up protection of Rondônia's remaining forests, to help establish "extractive reserves," and to boost other economic ventures more appropriate to local soils and forests than cattle ranching.

The first 150 miles clipped by on the new, all-weather highway. But the pavement ended abruptly at the border of Acre. For the next 150 miles, we banged through water holes in the road and spun along the muddy tracks left by trucks.

We arrived in Rio Branco during a big meeting of the Alliance of the People of the Forest, a coalition of indigenous people and rubber tappers, old foes now united against a common enemy—the cattle ranchers and their expanding deforested frontier.

The town swarmed with rainforest activists, indigenous rights advocates, journalists, filmmakers, and ecotourists from Brazil and far beyond. We wandered around the farmer's market down by the river with an anthropologist who was searching for products harvested from the standing rainforest. The tall, carrot-topped North American cut a comical figure, happily sniffing herbs and asking questions.

"What's this? What's it for?" he asked, rubbing between his fingers a coarse white flour made from manioc root. Dried and ground, *farinha* is a staple in the Amazon and sprinkled on nearly every meal in Brazil. "It might make a great base for a facial."

In Acre, trade in rubber, nuts, and other "extractive products," such as natural gums, oils, herbs, and fruits, still contributes more to the economy than cattle ranching or logging. But the trade has long been controlled by a mafia of traditional rubber and Brazil nut barons. With help from abroad, rubber tappers and indigenous people hope to cut out the middlemen and sell their products directly to consumers willing to pay a higher price to maintain the forest so necessary to their enterprise.

A few days later, we set out for Cruzeiro do Sul at the end of the highway, but soon the axle-deep mud on BR-364 got the best of our jeep. As we stooped to dig ourselves out of the oozing red muck and felt the sting of a hundred little red ants, we felt both defeated and relieved. We had, for all practical purposes, reached the end of the road. To continue, we'd have to go by plane.

Airborne over the state of Acre, we watched the forest stretch below us, interrupted only by a trace of BR-364 reflecting sun from its wet surface. We could see an occasional town where the road intersected one of the many tributaries below. The clearing of a ranch or farm appeared now and again along the banks. But the rest was an inscrutable carpet of green.

We landed in the tiny, waterlogged rubber-tapping community of Cruzeiro do Sul, which is accessible by road only nine months of the year. From there, we hitched a ride on a boat carrying goods up the Juruá River. We strung our hammocks on deck next to the rubber tappers traveling with us on the week-long voyage. The days began as light crept over the river, and José the boatman started hot water for coffee. Morning fog haunted the water and the edge of the forest. Then the sun appeared as a splash of gold on the towering *samauma* trees, and we heard the whooping and chattering of dozens of kinds of birds.

Before the sun got too hot, we sat on the roof of the boat, scanning the forest for signs of life. Caimans slid off the bank, slapping the water. Noisy flocks of parakeets and tricolor parrots accompanied us. We marveled at the occasional

Caiman

glimpse of a toucan or iguana, or a troop of monkeys flitting through the trees. When we passed a riverside settlement—a thatch house in a clearing, with an onion and manioc patch to one side, and a canoe or two tied in front—invariably a large family lined the bank like statues to watch our passing.

Calling for land reform, the tappers in the area were trying to organize a cooperative, and had refused to pay their customary "rent" to the landowners who claim vast tracts of forest where the rubber tappers ply their trade. We asked the rubber tappers on board where these first steps might lead, and the eldest smiled, "Everything will change." His friends nodded in agreement. They saw a spark of hope in the organizing efforts of the union and the cooperative. Although the bottom had fallen out of the government-subsidized rubber market, they talked of diversifying their products and markets and bringing in scientific and ecotourism ventures. The important thing, they said, was controlling their territory and their destiny.

We had only one mission left: to find the end of the road for ourselves. We pushed on in a borrowed jeep, straddling makeshift log bridges across raging creeks, until we could go no further. The highway ended here as a washed-out approach to an abandoned ranch. There hadn't been any road-building equipment in the vicinity for years. We laughed and took pictures of ourselves at the end of the legendary BR-364.

We talked of the many kinds of roads to be found in the Amazon—rivers, rubber trails, highways, and muddy paths—and how not all of them led where we expected. Where we had imagined an escape from the world we knew, an adventure on the road in a primitive wild land, we found a landscape not unlike the one we left at home, transformed on a human scale by cities, roads, and dams. Maybe we were part of the problem with our obsession about roads. But the people we met all seemed to want a highway, too. Just like us, they wanted to drive to their own destinies.

Jon Christensen traveled the Amazon reporting for Pacific News Service. *A freelance writer these days, he lives in the shadow of the Sierra Nevada on the edge of the Great Basin Desert in Carson City, Nevada, where he dreams of tropical climes. He and his wife Kit Miller, and daughters Annika and Lucia, scheme up periodic escapes. Lately, they have been crisscrossing the Great Basin working on a book about the region, which, aside from rainfall, shares intriguing characteristics with the Brazilian Amazon, a land of warm people, tough environmental issues, and road trips that beckon to the end.*

*

North on BR-364, a few miles out of Pimenta Bueno, the sawmill capital of Rondônia, traffic slowed to a near crawl. The sluggish procession wasn't due to a bridge out, a flash flood, or one of the scenic cattle crossings where cowboys drive their herds across the asphalt. What waylaid traffic on this November afternoon was craters. Cars, tractors, buses, and semitrailers formed a long line and, one after the next, descended gingerly into holes the size of small houses that pocked the Amazon superhighway. Some of the holes were dry and bare, reduced to the bare orange earth that underlay the asphalt and gravelly roadbed. Some were small lakes, filled with muddy water. The procession of vehicles crept in and out of these holes, like pack mules picking along a treacherous mountain switchback.

—Mac Margolis, *The Last New World: The Conquest of the Amazon Frontier*

JOHN KRICH

The Guy from Ipanema

Meeting the man who gave life to the "girl" is a musical treat.

GETTING TO KNOW A COUNTRY IS NOT THAT DIFFERENT FROM courting a member of the opposite sex. First impressions often count far too much. And, like so many North American men, my interest in Brazil began with a woman. No package tours ever tempted more tourists to book their vacations in Brazil than that unattainable beach bunny who was "tall and tan and young and lovely"—a twangy rendition of the Portuguese epithet *cheia de graça*, "full of grace." The difference is that I met her when I was just a boy. Which is all right, because she was only a girl.

Back in 1964, when I had reached that crucial threshold of thirteen, "The Girl From Ipanema" took the United States by storm—peddling the hot romance of cool samba to the tune of two million albums. My initial association with the bulk of South America was gawking at my customarily brainy parents, stripped down to beach towels on the deck of our vacation house, swaying along with this "new beat." They had no more idea of the proper dance steps than they did why this *bossa* happened to be *nova*. Or that these lightly plucked sambas were middle-class versions of the clattering, shattering originals by Brazil's poor blacks. North Americans caught up in the craze knew only that this sound conjured up a nation at once savage and knowing, whose seat of government had to be on the beach. Before my generation was wooed away by rock rebellion, Sergio Mendes and Lalo Schifrin, Stan Getz and Charlie Byrd whisked me off to a land I rarely heard about in junior high. Record-liner notes, not history books, first informed me and many others that there was such a place as Brazil.

Looking back, it is clear that far more was being reflected by this cross-equatorial invasion than a mere sharing of international bonhomie. In each American colossus, the early sixties provided a shining moment when it looked like democratic values might win out over barbarism. A generational change in political leadership led to a burst of sophistication in high places, symbolized by two dynamic presidents with the same initials: J.K. for John Kennedy, "Jota Ka," as it's pronounced in Portuguese, for Juscelino Kubitschek, still widely honored as the only honest civilian leader between two grueling stretches of dictatorship. There was idealism in the streets: the ferment of the civil rights movement in the United States, and the resurgence of industrial unions and peasant organizing in Brazil. There was a revitalized national purpose and confidence, symbolized by Kennedy's pledge to land a man on the moon and by Kubitschek's earthbound miracle, the long-dreamed-of construction of a futuristic new "capital of hope" in Brazil's lunar interior. It was no accident that the man asked to compose an orchestral work for the inauguration of Brasília was Antonio Carlos Jobim, the composer of "The Girl From Ipanema."

Soon enough, the dual Camelots would be snuffed out: in one case, through an assassination and the Vietnam War, in the other, through the 1964 CIA-sponsored military putsch that deposed left-leaning João Goulart and ushered in nearly two decades of the *ditadura*, military dictatorship. The period's musical movement, aimed at self-consciously paring down and melding the best of both America's traditions, continues to echo in our ears to this day. Brazil's "Americanized" bossa nova would come to embody a greater truth—that no two nations on the planet could be more alike than the continent size, frontier-driven, slavery-haunted, im-

migrant catchalls known as the United States of America and Os
Estados Unidos do Brasil.

The tunes that briefly united two hemispheres could only en-
courage my long-distance flirtation. Never mind that I was baffled
that there could be a Brazilian with the Nordic name Astrud, the
wife of singer João Gilberto, who won notoriety through her single English chorus of "Girl." Astrud Gilberto's voice certainly
handed me my earliest definition of the adjective "sexy." Turned to
song titles, places like Corcovado and Ipanema became idealized
teenage images of problemless playboy playgrounds. The very word
Rio took on an erogenous resonance. Poor Rio! The most common forms of deception on the planet are travel posters and girlie
pictures—to which might be added album covers. And since the
city's image has been formed by all three, it cannot help but be
thrice disappointing.

Am I let down because I've been led on for 25 years by a
musical pinup, a bikini-clad tease I can never meet? Of course, I
head straight for Ipanema Beach—at least the place really exists.
After a few hours of sodden jet-lag sleep, I am thrilled to get the
perfect Brazilian greeting. Above an air-conditioner's creaking last
gasp, through the drapes which work fine against a full-bore tropical morn, my modest hotel room is invaded by music. In floods an
onslaught of timpani, the binary clatter of bells, snares and shakers.
A wake-up call for the universe! But when I open the window to
chart the progress of this renegade marching band, I see nothing
but a storefront directly across the street featuring *Discos em
Promoção.* Recorded sambas for sale! A loudspeaker is giving the
neighborhood a free sample: the authentic sounds I crave turn out
to be canned. In the ethnographically quarantined tourist zone
where I've landed, the same rule applies to the authentic life of the
city as it does to the newest generation of Ipanema girls in their
skimpy swimwear. Look but don't touch.

In a ritual reenacted by many a *gringo,* I stagger out onto Rio's
hedonistic sands. As I've been warned, I carry nothing that can be
stripped from me but my swim trunks and my solitude. A pale cartoon ghoul, I feel utterly out of sync with the zillion frisky

Cariocas in the midst of another weekend's orgy of bodily display, beach volleyball, and beer. Along the promenade, numbered posts divide the sands into the varied subgroupings of Brazilian society. On one hot slice, the poets; on another, the high priests; at a third, the near-naked bureaucrats, the former political prisoners tanning at their customary waterfront turf. Brazil's Times Square-by-the-sea comes at me in all its predictable elements: the local beauties in their razor-thin loincloth *tangas* rightfully nicknamed "dental floss;" the equally undulating *calçadas*, black-and-white waves of sidewalk mosaic transplanted by the seafaring Portuguese; the incessant hawkers offering oversized towels and souvenir soccer shirts; the distant humps of coastal jungle sloping seaward, sole hints of an end to the mighty boomerang arc of bathers, this two-mile curve offering a whole city cooling consolation.

But what really makes this beach blanket Babylon different from all the others? As soon as my virgin feet begin to burn, I make for the shady oasis of a makeshift seaside tent, or *pagode* (from the Chinese *pagoda*, pronounced "pa-go-jee")—the name given to a stripped-down style of samba that has reappeared in recent years as a response to the overpromoted and overelectrified Carnaval themes. A back-to-the-basics jam is already in session, grouped around enough empty bottles of Antarctica lager to make a bonfire in brown glass. The refreshment I'm offered is all musical.

In the cool center of the shade, a half-dozen boys are fiendishly extracting all they can from the percussive building blocks of Brazilian music: perky, insistent *agogô* double-bell; squeaky, optimistic *cavaquinho*, a Portuguese mandolin we've come to know as the ukulele; impudent *caixa* snare drum and pompous *surdo* bass; moaning orgasmic *cuíca*, or African tension drum, as academics are wont to call this skin with a talking umbilical; attacking *atabaques*, tom-tom; versatile *pandeiro*, our tambourine, preferably tapped with an elbow, a hip, the tip of the nose; their *tamborim*, a miniature struck with machine-gun force; *reco-reco* scratcher and *xique-xique* shaker, sometimes just dry beans inside a soda can, always sounding just like their names. The overlays of staccato rhythm get everyone moving, a forced march deliciously stalled. A circle of

middle-aged mammas, shaking it in their G-strings, never runs out
of traditional melodies to accompany the drumming din. Where
few people carry beachside reading, every sun worshiper shows
high literacy in the oral tradition, a photographic memory for the
lyrical. From the start, I hear ample evidence of the average
Brazilian's encyclopedic capacity for song.

To begin my investigations into the music, I must find the creator of the lifelong infatuation that has led me here. In a nation
where flowery four-part Portuguese surnames are always reduced
to familiar diminutives, Antonio Carlos Jobim is known to all
Brazilians by the boyish
"Tom"—though the grand old
man of bossa nova is now in his
mid-60s. Five of the ten most-
recorded Brazilian songs of all
time bear his credit line—and
how about most hummed?—including "One-Note Samba" and
"A Felicidade." But Jobim is more
than a prolific tunesmith, a Latin Cole Porter. Nearly every aspiring Rio musician I meet, at whatever level of seriousness along the
pop spectrum, credits him with being the most innovative and imitated. Moacyr Luz, a singer of *musica popular Brasileira (MPB)*, the
term used to group everything in the wake of bossa nova, echoes
the popular sentiment: "Jobim is our great genius because he dared
to be simple."

*ntonio Carlos Brasileiro
de Almeida Jobim died
of heart failure on December 8,
1994, in a New York City hospital at the age of 67. He is buried
in Rio.*

—AH and SD

Daring to phone him at home, I'm astonished to reach the
composer after less than a dozen busy signals. "I'm sure you've noticed that our telephones are very whimsical," Jobim greets me
with the whimsy found in his finest lyrics. Amazingly, I haven't
had to fight my way past the jealous guard of some *empregada*
(maid), a law unto themselves in a country where even the maids
have maids. (One tells me her musician boss can't come to the
phone because he is resting in anticipation of Carnaval. Later, others will tell me their employers are resting in Carnaval's aftermath.)
Knowing that he splits his residence between Rio and New York,

I'm not expecting Tom Jobim to have time for me. "My friend," he declaims, "we'll *invent* time!"

It must have taken a genius to have invented so luscious a tribute to a locale as grubby as Ipanema. Strolling this narrow neighborhood squeezed between an inland lagoon and one of Rio's outer beaches, I find the air hazy, the condos heavily guarded, the avenues full of cut-rate juice joints and underpatronized malls. A block inland, we could be a million miles from the sea—except that Ipanema's bag ladies also tote folding beach chairs. But when Antonio Carlos Jobim's family transported him here, the trolley lines had just been extended from downtown. From the stretch of white sand praised by Isadora Duncan, branded by developers as the *Praia Maravilhosa* (Wondrous Beach), you could spy whales and great herons.

According to Jobim, real estate speculation ruined the whole town. Yet this nostalgic son of the neighborhood has said that real social justice will only come to Brazil once everyone can live in Ipanema. One afternoon, I follow the crowd to the very spot from which this locale became forever popularized. A block from the beach, a swarm of perfectly tanned types are striking tambourines and blasting trumpets in an attempt to squeeze every ounce of pleasure out of the waning day. The point of this promenade seems mainly to keep hopping about in Spandex fig leaves for as long as possible. T-shirts proclaim this group as *Furiosa*—a pun formed by the root of *furious* spelling *Rio*. They have paused to serenade beer swillers on the packed covered porch of a cramped corner bar whose sign reads *Garota de Ipanema*. *Garota* means girl, of course, but a very special sort of girl. At a table here, Vinicius de Moraes, the populist poet who lent respectability to Brazilian pop music by becoming bossa nova's prime lyricist, was moved to scribble down his tribute to one Heloisa Pinheiro, the lithesome, long-haired daughter of a Brazilian general. Riding her fame as the original "Girl from Ipanema," Pinheiro has gone on to become a roving gossipmonger during the television broadcast of Carnaval balls. She also posed nude alongside her daughter in the Brazilian *Playboy*. If you can elbow your way inside, the original draft of lyrics and music are enshrined in a frame over the bar—formerly called the Veloso. But I don't find Tom Jobim there. He has boycotted the place ever since it cashed in on his song's notoriety.

Waiting to catch up with him, I find nothing but an energetic facsimile of North American jazz fusion at People, Jazzmania, and the other fashionable *boîtes*. In similar elite enclaves, the bossa nova was born through the fusion of the '50s North American import—the "cool" sound pioneered by Miles Davis and Chet Baker—with native Afro-Brazilian rhythms. But the greater influence these days is rock, which Brazilians pronounce just like the sport hockey. MTV-style videos are used to teach English to teenagers on a popular nationwide show. The tabloids are full of Brazilian rock stars like the maniacal *Lobão* (Big Wolf) and the irreverent *Paralamas do Sucesso* (the Fenders of Success). At most public Rio events, rock, not samba, blares from civic loudspeakers. The Eagles and U-2 drown out the chants of Umbanda priestesses during New Year's celebrations on Copacabana Beach.

Fortunately, I'm tipped off that many veterans of bossa nova, Tom Jobim among them, are gathering for a rare reunion to benefit a terminally ill musician. Unfortunately, the show is being staged amid chandeliers and white linen at a ritzy nightclub usually reserved for *mulata* showgirls to shake their sculptural *boom-booms* at Argentine tour groups. The setting, and concert, point up how much the "new beat" has aged. At this benefit, both audience and performers have lost much hair and zeal. Johnny Alf, an ebullient black scat singer, reminds me of Johnny Mathis. Os Cariocas, once a breathtaking harmonizing quartet, sounds just like the Kingston Trio. I'm at a high school reunion of finger-snapping, jive-talking "hep cats." The classiest class of '59.

I'm hoping to find João Gilberto, more than the first interpreter of "The Girl From Ipanema," the pure quavering soul of bossa nova. As hard to track as his singing-by-speaking Zen vocals and his teasingly off-tempo guitar style, Gilberto has become that oddest of anomalies: the antisocial Brazilian. One of the many apocryphal tales surrounding this legendary recluse describes how the singer Elba Ramalho purposely moved into Gilberto's apartment building to befriend him. When shy João called her to borrow a pack of playing cards, he made her shove them under the door, one at a time. Gilberto has been the object of lawsuits for canceling shows at the last minute—and tonight he's a no-show. "The artist struggles all his life to become known and accepted," is how Antonio Carlos Jobim will explain his former partner's predicament. "Then when it happens, all he wants to do is crawl inside a cave."

The groundbreaking songs that Gilberto and Jobim helped establish in the '60s are today's standards, the slyest of elevator music. At the time of my arrival, a gossipy new book about the formative moment of bossa nova tops Brazil's best-seller list. Not only does interest in the music remain high but the passage of time has hardly alleviated the noisy controversy engendered by such softly flowing music. It's hard to believe that academics and columnists once hurtled every epithet at this gentle sound's pioneers: reactionary, escapist, sanitized, above all, Americanized. But I have only to look briefly around the invaded Brazilian social landscape to see why such a howl went up among the self-appointed protectors of cultural purity when Jobim's stream-of-consciousness classic "Waters of March" turned up as the basis for a Coca-Cola jingle. Now I know why envious critics still snipe at this leading ambassador of Brazil for acknowledging that one of his major inspirations has been George Gershwin.

That there should be such hypersensitivity to the question of "foreign influences" in Brazilian culture is, of course, a backhanded admission of susceptibility. Over and again, I will hear musicians boast of their ability to "metabolize" North American and European sounds into something distinctively their own. Brazilian music, like Brazilian art, poetry, or religion, grows through synthesis. Brazilian musicians are plagued by their tolerance, a fresh-eared approach to every incoming sound from hip-hop to the honking of cars.

I'm hoping to plumb Jobim's secrets on a lazy afternoon in some tropical backyard gazebo. Instead, I get a frantic lunch in a setting at least as characteristically Carioca: an old-fashioned boiler-plate *churrascaria* (barbecue house) called Plataforma. Doting old waiters replenish heaps of fresh-sliced steak and sausage, silver platters of onion rings and *petit pois*, the best French fries outside France along with obligatory beans and rice and *farofa,* the manioc flour that's a gustatory sawdust Brazilians sprinkle over everything.

"I'm composing every morning these days. I'm working much better than I deserve. The way I've been living, all I deserve is to sit on the beach and watch the pretty girls go by."

Jobim's evident cheer, his nonstop quips, are fueled with beer, Brahma or any other brand, and frequent chasers of the firewater distilled from sugarcane that is to Brazil as vodka is to Russia. "Have a *cachaça* with me, won't you?" The word, like so many in Brazilian Portuguese, is of African origin—Mozambique's *kachasu*. Though this son of Ipanema is not what's known quaintly as a *Carioca da gema*—"of the yolk," meaning born in the more authentic *centro*—he seems the very embodiment of the stereotypical Rio man: always testing out an angle, trying gambits in a world that's both evil and delectable.

"Yes, I'm a Carioca. How can you tell? I'm a son of the Atlantic forest. I love all her animals. I listen to the birds. When I was growing up, Rio was still 90 percent forest. The water of the lagoon here was crystal clear and we had all kinds of conches and mullets. No air pollution, no real estate speculation. Brazil was so bucolic. We had only 30 million people then. Teddy Roosevelt used to hunt jaguar in the Mato Grosso."

Compared to most of the world's major metropolises, Rio really is a frisky little girl. The sources of Rio's self-made myths are all quite recent: Copa's setting for seaside strolls, the Avenida Atlântica, wasn't laid until 1904; mass outbreaks of yellow fever came as late as 1906, the same year streetlights came to town; the first university didn't open until 1920, the same year as the city's mascot outspread Christ statue, erected from donations taken at Rio's churches.

In his music, and in his persona, Jobim revels in being a throwback to an earlier civility. He is the model of naïveté and the proof that tropical man can attain erudition. He delights in living with one foot in the jungle and one eye on the roulette wheel.

"In today's music, the chest vibrates with the electric bass. One is transported to paradise. In rock 'n' roll, there is strong reverence to the country of the downbeat. One-two, one-two, I know, I can count to a thousand! I don't come out of the fox-trot, the *lambada*, the *lambooda*, or the *lamboogie*! I come from the boogie-woogie, from the polyrhythmic and the unequal! I have this Jewish doctor in New York who said to me, 'Mister Jobim, I have a wife who works like a clock.' I never understood what he meant, but I like that! If something swings, everyone feels compelled to call it jazz. *Jazz* is the name for anything that swings, and because of the African element, there are three places in the world that swing: the States, Cuba, and Brazil. Rodgers and Hart, Duke Ellington, Jimmy Dorsey, Glenn Miller. I was exposed to all of them growing up, through the movies. And, of course, I love classical music, too.

"For the purists, even Pixinguinha"—the prolific king of the *chôrinho*, Brazil's lilting instrumental music derived from the Portuguese court—"is not pure enough. But the pure samba doesn't exist anymore. With big stadiums and electronic instruments, it had to change. They even say that my nickname 'Tom' is American. But my darling sister named me that. It was from Antonio, because in Portuguese the 'm' is pronounced like an 'n.' She was trying to call me a 'Ton-Ton.' Like those murdering fellows in Haiti! Yet everyone thinks it's American! Once, a gentleman in a bar accosted me, suggesting that my music was too American. As they say, 'I sold my soul to the company store!' I love Tennessee Ernie Ford! And country music, of course. My father came from the south of Brazil, from the land of the *gauchos*. So I told that gentleman, 'Yes, I'm an American! A South American!'"

Jobim's swagger rings as hollow as his defensiveness. He clings to the pose of the offended party in order to have some way to participate in the native dialogue, to break out of his isolation. For no matter how many drinking buddies you gather at your table, it really is lonely at the top—especially in Brazil, where the top is such a minuscule point of such a wide pyramid. Doing something as well as Jobim has done leaves him imitated, extolled, excoriated—but never with the proper company.

"Even here they discriminate against me!" Jobim roars, entirely aware of the irony, since the waiters keep heaping his plate with steak and *batatas fritas*, keep refilling both his glasses. "But my music is so Brazilian! Can't you feel it?" Jobim asks everybody and nobody at his long table. "If you listen to the music of Antonio Carlos Jobim, you will be saved! My music says, 'Live and let live.' Let the birds live, save the forest. I'm the original ecologist." Years ago, his sarcastic advice to the Indians was to get a striped shirt and a job in São Paulo. "My music isn't profane, it's profound."

Tom Jobim is one Brazilian whose garrulousness has gotten the best of him. He plays the court jester before crowds he knows perfectly well are not worth pleasing.

"Come on, my friend! Don't you want another *cachaça*?" I leave the greatest living Brazilian composer with a drink in each hand. "Just keep this in mind when you do your research! People think they are very intelligent when they can name things. Villa-Lobos used to say, 'I'm a neoprimitive concrete abstractionist.' Because all the labels are meaningless. When he was dying, you know, he was the one who told the press, 'I'm not composing, I'm decomposing!' He also told me, when he was working on scores for movies, 'The outside ear has nothing to do with the inside ear.' In other words, the way you dress the music isn't what makes it erudite or not. If you use orchestra, flute, or guitar. Villa-Lobos and Gershwin, what's the difference what you call it so long as it swings? You can say the same thing about the woman you love."

Is Jobim finally getting around to the Girl from Ipanema? Or is he referring to Rio, his lifelong passion? Or is he cautioning me before I plunge further into the music?

"You call the woman you love Maria, so you can go around thinking that you know Maria. But remember, my friend! That woman remains a mystery. Maria is only a name."

John Krich also contributed "Simply Irresistible" in Part II.

*

On my third day in Rio, spotting a bus that says Copacabana, I whip out past the modern art museum, the war memorial, the yacht club, the sweep of the harbor, Sugar Loaf, and find myself standing on the beach, a perfect curve of sand upon which timid breakers—exhausted as though they had been worn away to little slapping lake waves by the postcard cameras—slap. Behind the beach a mile or so of high cement apartment houses. This is supposed to be that spot where there are more people to the square inch than any other place on earth. But this morning the beach is almost deserted except for some youths tossing a ball and a handful of very old, very red and paunchy men, their chests white with tangled hair, jogging and gasping at the water's edge. Apparently everyone is still in his cubicle being dense.

—Moritz Thomsen, *The Saddest Pleasure: A Journey on Two Rivers*

PART FOUR

IN THE SHADOWS

SAM MOSES

Down the River of Doubt

*Retracing Theodore Roosevelt's historic Amazon journey,
an expedition makes a disturbing discovery.*

ON A MUGGY AFTERNOON IN FEBRUARY, ELIZABETH MCKNIGHT, co-leader of the Rio Roosevelt Expedition, was sitting on the porch of the Mirage Hotel in the Amazon town of Vilhena. Parked on the red dirt street was a vehicle that would have been at home in Arizona: an emerald green, turbocharged Ford truck with chrome wheels, fat tires, black leather upholstery, and a stereo with about a dozen dials. "I wonder who could possibly own that thing," Elizabeth mused.

Before the expedition would end nearly two months later, we would know the truck's owner well. It was Chief Oitamina of the Cinta Larga tribe, our escort through roughly 300 miles of wild Cinta Larga territory.

During the laborious planning of the expedition, an an-

*U*ntil 1914, the Rio Roosevelt was called Rio da Dúvida—River of Doubt—a name it acquired because no one outside the local tribes had descended it. Then Brazilian explorer Colonel Cândido Rondon located the river's headwaters and invited the former United States president to join him in a journey down the tributary. Their adventure claimed three lives; Roosevelt himself lost nearly 50 pounds during the eight-week journey and never regained his health.

—AH and SD

335

thropologist from the American Museum of Natural History had advised that we carry kazoos to humor startled primitives in the jungle, who might otherwise chuck spears or shoot arrows through strange and therefore threatening white people. The adviser never imagined that some of these natives might be wearing Pierre Cardin loafers and listening to Michael Jackson tapes.

Oitamina had driven from his home 88 miles away, bringing his best friend, Piu, a second Cinta Larga chief. They had come to warn the expedition of unfriendly rumblings downriver at the Captain Cardoza outpost, a Cinta Larga settlement on the river-bank. Oitamina and Piu added that outpost renegades had killed an intruder on the settlement's land a few years back.

When the meeting began, Elizabeth and the expedition's other co-leader Charles Haskell wore scowls, anticipating a request for money to settle the problem. As the expedition cameraman filmed—Haskell had commissioned full coverage—Oitamina walked to the corner of the lobby and opened a black case with the coolness of a pool hustler breaking out his stick, removed his own video camera and circled the room filming the filming. The leaders' scowls turned to astonished glares. Months later, Oitamina would laugh about the incident and admit it was deliberate one-upmanship.

Five weeks later, when the expedition reached the outpost, Oitamina guided the boats past it on the far side of the river quickly and stealthily; he instructed the lead boatman to, in effect, keep his head down, mouth shut, and back bowed over the oars. Fearing an attack by hostile natives and not wanting to offend Oitamina, Haskell remained silent in the lead raft, his six-shot Winchester shotgun at his side. None of the expedition members knew it at the time, but the nonincident at Captain Cardoza was not about gold, as Oitamina had claimed. It was not even about white men. And the story about the intruder being killed was a distortion. The tension in the area was between Oitamina and the Cinta Larga chief there, a man named Jacinto, and it was over ma-hogany. Spelled m-o-n-e-y.

Mahogany trees, now listed by the Brazilian government as vulnerable, rise majestically in the rainforest in a broad band across the southern Amazon. Brazilians have long taken the rich red wood for granted because it was once abundant, and the country boasts a century's worth of gorgeous woodwork—floors, ceilings, doors, cabinets, even coffins. Because so much mahogany has already been taken, logging companies now concentrate their cutting on Indian lands and biological preserves, where timbering is technically illegal. By 1988 a study showed that a total of at least $1 billion worth of timber had been removed from indigenous reserves in five Amazon states.

Since the trees grow widely scattered through the forest instead of in stands, cutting each tree requires bulldozing a new road. One study found that removing one mahogany damaged 28 other trees and more than a third of an acre of forest.

The government does very little policing, for a variety of reasons: lack of commitment, lack of budget, tangled bureaucracy, corruption, confusion, fear, lack of alternative income for the Indians. Some tribes mount their own efforts to stop timber poaching. The Nambiquara people, for example, neighbors of the Cinta Larga, have sworn not to sell their mahogany and have burned logging trucks that sneaked onto their lands. Oitamina and Piu themselves stated that they would like to slow down the cutting but it's difficult for some native Amazonians to resist the temptation to trade a few trees for a truck or a television, or a case of medicine to treat diseases brought to them by white men. Not to mention physically resisting the loggers, many of whom do everything in their formidable power—including trick, threaten, lie, cheat, seduce, steal, and kill—to cut as much mahogany as they can and pay the Indians as little as they can.

In Rondônia, the state where most of the Rio Roosevelt flows, logging companies pay the Cinta Larga $20 or $30 per cubic meter for mahogany that is sold in São Paulo for ten times that, and that price is doubled by the time the wood reaches Europe or the United States. But even at the share of ten cents on the dollar, the

Cinta Larga who actually sell the wood (invariably the few who speak Portuguese, such as Oitamina and Piu) can get rich if they sell enough.

As the expedition glides down the narrow twisty river, Oitamina rides the fat tube at the back of the raft as if it were a rocking horse. Jungle calls penetrate the steamy stillness cooled only by the gentle sloshing of the boatman's oars.

Oitamina absently raises his t-shirt, exposing a big, brown belly protruding over orange paisley jams. His dark eyes explore the tops of trees and his hands gesture skyward as he talks, softly telling a story which comes out in pieces that don't always fit.

Oitamina—in his native tongue the word means "we are men"—was born in 1958 and saw his first white men when he was about eight. The Brazilian government was contacting and "pacifying" Amazon tribes located anywhere near the path of BR-364, the oncoming billion-dollar World Bank-financed highway. One result of this contact was the spread of diseases such as measles or the common cold, which became deadly epidemics among indigenous tribes having no resistance.

Oitamina lost his parents to that side effect of progress, and some gold prospectors on the Rio Roosevelt took him in and named him "Roberto Carlos" after the Brazilian singing idol because the little boy had long hair like the singer.

His best friend was a boy named Piu, and the two eventually went to the city, Espigão d'Oeste, or "skyscraper of the West," a dusty boomtown carved out of the jungle, a glistening land of possibilities for the two adolescent Indians. They were smart and daring (though not unafraid), and they worked with their backs and survived by their wits, learning the white man's language and methods. Life was never easy; the boys were always exploited and often hungry—Oitamina remembers hunting rats to add to his monotonous diet of rice and manioc. But then in 1986 came a lucky break.

The government officially recognized the Cinta Larga lands, which gave the Indians control over their timber. Some loggers were caught cutting mahogany on Cinta Larga land, and the felled trees were turned over to the Indians to sell. Since Oitamina and Piu spoke Portuguese, the two were the sellers. It was probably a very large lightbulb that flashed in their heads. They began to cut deals on their own to allow loggers to take mahogany off Cinta Larga land. A single tree brought thousands of dollars, so the temptations and rewards have been great.

The problem that is catching up with them, not unlike the fate of loggers in British Columbia and America's Pacific Northwest, is that the supply is being exhausted. Cinta Larga land is divided into six regions, and Oitamina and Piu had already sold almost all the mahogany in their own Rio Roosevelt area. Now they had begun attempting to make deals with loggers to cut mahogany off the Captain Cardoza area. But Jacinto, the chief there, wanted to sell the trees himself and put the word out that Oitamina had better stay off his land. This is why Oitamina hurried the rafts past the outpost.

After five weeks on the river, the expedition had passed the last of Cinta Larga territory, and Oitamina returned to his home. Brazilian guide Mario Peixoto and I also left the expedition, planning to visit Oitamina in his village.

As we drove out of the jungle, we passed two trucks hauling bulldozers in. The expedition had announced to the Brazilian media that it planned to report on the state of the Rio Roosevelt at the Earth Summit, and the Federal Police, responsible for Indian land, did not want such a report (it was never written) to be negative. I was told later that some 90 trucks were moved out before the expedition passed. Now that the coast was clear, the equipment was flowing back in.

Peixoto and I spent three days in the town of Espigão d'Oeste

The United Nations Conference on Environment and Development brought together 178 nations and more than 115 heads of state in Rio's sprawling convention center in June 1992 for an unprecedented collaboration of rich and poor nations. When the meeting ended, it was hailed as a success, but most of its promises about protecting biodiversity and curbing global warming remain unfulfilled.

—AH and SD

asking questions about timbering. We knew we were being followed. An undercover policeman told us tales of massive poaching: one night he'd counted 30 log-filled trucks stealing out of the
jungle. Recognizing the risk in talking to us, he sat facing the open
door of his house, with a loaded .45-caliber automatic pistol on
the couch at his thigh.

Even high officials confirmed the problem. "There are 1,170
logging operations in Rondônia," explained Hamilton Casara, the
state's superintendent of IBAMA, the government agency that attempts to balance development and environmental concerns.
"Only 800 of them are legally registered, and 45 percent of those
operate in violation of regulations."

At first glance, the regulations appear unjust. Private landowners, who are often rich, are permitted to cut and sell mahogany on
their own property. Indians, almost always poor, are not. But the
issue is hardly simple. Casara says, "If [the Indians] ever came to
IBAMA with a proposal that showed that the whole tribe would receive benefits from the cutting of mahogany, and not just a few of
them, then I would seriously consider endorsing it."

The Cinta Larga, however, are fed up with the Brazilian government after decades of corruption and broken promises. Piu
seems truly confused when invited by IBAMA officials to present a
proposal for the above-board cutting of mahogany. He doesn't
know whether to trust them.

Meanwhile, in a bureaucratic twist of fate, Piu gained control of
a ranch with both mahogany and a sawmill on it. The government
had sold the land to settlers in the 1970s and is now nullifying its
own sale, reclaiming the land and giving it back to the Indians.

Piu sees it as an escape. He won't have to do business with ruth-
less, sometimes dangerous loggers any more; he'll be a logger himself. He can even buy mahogany at cut-rate prices from other
Indians. He'll go straight so he "can sleep at night," he says. Then,
maybe, he won't need the barbed wire over the picket fence nor
the two hair-trigger German shepherds chained to trees in the
yard of his lovely house with the wraparound porch, smooth tile
floors, and hand-carved doors and cabinetry inside, built at the

edge of the jungle that was pushed back when the BR-364 highway was built.

Nearby Oitamina conducts a tour of the *Associacão Pamaré* ("association of the people"), which he and Piu founded to sell mahogany in a more businesslike manner with benefits to more of the tribe. He walks through a complex of wood and tin buildings built by Piu, now a sort of senior adviser. On the payroll is an earnest and educated nineteen-year-old Brazilian boy who acts as an office manager, letter writer, and interpreter of business proposals. One recent addition to the association is a fax machine, a gift from the Rio Roosevelt expedition. Oitamina had installed it in his air-conditioned bedroom a few dirt streets away, until the newly elected association president reclaimed the machine for the office.

Behind a big table hangs a hand-drawn poster of a Cinta Larga man wielding a bow and arrow and wearing camouflage clothing with blood-red fringe across the shoulders and down the back of the arms. The trousers are skintight across the buttocks—"so people can see the physical strength of the Cinta Larga," says Oitamina.

Later, in Oitamina's bedroom where we watch his videotape of the Rio Roosevelt expedition, a familiar face glowers at me from the wall: Sylvester Stallone, tight camouflage pants and all. At the top of the poster are blood-red letters: "Rambo: First Blood."

If Theodore Roosevelt foresaw such culture clashes, they didn't dampen his (misguided) enthusiasm for exploiting the rainforest. "Surely such a rich and fertile land cannot be permitted to remain idle, to lie as a tenantless wilderness, while there are such teeming swarms of human beings in the overcrowded, overpeopled countries of the Old World," he wrote. But in his idealistic vision, electric trolleys powered by whitewater rivers moved inhabitants throughout the Amazon. One can only wonder what he would make of the Cinta Larga's current place in the harvest of that "rich and fertile land."

Sam Moses was a staff writer for Sports Illustrated *for seventeen years on the motorsports beat. As deputy editor of* AutoWeek, *he wrote high-perfor-*

mance road and racing car reviews. In 1998 he received automotive journalism's prestigious Ken Purdy Award. More recently he was creative director of a web site covering the Mount Everest climbing season, and he is the author of Fast Guys, Rich Guys, and Idiots, *a book about the two years he spent racing sports cars. An avid windsurfer, he lives in White Salmon, Washington, in the Columbia River Gorge.*

★

On February 27, 1914, shortly after midday, we started down the River of Doubt into the unknown. We were quite uncertain whether after a week we should find ourselves on the Paraná River, or after six weeks in the Madeira River, or after three months we know not where. That was why the river was rightly christened the *Rio da Dúvida*....

It was interesting work. No civilized man, no white man, had ever gone down or up this river or seen the country through which we were passing. The lofty and matted forest rose like a green wall on either hand. The trees were stately and beautiful. The looped and twisted vines hung from them like great ropes. Masses of epiphytes grew both on the dead trees and the living; some had huge leaves like elephants' ears. Now and then fragrant scents were blown to us from flowers on the banks. There were not many birds, and for the most part the forest was silent; rarely we heard strange calls from the depths of the woods, or saw a cormorant or ibis....

We started downstream again early in the afternoon of March 5. Our hands and faces were swollen from the bites and stings of the insect pests at the sand-flat camp, and it was a pleasure once more to be in the middle of the river, where they did not come, in any numbers, while we were in motion. The current was swift, but the river was so deep that there were no serious obstructions. Twice we went down over slight riffles, which in the dry season were doubtless rapids; and once we struck a spot where many whirlpools marked the presence underneath of boulders which would have been above water had not the river been so swollen by the rains. The distance we covered in a day going downstream would have taken us a week if we had been going up. The course wound hither and thither, sometimes in sigmoid curves; but the general direction was east of north. As usual, it was very beautiful; and we never could tell what might appear around any curve....

Inasmuch as the unknown river was evidently a great river, Colonel Rondon formally christened it the Rio Roosevelt. This was a complete surprise to me. Colonel Rondon had spoken to me on the subject, and I had urged as strongly as possible that the name be kept as Rio da Dúvida. I felt that the "River of Doubt" was an unusually good name; and it is always well to keep a name of this character. But my kind friends insisted otherwise, and it would have been churlish of me to object longer. I was very touched by their action.

       —Theodore Roosevelt, *Through the Brazilian Wilderness* (1924)

KATHERINE ELLISON

Unquestioned Authority

*Rio's crime scene is so bad that few seem to care when
its police serve as judge, jury, and, yes, executioner.*

I NEVER HEARD THE FIGHTING OR THE SCREAMS, BUT BY MORN-
ing it was front-page news. A noisy fight among some teenagers in
the small park outside my bedroom window had come to a bizarre
end. Someone in an apartment across the way had fired two hunting arrows into the crowd, puncturing the lungs and kidneys of a
twelve-year-old boy.

Even in a city whose out-of-control crime gets constant press
attention, the "Arrows Affair" quickly turned into a big story.
Aberrant and controversial, it had the added element of warning,
in that it told how Rio's general psychosis had seeped into one of
its protected neighborhoods—my neighborhood—Urca.

*T*he boy would survive his
wounds, and the police
would later arrest a Dutchman
who had lived in Brazil for several
years and who allegedly was seen
picking up arrows in the early
morning after the attack.

—Katherine Ellison

Cariocas, Rio's residents, call
Urca "privileged" for its quiet
avenues, shaded by almond trees,
its panoramic views of
Guanabara Bay, and its reputation as a crime-free haven, strategically sited between two military bases. Yet even residents of

the most violent United States cities might be slower to judge it an oasis.

Street people sleep on the cut-stone sidewalks; raw sewage pours into the scenic bay. Just a few days before the arrows attack, a resident was robbed of her car by a man with an AR-15 assault rifle.

Even a stroll on Urca's beach entails risks. One week after I moved in, my dog chanced to run after some chickens, which I came to realize were being raised by a grizzled man who lived on the beach. The man had run out and threatened to kill my dog if she bothered his livestock again.

Later I learned the troll calls himself "Corporal Dog," is said to be an ex-cop, and packs a .38, with which he has threatened other unwary dog owners. Urca's neighborhood association has made several complaints to police, but nothing has been done. The "corporal" is rumored to have a *pistolão*—a big gun, or protector—within police ranks.

Rio police are generally more aggressive with less powerful scofflaws, and usually with society's implicit approval. I remember reading two newspaper accounts of a mugging in Paineras, a mountain park near the famous Christ the Redeemer statue on Corcovado Hill. The first article merely told how a thief had stolen a bike, which was later recovered by police. The other mentioned—far down, almost in passing—that police had shot and killed the thief.

I once asked Jim Cavallaro, an American attorney who runs Rio's Human Rights Watch office, to name Brazil's worst human rights problem. Without hesitation, he said it was that people simply didn't care. The next week, we both found out how right he was, after he was mugged on a Copacabana bus. The robber took his watch and $6 in cash. But then Cavallaro—who had once told me that if something like that ever were to happen he would deliver all he had, down to his boxers—caught the guy in a half-nelson and got him off the bus and into the hands of two policemen.

There, however, to his horror, he watched the police savagely beat the man with nightsticks and their fists. When Cavallaro next saw the robber, he was trembling, with blood on his t-shirt and tears in his eyes.

Cavallaro announced that he wanted to file a human rights complaint, a request the police met with incredulity. A newspaper later quoted General Nilton Cerqueira, the head of security for Rio de Janeiro state, as saying, "I'd like him to go up the hill"—referring to the hilltop slum homes of Rio's toughest crooks—"and use his human rights to convince the bandits to give themselves up."

It seemed, in the wake of the Arrows Affair, that these stories have a common thread. They all describe a degeneration, not just of nice neighborhoods but of nice people's sensibilities. Terrified by crime, they give police carte blanche. But the police, even more strung out than those they are sworn to protect, end up adding to the violence. And then all that's left is the genuine law of the jungle—the anonymous arrows flying down through the dark from upper-middle-class apartment windows.

Witnessing this digression, I worry, both for Brazil and the home I hope to return to one day—the United States. The West refers to Brazil as a "developing country." But just what is it developing into? And, with regard to the United States—where many are growing increasingly impatient with immigrants, race relations, and above all, crime, we should ask ourselves: Is Brazil a portrait of our past, or of our future?

Katherine Ellison is the South American correspondent for The Miami Herald *and lives in Rio with her husband, her daughter, and her Samoyed (a great dog for the Tropics, despite what you hear). She has previously reported from Mexico, Japan, and the Philippines, and shared a Pulitzer Prize for international reporting for an investigation into the hidden wealth of Ferdinand and Imelda Marcos. She is the author of* Imelda.

★

Who can blame the underpaid cop who takes matters into his own hands when political leaders who are earning so much more enjoy near immunity. To be sure, more corrupt politicians, judges and police officers are being arrested these days than ever before. Still, crime in Brazil remains at a crisis level.

The country has the highest global per-capita rate for fatal shoot-ings—about 40,000 a year, or 88% of all homicides, according to a (2003) study by Fernand Braudel Institute of World Economics in Sao Paulo. Annual homicide rates in and around Brazil's biggest cities exceed 100 per 100,000 people, among the highest in the world. One in every 20 citizens in Sao Paulo was a victim of armed robbery in 2002, at a rate of 1,074 incidents a day.

Brazil's crime rate is also robbing its economy. The think tank's researchers found that crime is costing Brazil $100 million a day.

But a bigger problem, researchers say, is the general sense of impunity. In the state of Rio de Janeiro, for example, for every 100 cases of murder, just two to three are solved. To the bad guys, the threat of arrest is almost irrelevant.

—AH and SD

JOHN HARRISON

Malarial Misery

Tropical parasites are often more than a match
for the West's wonder drugs.

WHEN I FIRST CAME DOWN WITH MALARIA, I REFUSED TO BELIEVE it. I was still in that period of naïveté when I trusted implicitly in my antimalaria pills. "No, it can't be malaria," I told Brazilians who should recognize it when they see it. "I take Maloprim once a week." Anyway, I was twelve days from the nearest place where I could get a diagnosis so I had to let it run its course.

It started when I was riding on the top of a truck from the Mato Grosso up to Santarém, a city with a colorful history on the banks of the Amazon. Baked during the day and frozen at night it did not add to the fun, and the journey took five days instead of the normal two because we were delayed by a bridge that was collapsing.

Several trucks had drawn up on both sides of the creek, no one dared to cross the bridge that was tilting alarmingly. After a consultation, the drivers decided they would shore it up themselves rather than wait two weeks for the authorities to do it. They set to work, cutting medium-sized trees into 3-meter lengths with a chain saw, and carrying them the 200 meters to the bridge. I tried to help but as I'd had bad attacks of fever for the previous three days, I felt too weak and retired to the shade. The two drivers of my truck were fairly sympathetic, having seen that I was ill, but the others weren't at all. I've noticed this in Third World countries—sick people do not receive the pampering and fuss we in England have come to expect, and a sick *gringo* is often a source of entertainment. One of the drivers commented that no wonder the British economy was in such a state if everyone lay down instead of working! Another, when I said I'd had fever for three days, spat and said he had once had it for ten days but still drove his truck.

"Very macho," I snarled sarcastically, pulling the blanket over my head.

At Santarém the delays were not over—there was no boat to Manaus for three days—so I lay in a hotel room and continued to suffer every night from rigors and fever. The problems were compounded by a shortage of money. I had just come off the Rio Teles Pires, and all I had was $10. Saving some for the boat journey to Manaus (where money was waiting), I had to choose between a hotel and eating. Good thing I was not hungry, for the idea of lying in the streets in this condition made me choose the former. Even when treated to a meal by another traveler, I found I could not eat more than a mouthful anyway. Everything tasted unpleasant, and just looking at it or smelling it made me retch.

So I had not eaten for several days by the time the boat set sail. I slung my hammock and crawled into it, knowing that at least food was provided with the fare if I felt like it, and that within three days I would have money to see a doctor in Manaus.

However, South America always chooses such moments for delays. Twelve hours out from Santarém the propeller broke and another two days passed before we got under way again. By now I had had fever for nine days and each afternoon the attacks seemed more severe. Trying to fight the violent shivers left me totally exhausted, and then I poured with sweat until my shirt and trousers did not have a dry patch on them. After a few hours, feeling marginally better, I'd had to get up for a pee and to drink some water. By this time it was usually midnight and everyone was asleep.

The deck was completely obstructed by hammocks and the only way for someone of my size to get to the toilets at the far end was to crawl along the floor, over the luggage and under the low-slung hammocks. After risking other diseases by gulping a liter or two of untreated river water I returned the same way. Before retiring to my sodden hammock I dug out some aspirin from my backpack—although they did little to relieve the appalling headaches.

Perhaps it was paranoia, but the passengers on the boat seemed hostile and unfriendly—two very rare characteristics in Brazil.

> *It was funny, I thought, how gringos never talked about diarrhea when they talked and wrote about rain forests. White people from the northern hemisphere were always saying outrageous things about the jungles. In fact, gringos never called them jungles anymore. Kiss Tarzan of the Jungle, and darkest jungles, and steaming jungles, and savage jungles, good-bye. The P.R. crescendo had turned the dangerous, exotic places I had dreamed of in my youth into rain forests, an innocuous name more Tolkien than Edgar Rice Burroughs. Rain forests were mystical places filled with wise native peoples who talked to nature and understood life. Rain forests were groovy.*
>
> *But I stood by the rail of the boat and watched a young caboclo woman nurse a small child as three others—all hers, all born before the woman was twenty—sat quietly at her feet, and wondered which of them would die from diarrhea.*
>
> —Brian Alexander, *Green Cathedrals: A Wayward Traveler in the Rain Forest*

Perhaps it was partly explained by my lack of attempt to chat with my neighbors. I was not in the mood, and made no effort to pick up the conversational openers thrown in my direction. I wanted to lie there and suffer in peace and privacy.

On the second night of the renewed boat journey I crawled to the far end for the usual reasons, and found several men still up and playing cards. Finding the water container empty, I asked one of them if he would mind filling it for me. That meant hanging over the side of the lower deck and scooping it from the river, and I did not trust my strength and feared I would fall overboard.

"Fill it yourself," he replied, not looking up from his cards.

I must have looked ill; hair plastered to my head with sweat, clothes sodden, swaying on rubbery legs, but I explained I was sick and was afraid of falling overboard.

One of them got up reluctantly to fill the jug, but another commented that a fall into the river was the best thing that could happen to me. I burst into tears. I felt so bloody ill, miserable and weak, that this was the last straw.

That night the nightmares started; gold was hidden on me and everyone on board was out to kill me. My illness was their chance to get the gold and toss me overboard. The next morning I could barely distinguish between dream and reality, and with a temperature of 104 degrees those delusions continued all day. Everyone passing near my hammock was a potential assailant, and anyone regarding me with mild curiosity was a jackal waiting for my end. That end did not seem far away: my clothing after several pints of sweat poured over it had the sickly sweet odor of death. I imagined my body was beginning to rot already.

In the late afternoon when I started to shake, rattle, and roll in another attack, I became aware of a commotion around my hammock. Summoning reserves of strength I listened to the shouting voices.

"Every night I see him crawling around under the hammocks opening suitcases," said one.

"Let's search his pack to see if he's hidden it in there," suggested another.

People then grabbed my pack and began to pull out the contents. When they found my camera they let out a cry of delight.

"If we don't find the money, this must be worth something."

I sat up, shivering violently, asked what the hell was going on.

Someone had a large sum of money stolen from his suitcase, I was told, and I was the prime suspect. A large crowd had gathered—everyone shouting excitedly, so I asked who it was that was accusing me. Two men came sheepishly forward and I tried to conduct my defense through chattering teeth. I said they were welcome to look through my pack, and if it were really necessary I would even get up and let them search my clothing and body, too.

"Why do you open people's suitcases at night?" one asked me. So I explained that I was ill (they did not seem very perceptive, this lot), and that the only baggage I opened at night was my own to get aspirin.

Without even finishing the search of my luggage, the men departed and the passengers collected in little groups discussing the case out of earshot. I realized I was crying again, and I supposed I had been sobbing when replying to my accusers.

Later the captain himself came over, and said that I was cleared of suspicion, that they'd decided the thief must have got off at the previous stop.

"You've got malaria," he told me.

"Oh, no, it can't be. I take a pill called Maloprim," I replied and even refused some chloroquine that he offered me.

We got to Manaus the next day, and after collecting my money from the bank (and fainting twice in the street during the brief walk there), I got a taxi to the hospital where they diagnosed Falciparum malaria.

Now, when I think back on that boat trip, one thing bothers me. Did the incident of the stolen money ever happen? There is no doubt that I believed it at the time—and probably even sat up sobbing a defense. But did I imagine the rest? Three days after arriving in Manaus, when I felt stronger after some treatment, I spent half an hour searching my possessions for that gold. The nightmare had taken hold. Had it been stolen, or had it never existed? I still don't know.

John Harrison has spent the last twenty years traveling the world, concentrating on Latin America, and the Amazon in particular. A keen canoeist, he finds the Amazon's 1,000 tributaries hard to leave alone, and loves those empty areas of rainforest, devoid of humans, yet teeming with other life. When not traveling, he writes, lectures, produces TV and radio programs, and has his own construction firm. He lives in Bristol, England, with his wife and son.

⋆

Having spent two months traveling in the primary rainforests of Borneo, a four-month journey in the country between Orinco and the Amazon would pose, I thought, no particular problem. There are no leeches that go for you in the Amazon jungles, an absence which would represent, I felt, a great improvement on life in Borneo. But then there *are* much the same amoebic and bacillary dysenteries, yellow and blackwater and dengue fevers, malaria, cholera, typhoid, rabies, hepatitis and tuberculosis—plus one or two very special extras.

There is Chagas' disease, for instance, produced by a protozoon, *Tripanozoma crusii*, and carried by various species of assassin bugs which bite you on the face or neck and then, gorged, defecate next to the puncture. When you scratch the resulting itch you rub the droppings and their cargo of protozoa into your bloodstream; between one and twenty years later you begin to die from incurable damage to the heart and brain. Then there is *onchocerciasis*, river blindness, transmitted by blackfly and caused by worms which migrate to the eyeball; *leishmaniasis*, which is like leprosy and is produced by a parasite carried by sandflies (it affects eighty percent of Brazilian troops on exercise in the jungle in the rainy season): unless treated quickly, it eats away the warm extremities. And then there is the odd exotic, like the fever which erupted in the state of Pará in the 1960s, killing 71 people, including the research unit sent to identify it.

The big animals are supposed to be much friendlier than you might imagine. The jaguar kills you with a bite to the head, but only in exceptional circumstances. Two vipers, the fer-de-lance and the bushmaster, only kill you if you step on them. The anaconda is known to tighten its grip only when you breathe out; the electric eel can only deliver its 640 volts before its breakfast; the piranha only rips you to bits if you are already bleeding, and the giant catfish merely has a penchant for taking your feet off at the ankles as you do the crawl. The smaller animals are, on the whole, much more annoying—the mosquitoes, blackfly, tapir-fly, chiggers, ticks, scabies-producing *Tunga penetrans* and *Dermatobia hominis*, the human botfly, whose larvae bore into the skin, eat modest amounts of you for 40 days, and emerge as inch-long maggots.

—Redmond O'Hanlon, *In Trouble Again: A Journey Between the Orinoco and the Amazon*

MAC MARGOLIS

✦ ✦ ✦

Young, Down, and Out

For poor Brazilian children like Luciana,
life is a game of survival.

LUCIANA LOOKS UP AT ME AND PUTS ON A FROWN. SHE HAS BEEN interrupted while playing with her friends in a large plaza in downtown Rio de Janeiro. Her eyes narrow. She's thinking, is this a *boi*, a cow in Portuguese and street slang for an easy mark for a mugging?

Maybe it's *sangue bom*, "good blood," meaning a friend or an ally. But hang on, it just might be a *tira*, a cop. On the streets of Rio, the presence of an unknown adult can mean many things, and sizing up a newcomer quickly is a matter of survival.

Luciana is thirteen years old, but could easily pass for eight. Her small frame and mischievous eyes belie an experience that goes way beyond her years. A ten-inch scar makes an ugly seam down her left thigh, the result of an old "accident," when the driver of a bus she was clinging to swiped her off on a passing car, just as a horse might shake a fly. A swollen mound on her left foot marks the spot where a .22-caliber bullet sits, the result of a gang fight. Talk to Luciana for a little while and you'll learn a treasure of details about street life: where to sleep without getting bullied by cops, how to pick a pocket and melt away in the night, and where to buy cocaine.

Luciana and her friends are street kids—one of thousands, some say millions, of children between ages five and eighteen who roam Brazil's big cities, begging and stealing to survive. Her life is a window on the complex and dangerous existence of Brazilian youth. Many take to the streets to escape harsh discipline and abuse at home; others have parents simply too poor to house or feed them. The problems they cause, and their sheer numbers, threaten to tear Brazilian society apart.

The kids sleep wherever they can—under the marquee of a porno theater, in a vacant stoop, on a park bench. For escape, they sniff tins of shoemaker's glue for a mild high of dizziness and hallucinations. The glue causes permanent damage to their lungs and brains, but also dampens their hunger. Thousands fall prey to prostitution and disease. In Recife, on the northeastern coast, one in three prostitutes is between twelve and sixteen years old. In São Paulo, Brazil's largest city, 428 teenagers tested positive for the AIDS virus at a shelter for delinquent minors.

To many Brazilians, street kids are simply rats to be exterminated. Police figures show that over a ten-year period 6,033 children were murdered on the streets of Rio. The child murders are the most chilling response of scared and outraged shop owners and residents who have been robbed one too many times. Unable to count on the police, they turn to vigilante groups, mostly moonlighting cops or thugs for hire. They do not necessarily order up these murders; they simply "rent" these freelance gunmen and look the other way.

Lately, though, the death squads have given way to drug traffickers. More and more, drug lords have infiltrated many major

*O*ur hotel was on the Copacabana, where most of the children hang out, for there the wealthy tourists congregate. Anyone who owns a home, a complete set of clothes, who has access to hot running water, and eats regularly falls into the rich category for these children, who feel, quite naturally, that to take money, jewelry, or cameras from such people is no great hardship for them, for such things the rich can easily replace.

—Elizabeth Hillman, "Some Hope for Brazil's Abandoned Children," *Contemporary Review* cities, especially Rio, sucking children into the drug trade. To children of the shantytowns and poor areas, "nothing besides football players is so attractive as the drug lord," said anthropologist Alba Zaluar. "They are the ones with money, new cars, pretty girls, and authority."

The youngest children begin as lookouts, or "airplanes," tipping off the drug bosses when strangers, an enemy gangman, or the cops approach. Some may "graduate" to become security guards or partners in trafficking, peddling small quantities for the drug overlords. Many end up addicted or dead. Authorities say that involvement in drug trafficking accounts for at least half the child murders.

In 1988, legislators rewrote the constitution and drafted what is widely recognized as the world's most advanced child protection statute. But injustice persists throughout the society. Brazil has one of the widest income gaps in the world, with a handful of very wealthy people and a huge class of poor. Only ten percent of the nation's children even complete elementary school. With an entire generation lost to the streets, the future of Brazil itself is in danger. As Brazil's former president, Itamar Franco, said in his first speech to the nation in 1991: "In unjust societies like our own, the only thing distributed with equity is fear."

The stark contrast between rich and poor can be seen every night on Rio's *Cinelandia* (literally, "Cinema Land"), a broad boulevard named for its elegant movie houses. As night falls here, the Rio upper class files by Luciana and her friends, up the marble steps to the stately Teatro Municipal, modeled after the Paris Opera House.

Like most street kids, Luciana has a home of sorts. To get there you literally walk through a hole in the wall, up a dirt path to a row of wooden shanties, separated by an open sewage ditch. The shanties, made of tin, plywood, and plasterboard, sprout up on any unclaimed plot of city land, sometimes clinging impossibly to sheer slopes or standing on stilts above sewer water. Often they collapse under torrential rains or landslides.

Luciana's family moved to one of these shanties a little over a year ago, when the rent got too steep in Queimadas, a rural village not far from Rio. Once in a while, Luciana comes home from the street for a visit or a meal.

Unlike many of her street friends, she was not beaten or molested by her parents or relatives. Her mother, who is 48 and single, simply could not afford to support four children and a grandchild on the meager wage she earned sweeping up at a city hospital. Luciana first left home at age six, when she got tired of handing over to her mother the day's take from selling oranges and sweets in downtown Rio. One day she just pocketed the money. She has never looked back.

"The street is better," she says. "I have a lot of friends here. There are fights, but I'm friends with everybody." Now and then, her mother comes by Cinelandia to try to persuade her to come home. But Luciana doesn't stay long. "All she wants is to be on the street," her mother says, shaking her head sadly. "Nobody can hold her back anymore. She's going to die on the street someday."

Dangerous as it is, Luciana thinks of the street as a place of adventure, even of freedom. She is tenaciously independent and allergic to anything that smacks of authority. The day after she left the hospital, where she was being treated for the bullet wound in her foot, she defied doctor's orders to rest and hobbled onto a bus to Cinelandia. There, she showed off her new white cast. The next day she took a hammer and freed herself from the bulky plaster. When an older street "brother" announced he was taking her back to the hospital to replace the cast, she stormed off as fast as her bum foot would allow.

Weeks later, the cops ousted Luciana and the rest of the street kids from the broad steps of the municipal assembly building, where the children met nightly. I eventually found her in a half-lit, urine-soaked alleyway behind Cinelandia.

Luciana recognized me, and having already sized me up, turned on her charms. A smile and an outstretched hand quickly won her a Coke and a plate of chicken and rice. Satisfied, she leaned over to whisper a secret. She wanted a bicycle, a walkie-talkie, a trip to the amusement park, and, to top it off, a trip, say, around the world. She laughed at her own wish list, then limped away to her friends and the dark, dank alley that was her newest home.

Months later, I went back to Rio's rough downtown to find out about Luciana. I learned that she had tired of the street and the constant police raids, and finally retreated to the São Martinho shelter for kids, which offers warm food, a mattress, and a series of vocational courses for street kids. With new commitments from the government and aid from the United Nations, institutions like São Martinho are reclaiming dozens of street kids from the dangers of Rio.

But not Luciana. "She just didn't fit into our program," a social worker there told me. "We couldn't keep her here."

By the new year, she was back on the street again.

Mac Margolis also contributed "Patience, Patience" in Part II.

★

Yesterday I saw a man walking on his knees. His lower legs seemed to trail uselessly behind him like withered branches where no life flowed. He moved himself along by swinging his body between his hands, which acted as crutches. He was so inured to his plight that his naked knees had no protection and had hardened themselves, just as had the toughened bare feet of the poor. So his knees were now his feet, carrying him along the pavement, his view being the legs of the other walkers. He made his way along the rich, store-lined Avenue Copacabana, bobbing between the feet and dodging the traffic, and nobody took much notice, as if it was a familiar and tolerable sight, something you endure and even condone. Poor man should be a lesson in how sinful it is to be so poor and wretched. Somehow it was the man's fault. Nobody seemed horrified or to give him a second glance.

Rio's biggest symbol is the figure of Christ that holds out his stiff, concrete arms to the world beneath him. Never was a symbol more meaningless. Never did his words mean so little to those below. Never in my life have I seen so little charity or compassion in any city where extreme wealth and unendurable poverty lie side by side. I have seen no equivalent here to the War on Poverty or Oxfam—or any organization that could tap some of the enormous wealth rotting in banks. The man on his knees was an adequate symbol of Brazil. This is the figure that should be atop the giant hill and on all the postcards.

—Steven Berkoff, *A Prisoner in Rio*

WILLIAM R. LONG

✦ ✦ ✦

The Word Denied

"Civilization" is driving the Guarani to suicide.

TEN PEOPLE HAD KILLED THEMSELVES IN THE FIRST TEN MONTHS OF the year. That was a shocking toll for Caarapo, a rural community of 3,200 Kaiowa Guarani Indians in the western Brazilian state of Mato Grosso do Sul. Just as shocking was the tender age of some of the victims. The youngest was Fortunata Escobar, ten years old.

When she died, Fortunata's father had been away for more than a month, working for a distillery. Her mother had died of natural causes earlier in the year.

Eight brothers and sisters were staying by themselves in the family's rustic hut. Alone in the house with a four-year-old sister one August day, Fortunata strung herself up by the neck from a roof pole.

I wanted to find out why.

"I don't know," said Lourdes Escobar, Fortunata's oldest sister. Lourdes, twenty, wore bright lipstick, a new-looking red blouse, and a tight black skirt that was also fairly new looking. She had on a wristwatch, too. I wondered where she got money for this stuff, but there she was, all dressed up with nowhere to go on a sultry Saturday afternoon, standing in the open doorway of the family's new home. It was the same kind of hut, with thatched roof and dirt floor, as the one they had moved from to escape "bad spirits" after Fortunata's death.

Obviously uncomfortable answering a stranger's questions about a painful matter, Lourdes kept her answers brief. She said Fortunata hadn't seemed upset or sad. Could she have heard about other people hanging themselves and tried it herself in play? "I think so," Lourdes told me, but I wasn't convinced. And even if Fortunata's death could be explained as a copycat suicide, that didn't account for the alarming number of other Indians who had killed themselves.

Since 1990, a suicide epidemic has afflicted not only Caarapo but several other communities of Guarani-speaking Indians, members of the Kaiowa and Nandeva tribes, in the southern end of Mato Grosso do Sul. Since 1986, some 400 Kaiowa have committed suicide—51 in 2003 alone. In a Guarani population of about 30,000, that translates into a rate of 170 suicides per 100,000 people.

By comparison, the annual suicide rate among Navajos living on U.S. reservations is 17 per 100,000 population, according to a U.S. Indian Health Service report based on 1987–1989 data. Nationwide, the U.S. rate is about 12 per 100,000, and Brazil's is less than 4 per 100,000, according to 1991 statistics.

Obviously, something was deeply and desperately wrong in Mato Grosso do Sul. I went to Caarapo knowing that I probably would not find a clear and simple explanation for the tragic phenomenon but hoping for some understanding beyond what I had learned from articles in the Brazilian press.

I did background reading from a folder of news clippings and other documents on file in the *Los Angeles Times'* Rio bureau, with its picture-window view of yacht-sprinkled Guanabara Bay and the city's famous hillside *favelas*. Most analysts agreed that the Guarani suicides are related to a breakdown of old cultural patterns and a failure to adjust to new ones. Throughout the Americas, numerous native cultures are crumbling under the onslaught of outside pressures and influences. The toll in human suffering and degradation is often dramatic, but none more so than the Guarani suicides.

Brazil has a total of 250,000 to 300,000 Indians in many language and cultural groups. The Guarani are the largest group, but it is now tiny compared to their numbers centuries ago. Guarani-speaking peoples once dominated a large region of South America extending from northern Argentina through Paraguay and deep into southern Brazil. The total estimated Guarani population when the Spanish and Portuguese came to South America in the 1500s was two million.

Today, about 25,000 of the 30,000 Guarani Indians of the Kaiowa and Nandeva tribes in Mato Grosso do Sul live on 22 small reservations scattered over rolling plains of red earth that once was forested but now is mostly farm fields and pasture. Much of their land is overgrown with a deep-rooted weed called *colonião* that crowds out food crops and is stubbornly resilient. The Guaranis' farming methods are rudimentary, and the soils are weak from heavy use.

A 1993 study by Brazilian social researcher Olivio Mangolim says Guarani Indians occupied 40 percent of the territory in Mato Grosso do Sul two centuries ago but now are left with less than 1 percent, about 53,000 acres. "Today these small reservations continue to be invaded, their sacred territories exploited by big land-grabbers," Mangolim wrote. I knew from previous reporting that this was true of Indians elsewhere in Brazil, but it didn't explain why the Guarani have such an extraordinarily high suicide rate.

Communities that once lived by hunting, fishing, and subsistence farming are ruinously crowded onto reservations that don't have enough land for that kind of life. Cities have sprung up nearby, tempting the natives with consumer goods and urban diversions. Alcohol distilleries, which produce fuel from sugarcane to supplement gasoline in Brazil, recruit Guarani men for cane-cutting and other menial, low-wage jobs. Some women find work in town as domestic servants, some girls as prostitutes. Alcoholism has become widespread.

As the old ways of the Guarani have faded, their disorientation has increased. As their need for commercial goods has grown, their awareness of their poverty has sharpened. Family unity has weakened, community life has wilted, religious meaning has waned.

"For the Guarani, their life is not a life worth living," said Antonio Brand, a Brazilian historian who has done extensive research on Guarani culture. The collapse of the traditional Guarani economy, Brand explained, has meant the collapse of traditional religious life, because every act in the process of making a living from the land was a religious ritual. It is impossible to separate the economy from the religion, as we do in our culture," he said. Brand told me that the Guarani have been losing their ancestral forest lands for centuries, but that the most

The Indians are trying to live in two keys, ancient and modern. At the same time. But the Indians appreciate only the simplest traits in our culture, the ones that are—unfortunately—the weakest. They add these traits to their own culture without integrating, interpreting, or changing them. In this way, they create hybrid societies that are unlivable. Their passive resistance is not enough to sustain them, and they gradually lose even a sense of the injustice that is crushing them.

—Jacques Meunier and A. M. Savarin, *The Amazonian Chronicles*

devastating deforestation began in the 1950s and 1960s. In the 1970s, large-scale soybean planting for the export market dealt a final blow to the forests of Mato Grosso do Sul. "Finally, there were no more trees," Brand said disgustedly. "It is totally deforested. It is a crime."

For the Guarani, the crime may be lethal. Mauricio Souza Vilalba, a Guarani-speaking university student, said that because they no longer have enough land for their traditional lifestyle, "the people are being pulled away from their roots." Without those roots, life as the Guarani know it is difficult to live.

I met Mauricio in Dourados, a city about 40 miles north of Caarapo. He is active in the regional chapter of a Roman Catholic Church agency called the Indigenous Missionary Council, or CIMI, that does social and educational work among the Guarani. Hoping that more outside interest in the suicide epidemic would somehow help lead to a solution, he agreed to drive with me to Caarapo and introduce me to residents. The people were likely to be more open with me, he said, if I arrived with someone they know and trust. But he warned me that suicide is a subject that many are reluctant to discuss with anyone.

Before we left for Caarapo in my rented Fiat *Uno Mille*, an economy car made in Brazil, Mauricio primed me on the deeply spiritual nature of Guarani culture. Traditionally, Guarani religion was reinforced in a close-knit community structure led by a *cacique*, or religious chieftain, and by the family. As community structures have broken down and families have lost unity, the individual's sense of religious well-being has faded. Catholic and Protestant missionary work in Guarani communities has contributed to undermining the ancient faith.

The Guarani worship a divine family headed by *Nande Ru*, "the great father." Nande Ru speaks his truth through the souls and lives of the Guarani people. "The individual is a word of god," Mauricio explained. "The body is the home of the word." An individual's life is valid only when it expresses the word as the religion requires in all of its aspects—hunting, farming, family life, and community activities.

"The life of the people must mirror Nande Ru's way of life," he said, eager to help me understand the spiritual malaise of the Guarani. "Every aspect of life should be the expression of Nande Ru's word." Because they can no longer live their lives in the traditional way, many Guarani find life empty of meaning, he said.

"What they are living today is no longer what Nande Ru wants; it no longer is the word of Nande Ru. They feel that they have lost the way of Nande Ru."

Mauricio, a soft-spoken young man with expressive brown eyes, admitted that he does not fully understand the suicide epidemic but said it is related to those religious beliefs. "Suicide is a protest because a person can no longer express the word of Nande Ru. It is the word denied. When he sees that he is a word denied, he is asphyxiated. He commits suicide."

He said the use of hanging or poison in almost all Guarani suicides is a way of stopping the word, or spirit, from ascending through the throat. "The spirit stays on the ground, lost," he said. It becomes a "bad spirit" that seeks company, inducing others to commit suicide.

Although suicide is not encouraged by the Guarani religion, he said, it is sometimes admired as a final act of valor in a life stripped of the traditional ways. "The Guarani wants to show that he is courageous. He needs to be admired."

Guarani people also believe in hexes that can cause someone to commit suicide. Those whose lives do not follow tradition are considered to be vulnerable to such spells, said Mauricio, whose family is of Guarani origin.

We talked in an open shed at the back of the CIMI headquarters in Dourados, an old stucco house on a residential street. The shade of the shed took only a little of the wallop out of the afternoon heat. It was cooler when we left for Caarapo early the next morning. On the way, we drove across undulating plain, passing plowed fields and green pastures that reached the horizon. Here and there we saw clusters of zebu cattle, with their humped backs and sagging white hide. In Mato Grosso do Sul, Mauricio commented, a beef steer has a right to more land than an Indian does.

The Caarapo reservation is less than 9,000 acres of flat farmland, laced with dirt lanes that connect scattered huts made of rough planks, poles, and thatching. The bright heaviness of the day's increasing heat seemed to emphasize the squalor of the fragile little dwellings as we drove the heavily rutted dirt road into the community at midmorning. The well-trodden yards of most homes were bare of vegetation, but green *colonião* weeds choked roadside ditches and invaded fields, standing several feet high where it was left uncut. A few chickens, skinny dogs, and people were out and about in the lanes and fields, but there was no farm machinery to be seen, no cars or trucks. By Latin American standards, I quickly saw, this was rural poverty at its basic level.

The first person Mauricio introduced me to was Assunção Gonçalves, 36, who was hoeing patches of *colonião* weed from a field near his ramshackle home. Gonçalves came to Caarapo after repeated attempts to recover land on a ranch where his family had lived for generations. He and a few other Guarani tried to occupy the land three times, but each time, the police came and forced them to leave.

"I was born there," he said. "My mother, my grandparents, my great-grandparents all died there."

Gonçalves was wearing torn pants over worn-out boots and a tattered cap over uncut hair and scraggly beard. He and his wife have had seven children, but three have died of illnesses. He said many children in Caarapo are sick and hungry. Four had died in the past few months from eating spoiled food scavenged from the garbage dump of a neighboring town, also called Caarapo.

The twelve-year-old daughter of a neighbor committed suicide the year before, Gonçalves said. The father was away working at an alcohol distillery, and the girl's stepmother had scolded her one day, "called her lazy." The stepmother went out, "and when she came back, the girl was hanging in the house," Gonçalves said. The family burned the house and moved away "because of the bad spirits."

Mauricio helped Gonçalves hoe *colonião* for a while. Then we went looking for Jorge Paulo, Caarapo's *cacique*, or religious chief. We found him with his wife at the home of her sister. Paulo, 77, was wearing a straw hat, a black pin-striped suit jacket over a yellow t-shirt, and a pair of white rubber boots. He offered a variety of explanations for the suicide epidemic. In the cases of several youths who have killed themselves, he cited familial neglect: "Sometimes the father doesn't work, doesn't help his child. The child goes hungry at home and doesn't have a lunch to take to school."

The *cacique* said a widespread neglect of religious practice and prayer also leads to suicides. "If there are 1,000 Indians, only 8 or 9 remember God," he said. "Nande Ru is angry."

I asked him what the community could do to stop the suicides. "We would have to spend a whole day, two days, to pray and baptize the earth," he said. "In a year, two or three years, it wouldn't happen anymore."

Silvio Paulo, the community's *capitão*, or political leader, had other explanations for the suicides. He said alcohol often is involved, but that the drinking is caused by "a sickness of the spirit. People are desperate."

And the sickness seems to be contagious. Young people who have gone to see the body of a suicide victim sometimes commit suicide themselves soon after.

"Before, they didn't go to see the bodies. Only older people did," Silvio Paulo said outside his home, a bigger shack than most in the community but still made of the customary rough slats, planks, and sticks. The walls were flimsy, loosely fitted, unpainted, and full of unchinked cracks. "Today, children, youths, everyone goes."

Increased contact with city life has undermined Guarani customs, he said. "Children go to school, and they go to the city. They want diversions, they want shoes, they want watches." They become frustrated because they cannot afford many of those things. At the same time, traditional pastimes, such as hunting and fishing, have been lost.

But what is most lacking is religious practice and religious leadership, according to the *capitão*, who criticized the *cacique* for failing to teach and inspire religious faith.

"He no longer makes true prayers," Silvio Paulo said, not hiding his disapproval. "He's getting old. He doesn't bring people

A long time ago a Juruna visited Sinaá, the first Juruna. Sinaá was married to a huge spider that made dresses. Sinaá was very old, all white, but he became young again each time he took a bath, pulling his skin off over his head like a sack. After Sinaá asked how his people were, he took his guest to the top of a large rock, from which the Juruna could be seen down below, fishing in their canoes. Finally Sinaá showed the Juruna visitor an enormous forked stick that supported the sky and said, "The day our people die out entirely, I will pull this down, and the sky will collapse, and all people will disappear. That will be the end of everything."

—Orlando Villas Boas and Claudio Villas Boas, *Xingu: The Indians, Their Myths* together anymore. People don't get together anymore to sing."

It is clear that there is no single, simple explanation for the Guarani suicides. "There are a series of factors that add up," said historian Brand, who was preparing a doctoral thesis on the Guarani. Changes in economic and social patterns have had a magnified psychological impact on the Guarani because of their deeply mystical and sentimental nature, he said. "The supernatural is permanently involved in their spiritual life. They are fantastic people. Personal relations, family relations, kinship relations are fundamental in their day-to-day lives," and the breakdown in these ties can be devastating, he said.

Gonçalves Araujo, nineteen, was caught between the old ways and the new reality of the Guarani. He married Marta Martins when she was twelve and moved into his mother-in-law's household, as is the Guarani custom.

But Araujo went off to work for a distillery with a friend, Pedro Paulo Benites. Benites said the two returned after 50 days with money in their pockets, but by the time Araujo settled an old grocery store debt and bought some more food, his money was gone.

Araujo started drinking and kept at it for two days, Benites said. On the second day, his wife gave birth to a premature and sickly boy. Shortly after the baby was born, Araujo told his wife that he was going to go sleep in a thatch-roofed shed near his mother-in-law's house. Benites, a lean but sturdy young man, showed me where his friend's body was later found hanging in the shed.

"I guess he was angry because his baby was going to die," said Benites. The baby died a week later, the day I visited the family with Mauricio. The infant's body, wrapped in rags, was lying in a makeshift crib on the dirt floor of its grandmother's hut. Marta, the thirteen-year-old mother, appeared to be in shock. In the bright sun outside, she stared blankly when I asked her about her husband's suicide. As I drove away, Mauricio told me that the girl seemed likely to commit suicide herself.

"She will hang herself, almost certainly," he predicted.

Over the past twenty-five years, Bill Long reported from every country in

Latin America for The Associated Press, The Miami Herald, *and the* Los Angeles Times. *He lived in Brazil for a total of seven years, including four as Rio de Janeiro bureau chief for the* Times. *Since 1996, he has been a freelance writer, consultant, and journalism teacher based in Boulder, Colorado, where he grew up.*

✦

The Yanomami had always been there, shaman Davi Kopenawa Yanomami said, and had never moved away. "The Indian existed here before you came, before your father or mother existed," he said. "He does not come from another country. The first Yanomami is our creator, Omam. We were born here; Omam raised us and left us here. Then the Yanomami grew great and scattered over this land. Omam created everything, even you." Similarly, he said, the white did not discover Brazil, because it always existed, along with the Indians, its first inhabitants.

There are four main Yanomami groups, speaking different languages, each with its own dialect. The myth of creation perpetuated in this particular group of Yanomami said that the world was made of three superimposed layers. Originally there were only two, but the top one became old and worn, a large piece of it fell, taking with it two men. One of them was Omam, and he fathered Yanomami people when he was fishing in a stream and pulled out a woman. She did not, however, have genitalia, only a tiny hole, "like the anus of a hummingbird." Omam took the teeth of a piranha and cut out genitalia, after which he had many children.

The whites and other races were made from the foam or mist that lay along the river. A large bird pushed the foam to the shore and formed it into men, and the shading of the foam reflected the different colors of the human race.

I asked him to tell me more about Omam. "Omam is good for us," he said. "He is our chief. He is not like the gold prospector. He does not destroy the earth and the forest, he does not ruin the river, he doesn't look for gold. He doesn't bring sickness to kill others. Omam is respect, he loves us very much. He likes the Indian and the forest. Omam is very wise, not like the Brazilian government.

"It cannot see," Davi said, "because it is blinded by the gleam of gold."

—Augusta Dwyer, *Into the Amazon: The Struggle for the Rain Forest*

RYAN S. KELLY

Two *Fitas* and a Tattoo

Sometimes a lucky charm isn't enough.

I HAD BEEN FOREWARNED ABOUT THE STREET CRIME IN SALVADOR da Bahia. *"Tres dias, não mais,"* whooped Rumalho, a character paralyzed with a permanent leer that accentuated his gleaming white teeth against his caramel complexion. A combination of Bahian hospitality and financial duress had led him and his wife, Karla, to rent me a room of their cramped quarters a block away from the Avenida Sete do Setembro in Barra, Salvador's active beachfront district which commands the entrance to All Saints Bay. "Three days before you will be wearing the tattoo of a *ladrão!*"

Karla was more optimistic of my chances for survival, but by no means did she underscore the dangers present in Salvador, the colonial masterpiece of Brazil, a city that has been sliding into a miasma of poverty and obsolescence ever since gold was struck in the interior 250 years ago. Stories of victimization ranged from horrific to downright amusing:

> An uncle had been bested of his wallet late one night by two *ladroes* on the *Lacerda*, the pedestrian elevator that connects the lower part of Salvador to its upper neighborhoods. The thieves had been hiding in the shaft and had burst through the roof of the compartment.

The maid's sister had nearly bled to death when a *ladrão* on a motorcycle attempted to swipe her purse. The assailant, who had stolen up behind her with the intent of slicing her purse string with a filet knife, had hit an unseen pothole at the last moment and went careening into her, plunging the blade into her side.

A friend of a cousin, in the heat of the moment with his girlfriend, had been pistol-whipped by two thugs after dark on Praia Armação.

This last incident seemed to disturb Karla the most—that *ladroes* were now violating the unwritten code regarding the wide berth given to couples coupling after dark on the Bahian littoral was a sign of increased desperation and an omen of bad things to come. I, as a fair-skinned visitor, was known as "filet mignon" in the local *ladrão* lingo. At least if I were to be thought of as a piece of meat I was stamped as a quality cut. For my own protection Karla tied two blue ribbons, known as *fitas,* around my right wrist, taking care to secure each with three knots and a quick *beijo* on the cheek for emphasis. You will be hard pressed in Salvador to find someone without one. Leave it on your wrist (it falls off from natural wear and tear in a month or two) and it is a constant source of good luck. Cut the *fita* off and bad luck will hound you as persistently as the street kids on every Salvador street corner attempting to sell you a lifetime supply of these multicolored talismans.

My first two days in Salvador passed without incident, as did my third, to the relief and consternation of Rumalho. The con-

> *S*trangely, most residents of São Salvador da Bahia de Todos os Santos— "Holy Savior of the Bay of all the Saints," as the city is formally named—seem to dislike the sea. Windows opening on an ocean view are often kept shut, and are sometimes even blacked out; servants' quarters are generally on the sea side of the house. Bahia is full of art and artists, but nobody would ever dream of painting a marine landscape, although the coastline is extravagantly picturesque.
>
> —John Gunther, *Inside South America*

stant throng of activity along the Avenida Sete do Setembro made the threat of a violent assault seem impossible. Past travel experiences spanning the globe from India to Peru had proved that even in the worst neighborhoods of Calcutta and Lima a six-foot redhead, thoroughly unable to blend into the local populace, could avoid incidents through a simple regimen of dressing down, leaving the watch at home, and sticking to the major streets. As a general rule, I always kept a few dollars on me so in case the worst were to happen I would have something to give a desperate assailant.

I had visited the Morro do Cristo on a number of occasions on my daily walks along the Avenida Sete do Setembro. The *morro* juts out into the Atlantic by several hundred feet and, like its namesake, bears a statue of Christ atop its windswept summit, a miniature of Rio's fabled Corcovado. The *morro* was usually awash in activity: lovers intertwined along the base of the Cristo; corpulent old men putting short work to bottles of Brahma, the choice *cerveja* of Bahia; and a litany of *futebol* matches unfolding beneath the benevolent gaze of the Cristo. Today, however, the sky was overcast and the beaches and *morro* were silent. In Salvador, where everyone lives within shouting distance of the coast and the weather is picturesque year round, an invitation to go to the beach on a less than perfect day will be met with a smile and an *amanhã*—a decidedly Brazilian tomorrow that in Bahia can (and usually does) mean more than just a day.

A lone *Baiano* was atop the *morro* when I arrived, drinking what smelled like *cachaça*, the potent Brazilian homemade rum, out of a Coca-Cola bottle that would have long ago been sentenced to the recycling bin in the States. He eyed me contemptuously; he was quite drunk. I opted not to return the stare, instead focusing my attention on the far side of the *morro*, a rocky, precipitous drop into the Atlantic. A solitary fisherman stood at the edge of the bluff, casting for his lunch. I shinnied down the wall and began to negotiate the steep path through the rocks down to the edge of the ocean.

I claimed a perch that jetted out into the ocean some 50 feet from the fisherman and sat down. Below me was a frightening cavalcade of sharp rocks between which the raw sewage of Salvador sloshed about. The fisherman smiled and waved. I returned the greeting and gazed out to the distant horizon. Across this stretch of the Atlantic lay not Europe but Angola. I sat thinking about this perspective for quite some time, listening to the incessant crash of the waves against the rocks. A distant sound of breaking glass interrupted the harmony. I looked up to see where the sound originated, but there was nothing aside from the steep, charcoal escarpment of the *morro*.

When I turned again after a long period of silence I saw the drunk fumbling his way through the fractured maze of boulders. He was barefoot; I could not fathom how he could endure the razor sharp edges of the rocks. A fall was imminent. *"Cuidado!"* I called out, but he failed to heed my warning. Not wishing to witness his plunge, I turned back to the ocean. A minute later the fisherman issued a shrill whistle and urgently pointed a finger in my direction. Before I had time to react it was already too late.

My position on the edge of the bluff made it impossible for me to run. The drunk had covered the bottom half of the pitch in a flash. I could smell the *cachaça* on his breath, but by no means was he the drunk he appeared to be above; it had all been a guise. The bottle from which he had been drinking had been broken at the neck and filed down into a hideously sharpened glass dagger, which he pressed firmly against my chest. He held my right wrist with his left hand. Years of self-defense training evaporated. The stench of my assailant was overpowering; he had obviously not bathed for quite some time. He was both taller and heavier than me, uncommon for a Brazilian. He shifted his weight from his left foot to his right; I could see that he had torn the soles of both of his feet on the sharp rocks. I looked over at the fisherman. His back was now turned to my plight.

Never once did I look my assailant in the eye.

I quickly gained that I was to empty my pockets with my free hand. I produced a handful of local currency, totaling less than seven dollars (and dropping in value, no doubt, as the exchange took place). He let go of my right wrist, in the process tearing off one of the *fitas*, and made a rapid estimate of the loot. It seized me that he had gone through extraordinary trouble to create his weapon and to reach me, and that it was apparent the payoff was much less than he had expected. Thoughts of being pushed over the edge of the bluff onto the jagged rocks below were preempted by nightmarish scenarios of being taken to a local hospital and being administered a blood transfusion in a country where the supply is suspect.

"Não relogio!?" he barked. I shook my head that I hadn't a wrist-watch on me.

"Não documentos!?" I had long since taken to carrying a lami-nated photocopy of my passport when out on the streets. Again I shook my head no.

He jammed the cash into his pocket, and now began his own search of mine, certain I would have more than what I claimed. I could sense by the frantic movement of his hands his puzzlement, his rage that there indeed were no valuables on me. He flicked my passport photocopy into the ocean. The jagged end of the bottle pressed harder against my chest. *If he stabs me with it, we're both going for a swim,* I thought to myself.

He took a half step back, grabbed my right wrist again, eased back with the broken bottle, and made as if he were going to sprint away. I relaxed for a fraction of a second, and in that moment of inattentiveness he pulled me to him and lunged with the bottle, piercing me in the solar plexus. The impact of the thrust knocked the wind out of me and I staggered backwards, arresting my fall on a toehold a few feet below. My assailant was already midway back up the escarpment, climbing with swift, leaping bounds from boul-der to boulder.

The fisherman was upon me in a matter of seconds and helped pull me up. I instinctively clutched my hand to my chest. The wound had begun to bleed in earnest, painting a deep crimson stain on my white shirt. The two of us stood motionless watching my assailant traverse the rocks for the safety of the grass on the near side of the *morro*. Twice he looked over his shoulder to see if we were in pursuit. The remains of his weapon rested at my feet.

"É loco, este ladrão," the fisherman replied. *"Tudo bem?"*

I sat down heavily on the rocks and doubled over, warding off the sensation of shock. For once everything was not *tudo bem*. The unthinkable had finally occurred. I resisted the urge to harangue the fisherman for turning his back on the affair, fully aware I would need his assistance to reach the top of the *morro*. The fisherman offered me a rag, already stained with fish blood, to curb the flow. I lost any sensation of time passing.

The wound, as we discovered, was quite superficial, and eventually the bleeding ceased. It was a protracted climb to the top of the *morro* with the help of the fisherman. I felt weak, but convinced him I would be able to walk the kilometer back to my room under my own power and bade him a curt farewell.

A light rain began to fall. The boardwalk lining the Avenida Sete do Setembro was quiet save a young couple. The path of my assailant was marked by a set of bloody footprints that crossed the boardwalk and disappeared into the vast urban hovels that characterize the interior streets of Barra. It was impossible to conceal the stain, now a deep brown, and as the couple came closer they rushed me.

The young man immediately flagged down a passing taxicab and shoved me and his girlfriend inside. I insisted that it was nothing serious and implored that we bypass the hospital. The young man was visibly upset over my situation. The marked increase in violent street crime, the result of an ever growing disparity between Brazil's rich and poor, is a cause of grave concern in a nation that has seen the number of tourists decline in recent years. The unfortunate response to the increase in crime has been an increase in vigilantism, often directed against street kids as young as seven. Citizens hire off-duty police to kill street children under the pretense they are destined to become criminals that are best exterminated now instead of waiting for them to come of age.

After several minutes of roundabout travel through the backstreets of Barra I found myself at Rumalho's door. His wife helped me clean and dress the wound, after which we lunched over *xim-xim*, a Bahian dish of chicken, dried shrimp, peanuts, yellow squash, and *dendê* oil. We washed it down with several bottles of Brahma beer. Despite my misfortune Rumalho continued to smile. It was only after lunch had concluded and his wife had left the room his smile disappeared. Rumalho pulled up his shirt to reveal a chest and potbelly covered with salt and pepper fuzz, outlined by a wicked scar that stretched from beneath his right armpit to his navel. "Here is my tattoo," he began, his usual incomprehensible Afro-Portuguese drawl replaced with sharp enunciation. "It happened many years ago. They followed me home from the bus. One of them saw me leave the bank. You were quite lucky, *meu bem.*"

Karla insisted on my going to a hospital, hypothesizing worst-case scenarios of gangrene and a host of other bizarre infections, but her fears were unfounded. The wound healed quickly, and by the time I left Bahia there was no visual trace of its existence. As for my surviving *fita*, it has long outlasted its warranty. It has, in fact, endured for two years. Its longevity perplexes both Karla and me, and it has indeed brought good fortune and protection. I hope it continues to do so.

Ryan S. Kelly took a backpacking trip to the Tetons during the summer of 1988 and has been on the road every summer since. He has traveled widely and spent a year teaching English to high school students in Shizuoka, Japan.

★

"You can't imagine how things have changed in four years," our host Dilma lamented. "Now, you're never safe on the street." She repeated the advice most visitors get long before arriving in Rio. Don't wear a watch in public, or at least keep it under a long sleeve. Keep your money in a safe place, not in an outside pocket-except for a few hundred cruzeiros to placate a robber. Don't go to this neighborhood after dark, or to that neighborhood anytime.

Such concerns seemed far away as we made an obligatory promenade along the edge of the surf at Copacabana. The beach glistened and our wariness melted. We strolled back along fashionable Avenida Atlántica. Suddenly I felt a quick tug, like a fish taking a line, and Maria gasped in surprise; *pixotes* had grabbed her Microsoft fifteenth anniversary watch and my *Seattle Weekly* baseball cap.

The street seemed to explode. An undercover policeman who chanced to be walking near us pulled his gun and leaped, shouting, after the kids. Whistles blew, and uniformed policemen swarmed as though from the shop windows, guns drawn. Other pedestrians, apparently more used to such eruptions, darted into doorways or hit the pavement. We just gaped. The police never fired but, remarkably, rounded up all five of the *pixotes.* These looked to be about nine to fifteen years old; all wore identical, brand-new, blue Keds-type sneakers.

The cops found Maria's watch, which had been tossed under a parked car; I imagine my cap is still keeping the Brazilian sun from someone's eyes. They lined the kids up under a store awning and commenced their interrogation: "Which one took the watch? Tell us, or we'll take you all in. Are you going to go to jail just to cover up for him? Are you sure he'd do that for you?" The kids tried to look tough, like kids everywhere. One finally broke and nodded meekly at another, nearly the smallest of the gang. We couldn't help but hope the cops would let him go. They said they'd have to do just that, unless Maria would come in and sign a complaint. She tried to decline, but two young officers pleaded earnestly: the crime plague would never end until citizens took the trouble and risk of testifying. It was so frustrating for the police....

I remembered the reports of hundreds of street kids killed, usually after torture, by death squads that included off-duty policemen. The officers seemed to read my mind, and assured us that they would take their charge to the juvenile center, not to the regular jail. He would not be mistreated; he'd be sent to a juvenile home "for just a few months, where they'll try to teach him some kind of work."

—Eric Scigliano, "Robbed in Rio"

PAUL RAMBALI

✦ ✦ ✦

A Thou on the Dog

A fund-raiser for a zoo makes for some serious
monkey business in superstitious Brazil.

"WANT TO MAKE A LITTLE WISH?" THE MAN ASKS ME. HE IS SEATED at a table near the doorway of the bar.

He shrugs when I register only confusion. "*Tá legal,*" he says, giving me the Brazilian national gesture, a thumbs-up. That's fine. No problem. Here comes another one now.

"*Mil* on the dog," responds a construction worker in a lopsided hard hat who quickly drinks his glass of hot, sweet Brazilian coffee.

"You're barking up the wrong tree," someone jokes, and everybody laughs.

The man jots with a pencil on a slip of paper and gives it to the construction worker, who leaves a bill on the table. It's midday. By 3 p.m., the result will be out.

The *Jogo do Bicho* is a numbers racket based on animal characters, a system of signification that appeals to the Brazilian psyche. The Indians believe in the spirits of animals, and the *orixás*, the African saints, have characteristics associated with the animals they demand as sacrifices. There are other, official lotteries, including a weekly one based on the results of soccer matches. But the *bicho* is an obsession, combining aspects dear to the Brazilian heart of criminality, innocence, and folly.

Perhaps because it's illegal, people prefer the *bicho*. They distrust officialdom, but they know they can trust a crook to be honest. As well as handling more cash each week than some banks, the *bicho* is more reliable, too. A winning animal always pays out. Otherwise, who *can* you trust? In every neighborhood, there's a game. If it isn't in the bar on the corner, it's in the barber shop or the store.

"It's difficult to understand, to feel, to respect, to know Rio without the *bicho*," writes the author João Antonio. "Of all our institutions, it's the one that best reveals the soul of Brazil."

In Rio alone, the *Jogo do Bicho*—the Animal Game—is reckoned to have a turnover of US$10 million a week and employ 50,000 people, as many as Autolatina, the automotive giant formed by Ford and Volkswagen in the late 1950s to build cars in Brazil and Argentina. You can tell the employees of the *bicho* by their nice clean shoes, because this isn't working. They are agents, lookouts, runners, tellers, bagmen and maybe one day they might get to be bosses, *bicheiros*. You can tell the bosses by their heavy gold jewelry; stout, nervous types, you can see them in all the private boxes at the Sambódromo, alongside various civic notables, watching the parades of the samba schools that they've bought—along with the villas, yachts, and soccer clubs—with *their* winnings.

It all started, innocently enough, in 1892, at the zoo. The zoological park was the endeavor of Baron de Drummond, on his land at Villa Isabel, and, at first, it was generously endowed by the Imperial treasury. The Republicans, coming to power in 1889, saw no need to continue this largesse towards the cronies of Emperor Dom Pedro II, and left the Baron and his animals to fend for themselves. Having spent a great deal of money to acquire species from around the world, Baron de Drummond was in dire financial straits by the time a Mexican named Zevada proposed a scheme to run a lottery in the zoo.

Drawings of different animals were printed on the entrance tickets and, at the end of the afternoon, a placard was hoisted above the exit with the winning drawing. The lucky tickets were worth up to twenty times what they cost. This simple diversion rapidly caught on. Instead of tickets, families would ask for a lion,

By the early 20th century, Jogo do Bicho had spread throughout Brazil. Today, an estimated 400,000 bookies and runners handle US$2 billion in bets on the illegal game each year.

—AH and SD

a monkey, a snake, and a cat at the ticket booths, which had to be enlarged for the flood of visitors. The tram company didn't have enough cars to cope at the weekends.

Promenading in his zoo on crowded Sundays, amid the flags and laughter, the music and the cries of the animals, the Baron laughed at his good fortune.

The animal lottery became a daily diversion. It began to spread beyond the gates of the zoo—at which point, it was outlawed by the government. Driven underground, the *bicho* ceased to be a mere fad and acquired a fatal, illicit thrill for punters—many of them poor blacks, the descendants of slaves accustomed to sharing in secret rituals. For upwardly mobile mulattos not yet admitted to the Jockey Club, it provided a substitute for the pleasures of the turf. In the free and easy city, every shopkeeper became a bookmaker, taking orders for beans, onions, and tigers on the side. By the end of the month some households had run up bills for the *bicho* equivalent to those for their groceries. The lucky ones paid for their groceries from the *bicho*. There was no longer any need for extra tramcars to the zoo, the animals of the *bicho* roamed the city. Rio was one huge bestiary, and inside each animal was a potential jackpot!

The animals lurked everywhere, on illustrated signboards, in the configurations of words, and especially in dreams, providing much amusement for the urbane, superstitious Rio public. The backs of laundry tickets were printed with advice on how to divine the *bichos* from dreams. After lunch, a ruminative calm settled on the city, as the animals ran their secret race. The result of the lottery was announced—in secret—at 3 p.m. and, by a process of urban magic, was at once known by all. What is magic but a kind of contagion, an obscure or ill-read cause and effect? Even today, bets on soccer matches in Brazil are made not only out of loyalty or the evaluation of skills but by the accumulation of scattered portents. In the same way, the disparate ingredients of a Macumba ritual—stones, hairs, ointments, broken toys—combine in mysterious, irresistible formulae.

There are academic students of the *Jogo do Bicho*, including one, from the University of Pernambuco, analyzing the mathematics of a game that has spread to all the major cities, typically consisting of 25 animals and over a dozen types of bets. The multiplications involved are a daily test for Brazilians, who, even if many of them can't read, are inflation-trained in street mathematics and have little trouble keeping up.

During the first half of the century, the *bicho* became established in Rio, in factories, banks, insurance companies, department stores, even in the pages of a newspaper, *Mascotte*, which had a double language devoted to the game. Rings of bookies and runners were dismantled by the police. When they caught the bankers, the draw was divided in two; a disappointment for the punters, but an incentive for the police.

Today, the game has changed. The stakes are higher. The *bicheiro* on the corner has become the big shot in the Sambódromo.

One of these was Natalino José do Nascimento, who had only one arm, which made him no less fearful. He found time nevertheless to become godfather to 250 children. He was, in effect, an honorable member of the community of Portela, the president of the local samba school—renowned in the 1970s for its lavish, no-expense-spared Carnaval parades—and the owner of a professional soccer club.

Even as the manacles snapped around his remaining wrist once again, and he was led away, aged 70, to a retirement in the pen, he looked back with pride at his achievements.

"Here, there are 41 paved streets and thanks to me all these hills have running water," he said. "In this *favela*, of which I was the founder, more than 200 homes have been built thanks to me. I gave them the land and, what's more, the materials! All for the poor, for the people! The samba owes a lot to my profession and if

I wanted to, I could have been a senator!" He paused to consider the irony of this. "But it wouldn't have been long before they stripped me of office for some little infraction!" he joked.

Samba, football, *bicho*; here is the power nexus, delivering dreams and payoffs to the poor and votes to their smart new friends. The politicians give away beer and t-shirts and the *bicheiros* give away spectacle. João Antonio complains that they exploit paternalism, their good deeds mask bad deeds. [In fact, investigations by Rio's Attorney General Antonio Carlos Biscaia in 1994 uncovered evidence purporting to show a direct link between Colombia's Cali drug cartel and the lottery.] And what was once quaint, with overcrowding, has become murderous. The easy Cariocan values have been warped by the rural influx, by the dictatorship and inflation. Bodies in the bay now testify to deadly disputes over a lucrative pitch.

Want to make a wish?

Paul Rambali was an editor of The Face *and founding editor of* Arena *in London before moving to Paris, where he contributes to* Actuel. *His first book was the much-praised* French Blues: A Journey in Modern France. *This story was excerpted from his book,* In the Cities and Jungles of Brazil.

★

Side by side with the legitimate gamble is an illegal fascinating play called "The Beasts," in which the numbers from zero to ninety are split into groups of four, each group being presided over by an Animal God—Lion, Cock, Dog, and so on. If the beast you have staked on controls two or more of the final figures of the winning lottery number for the day, you are paid in proportion.

—Rudyard Kipling, *Brazilian Sketches* (1889)

PART FIVE

THE LAST WORD

* * *

The Real Brazil

Parting images of the country convince the author
that the nation's hopes are symbolized
by the regenerating heat of the jungle.

It was only right that my last impressions of Rio should
be visual ones. I traveled north-eastwards, along the road that
zigzags upwards to the Serra da Estrêla, past deep valleys, their sides
clothed with what my eye, trained by earlier custom, accepted as
grass, but which on closer inspection revealed itself as giant trees
packed as close as blades of grass: past other slopes where the trees
swept down like sloping rain, with no visible means of support. In
the distance, dominating everything, was the jagged stub of the
Dedo do Deus, the "Finger of God"—and round it other stubs,
some bare, some with a thick fur of green on their summits, others with merely a dab of green as if a giant's trowel had transplanted a clod of earth.

On beyond Petrópolis and towards the Serra dos Orgãos the
landscape became even more baffling, a chaos of tumbled rock and
mountain smoking with foliage and mist as if an earthquake had
just taken place. My eyes tried to find a pattern, but these mountains jutted this way and that; they didn't form a range; it wasn't
even possible to speak of "summits" or "peaks" for there was nothing so conclusive; they simply stopped, snapped off like broken
teeth. By the time I had reached 5,000 feet I had abandoned all

hope of forming a coherent pattern in my mind's eye: those fantastic contours must remain forever elusive.

Back in Rio, I drove along the Avenida Beira Mar, past Flamengo and Botafogo beaches, through the Botafogo Tunnel and on to Praia do Leme and then along the Avenida Atlântica. The white skyscrapers of Copacabana seemed to have edged closer to the beach and the breakers to have grown more restless since my last visit. Beyond Ipanema and Leblon the road was hemmed in by a towering rock-face on the right, and on the left the sea thundered and swirled through caves and galleries below it. Another road, blasted out of the solid rock, brought me to the Lake Rodrigo de Freitas, its shores overshadowed by Cantagalo, Cabritos, and farther to the northwest, by the Serra da Carioca.

I made my way, twisting and turning to the Alto da Boa Vista and Tijuca Forest, where the last emperor of Brazil loved to ride and picnic. Here, too, were mountains all around, soaring and swelling as if they were clouds kneaded by wind: Tijuca Peak, the *Pico do Papagaio*, or "Parrot's Peak," and the granite hump of the Pedra da Gavéa.

On again to the Corcovado range. Below me lay the panorama of Rio. Slopes and valleys, cascading with blue-green vegetation, scattered with pink, white and terra-cotta houses, and the *favelas* trailing like creepers down the gullies. The complicated crisscross, like a map of the moon, of avenues and roads and alleys with the traffic streaming along them like ants. Spires, roofs, towers, and the skyscrapers like clusters of white rock. The Jockey Club and racetrack like the board of a child's game. The cartwheel of the Maracanã stadium, where Garrincha and Pelé and his fellow footballers had won their spurs. The city cemetery, its tombstones glinting like chips of quartz. The vast expanse of Guanabara Bay, with its myriad inlets and islands, tilted up now, flat and luminous like the sea in Brueghel's "Fall of Icarus," the skyscrapers of Niterói quivering through a golden haze, and above me the Christ of the Corcovado, his arms outspread. Again I had failed to register any coherent pattern, but my eyes pricked as if with shafts of light. They, too, I felt, were beginning to grow new dimensions.

It was not quite the end. I thought it was when I boarded the plane for Europe at the Galeäo International Airport. I had decided to plunge straight back into my old world, not to subject whatever was stirring within me to the whittling away of a long sea voyage. But at Recife the plane came down for its last refueling before the Atlantic crossing. I stepped out on to the tarmac, and immediately the heat of the northern tropics closed around me like warm cotton wool. I felt the interminable jungles, as if I were standing at the edge of a green furnace. I could smell the muddy waters of the Amazon, the dirt and decay of the northern cities, the rotting palm-thatch of the huts and the sweat of emaciated brown bodies. This, I thought, was the reality. This was the real Brazil, in spite of the skyscrapers, factories, and machines of the south. This, as challenge, fulfillment, or defeat, was Brazil's future. This was where the raw materials of humanity in its continuous struggle with the forces of nature were to be found. This, moreover, was the reality as far as I was concerned. It answered to the chaos of hopes and desires I had brought with me when I first sailed into the Amazon, a century ago it seemed to me now. I was still not certain whether during the course of my travels through Brazil, and through the countries of my mind, it was seeing or feeling that predominated. Or did the two function now side by side? Perhaps the impressions that had poured through my eyes had worn fresh channels and planted in them new shoots of life. Perhaps one day a new flora and fauna would startle and delight me. Somewhere in the heat of this jungle lay the essence of human experience, the regenerating heat of a new Brazil. And this was something I could not see, but only feel.

Gilbert Phelps began writing when he was at elementary school. After winning scholarships to grammar school and Cambridge, and various spells of teaching, he was with the BBC for a decade. He now devotes himself full time to writing and is the author of many books, including The Heart in the Desert, The Winter People, *and* The Green Horizons. *He is married, with a son and daughter, and lives in Oxford, England.*

✳

Books for Further Reading

We hope *Travelers' Tales Brazil* has inspired you to read on. A good place to start is the books from which we've made selections, and we have listed them below. Many general guidebooks are also worth reading and the best ones have annotated bibliographies or sections on recommended books and maps.

Ackerman, Diane. *The Rarest of the Rare: Vanishing Animals, Timeless Worlds.* New York: Random House, Inc., 1995.

Alexander, Brian. *Green Cathedrals: A Wayward Traveler in the Rain Forest.* New York: Lyons & Burford, Publishers, 1995.

Banks, Vic. *The Pantanal: Brazil's Forgotten Wilderness.* San Francisco: Sierra Club Books, 1991.

Bates, Henry Walter, *The Naturalist on the River Amazon.* New York: Humboldt Publishing Co., 1880.

Beals, Carleton. *Nomads and Empire Builders: Native Peoples and Cultures of South America.* Radnor, Pennsylvania: Chilton Books, 1961.

Berkoff, Steven. *A Prisoner in Rio.* London: Century Hutchinson Ltd., 1989.

Bloom, Pamela. *Brazil Up Close: The Sensual and Adventurous Guide.* New York: Hunter Publishing, scheduled for publication in the fall of 1996.

Bodard, Lucien. *Green Hell: Massacre of the Brazilian Indians.* Translated by Jennifer Monaghan. New York: Outerbridge & Dienstfrey, 1971. Originally published as Le Massacre des Indiens. Paris: Editions Gallimard, 1969.

Boff, Clodovis. *Feet-on-the-Ground Theology: A Brazilian Journey.* Maryknoll, New York: Orbis Books, 1987.

Cahill, Tim. *Jaguars Ripped My Flesh.* New York: Bantam Books, a division of Bantam Doubleday Dell Publishing, 1987.

Crichton, Michael. *Travels.* New York: Random House, Inc., 1988.

Dos Passos, John. *Brazil on the Move.* New York: Doubleday & Company, Inc., a division of Bantam Doubleday Dell Publishing, Inc., 1963.

Draffen, Andrew, Robert Strauss, and Deanna Swaney. *Brazil - a travel survival kit.* Oakland, California: Lonely Planet Publications, 1992.

Dwyer, Augusta. *Into the Amazon: The Struggle for the Rain Forest.* San Francisco: Sierra Club Books, 1990.

Fleming, Peter. *Brazilian Adventure.* New York: The Press of the Reader's Club, 1942.

Guillermoprieto, Alma. *The Heart That Bleeds: Latin America Now.* New York: Alfred A. Knopf, Inc., 1994.

Guillermoprieto, Alma. *Samba.* New York: Alfred A. Knopf, Inc., 1990.

Gunther, John. *Inside South America.* New York: HarperCollins Publishers, Inc., 1966, 1967.

Harris, Jessica B. *Tasting Brazil: Regional Recipes and Reminiscences.* New York: Macmillan Publishing Company, 1992.

Harrison, John. *Up the Creek: An Amazon Adventure.* Bucks, England: Bradt Publications, 1986.

Harter, Eugene C. *The Lost Colony of the Confederacy.* Jackson, Mississippi: University Press of Mississippi, 1985.

Harvey, Robert. *Fire Down Below: A Journey of Exploration from Mexico to Chile.* New York: Simon & Schuster, 1988.

Hess, David J. *Samba in the Night: Spiritism in Brazil.* New York: Columbia University Press, 1994.

Kane, Joe. *Running the Amazon.* New York: Vintage Departures, a division of Random House, Inc., 1989.

Kelly, Brian and Mark London. *Amazon.* New York: Harcourt Brace Jovanovich, 1983.

Kipling, Rudyard. *Brazilian Sketches.* Kent, England: P. E. Waters & Associates, 1989.

Krich, John. *Why Is This Country Dancing?: A One-Man Samba to the Beat of Brazil.* New York: Simon & Schuster, 1993.

Lévi-Strauss, Claude. *Tristes Tropiques.* New York: Atheneum, 1974. First published in Paris by Libarie Plon in 1955.

Margolis, Mac. *The Last New World: The Conquest of the Amazon Frontier.* New York: W. W. Norton & Company, Inc., 1992.

Matthiessen, Peter. *The Cloud Forest.* New York: The Viking Press, Inc., 1961.

McGowan, Chris and Ricardo Pessanha. *The Brazilian Sound: Samba, Bossa Nova, and the Popular Music of Brazil.* New York: Billboard Books, an imprint of Watson-Guptill Publications, 1991.

McIntyre, Loren, with foreword by Catherine Caufield. *Amazonia.* San Francisco: Sierra Club Books, 1991.

McKibben, Bill. *Hope, Human and Wild: True Stories of Living Lightly on the Earth.* Boston: Little, Brown and Company, 1995.

Meunier, Jacques and A. M. Savarin. *The Amazon Chronicles.* San Francisco: Mercury House, 1994.

Mikes, George. *Tango: A Solo Adventure Across South America.* London: Andre Deutsch, 1961.

Minta, Stephen. *Aguirre: The Re-Creation of a Sixteenth-Century Journey Across South America.* New York: Henry Holt and Company, 1994.

Nugent, Stephen. *Big Mouth: The Amazon Speaks.* San Francisco: BrownTrout Publishers, Inc., 1994.

O'Hanlon, Redmond. *In Trouble Again: A Journey Between the Orinoco and the Amazon.* New York: Vintage Departures, 1988.

Phelps, Gilbert. *The Last Horizon: A Brazilian Journey.* London: Charles Knight & Company, Ltd., 1971.

Plotkin, Mark J. *Tales of a Shaman's Apprentice: An Ethnobotanist Searches for New Medicines in the Amazon Rain Forest.* New York: Penguin Books USA, Inc., 1994.

Popescu, Petru. *Amazon Beaming.* New York: Penguin Books USA, 1991.

Rambali, Paul. *In the Cities and Jungles of Brazil.* New York: Henry Holt and Company, 1993.

Roosevelt, Theodore. *Through the Brazilian Wilderness.* New York: Charles Scribner's Sons, 1924.

Scheper-Huges, Nancy. *Death Without Weeping: The Violence of Everyday Life in Brazil.* Berkeley: University of California Press, Ltd., 1992.

Shoumatoff, Alex. *The Capital of Hope.* New York: Coward, McCann & Geoghegan, 1980.

Shoumatoff, Alex. *In Southern Light: Trekking Through Zaire and the Amazon.* New York: Simon & Schuster, 1986.

Shoumatoff, Alex. *The Rivers Amazon*. San Francisco: Sierra Club Books, 1978.

Shoumatoff, Alex. *The World Is Burning: Murder in the Rain Forest— The Tragedy of Chico Mendes*. New York: Little, Brown and Company, 1990.

St. Clair, David. *The Mighty, Mighty Amazon*. New York: Funk and Wagnalls, 1968.

Starkell, Don. *Paddle to the Amazon*. Rocklin, California: Prima Publishing & Communications, 1989.

Thomsen, Moritz. *The Saddest Pleasure: A Journey on Two Rivers*. St. Paul, Minnesota: Graywolf Press, 1990.

Tomlinson, H. M. *The Sea and the Jungle*. New York: The Modern Library, 1928.

Topolski, David and Feliks. *Travels with my Father: A South American Journey*. London: Elm Tree Books Ltd., 1983.

Updike, John. *Collected Poems, 1953-1993*. New York: Alfred A, Knopf, Inc., 1993.

Villas Boas, Orlando and Claudio Villas Boas. *Xingu: The Indians, Their Myths*. New York: Farrar, Strauss and Giroux, 1970.

Wallace, Alfred Russell. *Travels on the Amazon and Rio Negro*. London: Melbourne, Ward, Lock & Co., 1889.

Winn, Peter. *Americas: The Changing Face of Latin America and the Caribbean*. New York: Random House, Inc., 1992.

Zalis, Paul. *Who Is the River?: Getting Lost in the Amazon and Other Places*. New York: Macmillan Publishing, 1986.

Glossary

acarajé	black-eyed pea fritter
adeus	good-bye
agogô	double cowbell used as musical instrument
alegria	joy
arrastão	dragnet
atabaque	single-headed drum
Bahiano, Bahiana	native of Bahia
bandeirante	Brazilian explorer during colonial era
bateria	drum and percussion section of a samba school
batida	cocktail made with fruit juice
beijo	kiss
berimbau	musical instrument made from wooden bow and gourd
bloco	organized group of singing Carnaval revelers
bodega	wine cellar, canteen; trash, garbage, a filthy house
bodó	Amazonian river fish
boteguim	tavern, bar or pub
búzios	shells
caatinga	scrub brush
caboclo	Brazilian of European and Indian descent
cachaça	sugarcane rum; Brazil's national drink
cachoeira	waterfall

caipirinha	cocktail made with rum, sugar and lime juice
Candomblé	African-Brazilian religion of Bahia
capoeira	martial art developed by slaves
caranguejo	crab
Carioca	native of Rio
cerveja	beer
chamada de benção	a call for a blessing
chapadas	mesa
chácara	country house
churrascaria	restaurant featuring barbecue meats
chuva	rain
ciclovia	bicycle path
corvée	unpaid laborer for a feudal lord; forced labor for the government
cozida	stew; also, cooked or boiled
curandeiro	quack, shaman or witchdoctor
curare	muscle relaxant derived from jungle plants
dendé	palm oil
destaque	prominence, eminence
Exu	spirit that serves as a messenger between gods of African-Brazilian religions and humans
faca	knife
fantasia	Carnaval costume
farinha	manioc flour
favela	slum
fazenda	ranch, farm
feijoada	national dish; made with black beans and smoked meat
festa	festival, party
figa	good luck charm depicting a fist with the thumb wedged between index and middle finger

filhos da Gandhi	Bahia's best-known Carnaval *bloco*
fio dental	dental floss; style of bikini
fita	ribbon; braid; string; band
fogo	fire
forró	music of the Northeast; incorporates accordion, harmonica and drums
garimpeiro	prospector or miner
gringo	foreigner
guaraná	Amazonian berry that contains caffine
Iemanjá	Candomblé goddess of the sea
jabiru	giant storck, indigenous to the Pantanal
jacaré	caiman
jagunço	gunman, assassin or hired killer
jeito	Brazilian way of getting something done
jogo do bicho	popular, though illegal, lottery
ladrão	thief
Macumba	African-Brazilian religion as practiced in Rio de Janeiro
madrugada	dawn, early morning
mai-de-santo	female spiritual leader of African-Brazilian religions
mandioguinha frita	fried manioc root, usually served as an appetizer
maravilhosa	marvelous, wonderful
mestre	master
moqueca	rich stew from Bahia region
morro	hill
mulatto	Brazilian of African and European heritage
oba	whoopee! Oh, what fun!
orelhão	big ear; phone booth
orixa	deity of the African-Brazilian religions

padaria	bakery
pagode	type of samba music
pai-de-santo	male spiritual leader of the African-Brazilian religions
pandeiro	tambourine
pantaneiro	native of the Pantanal region
Paulista	native of São Paulo
pelourinho	slave-era whipping post
pousada	inn
quadra	square, block (of street)
querida	darling, dear, beloved
repentista	improvisational musician from Northeast
roda	wheel, circle
rodoviária	bus station
sambista	someone who sings, writes, plays or dances samba
Sambódromo	Rio's open-air stadium for Carnaval parades
saudade	longing, yearning; homesickness
saveiro	long, narrow fishing boat, or person who uses one
sertanejo	native of the *sertão*
sertão	drought-stricken Northeast backlands
sorventeria	ice cream shop
tanga	bikini
telenovela	television soap opera
terreiro	house of worship in African-Brazilian religion
tesoura	scissors
trio electrico	musicians who play electrified instruments atop decorated trucks during Carnaval
trovão	thunder

Umbanda	African-Brazilian religion that incorporates elements of Candomblé and European spiritism
várzea	Amazonian floodplain
xixi	slang for urinate

Index

Index of Contributors

Acknowledgments

This book would have been possible without the help of many people. But many stepped forward and greatly eased its completion, and for that we are grateful. Our heartfelt thanks to: Julia Franco at the *Los Angeles Times* for her unswerving support during times of crisis, of which there were many; Don Montague, Saoirse McClory, and Leslie Katz at the South American Explorers Club for delivering on a moment's notice back issues of the Club's action-packed and info-filled magazine; José Guimarães and Ségio Mielniczenko at the Cultural Department of the Brazilian Consulate in Los Angeles for their invaluable advice and guidance; Professor Randall Johnson, co-chairman of UCLA's Program on Brazil, particularly for turning us onto the Brazilian Studies Association (BRASA), which supports Brazilian studies in the humanities and social sciences and proved to be a superb resource; Ohio State University Professor Edward A. "Ted" Riedinger, a wonderfully generous man whose extraordinary knowledge of Brazilian culture we frequently tapped; author Chris McGowan, whose expertise in Brazilian music we likewise took advantage of; Professor David George at Lake Forest College for providing many of the Brazilian proverbs that appear in the previous pages; Rio-based correspondents Mac Margolis of *Newsweek* and Katherine Ellison of *The Miami Herald* for obliging us with some highly valued reporting and fact-checking; Robert Falkenburg at Brazil Travel Service in Santa Ynez, California, for his excellent work in arranging our transportation and accommodations all over Brazil; Neise Cavini Turchin, whose native eye spotted and corrected subtle twists of Brazilian expressions that escaped our attention; and special thanks to Cindy Collins who took without so much as a groan the mounds of paperwork and computer disks we dumped on her and converted the mess into the polished product you hold in your hands, and the rest of the gang at Travelers' Tales Inc.—James O'Reilly, Larry Habegger, Raj Khadka, Susan Brady, and Linda Noren—for their essential support.

"*Bodó* Sing-Along" by Joe Kane excerpted from *Running the Amazon* by Joe Kane. Copyright © 1989 by Joe Kane. Reprinted by permission of Alfred A. Knopf, Inc.

"Argentino" and "Maracanã Whiz" by Terri Hinte reprinted by permission of the author. Copyright © 1996 by Terri Hinte.

"Once Upon a Time in Ipanema" by Edward A. Riedinger reprinted by permission of the author. Copyright © 1996 by Edward A. Riedinger.

"Tambourine Men of Recife" by Moritz Thomsen, copyright © 1990 by the Estate of Moritz Thomsen. Reprinted from *The Saddest Pleasure: A Journey on Two Rivers* by Moritz Thomsen with the permission of Graywolf Press, Saint Paul, Minnesota, and the Estate of Moritz Thomsen.

"Rio Risqué" by Cal Fussman reprinted by permission of the author. Copyright © 1996 by Cal Fussman. A version of this article originally appeared in *GQ*.

"Crappola" by Rick Geyerman reprinted by permission of the author. Copyright © 1996 by Rick Geyerman.

"Where the Wild Things Are" by Julia Preston reprinted by permission of author. Copyright © 1995 by Julia D. Preston. This article originally appeared in *Condé Nast Traveler*.

"Whose Vice Is It Anyway?" and "Where Life Comes in Slices" by Steven Berkoff excerpted from *A Prisoner in Rio* by Steven Berkoff. Reprinted by permission of Rosica Colin Limited. Copyright © 1989 by Steven Berkoff.

"Soul of the *Sertão*" by Alexander Shankland reprinted by permission of the author. Copyright © 1996 by Alexander Shankland.

"Aracaju Surprise" by Eric Scigliano reprinted from the July 21, 1991 issue of *The Washington Post*. Reprinted by permission of the author. Copyright © 1991 by Eric Scigliano.

"In Search of Miracles" by Alma Guillermoprieto excerpted from *The Heart That Bleeds: Latin America Now* by Alma Guillermoprieto. Copyright © 1994 by Alma Guillermoprieto. Reprinted by permission of Alfred A. Knopf, Inc. and Darhansoff & Verrill Literary Agency.

"Police Beat" by Arthur Dawson reprinted by permission of the author. Copyright © 1996 by Arthur Dawson.

"A Place for Living" by Bill McKibben excerpted from *Hope, Human and Wild: True Stories of Living Lightly on the Earth* by Bill McKibben. Copyright © 1995 by Bill McKibben. Reprinted by permission of the author, the Watkins/Loomis Agency, and Little, Brown and Company.

"Opium of the People" by Alma Guillermoprieto excerpted from *Samba* by Alma Guillermoprieto. Copyright © 1990 by Alma Guillermoprieto. Reprinted by permission of Alfred A. Knopf, Inc. and Darhansoff & Verrill Literary Agency.

"Where the Sun Dines" by Diane Ackerman excerpted from *The Rarest of the Rare: Vanishing Animals, Timeless Worlds* by Diane Ackerman. Copyright © 1995 by Diane Ackerman. Reprinted by permission of Random House, Inc.

"High on Iguaçu" by Scott Doggett reprinted by permission of the author. Copyright © 1996 by Scott Doggett.

"My Night of Candomblé" by Christopher Hall reprinted by permission of the author. Copyright © 1996 by Christopher Hall.

"Sailing Down to Rio" by Lori Nelson reprinted from the September 1987 issue of *SAIL Magazine*. Copyright © 1987 by Lori Nelson.

"My *Maravilhosa* Career" by David George reprinted by permission of the author. Copyright © 1996 by David George.

"A Walk in the Forest" by Alex Shoumatoff excerpted from *The World is Burning: Murder in the Rain Forest—The Tragedy of Chico Mendes* by Alex Shoumatoff. Copyright © 1990 by Alex Shoumatoff. By permission of Little, Brown and Company and the author.

"The Ultimate Road Trip" by Jon Christensen reprinted by permission of the author. Copyright © 1993 by Jon Christensen.

"Down the River of Doubt" by Sam Moses reprinted from the September-October 1993 issue of *International Wildlife*. Reprinted by permission of The National Wildlife Federation and the author. Copyright © 1993 by Sam Moses.

"Unquestioned Authority" by Katherine Ellison reprinted by permission of the author. Copyright © 1996 by Katherine Ellison.

"Malarial Misery" by John Harrison excerpted from *Up the Creek: An Amazon Adventure* by John Harrison. Reprinted by permission of the author. Copyright © 1986 by John Harrison.

"Young, Down, and Out" by Mac Margolis reprinted by permission of the author. Copyright © 1993 by Mac Margolis.

"The Word Denied" by William R. Long reprinted by permission of the author. Copyright © 1996 by William R. Long.

"Two *Fitas* and a Tattoo" by Ryan S. Kelly reprinted by permission of the author. Copyright © 1996 by Ryan S. Kelly.

"A Thou on the Dog" by Paul Rambali excerpted from *In the Cities and Jungles of Brazil* by Paul Rambali, originally published by William Heinemann Ltd. under the title, *It's All True* (1993). Copyright © 1993 by Paul Rambali. Reprinted by permission of Henry Holt & Company, Inc. and Reed Consumer Books Ltd.

"The Real Brazil" by Gilbert Phelps excerpted from *The Last Horizon: A Brazilian Journey* by Gilbert Phelps. Published by Charles Knight & Co. Ltd. Copyright © 1971 by Gilbert Phelps.

Additional Credits (arranged alphabetically by title)

Selection from *Aguirre: The Re-Creation of a Sixteenth-Century Journey Across South America* by Stephen Minta. Copyright © 1993 by Stephen Minta. Reprinted by permission of Henry Holt and Co., Inc.

Selection from *Amazon* copyright © 1983 Brian Kelly and Mark London reprinted by permission of Harcourt Brace and Company.

Selections from *The Amazonian Chronicles*, copyright © 1994 by Jacques Meunier and Anne-Marie Savarin. Published by Mercury House, San Francisco, California, and reprinted by permission.

Selection from *Americas: The Changing Face of Latin America and the Caribbean* by Peter Winn. Copyright © 1992 by Peter Winn and WGBH Educational

reprinted by permission of Orbis Books. Copyright © 1987 by Orbis Books.

Selections from *Green Cathedrals: A Wayward Traveler in the Rain Forest* by Brian
Alexander, reprinted by arrangement with Lyons & Burford, 31 West 21
Street, New York, New York, 10010. Copyright © 1995 by Brian Alexander.

Selection from *Green Hell: Massacre of the Brazilian Indians* by Lucien Bodard, published by Outerbridge & Dienstfrey. Copyright © 1971 by Lucien Bodard.

Selection from "Greenest City in the World!" by Curtis Moore. Copyright ©
1994 by the National Wildlife Federation. Reprinted with permission from
International Wildlife magazine's January–February issue.

Selections from *In the Cities and Jungles of Brazil* by Paul Rambali, originally
published by William Heinemann Ltd. under the title, *It's All True* (1993).
Copyright © 1993 by Paul Rambali. Reprinted by permission of Henry
Holt and Company, Inc. and Reed Consumer Books Ltd.

Selection from *In Trouble Again: A Journey Between Orinoco and the Amazon* by
Redmond O'Hanlon. Copyright © 1988 by Redmond O'Hanlon. Used by
permission of Grove/Atlantic, Inc.

Selections from *Inside South America* by John Gunther. Copyright © 1966, 1967
by John Gunther, renewed 1994, 1995 by Jane Perry Gunther. Reprinted by
permission of HarperCollins Publishers, Inc.

Selection from *Into the Amazon: The Struggle for the Rain Forest* by Augusta
Dwyer reprinted by permission of Key Porter Books. Copyright © 1990 by
Augusta Dwyer.

Selection from *Jaguars Ripped My Flesh* by Tim Cahill reprinted by permission of
Lowenstein Associates, Inc. Copyright © 1987 by Tim Cahill.

Selection from "Jungle Fever" by Richard J. Pietschmann reprinted by permission of the author. Copyright © 1994 by Richard J. Pietschmann.

Selections from *The Last New World: The Conquest of the Amazon Frontier* by Mac
Margolis. Copyright © 1992 by Mac Margolis. Reprinted by permission of
W. W. Norton and Company, Inc.

Selections from "Longing for Brazil" by Neise Cavini Turchin reprinted by permission of the author. Copyright © 1996 by Neise Cavini Turchin.

Selection from *The Lost Colony of the Confederacy* by Eugene C. Harter reprinted
by permission of the University Press of Mississippi. Copyright © 1985 by
the University Press of Mississippi.

Selection from "Lush Life in the Pantanal" by Scott Doggett reprinted by permission of the author. Copyright © 1996 by Scott Doggett.

Selection from "Malaria Aids?" by Scott Doggett reprinted by permission of the
author. Copyright © 1996 by Scott Doggett.

Selection from "The Meal is the Message: The Language of the Brazilian
Cuisine" by Roberto DaMatta reprinted from the May 1987 issue of the
UNESCO Courier. Reprinted by permission of *UNESCO Courier.* Copyright ©
1987 by *UNESCO Courier.*

Selection from *Nomads and Empire Builders: Native Peoples and Cultures of South
America* by Carleton Beals reprinted by permission of Bertha Klausner
International Literary Agency. Copyright ©1961 by Carleton Beals.

Selection from "One Day in Rio" by Arthur Dawson reprinted by permission of
the author. Copyright © 1996 by Arthur Dawson.

Selection from "Some Hope for Brazil's Abandoned Children" by Elizabeth
Hillman reprinted from the April 1994 issue of *Contemporary Review.*
Reprinted by permission of the Contemporary Review Co. Ltd. Copyright
© 1994 by Elizabeth Hillman.

Selections from *Through the Brazilian Wilderness* by Theodore Roosevelt published
by Charles Scribner's Sons. Copyright © 1924 by Charles Scribner's Sons.

Selection from *Travels* by Michael Crichton. Copyright © 1988 by Michael
Crichton. Reprinted by permission of Ballantine Books, a division of
Random House, Inc.

Selections from *Up the Creek: An Amazon Adventure* by John Harrison reprinted
by permission of the author. Copyright © 1986 by John Harrison.

Selection from "Villages and Beaches of Brazil's Costa Verde" by Larry Rohter
reprinted from the March 25, 1990 issue of *The New York Times.* Copyright ©
1990 by The New York Times Company. Reprinted by permission.

Selection from "Wet Again in Cachoeira" by Scott Doggett reprinted by permission of the author. Copyright © 1996 by Scott Doggett.

Selection from "Where They Are Now" by Katherine Ellison reprinted by permission of the author. Copyright © 1996 by Katherine Ellison.

Selections from *Who Is the River?: Getting Lost in the Amazon and Other Places*
by Paul Zalis reprinted with the permission of Scribner, a division of
Simon & Schuster and the Wallace Literary Agency, Inc. Copyright © 1986
by Paul Zalis.

Selections from *Why Is This Country Dancing?: A One-Man Samba to the Beat of
Brazil* by John Krich. Reprinted by permission of Simon & Schuster.
Copyright © 1993 by John Krich.

Selection from *The World is Burning: Murder in the Rain Forest—The Tragedy of
Chico Mendes* by Alex Shoumatoff. Copyright © 1990 by Alex Shoumatoff.
By permission of Little, Brown and Company and the author.

Selection from *Xingu: The Indians, Their Myths* by Orlando Villas Boas and
Claudio Villas Boas reprinted by permission of Souvenir Press Ltd. Copyright
© 1970 by Orlando Villas Boas and Claudio Villas Boas.

About the Editors

Annette Haddad and Scott Doggett met in 1986 while working as crime reporters for United Press International in Los Angeles. They soon discovered they had a mutual pastime—travel to exotic countries—and during the next few years visited two dozen nations on five continents. Annette recalls her first big trip—to Europe—at the age of nine as a seminal event because it was there, after heaving at the oracle of Apollo at Delphi, that she sealed her fate with the gods. They have been mostly kind, leading her to far and sundry and beautiful places. When not looking for beauty, she is searching for truth, as a journalist at the *Los Angeles Times.* She is fortunate to find a little bit of joy everyday with her menagerie of pets and her husband Scott.

Scott's interest in Latin America became personal when, in 1983, as a recent graduate of the U.C. Berkeley, he moved to El Salvador to work as a photojournalist. His initial career was followed by postgraduate study at Stanford University, reporting assignments for United Press International in Los Angeles, Pakistan, and Afghanistan; seven years as an editor for the *Los Angeles Times*; and six years writing guidebooks for Lonely Planet Publications. In 2003, Scott returned to the *L.A. Times* as a senior content producer assigned to the newpaper's Outdoor section. In early 2004, he received one of sixteen editorial awards the *Times* presents to staff members each year for excellence in jornalism

TRAVELERS' TALES

THE POWER OF A GOOD STORY

New Releases

THE BEST $16.95
TRAVELERS' TALES 2004
True Stories from Around the World
Edited by James O'Reilly, Larry Habegger & Sean O'Reilly
The launch of a new annual collection presenting fresh, lively storytelling and
compelling narrative to make the reader laugh, weep, and buy a plane ticket.

INDIA $18.95
True Stories
Edited by James O'Reilly & Larry Habegger
"*Travelers' Tales India* is ravishing in the texture and variety of tales."
            —*Foreign Service Journal*

A WOMAN'S EUROPE $17.95
True Stories
Edited by Marybeth Bond
An exhilarating collection of inspirational, adventurous, and entertaining stories
by women exploring the romantic continent of Europe. From the bestselling
author Marybeth Bond.

WOMEN IN THE WILD $17.95
True Stories of Adventure and Connection
Edited by Lucy McCauley
"A spiritual, moving, and totally female book to take you around the world and
back."   —*Mademoiselle*

CHINA $18.95
True Stories
Edited by James O'Reilly, Larry Habegger & Sean O'Reilly
A must for any traveler to China, for anyone wanting to learn more
about the Middle Kingdom, offering a breadth and depth of experience
from both new and well-known authors; helps make the China
experience unforgettable and transforming.

BRAZIL $17.95
True Stories
Edited by Annette Haddad & Scott Doggett
Introduction by Alex Shoumatoff
"Only the lowest wattage dim bulb would visit Brazil without reading this
book."   —Tim Cahill, author of *Pass the Butterworms*

THE PENNY PINCHER'S PASSPORT TO $14.95
LUXURY TRAVEL (2ND EDITION)
The Art of Cultivating Preferred Customer Status
By Joel L. Widzer
Completely updated and revised, this 2nd edition of the popular guide to travel-
ing like the rich and famous without being either describes, both philosophically
and in practical terms, how to obtain luxurious travel benefits by building rela-
tionships with airlines and other travel companies.

Women's Travel

A WOMAN'S EUROPE $17.95
True Stories
Edited by Marybeth Bond
An exhilarating collection of inspirational, adventurous, and entertaining stories by women exploring the romantic continent of Europe. From the bestselling author Marybeth Bond.

WOMEN IN THE WILD $17.95
True Stories of Adventure and Connection
Edited by Lucy McCauley
"A spiritual, moving, and totally female book to take you around the world and back."
— *Mademoiselle*

A WOMAN'S WORLD $18.95
True Stories of Life on the Road
Edited by Marybeth Bond
Introduction by Dervla Murphy

Lowell Thomas Award
—Best Travel Book

A MOTHER'S WORLD $14.95
Journeys of the Heart
Edited by Marybeth Bond & Pamela Michael
"These stories remind us that motherhood is one of the great unifying forces in the world"
— *San Francisco Examiner*

A WOMAN'S PASSION FOR TRAVEL $17.95
More True Stories from A Woman's World
Edited by Marybeth Bond & Pamela Michael
"A diverse and gripping series of stories!"
—Arlene Blum, author of
Annapurna: A Woman's Place

Food

ADVENTURES IN WINE $17.95
True Stories of Vineyards and Vintages around the World
Edited by Thom Elkjer
Humanity, community, and brotherhood comprise the marvelous virtues of the wine world. This collection toasts the warmth and wonders of this large extended family in stories by travelers who are wine novices and experts alike.

FOOD $18.95
A Taste of the Road
Edited by Richard Sterling
Introduction by Margo True

Silver Medal Winner of the Lowell Thomas Award
—Best Travel Book

HER FORK IN THE ROAD $16.95
Women Celebrate Food and Travel
Edited by Lisa Bach
A savory sampling of stories by the best writers in and out of the food and travel fields.

THE ADVENTURE OF FOOD $17.95
True Stories of Eating Everything
Edited by Richard Sterling
"Bound to whet appetites for more than food." — *Publishers Weekly*

THE FEARLESS DINER $7.95
Travel Tips and Wisdom for Eating around the World
By Richard Sterling
Combines practical advice on foodstuffs, habits, and etiquette, with hilarious accounts of others' eating adventures.

Travel Humor

SAND IN MY BRA AND OTHER MISADVENTURES $14.95
Funny Women Write from the Road
Edited by Jennifer L. Leo
"A collection of ridiculous and sublime travel experiences."
— *San Francisco Chronicle*

LAST TROUT IN VENICE $14.95
The Far-Flung Escapades of an Accidental Adventurer
By Doug Lansky
"Traveling with Doug Lansky might result in a considerably shortened life expectancy…but what a way to go."
— Tony Wheeler, Lonely Planet Publications

HYENAS LAUGHED AT ME $14.95 AND NOW I KNOW WHY
The Best of Travel Humor and Misadventure
Edited by Sean O'Reilly, Larry Habegger, and James O'Reilly
Hilarious, outrageous and reluctant voyagers indulge us with the best misadventures around the world.

NOT SO FUNNY WHEN $12.95 IT HAPPENED
The Best of Travel Humor and Misadventure
Edited by Tim Cahill
Laugh with Bill Bryson, Dave Barry, Anne Lamott, Adair Lara, and many more.

THERE'S NO TOILET PAPER…ON THE ROAD LESS TRAVELED $12.95
The Best of Travel Humor and Misadventure
Edited by Doug Lansky

—— ★ ★ ★ ——

Humor Book of the Year
— Independent Publisher's Book
Award

—— ★ ★ ★ ——

ForeWord Gold Medal
Winner — Humor
Book of the Year

Travelers' Tales Classics

COAST TO COAST $16.95
A Journey Across 1950s America
By Jan Morris
After reporting on the first Everest ascent in 1953, Morris spent a year journeying across the United States. In brilliant prose, Morris records with exuberance and curiosity a time of innocence in the U.S.

THE ROYAL ROAD $14.95 TO ROMANCE
By Richard Halliburton
"Laughing at hardships, dreaming of beauty, ardent for adventure, Halliburton has managed to sing into the pages of this glorious book his own exultant spirit of youth and freedom."
— *Chicago Post*

TRADER HORN $16.95
A Young Man's Astounding Adventures in 19th Century Equatorial Africa
By Alfred Aloysius Horn
Here is the stuff of legends—thrills and danger, wild beasts, serpents, and savages. An unforgettable and vivid portrait of a vanished Africa.

UNBEATEN TRACKS $14.95 IN JAPAN
By Isabella L. Bird
Isabella Bird was one of the most adventurous women travelers of the 19th century with journeys to Tibet, Canada, Korea, Turkey, Hawaii, and Japan. A fascinating read.

THE RIVERS RAN EAST $16.95
By Leonard Clark
Clark is the original Indiana Jones, telling the breathtaking story of his search for the legendary El Dorado gold in the Amazon.

Spiritual Travel

THE SPIRITUAL GIFTS OF TRAVEL $16.95
The Best of Travelers' Tales
Edited by James O'Reilly and Sean O'Reilly
Favorite stories of transformation on the road that shows the myriad ways travel indelibly alters our inner landscapes.

PILGRIMAGE $16.95
Adventures of the Spirit
Edited by Sean O'Reilly & James O'Reilly
Introduction by Phil Cousineau

ForeWord Silver Medal Winner
— Travel Book of the Year

THE ROAD WITHIN $18.95
True Stories of Transformation and the Soul
Edited by Sean O'Reilly, James O'Reilly & Tim O'Reilly

Independent Publisher's Book Award
—Best Travel Book

THE WAY OF THE WANDERER $14.95
Discover Your True Self Through Travel
By David Yeadon
Experience transformation through travel with this delightful, illustrated collection by award-winning author David Yeadon.

A WOMAN'S PATH $16.95
Women's Best Spiritual Travel Writing
Edited by Lucy McCauley, Amy G. Carlson & Jennifer Leo
"A sensitive exploration of women's lives that have been unexpectedly and spiritually touched by travel experiences…. Highly recommended."
    —Library Journal

THE ULTIMATE JOURNEY $17.95
Inspiring Stories of Living and Dying
James O'Reilly, Sean O'Reilly & Richard Sterling
"A glorious collection of writings about the ultimate adventure. A book to keep by one's bedside—and close to one's heart."
    —Philip Zaleski, editor,
    The Best Spiritual Writing series

Special Interest

THE BEST TRAVELERS' TALES 2004 $16.95
True Stories from Around the World
Edited by James O'Reilly, Larry Habegger & Sean O'Reilly
The launch of a new annual collection presenting fresh, lively storytelling and compelling narrative to make the reader laugh, weep, and buy a plane ticket.

TESTOSTERONE PLANET $17.95
True Stories from a Man's World
Edited by Sean O'Reilly, Larry Habegger & James O'Reilly
Thrills and laughter with some of today's best writers: Sebastian Junger, Tim Cahill, Bill Bryson, and Jon Krakauer.

THE GIFT OF TRAVEL $14.95
The Best of Travelers' Tales
Edited by Larry Habegger, James O'Reilly & Sean O'Reilly
"Like gourmet chefs in a French market, the editors of Travelers' Tales pick, sift, and prod their way through the weighty shelves of contemporary travel writing, creaming off the very best."
    —William Dalrymple, author of *City of Djinns*

DANGER! $17.95
True Stories of Trouble and Survival
Edited by James O'Reilly, Larry Habegger & Sean O'Reilly
"Exciting…for those who enjoy living on the edge or prefer to read the survival stories of others, this is a good pick."
    —Library Journal

365 TRAVEL $14.95
A Daily Book of Journeys, Meditations, and Adventures
Edited by Lisa Bach
An illuminating collection of travel wisdom and adventures that reminds us all of the lessons we learn while on the road.

THE GIFT OF RIVERS $14.95
True Stories of Life on the Water
Edited by Pamela Michael
Introduction by Robert Hass
...a soulful compendium of wonderful stories that illuminate, educate, inspire, and delight."
—David Brower,
Chairman of Earth Island Institute

FAMILY TRAVEL $17.95
The Farther You Go, the Closer You Get
Edited by Laura Manske
"This is family travel at its finest."
—*Working Mother*

LOVE & ROMANCE $17.95
True Stories of Passion on the Road
Edited by Judith Babcock Wylie
"A wonderful book to read by a crackling fire."
—*Romantic Traveling*

THE GIFT OF BIRDS $17.95
True Encounters with Avian Spirits
Edited by Larry Habegger & Amy G. Carlson
"These are all wonderful, entertaining stories offering a *bird's-eye view!* of our avian friends."
—*Booklist*

A DOG'S WORLD $12.95
True Stories of Man's Best Friend on the Road
Edited by Christine Hunsicker
Introduction by Maria Goodavage

Travel Advice

THE PENNY PINCHER'S PASSPORT TO LUXURY TRAVEL (2ND EDITION) $14.95
The Art of Cultivating Preferred Customer Status
By Joel L. Widzer
Completely updated and revised, this 2nd edition of the popular guide to traveling like the rich and famous without being either describes, both philosophically and in practical terms, how to obtain luxurious travel benefits by building relationships with airlines and other travel companies.

SAFETY AND SECURITY FOR WOMEN WHO TRAVEL $12.95
By Sheila Swan & Peter Laufer
"An engaging book, with plenty of first-person stories about strategies women have used while traveling to feel safe but still find their way into a culture."
—*Chicago Herald*

THE FEARLESS SHOPPER $14.95
How to Get the Best Deals on the Planet
By Kathy Borrus
"Anyone who reads *The Fearless Shopper* will come away a smarter, more responsible shopper and a more curious, culturally attuned traveler."
—Jo Mancuso, *The Shopologist*

SHITTING PRETTY $12.95
How to Stay Clean and Healthy While Traveling
By Dr. Jane Wilson-Howarth
A light-hearted book about a serious subject for millions of travelers—staying healthy on the road—written by international health expert, Dr. Jane Wilson-Howarth.

GUTSY WOMEN $12.95
More Travel Tips and Wisdom for the Road
By Marybeth Bond
Second Edition
Packed with funny, instructive, and inspiring advice for women heading out to see the world.

GUTSY MAMAS $7.95
Travel Tips and Wisdom for Mothers on the Road
By Marybeth Bond
A delightful guide for mothers traveling with their children—or without them!

Destination Titles

ALASKA   **$18.95**
Edited by Bill Sherwonit, Andromeda Romano-Lax, & Ellen Bielawski

AMERICA   **$19.95**
Edited by Fred Setterberg

AMERICAN SOUTHWEST   **$17.95**
Edited by Sean O'Reilly & James O'Reilly

AUSTRALIA   **$17.95**
Edited by Larry Habegger

BRAZIL   **$17.95**
Edited by Annette Haddad & Scott Doggett
Introduction by Alex Shoumatoff

CENTRAL AMERICA   **$17.95**
Edited by Larry Habegger & Natanya Pearlman

CHINA   **$18.95**
Edited by James O'Reilly, Larry Habegger & Sean O'Reilly

CUBA   **$17.95**
Edited by Tom Miller

FRANCE   **$18.95**
Edited by James O'Reilly, Larry Habegger & Sean O'Reilly

GRAND CANYON   **$17.95**
Edited by Sean O'Reilly, James O'Reilly & Larry Habegger

GREECE   **$18.95**
Edited by Larry Habegger, Sean O'Reilly & Brian Alexander

HAWAI'I   **$17.95**
Edited by Rick & Marcie Carroll

HONG KONG   **$17.95**
Edited by James O'Reilly, Larry Habegger & Sean O'Reilly

INDIA   **$18.95**
Edited by James O'Reilly & Larry Habegger

IRELAND   **$18.95**
Edited by James O'Reilly, Larry Habegger & Sean O'Reilly

ITALY	$18.95
Edited by Anne Calcagno	
Introduction by Jan Morris	

JAPAN	$17.95
Edited by Donald W. George & Amy G. Carlson	

MEXICO	$17.95
Edited by James O'Reilly & Larry Habegger	

NEPAL	$17.95
Edited by Rajendra S. Khadka	

PARIS	$18.95
Edited by James O'Reilly, Larry Habegger & Sean O'Reilly	

PROVENCE	$16.95
Edited by James O'Reilly & Tara Austen Weaver	

SAN FRANCISCO	$18.95
Edited by James O'Reilly, Larry Habegger & Sean O'Reilly	

SPAIN	$19.95
Edited by Lucy McCauley	

THAILAND	$18.95
Edited by James O'Reilly & Larry Habegger	

TIBET	$18.95
Edited by James O'Reilly & Larry Habegger	

TURKEY	$18.95
Edited by James Villers Jr.	

TUSCANY	$16.95
Edited by James O'Reilly & Tara Austen Weaver	
Introduction by Anne Calcagno	

Footsteps Series

THE FIRE NEVER DIES $14.95
**One Man's Raucous Romp Down the Road of Food,
Passion, and Adventure**
By Richard Sterling
"Sterling's writing is like spitfire, foursquare and jazzy with
crackle...."   —*Kirkus Reviews*

ONE YEAR OFF $14.95
**Leaving It All Behind for a Round-the-World Journey
with Our Children**
By David Elliot Cohen
A once-in-a-lifetime adventure generously shared, from the
author/editor of *America 24/7* and *A Day in the Life of Africa*

THE WAY OF THE WANDERER $14.95
Discover Your True Self Through Travel
By David Yeadon
Experience transformation through travel with this delightful,
illustrated collection by award-winning author David Yeadon.

TAKE ME WITH YOU $24.00
A Round-the-World Journey to Invite a Stranger Home
By Brad Newsham
"Newsham is an ideal guide. His journey, at heart, is into
humanity."   —Pico Iyer, author of *The Global Soul*

KITE STRINGS OF THE SOUTHERN CROSS $14.95
A Woman's Travel Odyssey
By Laurie Gough
Short-listed for the prestigious Thomas Cook Award, this is an
exquisite rendering of a young woman's search for meaning.

*ForeWord Silver Medal Winner
— Travel Book of the Year*

—— ★ ★ ★ ——

THE SWORD OF HEAVEN $24.00
A Five Continent Odyssey to Save the World
By Mikkel Aaland
"Few books capture the soul of the road like The *Sword of
Heaven,* a sharp-edged, beautifully rendered memoir that will
inspire anyone."
                        —Phil Cousineau, author of *The Art of Pilgrimage*

STORM $24.00
**A Motorcycle Journey of Love, Endurance,
and Transformation**
By Allen Noren
"Beautiful, tumultuous, deeply engaging and very satisfying.
Anyone who looks for truth in travel will find it here."
                        —Ted Simon, author of *Jupiter's Travels*

*ForeWord Gold Medal Winner
— Travel Book of the Year*

—— ★ ★ ★ ——